THE LAST HISTORIAN IN GALILEE

The Last Historian in Galilee

*Three Essays on Money, Truth,
and Power for Jews and Christians*

M. M. SILVER

WIPF & STOCK · Eugene, Oregon

THE LAST HISTORIAN IN GALILEE
Three Essays on Money, Truth, and Power for Jews and Christians

Copyright © 2025 M. M. Silver. All rights reserved. Except for brief quotations in critical publications or reviews, no part of this book may be reproduced in any manner without prior written permission from the publisher. Write: Permissions, Wipf and Stock Publishers, 199 W. 8th Ave., Suite 3, Eugene, OR 97401.

Wipf & Stock
An Imprint of Wipf and Stock Publishers
199 W. 8th Ave., Suite 3
Eugene, OR 97401

www.wipfandstock.com

PAPERBACK ISBN: 979-8-3852-4326-6
HARDCOVER ISBN: 979-8-3852-4327-3
EBOOK ISBN: 979-8-3852-4328-0

04/14/25

THE HOLY BIBLE, NEW INTERNATIONAL VERSION®, NIV® Copyright © 1973, 1978, 1984, 2011 by Biblica, Inc.® Used by permission. All rights reserved worldwide.

For old summer neighbors, through time, from Litchfield County
and close beyond: Harriet Beecher Stowe, Henry Ward Beecher,
Horace Bushnell, John Brown, Edward Robinson, Eli Smith.

There are, I believe, impossible historical situations,
and this is one of them.

—Albert Memmi, *The Colonizer and the Colonized*

Contents

Introduction | ix

1 Calling Saint Matthew: Capitalism, Jews, and Christians | 1

2 American Schmegegge: Truth, Jews, and Christians | 103

3 What Was Rabbi Jose Thinking?
   Colonialism, Jews, and Christians | 207

Bibliography | 305

Index | 321

Introduction

THIS IS A BOOK ABOUT NEITHER TRUMP NOR ISRAEL. BUT IT IS.

We live today in a world whose flaws are readily apprehensible but increasingly difficult to criticize. Liberal values have turned inside out, making their upholders a living and breathing contradiction in terms. Progressives who champion social inclusion and economic justice are intolerantly righteous and financially privileged. Were contemporary society to freeze in an ice age, after a century or two of thawing, it would be very difficult for any intelligent being left on earth to understand what happened to liberal-minded human beings during the first decades of the twenty-first century, before everything went cold. How did it happen that progressives who passionately fought for LGBTQ rights, who became environmental activists and animal rights activists, were also the most intolerant, sanctimonious people in North America since the Puritans, canceling anything in their present and past which was not to their liking? How political correctness became a rhetoric of tolerant inclusion and a cancel culture method of pseudosophisticated bigotry is a riddle, one that will puzzle historians for generations to come.

As to the self-understanding of liberals in our contemporary world, the fog is thick, almost asphyxiating. No generation of educated, liberal Americans has ever been so rigid in its convictions, and so oblivious about their implications.

When I drafted most of this book, a few weeks ahead of the November 2024 presidential elections in the United States, it was not entirely clear whether the most dire threat to liberal democracy was coming from the left or the right. Donald Trump's semiviolent shenanigans—his disregard for constitutional procedure, his well-publicized and adjudicated contempt for women, his authoritarianism, and his ignorance—were a dangerous but

INTRODUCTION

also tiresome topic, and I doubted whether I could say anything about it that was not being intoned relentlessly in liberal media outlets and blogs. Trump is far from the whole story, however. When I visited America in summer 2024, talking to people in old stomping grounds I have known since I was a little boy, it became clear (at least, to me) that the lingering popularity of Trump's MAGA movement is only one part of the crisis, and perhaps less weighty than its other main component, this being the self-serving perceptions of politicized progressives in the half of America that would never vote for Trump.

There are, I believe, plenty of reasons that explain the disillusionment and anger of Trump's supporters, who believe that the country's political system is rigged to their detriment. By the same token, in summer 2024 there were plenty of reasons that explained why Israel was waging a rough war with Hamas in Gaza and beginning to embark on another war against Hezbollah and Iran in Lebanon. But, on this United States visit, all I really heard from liberals was that Trump supporters are "idiots"; and even though, in deference to my sensibilities as an Israeli, my American friends and acquaintances parsed their words carefully when they spoke about the Gaza War, it was obvious that they blame Israel for genocide. If you support Trump, you are an idiot, and if you are a Zionist, you are a mass murderer— this was the progressive viewpoint in summer 2024, in a nutshell.

Since I myself am very critical of Trump and also very critical of Israel's West Bank settlement policies, I was suddenly viewing such progressives as my own doppelgangers (a concept that was fresh in my mind at the time, since I was reading Naomi Klein's clever, recently published book *Doppelganger*). That is to say, as a left-wing Israeli (and, yes, as a Zionist), the progressive wing of America's Democratic Party is indelibly and positively wedded to my outlook, just as in some ways it also repulses me.

Like any liberal anywhere in summer 2024, I did not want to be living in a world where an imbecile who boasts about groping women, who proposed that bleach injection be considered as a remedy to the Covid virus, and who legitimized the actions of neo-Nazis and KKK racists at the 2017 Charlottesville rally (not to mention his anti-Constitutional incitement leading to the January 6, 2021, assault on the Capitol) had a reasonable chance of being elected to a second term at the White House. While the prospect of a second Trump term was terrifying, the progressive fad of regarding half of the people in the country where I grew up and was educated through my early twenties as "idiots" was, for me, also repugnant.

In summer 2024, the same leftist doppelganger effect applied to Israel and its controversies at the time. Like any liberal anywhere (including about 40–50 percent of Israel's electorate, which is skeptical about, or outright

INTRODUCTION

opposed to, the West Bank settlements), I did not want to live in a world where American Jews, Evangelical Christians, and Israeli politicians secure lavish aid packages from the United States on the grounds that Israel is "the only democracy in the Middle East," while Netanyahu's right-wing governments nurture and expand illegal and illiberal Jewish enclaves on the West Bank.

In fact, as an Israeli who lives in a peripheral area within the country's pre-1967, internationally sanctioned borders that have been chronically neglected (and, in the past year, besieged and contracted), largely due to the Likud governments' disproportionately lavish support for the anti-democratic West Bank settlement movement, and also owing to my own American Jewish background and sensitivities as a historian, I thought I had earned a "special" right to speak out about distortions and false pretenses that have crept into relations between Israel and the United States over the past generation. But none of that meant that I would be prepared to regard Israelis of any stripe as "genocidal" murderers, and none of that meant that I would or should desist from advocacy for special annual aid packages necessary for Israel's survival as a democratic Jewish state in its inveterately hostile Middle East setting.

Here is the political catechism I had in my head, as a takeaway from this summer visit to the United States. As a progressive, I must oppose Trump because he is an authoritarian threat to democracy, and I must oppose Israel's West Bank settlements because they are an obstacle to a reasonable, two-state solution to the Israeli-Palestinian conflict. As a progressive, I also understand that my politics should be inherently inclusive and liberal toward people in a democracy who do not think as I do; and I understand that, from a practical standpoint, building coalitions across the aisle is the only way my politics will stand a chance of making a difference in an increasingly chaotic and authoritarian world. For such reasons, calling pro-Trump Republicans "idiots" and calling run-of-the-mill Israelis "mass murderers" is distracting and unhelpful.

In addition, I believed any judicious, empirical review of socioeconomic circumstances in America in 2024 would find a number of plausible reasons why reasons why middle and lower income people people believe that the system is rigged and have thus been disposed to join the MAGA movement. Similarly, I believed a fair, empirical review of military realities in what was then the 2023–2024 Gaza War would conclude that Israel can be faulted in many ways for the deaths of forty thousand Palestinians,[1] but

---

1. The war subsequently sprawled painfully into 2025, with thousands more victims added to this casualty number.

INTRODUCTION

its overall war action against Hamas was justifiably warranted by atrocities committed by this Islamic terror group on October 7, 2023, and was never genocidal in intention or effect.

Drawing such distinctions between reasonable left-liberal politics and self-defeating progressive radicalism ought to be a simple matter. If only it were.

As the summer ended, I did not see any point in writing a topical book about Donald Trump, or Israel's Gaza War. In today's chaotically overanalyzed public affairs scene, it could be assumed that a phalanx of journalists, politicos, pro-Israel and pro-Palestinian literary lobbyists, and others were hard at work, churning out manuscripts on such topics. Still, if you were Jewish, if you were liberal, if you were alive, and if you were writing in autumn 2024, how could you produce any text that was not, in some way, about Donald Trump or about Israel's war?

They are irresistible, unavoidable subjects. When I was sent out from a comfortable, middle-class, New York City suburb to a public elementary school, in the period when America first landed astronauts on the moon, the teachers did not tell us that when we became grandparents, the country would twice elect a man whose biotechnological savvy led him to propose that citizens ought to inject bleach in their bodies during an epidemic. When I was sent, kicking and screaming (because I wanted to play Little League baseball), from the same suburb to Hebrew school on weekends, they did not tell us that when we became grandparents, Israel, the Jewish state created in moral redress after the Holocaust, would be held accountable for genocide in reputable world tribunals, not to mention on North American and European college campuses.

I am a historian, and in that capacity I am always thinking about current events, even when the topic of my research and writing is necessarily from the past. This means that I am qualified to write a current events book. More precisely, I am competent to write a current events book that is not topical. If you are a historian, you simply cannot accept that contemporary problems should be diagnosed and addressed solely in contemporary terms. You cannot accept that the way to extricate ourselves from our self-made mess is to stay topical. Instead, historians believe, the path to individual and collective liberation begins by disentangling the roots of our recent and distant past.

This volume has three essays, written for Jews and Christians alike, which view current events from the standpoint of the past and vice versa. The three essays were prompted by particular developments and perceptions that arose in summer 2024, all of them portending a worsened world for my children as they make their way in it as adults, all of them portending

INTRODUCTION

a contraction in networks of mutual goodwill and respect between Christians and Jews that arose in North America and elsewhere after World War II and the Holocaust.

The first essay, "Calling Saint Matthew: Capitalism, Jews, and Christians," was prompted by my unease about reports of American Jewish billionaires flexing their philanthropic muscle to force university presidents into implementing illiberal crackdowns of campus protests, this being a new twist on the long-standing practice of American Jewish use of private capital to purchase sympathy for illiberal Israeli settlement policies on the West Bank and, beforehand (and perhaps in the future), on the Gaza Strip. The next two essays, "American Schmegegge: Truth, Jews, and Christians," and "What Was Rabbi Jose Thinking? Colonialism, Jews, and Christians," were provoked by the two aforementioned illiberal liberal platitudes: one holding that half of the American electorate is idiotic because it supports Trump, the other contending that the Jewish state is culpable of genocide for waging war against an enemy that murdered, raped, and kidnapped many hundreds of its citizens in an elaborately orchestrated terror attack on October 7, 2023.

Apart from the book's concluding sections, the particular problems that prompted these essays receive just glancing treatment in them. Nonetheless, anxieties caused by them are always in the background, motivating exploration of whether Judeo-Christian morality really mandates particular ways of thinking about political uses of private capital, about what counts as truth or fake news, or about what counts as abusive, or genocidal, uses of colonial power. Not topical discussions of current issues, the essays are investigations of how Jews and Christians have related historically to three broad problems that envelop our contemporary debates. These grand problems are money, truth, and power.

The three essays are equal in length and identical in method and execution. Each relates to a big subject (money, truth, power) with its opening sections analyzing ways Jews or Christians, in the period of Jesus and the crucifixion and of the destruction of the Jews' Second Temple, thought about the subject compared to the way it is discussed and debated in our time. Each has a middle part detailing how important thinkers, or admirable clerics, related to the problem about a century ago, meaning that this volume looks, historically, at contemporary issues by using two standards of measures: what Jews and Christians thought about the problem two thousand years ago and how they thought about it a century ago. Each essay ends by returning to the present, upholding a rather stern view of how the three issues of concern in this volume have transformed in Jewish-Christian interaction over the past generation. The censorious tone of these final sections might strike some readers as being objectionably moralistic, but I believe the volume's merits depend not on the question of whether its conclusions are particularly agreeable but rather on whether the way it relates to connections and severances between religion and liberalism offers a useful way of rethinking and reshaping discussions about divisive topics in contemporary, and future, public affairs.

In a few words, here is the book's argument. We will always be mega-perplexed by MAGA, flummoxed by the intractability of the Israeli-Palestinian conflict, and ill-suited to deal with other, similarly divisive topics unless we learn and think much more seriously about their religious and cultural foundations, in Jewish and Christian Scripture and in interactions between these groups over the ages. On the other hand, if we continue to allow specious, fool's gold rhetoric about "Judeo-Christian civilization" and its dictates to enter the public square, if we do not protect civil neutrality and bar subjective spirituality in our public spaces, liberal visions of American constitutionalism, of a democratic Jewish state, of modernity itself, will be ever more imperiled.

POSTSCRIPT AND DEDICATION

When I wrote these essays through the summer and early fall of 2024, I was feeling pretty certain about the likelihood of Trump's triumph in the upcoming elections and also rather doubtful about the prospect of a decisive Israeli victory in the northern part of the months-long war that began on October 7, 2023. The production process of bringing out a manuscript takes several months, and in that time I naturally garnered considerable information regarding parts of my expectations that were on target and others that proved to be unfounded. For one thing, a remarkable sequence of Israeli intelligence and military operations in the war's Lebanon phase caused the mood out of which this book's title emerged to seem, in retrospect, quite overwrought. Nonetheless, I have resisted the temptation to airbrush passages in this volume in view of events that transpired after its composition, principally because the measure of misbegotten expectation underlying some phrases and judgments has no bearing upon the book's analysis and arguments. Moreover, the mood responsible for this volume's title, and the passages enveloping it, emerged not only from the imminent threat of Israel-Hezbollah warfare but also, broadly, from the threat posed by global illiberal trends to universal, peace-oriented visions in the monotheistic cultures. In the absence of such visions, I doubt that history can be written credibly, anywhere.

INTRODUCTION

This book's writing had a dual, overlapping purpose: to capture the inner truth of a particular historic moment and to listen to echoes from centuries that preceded that moment. As it stands, this volume has a measure of self-referential irony. Also, some of its passages will likely not deepen my own friendship with professional colleagues. Nonetheless, I judged that editing the essays in the light of retrospective knowledge would defeat their dual purpose. With its Fabrizio-del-Dongo-at-Waterloo moments, the volume pays tribute to the central paradox of our postmodern lives. We live in an era when remorseless relativism insists upon the indeterminacy of immediate experience, but also when the widespread resurgence of religious faith encourages us to think in ambitiously long moral and historical frames.

This book is dedicated to a group of mid-nineteenth-century American Christians from Litchfield County, Connecticut, and surrounding areas, a region where I spent many happy summer days over almost six decades. Specifically, I dedicate it to the Beecher siblings (Harriet and Henry Ward), John Brown, Horace Bushnell, and, down the road from Litchfield, Eli Smith and Edward Robinson. Various beliefs and practices upheld and applied by these figures are quite unlike the liberal Jewish commitments I have pursued in Israel, where I have lived for most of my life; I have nonetheless drawn considerable inspiration from the way they combined scholarship, literature, politics, and spiritual idealism. They constitute a heroic subgroup in America's intelligentsia. Examples they set were on my mind when I wrote several passages of this book in their own backyard, as it were, before returning home to Galilee to finish the job.

I

Calling Saint Matthew
Capitalism, Jews, and Christians

MY NAME IN HISTORY

My parents never really explained why they called me Matthew. For someone raised as a good Jewish boy in the suburbs of New York City and Washington, DC, being named after one of the apostles might have been awkward, but it was not. Actually, I could have been dealing with a double whammy since my middle name is Mark, meaning that I am named after the first two Gospels. But nobody made a fuss about such things in Reform Jewish Hebrew schools, whose three or four hours of supplementary instruction on weekends were, as I experienced them, boring and meaningless. Before I immigrated to Israel in my early twenties, I do not recall ever wondering whether being named Matthew Mark was Jewishly sensible. Had I been paying attention, I would have noticed that my name was a little odd since there weren't many boys named Peter or Luke in Hebrew school, and though I had plenty of friends named John, they were all Christians. The truth is that I liked my first name because its accordion stretchability gave me an instant measure of where I stood in the world. I always knew whether or not I was in trouble depending on whether my mother called me Matt or Matthew; and I could sense whether a teacher cared less about me depending on whether he or she took the trouble to learn this accordion trick.

In contrast, living in the Jewish state made me uncomfortable about my given name. Eventually I signed my publications, in Hebrew and English, "M. M. Silver." For me, alternatives such as changing my name or adopting

"Kosherized" variants that sound as though they refer to Maccabean heroes or Hasidic reggae pop stars, Matityahu or Matisyahu, were disrespectful, derivative, or dumb. They were never on the table.

Maybe they should have been. As years went by in Israel, unease about my name crept into my professional life. In college classrooms I have been careless about my students' names in ways which, I hope, has struck them as being out of step with the effort I apply to other aspects of my job as a teacher. Self-centered and petulant, this has not been one of the finest parts of my career. It is as though I have been telling my students, "My name does not make sense, so why should I care about yours?"

As a historian, the New Testament's book of Matthew has heightened interest for me because I am interested in the Galilee region, and Matthew is the Gospel with the most intriguing descriptions of the area and its sociopolitical circumstances. It is also the Gospel most tellingly saturated with complicated evidence concerning how Jesus and his followers related to Jewish law and might (or might not) have been thinking about establishing a new religion. The Gospel of Matthew also provides the most sustained record of the Sermon on the Mount, a morally inspired document which challenges Jews like myself, and members of other religions, to reflect on how Jesus' Christian preaching is an extension of, or exception to, their own faith. These, and many other, characteristics render the Gospel of Matthew worthy of consideration.

Most learned commentators concur that this Gospel was not really written by the evangelist, Matthew, credited with its authorship.[1] Instead, they contend, the Gospel's composition began about half a century after the crucifixion, and it was taken up in Galilee by a group of commentators of mixed "Jewish" and "Christian" identity, who probably had never had direct, living contact with Jesus. Still, forgive me if it sounds facile, and writing as someone who has had a lifetime to wonder, inconclusively, about what's in a name, I suspect that the name of the Gospel matters. For me, as with (I am sure) countless other Christian and non-Christian readers over the ages, the Gospel's testimonial has a plotline that begins, logically, when the testifier is called forth by Jesus (Matt 9:9–13; also Mark 2:13–17 and Luke 5:27–28).

Jesus' selection of an ill-respected tax collector in Capernaum draws upon prophetic precedents in Scripture, which Christians later came to call the Old Testament (Abraham, burning bushes, and much else come to mind in this respect). The calling forth scene at Capernaum is part of a process that has an especially pronounced and polemical presence in the book of Matthew, whereby Jesus' doings recapitulate experiences in the Hebrew

---

1. Saldarini, *Community*; Overman, *Matthew's Gospel*; Kampen, *Matthew*.

Bible. As Christians found incentive to distance themselves from Jews, such echoes came to be thought of not as "recapitulation" but rather as "replacement," in a theology known as supersessionism. But, for now, let's overlook how the social and spiritual circumstances of these two figures, Jesus and Matthew, were subject to subsequent interpretation about where the Old Testament and New Testament converge or diverge. Let's consider instead the dramatic power inherent in all situations when one is unexpectedly called forth. In many lives, the experience of being called forth unexpectedly, and favorably, by some figure of authority is singularly memorable, sometimes even transcendent, no matter that the authority figure might hold a pedestrian role, as a teacher or sports coach or workplace boss. For Matthew, the moment is manifestly transformative: "As Jesus went on from there, he saw a man named Matthew sitting at the tax collector's booth. 'Follow me,' he told him, and Matthew got up and followed him," records the Gospel (Matt 9:9).

In Western culture, a well-known visualization of the moment is the Baroque oil painting *The Calling of Saint Matthew*, produced by Caravaggio in 1600 as part of a series of three works about the evangelist, which hang in the Contarelli Chapel in the Church of St. Louis of the French in Rome, close to Piazza Navona. The painting is accessorized in anachronism. The tax collector and his comrades are decked out in Baroque doublets, feathered caps, and slit-style breeches. Coins, an inkwell, and a sword are scattered around a table inside a dark, unpleasant room rendered by the artist as the first-century workplace of a tax collector. Capernaum is a sweltering locale on a northern lip of the Sea of Galilee (I know it well because as a kayak enthusiast, I launch jaunts to the Jordan River from a beach next to it, usually timing them to conclude before eight o'clock in the morning when the sun becomes inhumanly fierce). Starting in the early first century CE, when Jesus appears to have regarded Capernaum as his post-Nazareth home, this area of the Sea of Galilee has witnessed several different dress codes and styles. None of them have been nearly as florid as Caravaggio imagined.

The painting's physical unrealism accentuates its emotional authenticity, however. The "Who, me?" look on the face of the older, bearded man, who has presumably been called forth by Jesus, betrays a convincing mix of guilty remorse and redemptive hope. Based on his resemblance to the Matthew figures in the other two paintings at the French church, most commentators have assumed that this bearded figure is Jesus' designee. However, the crosswise angle of this older man's index finger seems to point not at himself but rather to an amusingly indifferent younger man, who is engaged greedily in coin-counting.

If Caravaggio's Matthew is this younger fellow, the scene's visualization has an unwitting 1960s feel. The young man's haircut resembles those of the Beatles around the time when George Harrison wrote the lyrics to "Taxman." Surely, the recoil felt by British citizens, who were obliged to heed this 1960s taxman, reflects the way Capernaum residents would have felt about Matthew two thousand years ago. When they sit, he taxes their seat, and when they're cold, he taxes their heat.

The young man theory also leaves autobiographical and inclusive traces on Caravaggio's canvas. The coin counter in the painting has a look of dull contentment, whereas the face in Caravaggio's self-portraits has a repressed scowl. So the artist did not exactly step into the painting, as Matthew himself, but he seems personally invested in the scene, in fraternal (perhaps homoerotic) and biographical senses. Having being born in 1571, he was roughly the same age as the coin counter and also Jesus. Caravaggio grew up in penury, but the commission he won for the Contarelli Chapel project was a windfall in his short, tempestuous life (he died in 1610). Perhaps the painter's alter ego, the young man at the far end of the table, has the task of verifying whether the San Luigi dei Francesi painting fee adds up. Disguised in some such way, Caravaggio's involvement in this anachronistically rendered New Testament scene underscores how the topic of capital accumulation crosses borders of space and time, implicating everyone—Jews and Christians, Romans, patrons of Baroque art, Americans.

Tax collectors are rarely well-liked figures, and the loathing of Matthew felt by Galilee Jews was exacerbated by his opportunistic engagement with the Romans, as a functionary employed in their colonialist oppression. Representing this widely felt incredulity, Pharisees interrogate Jesus' disciples, querying, "Why does your teacher eat with tax collectors and sinners?" Jesus replies that his mission as a physician of the soul is to treat the ailing, not the well: "I have not come to call the righteous, but sinners" (Matt 9:11–13). This explanatory phrasing in Matthew echoes the formulation in the partner Gospel, Mark (2:17), which refers to Jesus' festive dining with tax collectors and sinners in the house of Levi, son of Alphaeus. New Testament scholars such as Sean Freyne and John Dominic Crossan have elaborated on the "table fellowship" in this sort of sequence, arguing that it betokens moral innovativeness in the Gospels, by which Jesus challenged conventional norms of financial or sexual propriety and designed his mission specifically to benefit sinners, not the righteous.[2]

To a surprising degree, how we imagine the specifics of Matthew's vocation as a tax collector impinges upon how we explain the origins and

---

2. Freyne, *Galilee*, 54.

motivations of the Jesus group's eventual rupture with Judaism. How we account for nitty-gritty details of Matthew's occupation has major repercussions in our analysis of why monotheism fractured as two, and then three, religions—a fracture that produced considerable confusion and anguish in history, including violent anti-Semitism in the Crusades, the Inquisition, and the Holocaust and sprawling into the Jewish state's contemporary dispute in the Muslim Middle East.

The identity ambiguity in Caravaggio's painting is uncannily insightful. In this picture, as in the Gospel as a whole, the personal identity of Matthew is not germane. It does not matter whether he is the remorseful bearded man, who, to my eye, prefigures and resembles a tortured member of the Jewish council (*Judenrat*) in a Nazi death camp who collaborated under extreme duress, or whether he is the younger man, who, in addition to the 1960s look, prefigures and resembles an avaricious graduate of a university business administration program in the 1990s, on his way to a lucrative entry position at Goldman Sachs. Nor does it matter whether or not Matthew in the eponymous Gospel is also Levi, son of Alphaeus, in the book of Mark. The problem raised by the calling forth scene in Capernaum is not to be found in the realm of individual morality and personal behavior. Instead, the problem is to be found in the realm of economics and in the relationship between capital accumulation and the spirit of an era.

The book of Matthew revolves around the vexing mystery concerning the identity and motivations of the historical Jesus. Was Jesus an in-house reformer whose animus was to correct pharisaical rigidity and thereby perfect Jewish law ("Judaism," in today's parlance), as he himself attests in Matt 5:17 ("Do not think that I have come to abolish the Law or the Prophets; I have come not to abolish them but to fulfill them")? Or, alternatively, did this Jewish-born preacher and healer consistently harbor an intention of establishing a new faith, as suggested by the Great Commission sequence in Matt 28:19 ("Go and make disciples of all the nations")? Certainly, Jesus' excoriation of the Pharisees in Matt 23:33 as a "brood of vipers" sounds like the philippic of a man who is incontrovertibly disillusioned with his own birth religion. Even if you are not a doctrinaire Marxist, how you tackle such issues and questions depends upon how much revenue you think was pouring into Matthew's tax coffers at Capernaum.

CAPERNAUM, THE CROSSROADS OF WESTERN ANXIETY ABOUT MONEY

On one line of thought, whose extreme formulation is known as the theory of "Galilee of the Gentiles," Jesus operated in a northern milieu in the land of Israel that was ethnoreligiously far more diverse than the thoroughly Jewish milieu in the Judean area of Jerusalem and the Second Temple. The two centers in this Galilee region, Tiberias and Sepphoris, were newly built or rebuilt towns heavily immersed in Roman culture and politics. Jesus grew up in a provincial, neglected village, Nazareth; in the period when he engaged his spiritual mission, he regarded Capernaum as his home, and Capernaum has long been known as a middling fishing village. Yet Nazareth is not a long walk from Sepphoris (today's Tzippori), and many commentators imagine that he found work as a carpenter in this Romanized city. Also, conceivably, Capernaum's economy and society could have been uplifted by Roman-generated prosperity.

The upshot, on this interpretation, is that Galilee was an unusually gentile-influenced region in the Holy Land. The decision eventually reached by Jesus and his followers to break away from Jewish law, rather than "fulfilling" it, is therefore less nettlesome than it may seem. Jesus, in this view, may have been Jewish mostly in a nominal sense, much as many assimilated Jews in the United States today are primarily American and, at most, formally Jewish. If the term "Galilee of the Gentiles" (*Galil Ha-Goyim*, a phrase heard in the Hebrew Bible, or Old Testament, Isa 9:1 and then interpolated in Matt 4:15) is taken literally, Jesus came to the world in a demographically diverse region where anyone's true identity, including his own, was not unshakable and homogenous.

From the late nineteenth century, this last point about Galilee heterogeneity was diabolically exploited by anti-Semites like Houston Stewart Chamberlain. With their racial view of Aryan superiority threatened by Jesus' known affiliation with a Semitic religion, they searched for creative ways to vaporize Jesus' Jewishness. The scholar Susannah Heschel has shown how this Galilee of the Gentiles theory was manipulated by the Nazis.[3]

Aware of the theory's lugubrious political outcome, another scholar, Mark Chancey, authored a moderately persuasive book whose thesis is that this Galilee of the Gentiles theory has no credible footing in scriptural, demographic, and historic realms.[4] Chancey and many other commentators are undoubtedly correct when they insist that Jewish law, halakha, was

---

3. Heschel, *Aryan Jesus*.
4. Chancey, *Myth*.

upheld in Galilee essentially in the same way as it was practiced in Judea.[5] In this religious sense, Galilee was "Jewish," not gentile. However, Chancey soft-pedals the implications of the possibility that Jesus, or at least chroniclers of his preaching, may have been exposed, in places like Sepphoris, to cultural norms quite unlike those characteristic of what came to be known as "Judaism."

Also, it is worth keeping in mind that there is nothing intrinsically illiberal or anti-Semitic in any particular way of thinking about Jesus, and of the cultural milieu of his youth, in Galilee. Before the Holocaust enhanced the wariness of scholars regarding the wisdom of entertaining ideas that might be exploited by anti-Semites, many liberal-minded theologians endorsed soft or hard versions of the Galilee of the Gentiles theory. Traces of the theory, for instance, infiltrate the way Shirley Jackson Case, a liberal theologian who served as the dean of the Divinity School at the University of Chicago, wrote about Sepphoris and Nazareth in his 1927 biography of Jesus.[6] In such an instance, an emphasis on gentile traits in Jesus' home region does not attest to a commentator's anti-Semitic animus. Instead, they reflect daunting challenges posed to scholars, theologians, and laymen by sequences in the Judaism-Christianity rupture. One such interpretive challenge is raised by apparent contradictions in the book of Matthew. How are we to reconcile the inclusive messages in the Sermon on the Mount and the demonizing excoriation of a large Jewish group, the Pharisees, in the same Gospel?

Jesus preached that "it is easier for a camel to go through the eye of a needle than for someone who is rich to enter the kingdom of God" (Matt 19:24). How were Jesus' anti-materialist messages received? Possible answers depend upon how you view the socioeconomic circumstances in Galilee, Jesus' home region and the locus of most of his preaching. If aspects of the Galilee of the Gentiles theory are correct, many in the target audience would have been exposed to Hellenistic culture and had perhaps been enriched by Rome's rule. If so, Jesus' followers would have processed sermonizing, such as the "eye of the needle" exhortation, in a self-critical mood. Christianity would have consolidated as a religion that urges its believers to overcome the mundane lusts and greed of their bodily selves. Many, including non-Christians like myself who grew up watching televangelists on Sunday mornings operate in an affluent society like late twentieth-century America, believe that this is an apt description of Christianity, in general.

---

5. Schiffman, "Galilean Halakah?"
6. Case, *Jesus*, 202–12.

Yet relatively few people would accept what the Galilee of the Gentiles theory implies on a socioeconomic level. Instead, they assume that Jesus' first followers were rather poor fishermen and farmers, many of them living on death's edge because of low income and bad health.

This raises another possibility. Jesus might have been perceived as a social reformer by followers who lived on the margins and who were prepared to fight to gain their own small share of wealth that trickled down from Roman rule in Palestine. One New Testament scholar, Richard Horsley, spent much of his career at the University of Massachusetts trying to substantiate the idea that the Jesus movement arose in a rural milieu where residents were prone to follow Robin Hood–type leaders, whose social banditry methods promised wealth distribution on behalf of the poor.[7] Trying to apply the insights of the radical English historian Eric Hobsbawm, who studied "primitive rebels,"[8] Horsley offered suggestive descriptions about how rural Galilee Jews in the late Second Temple period suffered from double taxation pressures, being compelled to pay tribute and tithe both to the Jews' priestly elite in Jerusalem and also to Palestine's overall masters, the Romans.

As Horsley observes, once the dross of class bias in the writing of the Jewish-Roman historian Flavius Josephus is removed, Hobsbawm's portraiture aptly fits the actions and goals of Galilee's primitive rebel leaders who preceded Jesus. We know about the doings of these rebels from Josephus. An example is Hezekiah (Ezekias) who operated during Herod's term as military governor in Galilee (circa 47 BCE)—Hezekiah, Horsley wrote, was a "Jewish Robin Hood" whose actions "symbolized the Jewish peasants' basic sense of justice and their religious loyalties."[9]

Horsley, however, could never quite connect the dots leading to an appreciative image of Jesus as a "primitive rebel," in Hobsbawm's sense. One problem is that Josephus's descriptions of ebbs and flows of socioeconomic restiveness, or placidity, in Galilee are not in synch with the rise of the Jesus movement. Another problem is that a follower would have had to be selective about Jesus' preaching in order to uphold an image of him as a mix of Robin Hood and Che Guevara, as an advocate of wealth redistribution and political rebellion. How does the Sermon on the Mount's famous summons to turn the other cheek cohere with such an image ("I tell you, do not resist an evil person," Matt 5:39)?

---

7. Horsley and Hanson, *Bandits*.
8. Hobsbawm, *Primitive Rebels*.
9. Horsley and Hanson, *Bandits*, 75.

Despite such problems, the writings of some commentators cohere with the overall thrust of this primitive rebellion analysis. Such theologians and scholars interpret Jesus' anti-materialist preaching as a bona fide program of social reform designed for the benefit of poor peasants in Galilee and beyond. One of them was another American cleric, Shailer Mathews, an important figure in liberal Protestantism's late nineteenth-century Social Gospel movement, who, like Shirley Jackson Case, taught theology at the University of Chicago. In his 1897 volume *The Social Teachings of Jesus*, Mathews concluded that Christianity endorses the accumulation of wealth only insofar as it promotes fraternal brotherhood among men, and social justice.[10]

We are engaged here not in a scholastic survey of bygone or one-sided ideas about the origins of the Jesus movement, but rather in an attempt to uncover what people really have in their minds when they reflect upon what Jesus, or religion as a whole, is "really" about. For Americans, the social economy of the Jesus movement is not a topic of interest solely in forgotten, century-old treatises written by theologians at the University of Chicago. In fact, in America and elsewhere, the most popular contemporary expositions of Jesus and his movement are predicated upon imaginings of the socioeconomic circumstances of early first-century CE Galilee, particularly in the coastal town where Jesus apparently kept a home during his mission phase, Capernaum.

One example is Reza Aslan's 2013 best-selling volume *Zealot: The Life and Times of Jesus of Nazareth*.[11] Defending his attention-grabbing thesis about how Jesus was really a Jewish zealot wholly committed to the anti-Roman rebellion, Aslan accounts for Jesus' popularity by stressing how his anti-materialist preaching was tailor-fitted to a socioeconomic niche of first-century Galilee. Whereas the scholarly theologian Horsley relied on a leftist historian's theories about rural banditry, Aslan's discussion sounds as though it is predicated upon relative deprivation theory in twentieth century social science—according to this theory, social change dynamics are associated with the status-seeking aspirations of a semimarginalized social group which begins to notch some socioeconomic progress but feels slighted in comparison to the status of elites. Herod's son, Herod Antipas the Tetrarch, had promoted projects in Tiberias and Sepphoris that benefited urbanized Jewish elites; such progress was out of the reach of worried, perhaps resentful, persons in Jesus' target audience—largely Capernaum's fishermen and farmers, as Aslan observes. He writes, "The majority of Capernaum's

---

10. Mathews, *Social Teachings of Jesus*.
11. Aslan, *Zealot*.

residents had been left behind in the new Galilean economy."[12] As others have done, and will do, this author hinges provocative speculation about the identity of the "real" historical Jesus, and about dynamics in Christianity's rise, upon unprovable speculation about the political economy of Jesus' base in Capernaum.

Today, Capernaum is an attractive site on the Sea of Galilee filled with inspiring elements both for Christian pilgrim visitors and also non-Christians (it has also been underutilized in recent years, owing to the Covid epidemic and Israel's war against Hamas in Gaza and against Hezbollah in Lebanon). The site's administration, featuring cooperation between Israel's Nature and Park Authority and the Franciscans, seems a bit uneasy, but a visitor will find plenty to do and think about, exploring an excavated Jewish synagogue on the site, its St. Peter's Church, and a nature trail alongside the Sea of Galilee. Capernaum is a stimulatingly complicated place. Many visitors will leave with as many questions and answers regarding its main features—for instance, what might possibly be the relationship between the excavated synagogue and the consolidation of Christianity among Jesus' followers many decades after the crucifixion?

Through the World War I end of the Ottoman period in Palestine, nobody was really sure about Capernaum's precise location on the northern coast of the Sea of Galilee. Consider the example of Edward Robinson, an American from the Union Theological Seminary who, in a mid-nineteenth-century context of surging interest in archaeological and scholarly survey of Holy Land sites, stands out as an unusually prolific and reliable researcher.[13] Robinson misplaced Capernaum. He pinpointed a spot (Khan Minyah) on the Ginosar (Gennesaret) plain, a few kilometers south of Capernaum's now-accepted locale.[14]

Generally, scholars are locked in contentious disagreement about whether any relics at Capernaum or other Galilee sites can reasonably be traced to the first century CE period of Jesus' healing and preaching. Based on mid-twentieth-century excavations, archaeologists and scholars associated with the Franciscans, including Bellarmino Bagatti and Emmanuele Testa, hazarded suggestions about how Christian pilgrimage and related devotions can be followed in Holy Land locales back to the first century; this line of argument is hotly contested by scholars, as explained in a 1993 volume written by Joan Taylor.[15]

12. Aslan, *Zealot*, 95.
13. Goren, *Loss of a Minute*.
14. Robinson and Smith, *Biblical Researches*, 288–94.
15. Taylor, *Christians*.

These comments suffice as demonstration of how difficult it has been, and remains, to get a handle on possible realities in Capernaum, a key locale in the Jesus story. To make matters more confusing, Scripture itself is internally contradictory about Capernaum. Jesus, many will recall, remonstrates about the town at one point—in Matt 11:23 he fulminates about how Capernaum should be thrown "down to Hades."

For all these reasons, the strategy of predicating a controversial or counterintuitive theory about the "historical Jesus" upon a supposed reconstruction of Capernaum's political economy two thousand years ago seems precarious. Despite, or because of, its problematic character, this strategy remains popular, as demonstrated by Aslan's best-selling presentation of Christianity's demiurge as a Jewish zealot.

WAS THE HISTORIC JESUS A CORPORATE EXECUTIVE?

Jesus has been seen in many ways by different peoples. Innumerable commentators have remarked about how theologians and believers in a particular culture project their own self-interested ideas about wealth and poverty, war and peace, gender and race, and beauty and power in their evaluations of Jesus' life and its messages. For a fascinating study of the Americanized appropriation of Jesus' appearance, life, and preaching, readers can consult Stephen Prothero's 2003 volume *American Jesus: How the Son of God Became a National Icon*.[16]

One garish milestone in this process of Americanizing Jesus pertains to the issue we are highlighting in this essay: Jesus' critique of material wealth. In the mid-1920s, a Madison Avenue ad man, Bruce Fairchild Barton, turned Jesus into a corporate manager in his biography of Christianity's founder, *The Man Nobody Knows*.[17] The son of a Congregational minister, Barton won notoriety in American political history by serving a couple of terms as an isolationist Republican delegate from Manhattan in the House of Representatives. His political aspirations reached their acme in 1940, when he ran for a US Senate slot; President Franklin Roosevelt, who at this time was running for a third term at the White House, ridiculed Congressional isolationists in a rhyming quip about "Martin, Barton, and Fish."

In his book, Barton eschewed interest in the contents of Jesus' moral critique about material wealth. Instead, he focuses on how Jesus defused tensions about greed or economic inequality by dint of his corporate

16. Prothero, *American Jesus*.
17. Barton, *Man*.

managerial wizardry. Barton's pro-capitalist message is that Christianity proffered its new followers an attractive, limited liability arrangement with money because its founder knew how to take the contentious subject of materialism off the table. In the first chapter, tellingly titled "The Executive,"[18] Barton explained that the way Jesus recruited his disciples is a stellar example of executive organization—compared to this managerial issue, whether Jesus actually identified apostles as morally worthy initiators and emissaries of a new faith is a negligible matter. The "no discussion needed" manner by which Jesus headhunted Matthew is, in Barton's analysis, the quintessential example of how Christianity arose out of the adroit corporate management of its founder:

> And as Jesus passed by, he called Matthew. Amazing. No argument; no pleading. A small leader would have been compelled to set up the advantages of the opportunity. "Of course you are doing well where you are and making money," he might have said. "I can't offer you as much as you are getting; in fact you may have some difficulty in making ends meet. But I think we are going to have an interesting time and shall probably accomplish a big work." Such a conversation would have been met with Matthew's reply that he would "have to think it over," and the world would never have heard his name.[19]

Barton's biography of Jesus was an interlocked directorate of Christian belief and unabashed self-interest. Since his own professional field was relatively unknown to readers (his own firm, Barton, Durstine, and Osborn, was established just five years before this book's publication), Barton promoted advertising work by proclaiming to the world that Jesus was the first great ad man. Jesus and his followers knew how to package his good works in snappy, attention-grabbing headlines. In the first century, they promoted his messages in the open market squares of Galilee towns because "the market was a gathering place where everybody came at some time, the transfer place for all merchandise and for ideas." In the early twentieth century, ad men were following in Jesus' footsteps as the promoters of products; not open markets in Capernaum, but rather published newspaper advertisements had become "the modern thoroughfares. . . . The cross-roads where the sellers and buyers meet."[20]

---

18. Barton, *Man*, 1–31. Business terms in this chapter were modified in later editions of this book.

19. Barton, *Man*, 24.

20. Barton, *Man*, 139.

Jesus, Barton wrote, was a "sociable man" whose zest for life distinguished him from the stern asceticism of his erstwhile mentor, John the Baptist, and also from his predecessors in the Hebrew Bible. Jesus' sociability, in fact, is the divider between the Jews' part of the Bible and the Christians' part: "The Jewish prophets were stern-faced men; there are few if any gleams of humor in the Old Testament from beginning to end." Jesus was also a strong, powerful outdoor man. The key to Jesus' executive style was his manliness because, Barton explained, "since the world began no power has fastened the affection of women upon a man like manliness."[21]

Much can be said about the subtext messages packed into Barton's presentation of Jesus as a corporate manager. For a start, the images of Jesus' rugged outdoors manliness reflected myths of frontiersman power that lingered in prominent examples, such as Theodore Roosevelt's much-publicized hunting exploits, years after the historian Frederick Jackson Turner formally proclaimed that the frontier had closed at the end of the nineteenth century. Also, just as he claimed that Jesus' sociability ought to be seen as a line of demarcation separating the Christian New Testament from the Hebraic Old Testament, Barton's patriarchal words about Jesus' manliness evoked a distinction. They differentiated between the way ideas of power in America were reconsolidating in the 1920s in a corporate business format, as opposed to the more motherly, forgiving images of power that had helped the country heal its wounds after the Civil War. By far the most important religious book of the postbellum era, Lew Wallace's *Ben-Hur: A Tale of the Christ* (1880) had associated national reconciliation with feminized images of Jesus. Inevitably, this notion of Christianity's founder as a forgiving mother stirred a backlash. In the last year of the nineteenth century, a Protestant weekly, *Outlook*, surveyed some seventeen clerics, asking whether medieval and modern artistic renditions of Jesus' visage satisfied their idea of a "strong face." Most replied in the negative, and several volunteered additional criticism of Jesus' feminization.[22] Such values and concerns are vividly reflected in Barton's biography of Jesus.

Since the onset of secularized thought in the Enlightenment era, toward the end of the eighteenth century, theologians and other commentators who have engaged searches for the "historical Jesus" have anachronistically relativized his messages. Many of these commentators believed they had uncovered timeless insights about the preaching and activity of the "real" Jesus. Nonetheless, for a scholar who took a bird's-eye view of the entirety of this quest, it was not very hard to show how theologians kept finding the

21. Barton, *Man*, 66, 48.
22. Morgan, *Protestants*, 298–300.

historical Jesus whom they were predisposed to find from the start. Jesus, in their interpretations, was saying what they wanted him to say, based on their own contemporary interests and value systems in nineteenth-century Europe, in interwar America in the era of the Roaring Twenties and the Depression, or wherever and whenever.

Jesus' Critique of Materialism: The Eschatological Interpretation

The scholar who launched this sort of critique—Albert Schweitzer, in his *The Quest of the Historical Jesus*, originally published in German in 1906— was neither a cynic nor a relativist.[23] Schweitzer, who led a remarkably active and diverse life as a Lutheran minister, music devotee, philosopher, and physician, and who won acclaim for his humanitarianism and moral commitment (as acknowledged by the conferral of the Nobel Peace Prize to him in 1952), believed that authentic intents and meanings in Jesus' words and deeds could be found, no matter that they had been bowdlerized by modern commentators and critics. The problem was not really that these nineteenth-century commentators, primarily German Protestant theologians, lavished anachronism on the subject because they were moderately self-centered, or outright opportunists (Schweitzer had relatively little to say about Catholic interpretations of the historic Jesus, and he roundly bypassed Jewish reckonings with the same issue[24]).

In truth, Schweitzer had little regard for many of the theologians surveyed in his groundbreaking study. But he judged that the flaws in their commentaries on the historical Jesus stemmed not from defects in the theologians' own analytic abilities but rather from the esoteric quality of Jesus' messages. Schweitzer's own interpretation can be called "eschatological." He argued that Jesus' exhortations about money, and about fundamental issues such as family, loyalty, and marriage, belonged on the other side of a moral-metaphysical divide—one not really accessible to modern commentators whose earthly outlooks were tempered by bourgeois considerations of investment and effort. In contrast, Jesus and his followers lived according to an apocalyptic mindset, whereby the countdown toward the end of days had already started.

"The historical Jesus will be to our time a stranger and an enigma," concluded Schweitzer.[25] The eschatological volatility of his preaching would

23. Schweitzer, *Quest*.
24. Paget, "Albert Schweitzer."
25. Schweitzer, *Quest*, 397.

never be processed by modern clerics and thinkers whose thinking about effort investment, and material or spiritual profit, is tempered by middle-class culture. Schweitzer's eschatological interpretation borrowed from the findings of one or two iconoclastic thinkers he surveyed in his book, such as Johannes Weiss, a New Testament scholar who ended his career at the University of Heidelberg, and whose 1892 booklet on *Jesus' Proclamation of the Kingdom of God* became available in English in 1971.[26]

While this eschatological view defuses various tensions and riddles caused by the impractical severity of Jesus' preaching about material wealth and other issues, it nonetheless creates as many problems as it solves. In the book of Matthew, passages like the one referring to the "eye of the needle," or the stricture about debt forgiveness in the Lord's Prayer, often have an unworldly, anti-capitalist severity. Some passages convey summary proclamations against material accumulation, for example: "Do not store up for yourselves treasures on earth, where moths and vermin destroy, and where thieves break in and steal" (Matt 6:19). The Sermon on the Mount's abjuration about serving two masters ("You cannot serve both God and money," Matt 6:24) sounds as though it is telling latter-day followers to ignore the company's boss and listen instead solely to the priest in church. The intimidating impracticality laden in such exhortation is neutralized insofar as we imagine that Jesus was preaching on a hilltop to a few disciples who sat in a circle around him, and perhaps to some noninitiates positioned at lower depths of the mountain, who were possessed eschatologically by the idea of their imminent transition to another realm of existence.

The same point can be made in application to passages in the Gospels that relate to issues other than material gain. If we are able to read the Gospels within this frame of apocalyptic expectation, the onus in Jesus' peremptory demand of absolute devotion among his followers, one which theoretically unhinges their family ties, is mitigated (we are referring here to difficulties raised by passages such as, "Anyone who loves their father or mother more than me is not worthy of me.... Whoever does not take up their cross and follow me is not worthy of me," Matt 10:37–38).

Modifying Schweitzer's rather extreme proposal, we might regard eschatological volatility as *one* of a few essential elements addressed in a New Testament hermeneutic. This approach mollifies a prominent stumbling block in the reading of Scripture like the book of Matthew—namely, the seeming glare of its internal contradictions.

Howard Clarke, the author of a useful survey of the historical reception of Matthew's Gospel, comments on its inspiring centerpiece, the Sermon

---

26. Weiss, *Jesus' Proclamation*.

on the Mount: "Over the ages, its sentiments have inspired, frustrated and puzzled its readers"; and the remark refers aptly to apparent inconsistency in the Gospel as a whole.[27] Whereas he recommends "turning the other cheek" in the Sermon, Jesus later casts off the peacemaker's garb and speaks in an idiom of apocalyptic militancy: "Do not suppose that I have come to bring peace to the earth. I did not come to bring peace, but a sword" (Matt 10:34). Similarly, Jesus' preaching against capital accumulation in the book of Matthew is not uniformly consistent. Readers familiar with the parable of the unprofitable servant (Matt 25:14–30) will recall how its moral undermines, to some extent, the Gospel's unsparing critique of materialism. Jesus hints in this parable about how capital accumulation will serve Christianity's interests. Traditionally, Christian theology tried to resolve such apparent contradictions by developing a multilevel interpretation wherein Jesus' messages had literal applicability for some audiences (eventually located in monasteries, among other places) and a figurative, exhortative quality for other (laymen) audiences.

This two-level/two-audiences view has firm footing in some scriptural passages. Consider, for instance, Matt 5:1–2, which encourages the reader to visualize the Sermon on the Mount concurrently as private counsel for initiated disciples and also as public performance for Galilee's masses ("Now when Jesus saw the crowds, he went up on a mountainside and sat down. His disciples came to him, and he began to teach them"). This two-level interpretation resolved issues for theologians, but it had limited appeal for less scholarly Christians who appreciated the universalism of their religion as opposed to a view of it as a faith of two branches—one of ritualistic and disciplined daily severity for a spiritual elite and another, relatively latitudinarian, stream for the masses.

Writing as an enthusiastic amateur collector of artistic renderings connected to the Sea of Galilee, I am impressed by how many paintings of the Sermon on the Mount neglect the two-tiered structure that Matt 5:1–2 seems to evoke. Artists do not picture the Sermon as a bifurcated performance: one part being private counsel for select disciples, the other part being public message. Instead, they typically present Jesus' revered sermon as a univocal broadcast on a sloping, open field appreciated by an undifferentiated audience.

I am suggesting here that multilevel hermeneutics for the New Testament need not refer to segregated *audiences*—that interpretation seems emotionally unsatisfying. Instead, the two levels might apply to differences of existential expectation, where one stratum refers to relatively pedestrian

---

27. Clarke, *Gospel of Matthew*, 111.

understandings of investment and profit along the timeline of an ordinary lifetime, and the other level is saturated eschatologically in end of days expectation. Apparent contradictions in the Gospels can be explained via this possibility that Jesus is addressing both levels at once, or referring to one level in some passages and another level in other scriptural moments.

Schweitzer's eschatological interpretation ties some loose ends, but it fails as an overall explanation of Christianity's appeal and consolidation. Belief systems based on the expectation of some apocalyptic event face dire challenges when the event's designated date quietly comes and goes. In fact, an entire field of social science research, dating from studies about what happens when prophecy fails published by Leon Festinger in the mid-1950s, deals with this phenomenon of disappointed expectation, whose manifestations came to be known as "cognitive dissonance."[28] Religious history does not incontrovertibly show that a movement, such as the one promoted by Jesus' followers toward the end of the first century CE, must necessarily have failed had it been based on an eschatological expectation that remained unfulfilled as decades went by. For instance, in the North American case, in the 1830s, around the time Edward Robinson was correctly identifying a breathtaking number of Holy Land sites but misplacing the town where Jesus had a home, a farmer from northeastern New York, William Miller, inspired a spiritual movement by proclaiming that Jesus' second coming would happen within a few years. This never happened, of course; but after the "Great Disappointment" of this second advent's non-materialization on the designated date in October 1844, Millerism did not exactly perish. This was the era of America's Second Great Awakening, a time of religious excitement and tenacity. In the spirit of the times, some of the Millerites persisted and ended up forming the Seventh-day Adventist Church.

Theoretically, if we assume that Jesus' followers originally assembled in a mood of apocalyptic imminence, the spread of their faith after this expectation was never met can be understood in view of later examples, like Millerism. No faith that arises in a remote province like first-century Galilee can ever become a world religion without a capable bureau of eschatological administrators. However, this paradigm explaining Christianity's history as the creative management of cognitive dissonance is nonetheless reductive. The story of the rupture between Judaism and Christianity, and the latter faith's subsequent institutionalization and spread throughout the Roman Empire, cannot be fit into a one-size-fits-all paradigm.

---

28. Festinger, *When Prophecy Fails*.

The Canon Will Always Be with You

The nature of the allure generated by the record of Jesus' words and deeds will always remain in dispute whenever Christians discuss religion with others, of course. Trying to separate our discussion from this metric of subjective faith, I am arguing for as "regular" a reading of the Gospels as can be allowed, once relatively uncontroversial judgments and findings from modern studies in fields of archaeology, religious studies, and history are taken into account.

We are now exiting an unusual, post-Holocaust era of relative amicability between Judaism and Christianity, perhaps the first and last time when people spoke about "Judeo-Christian civilization" in a tenor of innocuous sincerity. This was also an era when it seemed interesting to "deconstruct" the West's cultural canon by stressing omissions and power dynamics in admired texts. Deconstructionism felt like responsible business because treating canonical texts the way they had been handled for centuries had become tedious in practice and, in view of the Holocaust, genocidal in effect. Thus, consolidating in deliberate opposition to the Western canon, new fields like postcolonial studies evolved.

After a generation of operation, practitioners and students in these new fields reached the conclusion that out of all flawed state projects in the twenty-first century, the Jews deserve special marks of opprobrium for promoting genocide in their Zionist state. Whatever you think about Israel's policies, this outcome can only mean that even though a generation of "deconstructing" the West's canon might have thankfully eliminated many offensive things, the new, radical school of interpretation remained ensnared by old anti-Semitic tropes. It never developed inclusive, liberating ways of relating to the most dangerously portentous points of contention in the Western world's canon.

The canon will always be with us. This is because the issues it addresses with beguiling power and ambiguity, such as the problem of wealth accumulation raised by the book of Matthew, will always be with us. Whether you are happy about them or not, trends in our time summon us to revisit such issues and to try to work through them in a way that yields better results.

What are the trends? Generally, they are seen in a mounting discussion about iniquities caused by the power of the superrich "1 percent"; specifically, they are pungent, ever-amplifying accusations about the antidemocratic behavior of the Jewish superrich, who allegedly control the pro-Israel "Jewish lobby." One way or another—many fair-minded people would suppose—the shape and subtexts in social media and in public discussions of these trends come from the canon. The most intelligible, promising way of dealing with this supposition is to relate to the canon more or less on its own terms—not to "deconstruct" it, but rather to assume that its narrative dramas and moral contrasts have been apprehensible to believers and readers in a roughly similar fashion, from one era to the next. This means restoring faith in the canon, not necessarily as a guidebook enjoining ritual and belief systems, but rather as a reliable record of how the same set of moral and political issues continually engage persons, their own differing rituals and belief systems notwithstanding.

The postmodern critics have argued that contemporary readers ought not passionately engage with texts like the Gospels because doing so submissively reinforces power manipulations wrought by white male elites. Looking at the same issue from another angle, a century before the late twentieth-century culture wars, Schweitzer, Weiss, and a few other clerics and theologians urged a similar conclusion. They suggested that readers and believers in the modern West could not effectively engage with Gospel scripture since the disciples who compiled it dwelled, so to speak, on another eschatological planet.

In practical terms, the thrust of both these critiques is to insulate canonical religious writings from the positive engagement of unassuming, regular readers, Christians and others. The deconstructionists insist that the canonical texts must first be purged of toxicity embedded in them by class, gender, and race interest, whereas the second school demands that the entire eschatological culture, one quite exotic by modern standards, must be reconstructed before anyone, Christian believers or others, can penetrate to the gist of Jesus' messages. Such approaches preempt, or significantly defer, reasonable discussion between Jews and Christians (and others), based on relatively straightforward efforts to read and process Scripture considered sacred by one side or the other.

In theory, there is no prima facie reason to conclude that interfaith dialogue between members of different religious groups must ameliorate tensions that weigh upon their interaction. In a perfect world, the canon—defined not as the dogma of a particular church, but rather in the post-Enlightenment sense of a textual corpus that aspires to engage persons of differing value and belief systems—could be set aside. In such a world, anyone could proceed with his/her own business, engaging texts whose cultural or spiritual import is mainly appreciated by his or her group. However in our imperfect world, we might set the canon aside, for sheer neglect or for deconstruction, but the canon will not put us aside. Jews and Christians are still talking and thinking about one another in the same age-old modes, using the same metonyms and metaphors. For a generation we tried to obliterate, or just plain forget, the canon. But it was paying attention to us. Below are some examples.

The Book of Matthew and Twentieth-Century American Debates About Capitalism

In the political economy of worldwide Jewry in the post-Holocaust era, the decisive period was the mid-1980s when new opportunities for private capital accumulation arose, thanks to the privatization and deregulation policies adopted by the Reagan administration in the United States, and in step with trends in Europe shaped out of the philosophy and doings of Maggie Thatcher's governments in Great Britain. Generally, wealth has been concentrating heavily in the hands of a mega-elite since that time, and this capital concentration phenomenon has vast social and political implications in America and elsewhere. In Jewish life, the creation of a financial super-elite in the 1980s was coterminous with the skyrocketed rise in the power of pro-Israel lobbying groups, particularly AIPAC (the American Israel Public Affairs Committee). This was not a coincidence—through the present day, the muscle behind AIPAC's lobbying belongs to its megadonors, largely a class of nouveau riche parvenus whose wealth accumulated as a result of this 1980s turning point.

Since the late 1970s, when the right-wing Likud party grabbed the reins of power in Israel (it has relinquished them for just a few relatively short periods since 1977), AIPAC has lobbied in favor of governments in the Jewish state that have built and amplified an antidemocratic, colonialist settlement movement in areas wrested in the 1967 Six-Day War. Connections between private capital formation among superrich American Jews and the settlement movement, located today on the West Bank, are multitudinous and conspicuous.

Also conspicuous in this mid-1980s period, precisely when AIPAC became politically important even though it was established three decades earlier, was a trend of well-publicized insider trading and related white-collar crime scandals, featuring American Jews who had become prominent in this new financial elite. One of them, Ivan Boesky, became a symbol of unbridled avarice and shameful corruption in the Reagan era. Partly, this was thanks to a line proclaimed by Gordon Gekko (played by the actor Michael Douglas) in the *Wall Street* film, which reportedly reworked a statement made a year earlier by Boesky at the graduation ceremony of the University of California, Berkeley, business school. "I think greed is healthy. You can be greedy and still feel good about yourself," declared Boesky (Gekko's diction was pithier).[29]

Forty years after the Holocaust, the roles and reputations of Jews in the economy of the United States, which has historically been a philosemitic country, were not nearly as volatile as they had been in other places and eras, including pre-Holocaust Europe, primarily an anti-Semitic milieu. But this does not mean that America is exceptionally impervious to views and prejudices about Jews in the economy that draw from the West's religious canon. In fact, in this economics sphere, Jewish history in America is not an absolute exception. This fact remained muffled for decades, at least until the 2023–2024 Gaza War crisis, partly because of latitude extended to Jews by guilt-ridden Christians after the Holocaust. Nonetheless, here and there blips of publicly articulated anxiety about the political economies of American Jews pinpricked the silence, particularly at times of economic downswings. One such moment was the 2007–2008 financial crisis, which pivoted around the questionable practices in real estate and other spheres undertaken by investment banks, some of them, such as the ill-fated Lehman Brothers and also Goldman Sachs, known for having heavily Jewish executive personnel rosters and heavily Jewish organizational histories. Not as a causal determinant but rather as a spin-off of the 2008 financial meltdown, Bernie Madoff's unprecedentedly profligate Ponzi scheme attracted considerable attention as an American Jewish corruption scandal. Meantime public discussions sprawled in new, uncontrollable ways on social media.

Whereas through the 1950s and 1960s, American Jews had not really managed to wrest top managerial posts in major corporations, suddenly in the mid-1980s their innovative use of new techniques in finance, and in the corporate mergers and acquisitions field, propelled them toward the top of the country's economic pyramid. Abruptly several American Jews were positioned to buy emblematic companies in the country's economy. "We're going to tee-up GM, Ford and IBM, and make them cringe," exclaimed Michael Milken,[30] whose fortune at the Drexel Burnham Lambert investment bank came from his hugely successful use of junk bonds and from involvement in company takeovers (LBOs, leveraged buyouts) that were leveraged by junk bonds. Junk bonds, LBOs, and risk arbitrage (the favored field of Ivan Boesky, Milken's confederate in one of the era's notorious insider trading scandals) were financial practices developed with unusual intensity by Jews, mostly because the "white shoes" executives at gentile-controlled banks shunned them as overly aggressive or risky ways of making money.

---

29. Stewart, *Den of Thieves*, 261.
30. Stewart, *Den of Thieves*, 67.

As it turned out, these new financial practices straddled a thin line between the fulfillment of the American dream and white-collar crime. We will return to this story later. Here, our purpose is to show how new trends in the political economy of any era are inevitably processed within biblical frames.

The biblical canon followed these insider trading scandals. It was as though American commentators, who, justifiably, would have been incensed had anyone accused them of anti-Semitism, had no other way to format their coverage and understanding of what was happening in American finance in the 1980s. Though some of its findings, and aspects of its methodology, have been called into question, James B. Stewart's 1991 Pulitzer Prize–winning account of the mid-1980s insider trading scandals remains the most readable and influential survey of the subject.[31] Its focus is on the law-breaking of four American Jews: Milken, Boesky, Martin Siegel, and Dennis Levine. Taking its cue from Matt 21:13,[32] Stewart called his book *Den of Thieves*.

If you reread that biblical quotation ("'My house will be called a house of prayer,' but you are making it 'a den of robbers'") and transpose it to the subject of Stewart's report, the devastatingly harsh implication is unmistakable. The author is saying that economic opportunity in America, and the realization of dreams through honest labor and fair investment, is the secularized equivalent of holiness in the ancient Jerusalem temple. Just as Jesus upset the money changers' table (reversing the approach he deployed with Matthew in Capernaum) and accused Jewish greed and Pharisaical rigidity of despoiling God's temple in Jerusalem, so too is investigative reporting revealing how the Junk Bond Jews of the 1980s befouled the American dream, as articulated in Reagan's popular homage to the shining city on the hill. Such innuendo is packed within the title of Stewart's book.

Traces of the Gospel format arise whenever the topic of political economy arises in discussions between Jews and Christians. Also recapitulated is the ambiguity of Jesus' situation in episodes such as his upbraiding of the Pharisees. Historically, the diatribes provided ammunition for anti-Semites, but this result accorded only with the intentions of members of the Gospel of Matthew composition team, who favored a breach with Judaism. In contrast, members of this team who recorded and emphasized Jesus' proclamation about "fulfilling" Jewish law must have seen the implications of

---

31. Cohan, *Money and Power*, 267–70. This criticism of Stewart's coverage focuses on its assessment of Kidder, Peabody, and Goldman Sachs employees implicated in the prosecution of the era's major insider trading scandal, supervised by Rudolph Giuliani, then US attorney for the Southern District of New York.

32. It bears mention that this dramatic New Testament passage, Matt 21:13, reworks the Old Testament (Hebrew Bible) reference in Jer 7:11.

this anti-Pharisee philippic through a different prism. How would history have changed had Jesus been seen as an in-house critic concerned about Jewish internal reform at the temple and in everyday life when he kicked over the money stalls, or when he lambasted the Pharisees' "greed and self-indulgence"!?

It never changed history, but Jewish critics sensed the ambiguous malleability of Jesus' circumstances and preaching in the Gospels. Sometimes they stood his criticisms on their head by using them to censure emblematic Christian institutions.

One example, also taken from the context of American finance, can suffice. In American history, the period whose political economy most closely resembles our contemporary, iniquitously lopsided, situation occurred around World War I, in a transitional stretch between the corrupt Gilded Age and a Progressive Era that was marked by experimentation in public regulation and trust-busting. This was a time when wealth and power was intolerably consolidated in the hands of an economic elite, as is the case today; but it was also a period of robust public discussion about economic opportunity and fair play, which, if truth be told, sometimes veered toward paranoiac hysteria (investigative journalists, famously known as "muckrakers," were not particularly discriminating in their use of terms like "monopoly" or "robber barons").

In the Progressive camp, one of the foremost critics of financial foul play and capital concentration was Louis Brandeis, who first gained public renown as the "people's attorney," filing innovative legal briefs on behalf of male and female workers' rights, fair administration of public utilities, and many other public-spirited causes.[33] In my own world of scholarly work and ideological interest, Brandeis is a uniquely inspiring figure because he climbed to the most prominent post attained heretofore by an American Jew, as a Supreme Court justice, precisely in the politically tumultuous World War I era when he also did more for the world Zionist movement than had been accomplished heretofore by any other American Jew.

After the devastating financial crisis of 2007–2008, when the public realized how executives from major investment banks had stacked the deck, awarding themselves fat Christmas bonuses exactly as taxpayers surrendered hundreds of millions of bailout dollars to forestall the collapse of corporations and banks that were "too big to fail," historians and journalists followed the liberal-Progressive track back to Brandeis. Belatedly they appreciated how prophetic a critic of monopolization he had been.[34] In his

---

33. Urofsky, *Louis D. Brandeis*.
34. Wu, *Curse of Bigness*.

attacks against what he called "the curse of bigness," Brandeis presciently foreshadowed the crisis of political economy in America a century later. He anticipated how the vicious circularity of "too big to fail" arguments articulated on Wall Street in the twenty-first century invariably costs the everyday citizen on Main Street. As often happened among the muckrakers and the Progressives, a strain of overwrought zealousness militated against Brandeis's insights, to some degree (his predilection for unmitigated condemnation of "bigness" betrayed an unrealistic refusal to acknowledge some advantages of economic consolidation, and the possibility that a "natural monopoly" might arise in particular economic spheres).

At the edgiest pinnacle of this World War I phase of his career, Brandeis recalibrated the conventional structure of financial critiques and conversations pertaining to Jews and Christians. In a series of articles published in 1913–1914 in *Harper's Weekly*, America's foremost Jewish figure berated the country's Christian bankers for Pharisaical greed and self-indulgence.[35]

We call attention to this critique because its centerpiece article is formatted straight out of the book of Matthew. In 1914, Brandeis's articles were reprinted as a one-volume collection under the sublimely cheeky title *Other People's Money and How the Bankers Use It* (we will return to this phrase). Throughout the book's chapters, the banker J. P. Morgan (an Episcopalian) emerges as Brandeis's archnemesis, the personification of various ills of financial concentration, such as interlocking directorate arrangements.

In irately layered prose, which presaged the way outraged commentators on the 2007–2008 fiasco wrote about Goldman Sachs, Brandeis accused Morgan of exercising sprawling, octopean control over the entirety of the American economy. In a two-page section, called "The Endless Chain," Brandeis imputed unfair influence to Morgan with respect to these companies (the list is not complete): the New York, New Haven, and Hartford railroad; Penn Mutual Life Insurance Company; Guarantee Trust Company; the United States Steel Cooperation; the General Electric Company; the Western Telegraph Company, a subsidiary of the American Telephone and Telegraph Company; the Pullman Company and the Baldwin Locomotive Company.[36] Brandeis's corrective for such iniquitously interlocked directorship was taken straight from Jesus' mouth: "No one can serve two masters" (Matt 6:24). Indeed, didactic chapter headings in Brandeis's book (e.g., "Serve One Master Only") created the sense that his critique of the curse of bigness came straight from the Sermon on the Mount.[37]

35. Urofsky, *Louis D. Brandeis*, 321–25.
36. Brandeis, *Other People's Money*, 52–54.
37. Brandeis, *Other People's Money*, 69.

CALLING SAINT MATTHEW

THE BACKWARD GLANCE AT THE PERILS OF CAPITALISM

Gospel discussions about issues of capital accumulation have served as a lasting format, as the frame of highly contentious subjects such as corporate takeover mania in the mid-1980s or "too big to fail" phenomena twenty years later, because of their own innate narrative drama. Even in religiously unlearned, secularized periods, readers have enough knowledge of Judaism's evolving crisis in the late Second Temple period to appreciate the high drama of Jesus' strictures about the consequences of the Pharisees' greed and self-indulgence.

Specifically, the narrative power of the book of Matthew derives from what commentators have called its "backward glance."[38] According to scholars such as Anthony Saldarini and J. Andrew Overman, this Gospel was compiled toward the end of the first century, in some Galilee venue, by a group of chroniclers who had conflicted ideas about the desirability of continued fidelity to Jewish law and whose spiritual confidence had been jarred by the failed Jewish rebellion and the Second Temple's destruction, perhaps less than a generation before they took up the Gospel's composition.[39] Their backward glance vantage point packed power into Jesus' warnings about the consequences of material greed: the Jews were putting the entirety of their religious civilization, their temple, at risk. The Swiss theologian Ulrich Luz, a respected authority on the book of Matthew, insists that backward glance, prophetic passages in this Gospel "clearly refer to the events of the Jewish War" which occurred some thirty years after the crucifixion.[40] The prime example here is the apocalyptic passage, Matt 24:15–22 ("Let those who are in Judea flee to the mountains.... How dreadful it will be in those days for pregnant women and nursing mothers"). No sanction against wanton capitalist greed could have ever been more imposing than this Armageddon threat of the temple's impending destruction, what Jews call the *hurban*.

In the secularizing modern period, the grip on believers held by Gospel accounts of supernatural, miraculous occurrences in Jesus' mission loosened. In contrast, as moral and political challenges posed by capitalist accumulation expanded exponentially, there was growing incentive to relate to socioeconomic aspects of Jesus' preaching.

In the mid-nineteenth century, at the height of the first search for the historical Jesus surveyed by Schweitzer, bestselling commentators focused

---

38. Silver, *Galilee, 47 BCE to 1260 CE*, 53.
39. Saldarini, *Community*; Overman, *Matthew's Gospel*.
40. Luz, *Gospel of Matthew*, 126.

on issues of Jesus' divinity and his personal character. This angle of interpretation was rather traditional, even though the commentators sometimes reached provocative conclusions attuned to the secularizing temper of the period. Probably the book which best captures the spirit of this time is Ernest Renan's sensational *Life of Jesus* (1863).[41] The volume provoked interest among readers by unpacking a psychologically complicated situation wherein Jesus privately disregarded miraculous traits that were attributed to his doings by his followers.

Today, unlike Renan's time, readers are rather desensitized to supposed revelations about the "real" character of the historical Jesus, as a Jewish zealot, a shaman, a corporate executive, or many other guises. They want to know about the socioeconomic status of followers who trudged up from Capernaum to the sermon hilltop. In its aspiration for a better world, how invasive should religion be, with respect to the investment portfolios of its believers? Today, in settings like the United States where the top 1 percent controls 26.5 percent of all household wealth, the same share (26 percent) that is controlled by 60 percent of Americans who are defined as comprising the middle class, incentive to ponder the socioeconomic dimensions of Jesus' career and preaching is obvious.[42] We are left wondering about how much tax coinage Matthew collected at his booth in Capernaum, and whether the state-imposed rates George Harrison sarcastically complained about on the opening track of the Beatles' album *Revolver*, "Taxman," were really quite so unreasonable.

JEWS AND THE CAPITALIST SPIRIT, 1911

When Brandeis unleashed his scathing attack on J. P. Morgan and the banks just before World War I, he relied heavily on data and testimony accumulated in a congressional investigation of the "money trust" that was known as the Pujo Committee. The theory animating this subcommittee was that the big banks indulge dubious profit-making tactics and threaten or damage the public interest in multifarious ways.[43] Without question, the revival of the same theory a century later, following the 2007–2008 financial crisis, underlies the emergence of specific militant left phenomena, such as the Occupy Wall Street movement.

More broadly, a reasonable case could be made holding that the entirety of US politics in the third decade of the twenty-first century, defined

41. Renan, *Life of Jesus*.
42. De Vise, "Top 1 Percent."
43. Brandeis, *Other People's Money*, 109.

by populist-spirited fracture between the Bernie Sanders's left wing of the Democratic Party and Donald Trump's MAGA movement, is unfolding under the shadow of the Pujo Committee's thesis. The left holds that since the thesis is obviously true, the fundamental structure of the economy ought to be transformed via aggressive taxation policies, free college tuition, and so on. The center recognizes the truth of the thesis but pretends that it does not enjoin major policy reform. The right celebrates the reality of big bank and big corporation profit-making, and vows that it is un-American to ask questions about it.

The Pujo Committee's driving force was a New York City attorney named Samuel Untermyer, whose ethnic and professional profile resembled that of Louis Brandeis. Like Brandeis, Untermyer was an American Jew who descended from immigrants from Central Europe and who grew up in the south, and then made a fortune in the northeast as a corporate lawyer while becoming deeply engaged politically in public campaigns against the "trusts"—that is, the consolidation of capital among banking and corporate elites. Not only was Untermyer Jewish, but his law firm was heavily involved in the establishment and support of American Jewish initiatives and organizations whose paramount purpose was to combat anti-Semitism. This organizational work for American Jewry, ably promoted by Untermyer's law partner Louis Marshall, was voluntary, idealistic, and untainted by corruption; often this work was crucially beneficial for many non-Jews, as exemplified by Jewish organizational lobbying for open immigration through the early 1920s, before America closed its doors. That said, such organizational work can also be seen as a confusing and complicated entanglement of private philanthropy, communal lobbying, white-collar professional success, and political struggle.[44]

Unlike a widely held misconception, the common denominator linking these World War I circumstances and peptic discussions of the "Jewish lobby" a century later is *not* American Jewry's attachment to Zionism, an ideology that came to be loathed by Palestinians, among others. Until the start of the 1920s, the mainstay of the evolving American Jewish political philanthropy network was Jacob Schiff, a banker from Kuhn, Loeb, an investment house which, through a 1970s merger, became Lehman Brothers, the financial services giant whose bankruptcy and dissolution symbolized the chaos and wreckage of the 2007–2008 financial meltdown.[45] Schiff, whose bank was a major client for Untermyer's law firm, was an adamant

---

44. For the Pujo Committee, see Urofsky, *Louis D. Brandeis*, 281–85; for Untermyer, see Hawkins, *Progressive Politics*; for Marshall, see Silver, *Louis Marshall*.

45. Cohen, *Jacob H. Schiff*.

anti-Zionist (his objections to Jewish nationalism shaped the ethos and early organizational history of a whole series of signature American Jewish organizations, such as the Conservative religious stream's institutional backbone, the Jewish Theological Seminary). In this pre–World War I era, much as is the case today, the crux of controversy or confusion about organized American Jewish effort was not Zionism but rather the age-old discussion between Christians and Jews about materialism and earthly power.

When Untermyer, via the Pujo Committee, and when Brandeis, in *Other People's Money*, stigmatized J. P. Morgan as the quintessential robber baron, they were shifting public attention from one, Jewish, side of Wall Street toward its other, much more solidly established, Wasp side, where Morgan was the era's major player. Morgan thought such maneuvering was rich, to turn a phrase. From Morgan's standpoint, the public Progressive crusades of such Jewish "people's attorneys" were a smokescreen—Untermyer and Brandeis were corporate attorneys who made their daily bread by representing clients such as Schiff, who was a prominently minted member of one (Jewish) side of the money trust that was targeted by the Pujo Committee. White-shoes bankers on gentile Wall Street believed that the Pujo Progressives caused Morgan to die from stress, and Morgan's son called Untermyer, "the Beast."[46]

In 1911, exactly as Untermyer brushed up his arguments for the Pujo Committee's assault on the alleged greed and self-indulgence of Wasp banking houses on Wall Street, academics in Europe were staging a comparable discussion about the same subject. Who was responsible for capitalism's record of unfair practices and social injustice? In America, in the Roaring Twenties decade that ensued after World War I, discussants who identified "Jews" as the answer to this pointed question spawned anti-Semitic campaigns that were egregiously obnoxious in content but relatively short-lived and ineffectual—Henry Ford's dissemination of an Americanized version of the *Protocols of the Elders of Zion* in the *Dearborn Independent* is the leading example.[47] In Europe, even though it was sometimes staged by talented, mostly empirical academics, the discussion was far more volatile, and it can be associated with genocidal catastrophe, the Holocaust.

In his 1911 treatise *The Jews and Modern Capitalism* (*Die Juden und das Wirtschaftsleben*), Werner Sombart, a Berlin-based professor whose work combined history, economics, and sociology, proclaimed that Jewish religious culture, as it had evolved from antiquity through the early modern period, lacked the anti-materialist core that the Gospel record of Jesus'

---

46. Chernow, *House of Morgan*, 159–60; Silver, *Louis Marshall*, 222.
47. Baldwin, *Henry Ford*.

preaching had embedded in Christianity.[48] Citing Matt 19:24, Jesus' stricture about the camel and the eye of the needle, Sombart declared, "This is the keynote of Christianity on the point, and the difference between it and Judaism is clear enough. There is no single parallel to the saying of Jesus in the whole of the Old Testament, and probably also none in the entire body of Rabbinic literature."[49]

Read over a century later, Sombart's book displays the best and worst features of discussions about Jews, Christians, and economics. Its early parts, written as economic history, are grounded in empirical research.[50] They present a provocative thesis about how the expulsion of Jews from the Iberian Peninsula during the Inquisition, and their migration northward toward commercial centers like London and Amsterdam in the sixteenth and seventeenth centuries, contributed significantly to the development of capitalism in this early modern period. To be sure, Sombart's formulations in this part of the book exaggeratedly convey a sense of capitalism's consolidation as being almost exclusively a result of Jewish migration and activity. Also, the writing compresses and expands in a dizzying blur when Sombart pushes his thesis to South America and North America, glossing the differing circumstances, motivations, and skill sets of various Jewish subgroups, such as the Sephardic departees from the Inquisition and a much later group of Jewish arrivals to mid-nineteenth-century America from Central Europe (also, we will not elaborate here on the accuracy, or lack thereof, of specific claims made by Sombart about Jewish financial wizardry and the unfolding of political events like the American Revolution). Still, particularly in his analysis of the European situation in pre-nineteenth-century eras that were less saturated by ideological discussion of the so-called "Jewish problem," Sombart's discussion of how the contrasting economic performances of towns in the Netherlands, German-speaking principalities, and elsewhere depended on whether their policies toward Jewish traders were restrictive or inviting is suggestive.

Sombart has a spotty reputation among Jewish scholars.[51] "The principal claims" in Sombart's book "are at best inaccurate and at worst breathtakingly silly," wrote Derek Penslar, in his 2001 study on Jews and economics in

---

48. Sombart, *Jews*.

49. Sombart, *Jews*, 221.

50. Sombart, *Jews*, 11–153. This part is called "The Contribution of the Jews to Modern Economic Life."

51. For the complicated array of contemporary responses, pro and con, among Zionists and other Jewish (and gentile) commentators, see Samuel Klausner's introduction in Sombart, *Jews*, xv–xx, c–cii.

early modern Europe.⁵² On the other hand, scholars use Sombart's findings and claims as a launching pad in their discussions of Jewish migration and capitalism's consolidation in the early modern period, not only in European venues. One example involves Sombart's claim that Jewish immigrants were traders, rather than heavy-lifting pioneers, in the settlement of North American colonies in the early modern period. Its gist undergirds the description of the subject in a recent (2017) one-volume study of American Jewish history published by Cambridge University Press.⁵³ But just as Sombart's discussion provided inspiration to future scholarship, his formulations invited manipulation by anti-Semites. Here is how he wrote about Jews and the settlement of North America (Jews are the twentieth family group referenced in this passage):

> We may picture the process of colonizing somewhat after this fashion. A band of determined men and women—let us say twenty families—went forth into the wilds to begin their life anew. Nineteen were equipped with plough and scythe, ready to clear the forests and till the soil in order to earn their livelihood as husbandmen. The twentieth family opened a store to provide their companions with such necessaries of life as could not be obtained from the soil, often no doubt hawking them at their very doors. Soon this twentieth family made it its business to arrange for the distribution of the products which the other nineteen won from the soil.⁵⁴

In the final part of the book, stereotypical writing overtakes Sombart's earlier commitment to empirically reasoned analysis.⁵⁵ Conscious of how these concluding chapters might lack appeal to readers who had not succumbed to the fad of racial-based theorizing, which remained popular in many intellectual circles a decade into the twentieth century, Sombart inserted orotund explanatory prefaces, euphemistically describing their essentialist-racist methodology as "genetic." He made sure that the traits he associated collectively with the Jews had an objective or even complimentary ring (he attributed "high intellectuality" to the Jews, a goal-directed, *tachlis*, orientation, and so on). Sombart died in 1941. He ended his career writing pseudoscientific panegyric about Nazi National Socialism, favorably comparing its *volksgeist*, "national folk spirit," to the capitalist egoism

---

52. Penslar, *Shylock's Children*, 165.
53. Lederhendler, *American Jewry*, 5–13.
54. Sombart, *Jews*, 44.
55. Sombart, *Jews*, 281–355. This part is called "The Origin of Jewish Genius."

of the Jewish spirit.[56] We might overlook this late phase, assuming it happened under professional and political duress of some sort; but, whatever Sombart's innermost motivations thirty years earlier, when he wrote *The Jews and Modern Capitalism*, can we plausibly overlook how the politely formulated generalizations at the end of this 1911 volume camouflaged blunt, simplistic thinking about Jews? Sombart ended his book with lazy generalizations ready-made for exploitation by anti-Semites. Jews are capitalism's progenitors and beneficiaries (Sombart repeatedly insists that Jews are richer than Christians, even though there are many impoverished Jews). This is because the Jews are smarter than the brawny gentiles, Sombart concludes. He quotes a folk saying, "Heaven protect us against Jewish mooch (brains) and Gentile koach (physical force)," and elaborates, "Mooch v. Koach—that is the Jewish problem in a nutshell. It ought to be the motto of this book."[57]

The middle part of Sombart's study, written with more analytic rigor than its last part, is sociological in character and complements the economic history approach of its first part.[58] Its thesis is a bald generalization—Judaism is a rationalist creed and culture. Sombart argued that Judaism bred among its adherents capacities for forward-thinking investment activities, and computational skills in innovative capitalist fields, like stock market trading. This discussion focuses on how Western culture changed after capitalism arose and how religion might have wedged this transformation (in lieu of forces like class struggle that were emphasized by critics of capitalism such as Marxists, whose analyses had interested Sombart earlier in his career).

For all its semi-racist generalization, on the eve of the world wars, Sombart's book on Jews and capitalism was at the cutting edge of academic-intellectual discussion about the nature of modernity itself. Two or three times in his book, Sombart explained that its impetus was Max Weber's booklet *The Protestant Ethic and the Spirit of Capitalism*, originally published in German six years before Sombart's volume.[59] Weber contended that Calvinism ushered in capitalism by altering the cultural values, or the "spirit," of early modernity. Sombart countered, arguing that Jews actually served the functions attributed by Weber to Calvinist Puritans. Sombart

---

56. In a 1937 publication, Sombart declared that Jews ought not to have equal rights with citizens of the Reich. See Klausner's introduction in Sombart, *Jews*, cii. See also, Mitzman, *Sociology and Estrangement*, 135–264.

57. Sombart, *Jews*, 260.

58. Sombart, *Jews*, 157–280. This part is called "The Aptitude of the Jews for Modern Capitalism."

59. Sombart, *Jews*, 191, 248; Weber, *Protestant Ethic*.

then diluted the intellectual seriousness of his debate with Weber.[60] He fatuously claimed that there could not be much difference between the two publications because the Calvinist Puritans were, for all intents and purposes, Jews. (Examples cited by Sombart in defense of this droll claim later entered volumes written by scholars of American Jewish history, who noticed that Puritan culture in the early North American colonies was suffused with Hebraic references and images; but, for Sombart's purposes, details in this line of analysis are irrelevant because Weber stressed how precepts in Calvinism's belief system, like predestination, encouraged capitalist orientations, and these Calvinist notions are completely foreign to Judaism.)

In fact, the relationship between Weber's famous publication and *The Jews and Modern Capitalism* was more interestingly complex than Sombart seemed to understand or acknowledge.[61] In his essay, Weber recognizes that Sombart's earlier work about rationalism as the motor of capitalism intrigued him and almost became a key idea in a series of sociological works about religion and economics, to which his *The Protestant Ethic* was an introduction.[62] However, Weber decided that rationalism is an insufficiently unitary and coherent concept. The "capitalist spirit" could not reasonably be called "rational," Weber decided. In fact, what Weber chose as the archetypal example of such Calvinist-molded spirit—i.e., passages from Benjamin Franklin's autobiographical writing that refer to the relentless management of time, work, and money for the cause of profit accumulation—could be seen as profoundly irrational.[63] After accumulating enough revenue to spend his days in comfort, would a man like Franklin continue to invent and trade in order to accrue yet more capital if he were motivated by purely rational calculations? The only explanation for capitalism's relentless pursuit of new markets, growth, and profit could be that innermost individual motivations were induced by religious beliefs founded on nonempirical ("irrational") ideas about afterlife destiny, Weber concluded.

Nothing in Sombart's book was comparable to Weber's penetrating theological and sociological examination of how a religious idea sometimes breeds counterintuitive socioeconomic results. Calvinist doctrine about predestination might have bred socioeconomic lassitude (if your afterlife fate is predetermined, why bother during a few decades of earthly life?), but Weber's point was that the opposite happened. Calvinism, a coldly dour

---

60. Sombart, *Jews*, 248–51.

61. For an overview of interaction between the two, see Klausner's introduction in Sombart, *Jews*, ixxiv–ixxxv.

62. Weber, *Protestant Ethic*, 36–38.

63. Weber, *Protestant Ethic*, 14–16.

creed, and Puritanism, a notoriously ascetic way of life, ended up generating the booming gluttony of capitalism, essentially what most people are thinking of when they imagine life in twentieth- and twenty-first-century America.

While Sombart was not the type to delve into such theological dialectics, his work shared a number of key traits with Weber's. As the historian Jerry Muller points out in his 2010 book *Capitalism and the Jews*, both researchers assumed that modernity and capitalism jumped out of the Middle Ages and that some specific group could be identified as the catalysts or cause of this rupture and transformation.[64] Both stressed how they were not talking about profit drives and market mechanics that exist in many settings outside of Western modernity; both thought about capitalism as something definably new in the world. However, neither writer seemed particularly enthusiastic about attempts to define the essence of modern capitalism in a sentence or two ("We will define a capitalistic economic action as one which rests on the expectation of profit by the utilization of opportunities for exchange, that is on formally peaceful chances for profit," wanly declaimed Weber[65]). Also, as Muller points out, neither writer really proved that "capitalism" represents something qualitatively new in the world, rather than the quantitative expansion of market dynamics that had existed in cruder forms in ancient and medieval settings. In fact, Sombart's delineation of premodern economic practices and their transformation was more detailed and persuasive than anything found in Weber's essay. When all of these points are put together, it appears that the only essential difference between these two publications was the identity of the agent of capitalism's rise, Calvinism or Judaism.

Sombart viewed the transition to modern capitalism in moral and mechanical terms, as though it were all a matter of velocity and values. Before modernity, economic activity was slow and circumscribed by communal ties. Capitalism, in contrast, was fast and impersonal. Jews facilitated the transition to modernity because their religious (Talmudic) training trained them to think quickly about pros and cons in trading, because their social experience of migration and their legal status as semi-aliens taught them to move quickly, and because their dispersion over the globe enabled them to form multinational trade networks wherein they moved goods with a speed and scope unmatched by competitors. Jews had a precocious ability to identify and secure assets, products, and services, starting with gold and silver, which would be valued by important clients and purchasers. (Sombart

---

64. Muller, *Capitalism and the Jews*, 53–61.
65. Weber, *Protestant Ethic*, xxxii.

tended to stress Jewish evolution from court Jews into elite bankers like the Rothschilds, whose trading and services focused on leisure markets and prominent clients.) Because of their semi-alien status and far-flung circumstances, Jews catapulted economically as contractors during wars.

Sombart cited numerous examples of Jewish theorists and traders who published treatises and implemented new trading practices in ways which overcame traditional Christian inhibitions about usury and profit accumulation. A text like Don Joseph de la Vega's 1688 *Confusion de Confusiones* demonstrated "that if the Jews were not actually the 'fathers' of Stock Exchange business they were certainly primarily concerned in its genesis."[66] All the details and examples whittled down to a perceptible argument: the premodern economy was "slowed" by traditional inhibitions and communal constraints, whereas the pace of modern capitalism accelerated because of the impersonal character of transactions and the precedence taken by the profit motive, at the expense of communal solidarity.

Weber thought exactly the same way about premodern economic activity. In premodern times, men retired from work when they had accumulated enough to live on. Piecework employment mechanisms could not be relied on for mass manufacture and profit accumulation because workers simply slowed down and quit when they had produced a number of pieces equivalent to the wage they traditionally viewed as sufficient. Price-cutting or even advertising was shunned because erstwhile competitors put a premium on community fellowship, not profit.

While a much-circulated anti-Semitic canard held the Talmud responsible for Jewish ethnocentrism and irrationality, and for the Jews' seclusive alienation from modernity, Sombart's diagnosis went in the opposite direction. The Talmud, he believed, turned Jews into rationalists who pushed open the doors of modern capitalism for themselves and for everyone else. "The most learned Talmudists," proclaimed Sombart, "were also the cleverest financiers, medical men, jewelers, merchants."[67] The Talmud drew distinctions between how Jews should interact among themselves and how they should relate to gentiles; its teachings on this second track cultivated among Jews a penchant for regarding transactions instrumentally and impersonally as a means to obtain defined goals, with no regard for what they might do to other parties. When Sombart cited examples to defend this proposition, holding that Judaism sanctions impersonal, profit-seeking behavior in trade with gentiles, he drew mainly from Talmudic texts but also

66. Sombart, *Jews*, 87.
67. Sombart, *Jews*, 196.

sprinkled his analysis with a few references from halakha (Jewish law) codifications, such as *Chosen Mishpat* from Jacob ben Asher's *Arba'ah Turim*.

In his explanation of how Calvinist faith in predestination ultimately bred desire for profit accumulation among Puritans, Weber deftly wove through a labyrinthian maze of convoluted motivation and counterintuitive result. In contrast, Sombart's argument about Judaism and profit was straightforward: the Jews' religion taught them that riches were God's reward. So did Protestantism's Calvinist stream, but to understand how, according to Weber, you had to insert ten or fifteen steps. Sombart confessed that rabbis and other learned Jews, who had heard him lecture, vociferously objected to his thesis.[68] They alerted him to various passages from the Tanakh (the Hebrew Bible) and the Talmud that regarded wealth as a danger to the righteous. In such matters, Sombart insisted, quantity counts; Jewish religious sources extolling wealth as a reward for piety outnumber those that warn about private profit by a factor of ten to one, he claimed.[69]

At this stage, Sombart brought in the Rothschild family, a symbol of Jewish capitalist success in nineteenth-century Europe which fanned considerable friction and tension in discussions between Jews and Christians, to reinforce his thesis about how nothing in the Old Testament or the Talmud compared to Jesus' admonitions about wealth in the Gospels:

> Let us imagine old Amschel Rothschild on a Friday evening, after having "earned" a million on the Stock Exchange, turning to his Bible for edification. What will he find there touching his earnings and their effect on the refinement of his soul, an effect which the pious old Jew most certainly desired on the eve of the Sabbath? Will the million harm his conscience?[70]

By characterizing Judaism as an entirely "rational" religious culture, Sombart downgraded phenomena such as kabbalistic mysticism, which had engaged a significant portion of Jewish spiritual energy after the expulsion from the Iberian Peninsula starting in the sixteenth century, precisely the era pinpointed in this discussion as the point of origin for modernity and capitalism.[71] Hence, Sombart did not think about Judaism as many do in the twenty-first century—that is, as a complicated amalgam of rationalism and mysticism. However, it can be anachronistic to blame Sombart for his dissimilar perception. By stressing Judaism's rationalism, he apprehended the

68. Penslar, *Shylock's Children*, 165–70.
69. Sombart, *Jews*, 217.
70. Sombart, *Jews*, 217.
71. Klausner alludes to contemporary commentators who criticized Sombart for downplaying Jewish mysticism in Sombart, *Jews*, xv.

religion exactly as he was told to do by enlightened, in-house commentators of Jewish history and Jewish thought who exerted influence in Germany from the end of the nineteenth century through the date of the publication of *Jews and Modern Capitalism*. For instance, the historian Heinrich Graetz, whose name appears over forty times in Sombart's book, aggressively ridiculed and devalued Kabbalah and related mystical phenomena.[72] Meantime, the most influential Jewish thinker in Sombart's milieu, Hermann Cohen, related to Judaism as a "religion of reason," eventually publishing, after World War I, a treatise with that title.[73] Much could have been said about how Hasidism, the Jews' mass spiritual movement in early modernity, contradicted Sombart's thesis about Judaism as rationalism, both because of the way the Hasidic masters, *tzadikim*, cultivated styles of humility and advocated anti-materialistic concepts of bodily transcendence, and also because, in the eyes of some historians, Hasidism developed as mystified social protest against anti-Semitic harassment and persecution sanctioned by early modern economies, not at all as a rational-minded endorsement of capitalist accumulation. But from Sombart's standpoint, such arguments, originally developed by the historian Simon Dubnow,[74] emanated out of a remote, mostly unknown Eastern Europe milieu.

Another criticism that is often made of Sombart's book is that he seems to be identifying Jewish religion in places where he should have discussed Jewish secularity. That is, many of the figures he cites as Jewish pioneers in capitalism's development were outright secularists, or semisecularized Jews who loathed the traditional *heder* education they had received as youngsters, and who were not learned about Talmud. But this critique is also not very compelling. Its basic point, suggesting that Sombart was not as gifted a sociologist as Weber, is correct but not pertinent. Secular Jewish innovators who contributed to capitalism's consolidation were typically the children or grandchildren of pious Talmudists, and a number of plausible sociological-cultural models can be applied in an explanation of how religious outlooks and modes of thought of ancestors in earlier generations permeate and help shape how descendants relate to challenges in their own contemporary worlds.

That such models are plausible is exemplified by a book that many might view as the opposite of Sombart's. Isaac Deutscher, a left-wing critic and historian, relied precisely on these models in an interesting volume, *The Non-Jewish Jew*, whose chapters often reach a conclusion antithetical

---

72. Brenner, *Prophets*, 68–73.
73. Cohen, *Religion of Reason*.
74. Biale et al., *Hasidism*, 2–5.

to Sombart's.[75] It was the Jewish backgrounds of activists and thinkers who were not themselves thought of as Jews that propelled them toward significant forms of resistance to aspects of modernity, including capitalism, Deutscher argued. Whether one agrees with Deutscher or Sombart, the methodologically important point is common to them both. Outlooks and experiences of Jews before modernity lingered in the activities and ideologies of their secularized heirs in modernity.

From the standpoint of our discussion, the most cogent criticism of both Weber and Sombart is this: both believed that they were writing about the transition to something that was entirely new, capitalism in the modern West, yet in many ways their discussions reinforce how Jews and Christians keep saying the same things about themselves and their economies, from one era to the next. Sombart, in particular, suggested that the Jews' hypercapitalist performances in modern times were preordained because their own religious tradition, in the Tanakh and the Talmud, bequeathed no guardrails against self-centered, rampant profit accumulation. The book of Matthew and other New Testament sources, in contrast, manifestly produced inhibition about capitalist excess among Christians, Sombart believed. The main difference between Jews and Christians is the way they relate to capital and the pleasures or pitfalls, impiety or power, that come with it. That there is nothing necessarily modern about this difference means that Sombart's revision to Weber's theory about the spirit of capitalism was nothing new. It was another chapter of a long-standing polemic.

JEWS AND THE CAPITALIST SPIRIT, 1999

Less than a century after the Sombart-Weber discussion about whether the Jews or anyone else can be identified as the driving force behind modern capitalism, another great debate about the spirit of modern capitalism erupted. This time, in 1999, the specific question was the world economy's likely direction in the new millennium. The debate featured two Jewish commentators, Naomi Klein and Thomas Friedman. The two journalists released much-discussed books on the eve of the twenty-first century.[76] This was a decade after the end of the Cold War inspired thinkers and activists to come up with a big paradigmatic idea describing the likely direction of the world now that it was not divided between a capitalistic, democratic, America-led "Free World," and the centralized authoritarian communist corruption of the Soviet camp.

75. Deutscher, *Non-Jewish Jew*.
76. Friedman, *Lexus*; Klein, *No Logo*.

In writings both before and after this 1999 debate, Klein and Friedman have had a lot to say about Israel. Klein speaks in uncompromising condemnation of Israel's colonial occupation in the 1967 territories, and her writing on the subject does not heed the precepts and rules of the organized "pro-Israel" community. Friedman maintains a liberal pro-Israel mode that is critical of settlers and Israeli policy on the West Bank but is nonetheless deeply committed to Israel's founding principles, enthusiastic about its accomplishments in high tech and other noncontroversial spheres, and supportive of formulas such as a two-state solution that remained, formally, pillars of the Israel–United State special relationship up to the 2023–2024 crises. (A columnist for *The New York Times* who had headed some of its bureaus in the Middle East, Friedman won the National Book Award for his 1989 book *From Beirut to Jerusalem*, which was an outgrowth of his groundbreaking reportage of events such as the 1982 Sabra and Shatila massacre.)

Ostensibly, Israel and other Jewish matters were nothing more than incidental issues in this 1999 discussion. But the 1999 books authored by Klein and Friedman recycle and reiterate orientations on dilemmas of capital accumulation whose roots stretch back to the late Second Temple era of the rupture between Judaism and Christianity. Klein was bearish about the impending twenty-first-century economy whereas Friedman was bullish. Klein wrote openly in advocacy of a "No Logo" anti-corporatist attitude whereas Friedman was emphatic about the necessity of the world's transformation by "globalization," and despite attestations about his journalistic objectivity, he often sounded like a gleeful booster for globalization. Both had a knack for synthesizing contemporary trends whose connectedness was opaque to almost everyone else, and so both wrote influential books; but neither Klein nor Friedman published a treatise whose premises and conclusions retained sweeping credibility over time. On the eve of World War I, Weber and Sombart debated whether Jews ought to be regarded as modern capitalism's big story. On the eve of twenty-first-century postmodernity, Friedman and Klein discussed what might be capitalism's big story in the next millennium. Many of the findings and insights proffered by these four discussants in a decades-long conversation were provocatively original; nonetheless, nothing in this discussion was ever satisfactorily resolved. The common denominator in the pre–World War I debate and the pre-twenty-first-century discussion about capitalism is the conspicuous roles played by Jews, as objects analyzed critically or as the producers of critical commentary.

Mad with Greed in the Golden Straightjacket: Friedman and Globalization

"Globalization" conjures innumerable images, many of them connected to the rapid flow of information. This information technology emphasis was shared by readers of Friedman's *The Lexus and the Olive Tree* a quarter century ago, even though dimensions of the internet's impact were just hazily perceptible at the time of his volume's original 1999 release. As the foreign affairs columnist for *The New York Times*, Friedman had license to roam globally; as a perceptive, energetic journalist, he collected state-of-the-art examples about how the world was shrinking, thanks to technological innovation. However, as it turned out, the images he used to evoke this sense of a shrinking globe (e.g., "a world without walls"[77]) attracted attention, but they could not always be associated reliably with particular technological innovations or even with specific changes in managerial techniques. The reason why actually reinforced Friedman's basic point: mainly because of rapid innovation in home computer and internet technologies, the world was changing with dizzying velocity on the eve of the new millennium. The only reliable way to write about globalization, Friedman himself hinted in the introduction to later editions of *The Lexus and the Olive Tree*, would have been to publish an interactive volume that would have allowed the author to update sections on an annual, or even monthly, basis.[78]

The fate of Compaq Computer exemplifies this problem. In the book's original edition, Friedman touted this computer's adaptive marketing tactics as a globalization success story. But just a few months after the publication of *The Lexus and the Olive Tree*, Compaq was outmaneuvered by Dell (Compaq was effectively put out of business when it was acquired by Hewlett-Packard in 2002), thereby requiring Friedman to rewrite relevant passages in later editions of his book. Thus, even at the time of its publication, this landmark publication about globalization could not be read as reliable testimony about technological innovation, or about managerial and social adjustments to a new era of information technology—no writer could possibly keep up with such changes. Instead, the book was about free markets.

"The driving idea behind globalization is free-market capitalism," announced Friedman. "The more you let market forces rule and the more you

---

77. Friedman, *Lexus*, 45.
78. Friedman, *Lexus*, x.

open your economy to free trade and competition, the more efficient and flourishing your economy will be."[79]

Friedman admitted that his measuring stick in the evaluation of globalization's present and likely future was neither a diplomat's assessment of behavioral patterns, interests, and motivations of superpowers, nor a historian's prediction of what might happen in the world tomorrow based on study of what happened in it yesterday. Instead, Friedman looked out to the world from the standpoint of hedge fund managers. Such profit-seeking fund managers constituted "the only real thriving school of globalists in the world today," he said.[80] Hedge fund managers wanted to put their money in countries that were stabilizing their currencies, clamping down on inflation, repealing tariffs, reducing their national budgets by cutting back on social spending, and removing collective, protective agreements for workers.

Fond of frontier imagery which projected a sense of globalization as an open frontier for prosperous settlement, Friedman depicted hedge fund managers as big ranchers at the forefront of a global investment cattle drive, one comprised of an "electronic herd" whose calculations were driven by profit considerations alone.[81] The herd demanded that developing countries put on a "Golden Straightjacket," meaning the enactment of measures annulling extant unionization, social welfare, and tariff protection policies in a particular country.[82]

Delving into the realm of mental illness therapy, this straightjacket metaphor was no less revealing than Friedman's Wild West frontier imagery. It implied that it was clinically insane for a country to try to resist wrenching trends of unemployment and sudden impoverishment (prompted by rising prices) caused by the wearing of the straightjacket. Similarly, Friedman's writing implied, it would be sheer lunacy for a country not to privatize—that is, denationalize—key resource sectors and make them available for purchase by foreign private investors or multinational corporations. As happens to patients who have emotional illnesses, severe therapeutic measures might cause temporary, aggravated pain; but, in the long run, putting on the Golden Straightjacket would bring prosperity to a particular country, insisted Friedman.[83] True, globalization left losers behind—both businessmen who could not adapt to new competitive economic circumstances and citizens in countries victimized by initial shocks precipitated

79. Friedman, *Lexus*, 9.
80. Friedman, *Lexus*, 26.
81. Friedman, *Lexus*, 112–42.
82. Friedman, *Lexus*, 101–11.
83. Friedman, *Lexus*, 105–6.

by the donning of the "straightjacket." But these were tolerable losses in the making of a new era.

This theory seemed to undermine free market neoliberalism's objection that socialism endorses violent revolutionary authoritarianism (á la discussion by Marx and Lenin about a "dictatorship of the proletariat"). Looking for theoretical authority that would mitigate or rationalize this issue arising from his description of globalization as a revolutionary process that necessarily causes real injury to persons, Friedman now and then quoted respected academics, as exemplified by his allusions to the phrase "creative destruction," which circulates in the writing of Joseph Schumpeter, a Harvard Business School professor (who also had political experience as a former finance minister in Austria). However, a journalist who frequently depicts academics as self-involved sophists who are detached from reality, Friedman never really relied on any scholar's theory to bolster his enthusiasm about globalization. He sprinkled his endorsement of globalization's "creative destruction" with quotes and insights culled from a high-tech guru, Andrew Grove, a Jewish-Hungarian émigré who became CEO at Intel. However, even the title of Grove's memoir of his Silicon Valley experiences, *Only the Paranoid Survive*, subverted the pro-business, free market boosterism that filled most pages of *The Lexus and the Olive Tree*.[84] Why, exactly, in a world liberated by globalization, where there were no more walls, would citizens be happily thrust into a Darwinian contest for survival where "only the paranoid survive"?

Nothing in Friedman's analysis related to scenarios whereby local elites cash-in by enacting privatization policies, selling their country's public assets to foreign buyers at bargain-basement prices which do not reflect how the resources' value was enhanced by the hard labor of the nation's own population. Nor does the author give credence to anti-globalization skeptics who were at the time (as they have been doing since 1999) arguing that international organizations like the World Bank and the IMF manipulate interest rates and policy demands in ways designed to benefit the interests of foreign investors, particularly (but not exclusively) American-based entities, and thereby, in contravention of their own organizational mandates, deprioritize the interests of local groups in the developing countries.

To all such objections, Friedman had a compelling point. His book's basic contention is powerful: leaders and citizens of a country might grimace or smile as they put on the straightjacket, but if they refused to wear it, or if they put it on too late, the electronic herd would just move on. The herd acted on objective free market parameters—currency stability, national debt

---

84. Grove, *Only the Paranoid Survive*.

management, and so on—and it had a world full of investment options. So a country that ignored the herd's demands would be stampeded into poverty and despair.

As he opened the gates for free market globalization, Friedman either merrily applauded its expected benefits or soberly analyzed the process's inception as an unavoidable necessity. That he delivered the first full-length popularization of a process that would, within a few decades, result in what many regard as the most iniquitous and unbalanced distribution of global wealth in history encourages a suspicious retrospective reading of *The Lexus and the Olive Tree*.[85] The snappily upbeat tone of most (though not all) of the book's chapters aggravates this suspicion.

When reviewed with this Monday-morning quarterback sort of hindsight, the most inculpatory aspect of Friedman's writing is its arrogantly dismissive attitude toward anybody or anything that did not agree with its premises. In a mood of post–Cold War triumphalism, Friedman argued that American capitalism bred mostly beneficial homogenization effects around the globe (this premise's most notorious exemplification in the book is its "Golden Arches Theory of Conflict Prevention," holding that two countries that host McDonald's franchises do not go to war against one another).[86] Some countries around the world, such as France, could be expected to have especially strenuous cultural and socioeconomic objections to this idea of McHappy global homogenization. With preemptive intent of denying such anti-globalization critics a seat at the discussion table, Friedman wrote with noticeable severity about leaders from such prideful nations, as in this example: "While certain French government officials and intellectuals say a lot of silly things about and against the globalization system, French industrialists and entrepreneurs are putting on the Golden Straightjacket with a vengeance."[87]

Friedman filled many pages with descriptions of how attachments to local traditions and local interests could be expected to create yin and yang dynamics in the new era of globalization. This locality is symbolized by the olive tree. It is planted in the title of the volume as a contrast with the multinationally produced Lexus automobile, as though globalization is a creative dialectic where locality will have its place. However, most of the book's examples of "olive tree" locality are anecdotal. They lack the analytic incisiveness characteristic of Friedman's writing about globalizing "Lexus"

---

85. For a study that highlights contemporary income inequality issues and proposes creative ways of comparing them to past periods of vast economic disparity, see Milanovic, *Haves*.

86. Friedman, *Lexus*, 248–75.

87. Friedman, *Lexus*, 232–33.

phenomena. One example caught my eye both because Friedman describes it as his "favorite" parable about the prime "challenge" in the new era of globalization of finding "a healthy balance between preserving a sense of identity, home and community and doing what it takes to survive within the globalization system," and also because its protagonist, an old college friend of the author's, was for several years a colleague of mine on the teaching staff of a public college in northern Israel.[88] The story is about how this academic accidentally left a briefcase packed with cutting-edge computer equipment, circa 1995, at a bus station in a small Israeli town. Classified as a suspicious, possibly terror-related object, the bomb squad came and drilled a bullet into the briefcase, which the academic later proudly brought into his classrooms to enhance his street credibility. Though amusing, the anecdote lacks a punch line of any sort (if the olive tree is Israeli hypersensitivity about terror and the Lexus is my colleague's small PC in a briefcase, what's noteworthy about the contrast?).

As long as the olive trees are local schlimazels whose meandering does not have clear political or ideological ramifications, Friedman's writing is diffusely ironic. In contrast, it becomes focused, punchy, and averse whenever it refers to olive trees that have political ideas of their own. Witness the way Friedman mocks Malaysia's prime minister, Dr. Mahathir Mohammad, who in September 1997 berated globalization after his country's stocks and currency were savaged by the electronic herd of global investors. Friedman ridicules Mahathir, who described late twentieth-century global markets as a "jungle of ferocious beasts," and stridently condemned financiers such as George Soros for compelling Asians to open their markets to currency speculators (a strain of anti-Semitism laced through Mahathir's philippic).[89] As though he were speaking in the voice of then US Secretary of the Treasury Robert Rubin, Friedman acidly asked Malaysia's leader, "What planet are you living on?" thereby reiterating the book's pungent thesis, holding that political resistance to globalization is outright insanity, literally alien consciousness.[90]

The choice of Rubin as the mouthpiece for this broadside is revealing. Of all the investment bankers in the Goldman Sachs/Lehman Brothers/Bear Stearns crowd who published memoirs before or after the 2007–2008 financial crisis, Rubin's 2003 autobiography, *In an Uncertain World*, is noteworthy for its occasionally sober tone and for its passing confessions about the moral ambiguity of being a big-time rancher in the global

88. Friedman, *Lexus*, 42–43.
89. Friedman, *Lexus*, 112–13.
90. Friedman, *Lexus*, 112.

electronic herd.[91] One, unexpectedly moving, part of the memoir describes Rubin's emotional struggles after his undergraduate studies at Harvard (he was advised by a dean to see a psychiatrist), and a Bohemian year off the grid in the early 1960s as a nondegree student at the London School of Economics. In prose whose syncopated beat does not march in step with Friedman's triumphalist determinism, Rubin suggests that breaking from the globalization herd was always on his mind, even as climbed the ladder and reached Clinton's cabinet. Thanks to this gap year in England, Rubin confessed, "even as I became part of the establishment, I continued to feel that I could always opt out of the system if I wanted to."[92]

In a 2009 book (*The Return of Depression Economics and the Crisis of 2008*), another *The New York Times* columnist, Paul Krugman, who is a Nobel Prize laureate in economics, retrospectively questions Friedman's penchant for peremptory dismissal of world leaders who were critical of globalization in the 1990s.[93] Skeptically relating to Friedman's contention that economic downswings in the new globalization era are entirely the fault of obstreperous local leaders, who resist outfitting their national economies in the Golden Straightjacket, Krugman partially rehabilitates Mahathir: "As time passed, Mahathir's demonization of hedge funds started to look a bit less silly than it did when he first began his ranting."[94] This revision cracks open the door for anti-globalization critics who suspect that the 1997 Asian Financial Crisis was deliberately induced by profit-hungry global speculators, who acted in concert with the IMF and other outside entities—Naomi Klein, for instance, supports this scenario in her survey of "shock doctrine" policy.[95]

Krugman, for his part, bitterly critiqued hedge fund managers. Whereas Friedman used them as the prime source for information and analysis in a book championing the triumph of a new era of prosperity, Krugman's 2009 book declared emphatically that hedge fund management was a leading source of economic *instability* in the 1990s decade that served as a dress rehearsal for Friedman's proclamatory manifesto about globalization. "One of the most bizarre aspects of the economic crisis of the 1990s was the prominent part played by hedge funds," wrote Krugman. "Without

---

91. Rubin, *In an Uncertain World*.
92. Rubin, *In an Uncertain World*, 62.
93. Krugman, *Return*.
94. Krugman, *Return*, 95.
95. Klein, *Shock Doctrine*, 267–80.

question hedge funds, in both their success and their failure, rocked world markets."[96]

Krugman's critique stiffened after the 2007–2008 financial crisis debacle, but it does not appear that it was the shock of any particular twenty-first-century event that flipped open the lid of admiring popularity for Friedman's book, allowing much of its effusive endorsement of globalization to drain out. Globalization boosterism leaked away for a number of reasons. Written out of an array of agendas and motivations, a mounting corpus of scholarly literature, some of it packaged in readable books for the nonspecialist public, undermines fundamental premises of *The Lexus and the Olive Tree*. The common concern uniting these discussions relates to mounting inequality in world economies, a trend that became painfully conspicuous in the twenty-first-century era of globalization that was so bullishly anticipated and heralded in Friedman's book.

Interestingly, one academic publication that could have been seen as a genuinely dire warning predating Friedman's globalization predictions was authored by a conservative, anti-Keynesian economist from the University of Chicago, Robert Lucas. In a 1990 paper—that is, almost a decade before *The Lexus and the Olive Tree*—this economist argued that contrary to a premise underlying extant economic paradigms, capital *does not* naturally flow from rich countries to poor countries.[97] In the mindset and lexicon of economists, whose analyses do not put a premium on cultural and psychological variables (i.e., the cultural bias tendency of investors to put their money "with people like us," or their recoil from investment fields which operate under unfamiliar political systems), Lucas's finding was termed a "paradox." In his 2010 book, Branko Milanovic, an academic who once worked as lead economist at the World Bank's research division, surveyed the results of the Lucas paradox. "Of the total amount of direct foreign investments in the period 2000–2007 (almost $9 trillion)," Milanovic wrote, "no less than three-quarters went to the rich nations." During this same period, foreign investment amounted to "only about $20 per person in Africa, $6 in India, $45 in China, and about $800 per person in rich countries."[98]

If Friedman was right and if we have been living in an era of "globalization" for the past quarter century, most voices in this corpus of critical economics publications do not sound very happy about it. The fulcrum of the dissent is anxiety about the concentration of wealth in the hands of an economic elite; since this critique about the mega-rich 1 percent has

---

96. Krugman, *Return*, 119.
97. Lucas, "Why Doesn't Capital Flow."
98. Milanovic, *Haves*, 105.

entered public square political debates, starring figures like Bernie Sanders, we need not regurgitate it here in detail. What deserves brief discussion is whether globalization policy, as popularized by Friedman, emanates out of a kind of deep state doctrinaire ideology that is indifferent towards, or even supportive of, rising income inequality around the world. To what extent are globalization's enthusiasts and discontents talking about some sort of neoliberal deep state doctrine, whose proponents might possibly have anticipated and condoned the grossly lopsided distribution of capital that arose after many world countries agreed to don the Golden Straightjacket?

Some of the most engaging discussions in this critical literature about twenty-first-century world economics attack paradigms somewhat dissimilar to the neoliberal doctrine articulated by F. A. Hayek and Milton Friedman, which, many suppose, undergirds the free market euphoria in books like *The Lexus and the Olive Tree*. For instance, Timothy Noah's engaging 2012 book, *The Great Divergence*, is filled with information about rapidly accelerating income inequality in the United States.[99] The book's baseline refers to the Gini coefficient, the accepted measure of national income equality. In 2005, America's Gini score ranked twenty-seventh out of the world's wealthy OECD (The Organization for Economic Co-operation and Development) nations; only Portugal, Turkey, and Mexico had more lopsided, unequal economies.[100] Unforgettably, Noah showed that genetic heritage has become a less accurate predictor of an American's future than economic heritage.[101] That is, if you are an American youngster who has tall parents, the probability that you will be tall is lower than the probability that you will be wealthy if your parents are wealthy. Though the country's citizens still believed wholeheartedly in the social mobility connotations of the American dream, a much more promising place to achieve the American dream in North America was Canada, Noah argued (he brought out a chart of "Income Heritability by Country" to prove the point).[102]

Noah's critical survey cast a devastating retrospective spotlight on Friedman's 1999 book, which repeatedly described globalization's result as a "fast world."[103] Instead of "fast" dynamics of socioeconomic transformation, commentators like Noah discovered unprecedented trends of social stagnation in America, the superpower regarded as the driving engine of globalization. Elites in the United States were reproducing themselves with

---

99. Noah, *Great Divergence*.
100. Noah, *Great Divergence*, 7.
101. Noah, *Great Divergence*, 40.
102. Noah, *Great Divergence*, 50.
103. Friedman, *Lexus*, 331–2, 342–3, 375–6.

increasingly obstinate inflexibility; the most discernible process of "mobility" in the country was in a downward direction, with disturbing numbers of Americans falling out of the middle class toward genuine socioeconomic hardship.

As he developed his arguments and presented his findings, Noah's main quarrel was not with neoliberal (i.e., conservative) economists like Hayek and Milton Friedman, whose work apotheosized free markets. Noah's view was unlike that articulated in books like Naomi Klein's 2007 volume, *The Shock Doctrine*, or the pithy 2024 booklet published by George Monbiot and Peter Hutchison, *Invisible Doctrine: The Secret History of Neoliberalism*.[104] Such studies present globalization as a semi-conspiracy, as a smokescreen deliberately cast by corporations, governments, and international organizations, behind which they aggressively promote the free market aims of Hayek-Friedman neoliberal policy.

Whether or not he was naïve, Timothy Noah tended to view the rampant growth of income inequality in the United States as the result of tragic mistakes of genuinely liberal economic theory. In particular, in contrast to "convergence" ideas of middle-class expansion in America after the Great Depression and World War II, America's economy in the twenty-first-century globalization era was marked by "great divergence," that is, a shrinking middle class, Noah explained. The theoretical revision here applied to the post–World War II work of the economist Simon Kuznets, whose Jewish family immigrated to the United States from Eastern Europe in the early 1920s. Illustrating his idea by using an inverted "U," the so-called Kuznets curve, this economist predicted that following industrial revolution periods of economic instability and inequality, modern society would be marked by increased growth, and by socioeconomic equality and homogeneity furnished by the expansion of middle-class groups.[105]

For Thomas Friedman and many others, the Soviet Union's collapse validated patriotic belief in the power and rectitude of America's capitalist democracy. Friedman wrote on the eve of a new millennium, when it was fashionable to believe in a state of semi-utopian enthusiasm, that the international socioeconomic system which seemed to be locking into place in the 1990s would last for a long time, if not forever. Francis Fukuyama's 1992 book, *The End of History and the Last Man*, is the best-known manifestation of this mood (Friedman laced *The Lexus and the Olive Tree* with warnings issued by Fukuyama during this 1990s decade, regarding the perils awaiting

---

104. Monbiot and Hutchison, *Invisible Doctrine*.
105. Kuznets, "Economic Growth."

countries which dare to resist free market globalization).[106] Some of the more trenchant critiques of Friedman-esque globalization theories focus on this dimension. Such critics dismiss the perception of globalization as an everlasting mode produced by the "end of history." Instead, they insist, globalization is a passing fad, part of a boom and bust cycle of market regulation and deregulation that has been repeating itself since the South Sea Bubble, a financial crash that occurred four hundred years ago at the onset of modernity. Some scholars even identify the cycle's origins in periods long before then.

The cyclical view is conveyed in another book released in the fallout from the 2007 financial crisis, a 2009 volume entitled *This Time Is Different: Eight Centuries of Financial Folly*, authored by Carmen Reinhart and Kenneth Rogoff.[107] These authors contend that financial busts are followed by stiffened governmental regulation policies aimed at correcting abuses held responsible for the downswing. Subsequently, after a period of relative stability in the economy, profit-seeking financiers lobby for deregulatory policies, whose eventual implementation invites another cycle of bust and boom (no doubt the Clinton administration's repeal of the Depression-era Glass-Steagall Act, which circumscribed activities of investment banks, and this repeal's apparent link to the 2007 financial debacle, was on the authors' minds when they developed this analysis).

Relying on sophisticated computer modeling, what he calls "cliodynamics," Peter Turchin has recently popularized his thesis holding that twenty-first-century American reality reflects a cyclical pattern by which superpowers decline after an identifiable length of time.[108] Returning to the same critical premises that inform studies such as Timothy Noah's *The Great Divergence*, Turchin views contemporary America as a stagnant, stratified society that affords no constructive outlets for accumulated capital. The country, he writes, is a "plutocracy" where a tiny elite holds an untoward portion of capital and political power. Thousands of Americans who belong to the top 10 percent, or the top 1 percent, of the socioeconomic elite can find no constructive use for their newfound power; "elite overproduction" factors as the prime determinant of the impending erosion of America's superpower status. Whether or not one agrees with such gloomy prognostication, or views the author's effusive description of methodological "cliodynamics" as hollow showmanship, the cyclical determinism in such

---

106. Fukuyama, *End of History*.
107. Reinhart and Rogoff, *This Time Is Different*.
108. Turchin, *Elites*.

studies is noteworthy as a contrast to the linear "end of history" utopianism in Friedman's book.

It is not entirely fair to judge Friedman's 1999 book on the basis of developments in world economies that occurred after its publication. In fact, were we to track this retrospective line of analysis to its end, we would likely conclude that *The New York Times* columnist got as many things right as he got wrong. The world is a much faster, smaller place than it was a quarter century ago, and much of the hyped-up enthusiasm of writers who wrote on the eve of this transformation was warranted. Persons like myself, who were already into their thirties by the mid-1990s when all of the pro-internet hoopla started and who only "went with the program" after considerable teeth-gnashing and hesitation, were privately resentful about how all the globalization technologies everyone was talking about were really a younger person's game. But today, even those of us whose attitudes were just one shade short of Luddism at the start of the millennium understand how getting into the game made us smarter, better connected with friends and family, and much more proficient producers and discerning consumers.

Imperious, one-sided sections of *The Lexus and the Olive Tree*, such as Friedman's love sonnet to the Golden Straightjacket, do not read well today, but it would be hard to deny that many national economies have benefited by adopting measures dictated by the book (more precisely, measures dictated by the electronic herd described by the book). I live in one of them—Israel. Starting with its egalitarian ethos, many things about the state-controlled economy I briefly sampled when I immigrated to the country in the mid-1980s were laudable and preferable to the privatized socioeconomic reality that firmly took shape in Israel by the twenty-first century. But it is also true that inefficient, corrupt cronyism was rampant in sectors of the economy dominated by public companies (if you doubt this, ask any elderly Israeli about what he or she remembers regarding how a phone line was obtained in his/her family home from the state-run Bezeq company in the 1960s). In fact, Israel's twenty-first-century prowess as a high-tech wonder, the "Start-Up Nation,"[109] is readily traceable to its adoption of Golden Straightjacket reforms, many of them enforced by Benjamin Netanyahu during his 2003–2005 term as the country's finance minister. Much as his policies on Palestinian and related political issues have been widely castigated (Thomas Friedman himself being one of the more vociferous critics), Netanyahu's career arguably adds another layer of justification to the free market/privatization agenda Friedman articulated in his book about globalization. In a country positioned as Israel is, the development of

---

109. Senor and Singer, *Start-Up Nation*.

some advanced technology sectors via Golden Straightjacket reform policies can be seen as a strategic matter of life or death.

Furthermore, the most grievous economic development of the globalization era, the intolerable rise of income inequality in innumerable countries, including well-rooted democracies, has a complicated relationship to the sort of analysis developed by *The Lexus and the Olive Tree*. Friedman can, and should, be faulted for presenting the profit-seeking agenda of hedge fund managers as though it were unqualifiedly a public-spirited program for global improvement. In some cases, most notoriously post–Cold War Russia, by donning the Golden Straightjacket, a country delivered formerly public resources straight into the hands of local oligarchs. More commonly, privatization, the elimination of tariffs and collective worker protections, and other Straightjacket policies put a country's resources up for sale to foreign financial elites. Such developments are at the core of the anti-corporatist critique articulated by Naomi Klein (and many others), and we will turn to them in the next section. Here it suffices to point out that globalization, as Friedman depicted it, undeniably promoted the concentration of wealth among financial elites and thus exacerbated the gravest threat posed to democracy as the twenty-first century approaches middle age, i.e., iniquitous income distribution.

Developing this point would be tricky, however. Friedman's 1999 book is filled with empirically grounded sections about subjects like the "democratization of finance," which show how regular folks like you and me were expansively getting involved in mutual funds and other investment practices, thus joining the "electronic herd" toward the end of the twentieth century.[110] Why, then, was the herd's self-interested, peripatetic practice of roaming the globe and identifying solid investment opportunities in properly straightjacketed economies not conducive to the *growth* of the middle class rather than what actually happened, i.e., its alarmingly drastic contraction? Many explanations could be applied to this question, but the most convincing argument about the causes of income inequality puts the onus in places outside of the realms discussed in *The Lexus and the Olive Tree*, expansive as that book was in its ambitions and descriptions. The most serious commentators on income inequality in the twenty-first century, like Milanovic and Noah, reach the same conclusion: capital concentration among elites has many determinants (immigration policy, anti-union measures, and so on), but by far the most important culprit is national tax policy. If you want a more reasonable distribution of wealth in your country, vote for the political party that favors increased taxation of the upper middle classes

---

110. Friedman, *Lexus*, 53–60.

and the rich. You should vote for the party which asks Saint Matthew to put aside the evangelizing for a while and get back to his first job.

The opposite has happened in the era of globalization, but obviously not because world leaders and their constituencies were reading free market booster books, like *The Lexus and the Olive Tree*. In this connection, Klein's "shock doctrine" analysis has interpretive validity, but its global applicability is limited (as we will argue). The basic problem is that tax reduction programs are popular in democracies; and there are always parties, like the Republicans in the United States, who exploit this fact without being very conscientious about telling the public which income sectors will really benefit from the tax cuts.

Over the last quarter century, the world has been irreversibly changed by the birth and growth of virtual reality activity facilitated by social media technologies. Never again will thinkers and activists talk about the future of the world on the basis of assumptions and precepts that girded the field of political economy, within which writers like Adam Smith, Karl Marx, and John Maynard Keynes articulated contrasting conservative (pro–free market), radical, and liberal visions. In our new era, consumer patterns, the supply of services, and production processes are, in quantitative and qualitative respects, unlike dynamics known to these giants in the bygone field of political economy. The end of the twentieth century, the moment when the internet revolution was just taking off, represented the last time when writers like Friedman and Klein might conceivably have still been in conversation with celebrated theories of nineteenth- and twentieth-century political economy. The thesis I am pursuing here is that up to this end-of-the-millennium (1999) endpoint, the frame through which writers like Friedman viewed issues of capital flow and profit remained what it always had been, since the days of the Gospels when Jews and Christians first started to talk about them. When Friedman's mesmerizingly perceptive and confused book is understood in its own terms, without the hindsight (Monday-morning quarterback) vantage point we have just discussed, its "Jewish" dimension remains the only plausible explanation of its mysteriously doctrinaire quality.

Consider Friedman's diatribe against semisocialist, mixed-economy states, which appears in the book's pivotal Golden Straightjacket chapter. "People can talk about alternatives to the free market and global integration, they can demand alternatives, they can insist on a 'Third Way,' but for now none is apparent," he proclaimed. "There is only one thing to say about those alternatives: *They didn't work*."[111] In the era of globalization, there will

---

111. Friedman, *Lexus*, 103–4.

only be free market democracies, quite like Reagan's America in the 1980s (and very much not like FDR's social welfare New Deal economy); or there will be dictatorial regimes. Homogeneity bred by globalization is a little regrettable, but living in a country privy to it sure beats living in a dictatorship. This is what Friedman meant when he announced, "Today there is only free market vanilla and North Korea."[112]

These are pronouncedly not empirical judgments. Instead, they are doctrinaire statements.

Plenty of countries maintained mixed economies in the 1990s and thereafter. The social welfare parts of their national systems might not have been popular with the electronic herd, and Friedman might have jettisoned as "silliness" the orations of leaders in places like France, who tried to protect local customs and local production processes in the hope that they would yield more than "vanilla" flavor to their countries' national experiences, but the world is always complicated; there are always alternatives in it, however objectionable they may seem to ideologues. In retrospect—that is, in light of many things that have occurred over the past quarter century—the sophomoric and misguided determinism of pronouncements like "There is no Third Way" can be elucidated; but, in the context of political and socioeconomic realities known to him in 1999, why would a writer like Friedman have unleashed such anti-empirical, exaggerated judgments?

Here, I am not sure that the semiconspiratorial status attributed to neoliberal theory by recent writers like Monbiot and Hutchinson is very helpful (much as their volume *Invisible Doctrine: The Secret History of Neoliberalism* is worth reading for other reasons).[113] A seasoned journalist, Friedman has never been an ideologue in the service of anyone's academic theories—in fact, the names Milton Friedman and F. A. Hayek appear just one time in the index of *The Lexus and the Olive Tree*. More plausibly, excesses in this popularization of globalization theory can be seen as symptomatic reflections of Cold War culture, particularly its triumphalist final phase in America. A staunchly patriotic, liberal American, Friedman subscribed, to some extent, to rules of public discourse that consolidated in the 1970s and 1980s, whereby discussion of third way alternatives around the globe was invariably seen as being pro-Soviet. Anyone in North America or Western Europe who displayed sustained concern about how, from Iran in the 1950s to Chile in the 1970s, the CIA and corporations helped topple democratically elected third way leaders who threatened to nationalize key local resources, was dismissed as a malcontent, if not a Communist fellow

---

112. Friedman, *Lexus*, 104.
113. Monbiot and Hutchison, *Invisible Doctrine*.

traveler. Atavistically, this "you're with us or you're against us" Cold War way of dichotomizing reality influenced Friedman's writing.

So too did his inclusion in a 1990s era "Inside the Beltway" elite, comprised of programmatic-minded, intellectual writers who were convinced that history was necessarily on the side of the way Americans saw the world and operated in it. The outcome of the Cold War validated this supposition. Red-hot sunbeams of self-congratulatory American patriotism shot through this brief historical window, blinding influential writers; they could not see the contradiction between the grandiose authoritarianism of their pronouncements and their own self-image as liberal-minded proponents of free debate. History had ended because Francis Fukuyama said it had. In the new globalized millennium, there would never be a third way between free market capitalism and dictatorship because Thomas Friedman said so. Thankfully, the internet's digital trails were, at this time, clicking into place, and bloggers and trolls would soon find their way to mock and expose such triumphalist hubris.

Friedman wrote publicly as a patriotic American, but his private instincts about globalization were Jewish. While this point is impossible to prove (who knows anything for certain about anyone else's inner motivations), we can identify Friedman as the last in a very long line of theorists and journalists who were Jewish, and who wrote about the transition from one socioeconomic era to a new one as though everything was predetermined and would proceed on the basis of scientifically adducible laws. Not all Jews who wrote about such transitions were free market enthusiasts—of course, names like Marx and Trotsky are reminders of an imposing lineage of Jewish socialists, or socialists who had Jewish ancestry. Zealous critics of free market economics, and their adversaries, shared the same belief about how transformation in historical eras was caused by anonymous forces (Friedman's electronic herd being the last in a very long list) rather than by cultural myths and stereotypes or by power politics arrangements between a majority and a minority. Why Jews, a vulnerable minority who typically suffered pain and humiliation in a particular era, would be drawn toward political economy ideas which deterministically projected mankind's entry into new, improved historical periods and negated the impact of human subjectivity in this transition, is self-evident.

In 1990s America, the country's free market democratic system was enthusiastically believed to have been responsible for victory in the Cold War. In this climate, the tendency of Jewish thinkers and writers to uphold "neutral" mechanisms, like the free market, synergized powerfully with their surging American patriotism. This is the psychological and political background of the circle known as Jewish "neoconservatives" (confusingly, the term has become synonymous with neoliberals).[114] Friedman has never been considered a member of this circle because his views on an array of issues in domestic politics and global politics are center-left, whereas the neocons are typically affiliated with the political right (among many other things, Friedman's pro-Israel orientation is much more critical of policies adopted by the country's Likud-dominated governments than is the zealously pro-Israel view of the neocons[115]). But the free market enthusiasm in Friedman's groundbreaking book about globalization is drawn from the same well of Jewish, and American Jewish, sentiment and outlook whose water has slaked the right-wing thirst of the neocons.

The central dilemma in *The Lexus and the Olive Tree* is whether the transition from the Cold War to globalization would, or should, cause rupture, both on the macro level of national economies and also on the micro level of personal identity. Friedman identifies his approach to this dilemma as "glocalism."[116] Glocalism, it seems, envisions some sort of hybrid mixture of Lexus automobiles and olive trees. Friedman recommends that persons in globalized economies craft their identities in line with the homogenized workplace style enforced by multinational corporations, but also retain some sense, however inchoate, of the particular locale where they came from and of its traditions and style. In the end, glocalism seems to have much more Lexus than olive tree.

The term "glocalism" started to circulate at the end of the 1980s. However, in Friedman's book it sounds like a neologism that deliberately bypasses nomenclature and formulas that were evolving in the 1990s in campus "culture war" arguments about multiculturalist diversity. It gives precedence to homogeneity and allows very little room for ethnonational (not to mention, gender-sexual) diversity. The most that the glocalist Friedman can say for the olive trees is that he would want a Japanese child in Tokyo to understand that McDonald's is an American company, just as he would not want the child of an immigrant Japanese family in Los Angeles to believe that sushi originates in American cuisine. In the end, Friedman is inconclusive about his book's big dilemma. How much rupture will be brought by globalization? The reader never knows because the author's formulations are vague: "An unhealthy glocalization is when you absorb something that isn't part of

---

114. Friedman, *Neoconservative Revolution* (the author here, Murray Friedman, is not to be confused with Thomas); Fuller, *Taking the Fight*.

115. Fuller, *Israel and the Neoconservatives*.

116. Friedman, *Lexus*, 295–97.

your culture, doesn't connect with anything latent in your culture, but you have so lost touch with your culture, you think it does."[117]

Thus speaks the globalization "Gospel of Thomas" in the same mode as the Gospel of Matthew. The problem is irresoluble, everlastingly puzzling. Does capital accumulation among the money changers at the temple, or among the hedge fund managers in globalization, beckon radical change in human identity? Should it? Must Jews who resist pharisaic materialism become Christians? wonders Matthew. Should Japanese resist Americanized globalization by assertively cultivating fundamentals of their own separate identity, their own olive trees—that is, cherry blossoms? wonders Thomas. In moral terms the question is, Will we trade our souls for money? Should we?

In modernity, whenever the elementary problems of political economy arose, there arose a Jewish-Christian question rooted in the Synoptic Gospels. In the nineteenth century, the question was whether the socioeconomic integration of Jews in the liberal nation-state would create a new reality, where everyone was united homogenously by the new secular liberal creed. Alternatively, critics wondered, ought not there be space left in the modern world for separate religious-national identity? Anti-Semites, Zionists, and many others ruminated about this question. On the eve of postmodernity, the American-Jewish writer addressed the same sort of issue in *The Lexus and the Olive Tree*: Should all of humanity put on a straightjacket to gain access to material prosperity yielded by Americanized globalization? Must everyone speak, smile, and hold their bodies the way it is done by newscasters on CNN? Is becoming American in this corporate CNN sense the destiny of all mankind? Ought not there be space left in globalized reality for olive trees?

Must we all become our own earthquakes, convulsing and eradicating our own identities? Is that what our prophets and saviors are really asking of us? The question has been lurking since it was posed in the narrative of the book of Matthew, where Jesus imposes an astonishingly taxing, anti-materialist program upon his followers ("It is easier for a camel to go through the eye of a needle," Matt 19:24) while also comforting them by disavowing any intention to fundamentally alter their spirit and way of life, their religion ("Do not think that I have come to abolish the Law," Matt 5:17). As long as political economy was studied in modern times, it was always rattled by the tension inherent in these contradictory directives, ones which evoke an earthquake that perhaps may not convulse. It is a tension apt to drive one crazy with greed, or against greed. Reflecting this tension, the fundamental

---

117. Friedman, *Lexus*, 297.

images of political economy long evoked a bewildering mix of madness and materialism, culminating in the Golden Straightjacket that we are to wear into our globalized future.

Jamming the Message to Garcia: Naomi Klein's Anti-Corporate Dissent

In an edition of his magazine *The Philistine*, published on Washington's birthday in 1899, Elbert Hubbard prognosticated that the ensuing century would belong to self-motivated individuals who, out of unstinting loyalty to their employers and out of unswerving allegiance to the objectives and values of the company they work for, would carry out their assigned tasks, no matter how strenuous they might be, without any consideration of direct personal benefit.

Hubbard's short essay was inspired by the story of a US army officer who unquestioningly carried out a dangerous reconnaissance mission during the Spanish-American War, delivering a request for information from President McKinley to an anti-Spanish insurgent in Cuba, named Garcia. Hubbard forecasted that the health of America's society and economy in the forthcoming century would depend upon the proliferation of strongly motivated individuals who show initiative and unreservedly deliver "messages to Garcia" whenever their bosses tell them to do so.

Writing at a time of thickening anxiety about the rise of urban society, mass immigration, and the decline of an agriculturally based economy, Hubbard switched the focus of social commentary. Rather than writing from a standpoint of humanitarian pity for the plight of untrained, would-be factory workers who lacked income and tolerable shelter in the cities, he took up the viewpoint of employers who found their energies and ambitions hamstrung by a workforce of undisciplined slackers.

The country's welfare in the coming century, Hubbard prophesied, will depend upon the recruitment of laborers who will "take a message to Garcia." In retrospect, there can be little doubt that Hubbard was writing about the development of corporate personality, of workers so personally identified with their companies that they would view any breach of assigned tasks as being tantamount to ignoble military disobedience, or treason. Hubbard wrote,

> My heart goes out to the man who does his work when the "boss" is away, as well as when he is at home. And the man who, when given a letter for Garcia, quietly takes the missive, without asking any idiotic questions, and with no lurking intention of

chucking it into the nearest sewer, or of doing aught else but deliver it, never gets "laid off," nor has to go on a strike for higher wages. Civilization is one long anxious search for just such individuals. Anything such a man asks shall be granted; his kind is so rare that no employer can afford to let him go. He is wanted in every city, town and village—in every office, shop, store and factory. The world cries out for such: he is needed and needed badly—the man who can carry a message to Garcia.[118]

Elbert Hubbard, the author of this pro-corporate manifesto was a fascinating character.[119] As a young man, he accrued a hefty seventy-five thousand dollars from selling his share of a soap factory. Hubbard then studied at Harvard College and toured Europe, where he became entranced by William Morris, the charismatic English poet, decorative arts maker, and radical socialist. Influenced by Morris's devotion to the Arts and Crafts Movement and to worker communalism, Hubbard founded Roycroft in the mid-1890s in Erie County, New York, not far from Buffalo.

Hubbard's Roycrofters worked as bookbinders, furniture makers, and metalsmiths, winning a modest amount of admiration for quality work produced in a cheerfully positive environment. However much it reads as a precocious exercise in proto-twentieth-century corporate cheerleading, and thus as a kind of crass commercial inverse of the esthetic finery of the Roycroft shop (and of the communist mentorship of William Morris), Hubbard's essay, "A Message to Garcia," actually emerged straight out of the same concern that drove Roycroft. Hubbard was looking for creatively positive ways to impose discipline upon restless American youngsters who could no longer deposit their frontier energies on farms.

Nothing in Roycroft's modest impact prepared Hubbard for the storm stirred by "A Message to Garcia." The short essay can be regarded as the first writing about modern American capitalism to go viral. This happened because manufacturers recognized the piece's potential as a guide for developing corporate morale and initiative. George H. Daniels, of the New York Central Railroad, reprinted the essay endlessly in multiple editions of one hundred thousand booklets. Some one hundred million copies of the essay are said to have been printed.[120] Published in thirty-seven languages (and the basis of two movies), it found motivational uses around the world. In

---

118. Hubbard, *Selected Writings*, 252–59.
119. Biographical details are drawn from Shay, *Elbert Hubbard*.
120. Shay, *Elbert Hubbard*, 160.

the 1920s, more copies of "A Message to Garcia" were said to have been in print "than any other publication except the Bible and the dictionary."[121]

Naomi Klein's *No Logo*, published exactly a century after "A Message to Garcia," reverses the essay's platitudes and conclusions, lobbying for an anti-corporate orientation whose components seem more esthetic and behavioral than industrial.[122] Writing in the midst of America's transition from farm life to city-based industrial production, Hubbard proposed, at Roycroft and in the "Message to Garcia" essay, two possible remedies to issues of disorientation produced by this urban-industrial shift: commitment to high quality craftsmanship and unswerving loyalty to corporate management. After the ensuing century of mass production, city life, and national prosperity, Klein wrote for a generation of young, recent college graduates who felt that there were far too many Garcias in the country. Twentieth-century corporate culture had produced circumstances wherein this young generation felt it had "No Space" and "No Choice" left for personal freedom.

Klein's topic was an accelerating trend of corporate branding and marketing. Not without traces of claustrophobic paranoia, she contended that such branding was everywhere: on city billboards, in elementary school cafeterias, in university research labs, at Rolling Stones rock concerts.

Late twentieth-century corporatism, as Klein depicted it, had damaging effects in areas of traditional concern in political economy. In addition to chapters in her challenging book whose headings and contents evoked existential and esthetic laments (e.g., "No Space"), Klein wrote probingly about issues of employment faced by members of her own generation in America, and also about worker exploitation in outsourced sweatshops in underdeveloped countries in the world. Because Klein's critique of corporate branding was so original, it is easy to forget these more conventional, political economy sorts of sections on "No Jobs," in which she analyzed how corporations were saving millions of dollars by structuring service positions as temporary posts designed for young people who theoretically were just passing though, on to greener socioeconomic pastures.[123] The book shows how many such part-time, temporary jobs ended up as years-long traps for their possessors. Meantime, corporations avoided paying pension and social benefit costs owed to workers who put in full, forty-hour work weeks.

No Logo's most provocatively chilling chapter relates to "Export Processing Zones" (EPZs), where multinational corporations outsourced key production processes to zones in underdeveloped countries that were

---

121. Shay, *Elbert Hubbard*, 159–60.
122. Klein, *No Logo*.
123. Klein, *No Logo*, 194–277.

exempted from local labor regulations and socioeconomic protections.[124] Klein researched on-site a few such EPZs, finding that they were filled mostly with young teenage girls from the countryside who seemed too bewildered to grasp how comprehensively they were being exploited. In the book's most memorable, poignantly ironic passage, Klein observed that the only place in the world where corporations were not blazoning their logos was at factory sites in these EPZs, in order to avoid conspicuous association with their derelict, inhumane character.

Along with many other parts of *No Logo*, Klein's EPZ depiction should be read in conjunction with Friedman's concurrent publication, *The Lexus and the Olive Tree*. In Friedman's book, anonymity basically recapitulates the function of Adam Smith's invisible hand—that is, the faceless electronic herd is portrayed as steering the globe toward a state of somewhat blandly homogenized, but nonetheless comfortable, prosperity ("vanilla ice cream"). Furthermore, Friedman casts the downside of globalization, the hardships created by donning the Golden Straightjacket, as temporary birth pangs. He assumes that foreign companies, or local financiers and managers, who take over production processes in countries that have privatized and annulled collective labor agreements and protections will behave with restraint. They will not rejuvenate the exploitative depravity of the early days of the industrial revolution, the "Coketown" landscape of Dickens's novel *Hard Times* (Friedman never exactly explains why such manufacturer restraint would arise and remain intact; his book is tacitly predicated on a roseate liberal Enlightenment view of human nature).

In Klein, corporate branding is everywhere, and anonymity is nowhere to be found, apart from remote, outsourced regions, the EPZs, which are outside the ken of Western middle classes. In Klein's world, it is horrendously unempirical to think of hardship borne by working classes as mere temporary setbacks in a shining gold straightjacket. Her book is thus founded on a Hobbesian view of the nature of corporate management classes (more on this subject in a second). *No Logo* leaves no room for thinking that hardship caused by globalization is a passing phenomenon. For instance, Klein noted that in the Philippines in 1999 there were fifty-two EPZs employing 459,000 workers, a leap from 23,000 EPZ workers in the country just thirteen years before.[125]

Read a quarter century later, many of the descriptions in *No Logo* seem quaintly passé. Implying that corporate branding was leaving no space for conscientious young citizens to breathe, the book often has a claustrophobic

---

124. Klein, *No Logo*, 204–30.
125. Klein, *No Logo*, 205.

feel. Younger readers who cannot imagine what the world felt like when internet communication was still somewhat indefinite, and when social media apps were unknown, would (I suspect) have trouble empathizing with the feeling of cultural suffocation evoked by Klein's writing about corporate branding. For better or worse, many new realms of cultural expression (not to mention corporate marketing) opened up in twenty-first-century high-tech virtual realities; published in 1999, *No Logo* could not possibly have said anything about them. However, just as *The Lexus and the Olive Tree* is often thought of as a book about the advancement of information technologies in globalization but is really about free markets, *No Logo* is usually thought of as a critique of corporate branding but is actually a book about power and responsibility. Ultimately, Klein did not recoil from corporate branding because it was often ugly and, at least in her readers' daily landscapes, ubiquitous. Instead, her critique centered on how the turn to branding allowed corporate elites to escape responsibility for matters conventionally discussed in political economy (e.g., worker welfare) and also for problems of growing concern in the late twentieth century, particularly in the environmental sphere.

No Logo is filled with examples of how corporate executives were at the time preening about how their companies were producing "nothing," and about how their own jobs were conceptual, not industrial or economic. While they were making fortunes by outsourcing product manufacture to EPZs, where their own corporations avoided liabilities and profited from rank worker exploitation, these executives were pretending that their jobs were to cultivate, via branding, an original vision of contemporary life to which consumers would become indelibly connected, in lieu of appreciation of the quality of particular products.

Hubbard, at Roycroft, was personally committed to high quality, esthetic craft production. When he penned "A Message to Garcia," he believed that corporate managers were reliable citizens responsibly committed to their country's twentieth-century future. Ordinary citizens ought to become loyally disciplined workers, Hubbard suggested, because corporate managers were responsible and would never turn the world into an ugly, cramped place. *No Logo* reverses all of these assumptions and expectations. Ordinary citizens, Klein declared, ought to disengage from corporate discipline because management elites were irresponsibly recalcitrant outsourcers who were turning the world into an ugly, cramped place.

Though in some ways it became instantly outdated when social media virtual realities overturned the "No Space" and "No Choice" circumstances it depicted, *No Logo* nonetheless warrants serious consideration as a bookend in a century-long debate about corporate discipline. Their debate on the far edge of political economy discourse, Hubbard and Klein were talking about a modern (or postmodern) economic behavioral issue that is only partly subsumed in the influential discussion staged by Sombart and Weber. When these two European discussants talked about the "capitalist spirit," they were thinking about how religion, and its age-old concerns about vices like greed, might or might not have prepared adherents for the challenges of modern life. In their secularized discussion, Hubbard and Klein were still talking about virtue and vice, but their concern was how individual morality might, or might not, be regulated by corporate engagement.

In 1899, Roycroft and corporate discipline were correctives to what Hubbard called "hoodlumism." His viral, unprecedentedly impactful "Message to Garcia" suggested that the world's worst problem was young employees who came to work with "a lurking intention" of taking corporate materials, and "chucking [them] into the nearest sewer." In writings that complemented his Garcia letter, Hubbard elaborated on this affliction of hoodlumism. A hoodlum, an appalled Hubbard explained, "bombards with tomatoes a good man taking a bath, puts ticktacks on windows, ties a can to the dog's tail, takes the burs off your carriage wheels . . . and scares old ladies into fits by appearing at windows wrapped in a white sheet."[126] Naomi Klein, for her part, ends *No Logo* with extended sections praising hoodlumism, albeit by using a different term, cultural "jamming."[127]

In 1899, one writer forecasted that democratic freedom and prosperity in the coming century would be facilitated by the eradication of hoodlumism, by the training of young corporate employees who would cross a dark, dangerous jungle to deliver company goods to Garcia. In 1999, another writer forecasted that democratic freedom in the coming century would be regained thanks to jamming hoodlumism. Klein reveled when describing the street pranks of young jammers who were scratching clever puns and put-downs on corporate billboards or taxi rooftops ("Virginia Slime" instead of "Virginia Slims"), pasting a likeness of Charles Manson on a huge ad for Levi's jeans, and turning Apple rainbow logos into skulls.[128] Of course, between Hubbard and Klein, many American sociologists and commentators offered important critical insights about corporate organizational discipline (names like C. Wright Mills and David Riesman come to mind in this connection), but the frame for this century-long discussion about American corporatism is set by the thought-provoking contrast yawning between Hubbard's polemic against hoodlumism and Klein's

126. Hubbard, *Message to Garcia*, 45–46.
127. Klein, *No Logo*, 279–301.
128. Klein, *No Logo*, 279–311.

polemical advocacy of jamming. Writing on the eve of a new era of mass production, Hubbard believed that anti-esthetic vandalism belonged to the passing, premodern era. Writing at the end of that same century of mass production, Klein believed that artful vandalism might usher in a liberated era of postmodernity.

How much would human identity transform in the transition from one era to the next? As in the case of Friedman's influential 1999 book, Klein's *No Logo* can be evaluated as part of a "Jewish" conversation about socioeconomic transformation, even though neither author directed his/her writing to any particular religious readership. For one thing, there is the fact that in 1999 two North American Jewish journalists wrote groundbreaking books that set guidelines and borders in a "pro and con" debate about the future of corporatism and globalization in the new millennium. More importantly, both commentators wrote within the same frame of Christian-Jewish discussion of whether newly powerful modes of capital accumulation are necessarily convulsive to spiritual identity, both on individual and collective levels. Friedman, as we have seen, offered a rather benign remedy to this problem, proposing that reasonable "glocalist" solutions would balance between local traditions and global economic processes. Klein's vision, of course, was far more somber and dark. As she saw it, corporate branding (a kind of correlate to Friedman's globalization) was decimating creative identity, both on individual and community levels. In her analysis, culture jammers are akin to Jesus' disciples, a small band of spiritual visionaries with a message to disseminate to the world—Christianity in one case, anti-corporatism in another.

We have limited the discussion here to 1999 books that were produced just before information technologies stretched modes in consumerism, marketing, and service production well beyond the conventional frames of political economy. Passingly, it bears mention that Naomi Klein's later work continues this discussion about convulsive rupture in transitions to globalized free markets, and usefully demarcates clear moral and practical differences between leftist opposition to globalization and liberal accommodation with it.

In brief, whereas the liberal Friedman viewed globalization as a technical process promoted by neutral agencies (the electronic herd), Klein's work, as exemplified by her well-publicized 2007 volume *The Shock Doctrine*, views globalization as a coercively political process.[129] Filled with images of violent convulsion, the 2007 book develops an argument about twenty-first-century disaster capitalism. *The Shock Doctrine* argues that

---

129. Klein, *Shock Doctrine*.

profit-interested corporate elites, taking signals from neoliberal free market ideologues like Milton Friedman, deliberately annihilate the socioeconomic foundations of nations across the globe for the purpose of imposing a market-based system devoid of governmental regulation or intervention. Whereas Thomas Friedman took cues from hedge fund managers as he developed an analysis of Golden Straightjacket globalization motored by relatively innocuous agencies like global investors, Klein's source base was comprised of exiled outcasts of third way socialist regimes, such as the recorded testimonials of Orlando Letelier from Salvador Allende's ill-fated early 1970s Chilean government.[130] These sources taught her about how a collusion of private capital, international economic agencies like the IMF, and CIA operatives (who acted on policy directives furnished by the White House), brutally imposed free market policies in their countries under the auspices of dictatorial regimes. This is to say that in Klein's later work, Friedman's relatively innocuous Golden Straightjacket transmogrifies and becomes politically dictated electroshock torture.

Many readers will feel, as I do, that the way Klein's *Shock Doctrine* pulls together 1950s pseudo-therapeutic shock therapy, Milton Friedman's free market ideological zeal, corporate profit motivations, and various US foreign policy misadventures, culminating in the Second Persian Gulf War, can be strained. Some parts of *The Shock Doctrine* are very hard to process, both because of their excruciating descriptions of political torture and also because the way the text ties together analytic loose ends testifies to Klein's own anti-corporate militancy, rather than solidly defensible empirical research. On the other hand, *The Shock Doctrine* can be credited positively for the way it nudges twenty-first-century anti-corporate activism back toward accepted frames in political economy. Klein's basic point accords with staples of respected critical branches of political economy. *The Shock Doctrine* argues that the transition to new socioeconomic regimes and eras is ushered in by the use of political violence. Such violence is motivated by class interest (or corporate interest, in Klein's case) and deployed brutally against a particular group of people. Marx's *Capital* similarly views the early modern Enclosure Movement in England.[131]

For the purposes of this discussion, it suffices to point out that however militant its aims and conclusions, *The Shock Doctrine* belongs to an ongoing discussion about profit accumulation and wrenching identity change, about greed and madness, which we are following in this essay and which is

---

130. Klein, *Shock Doctrine*, 86.
131. Marx, *Capital*.

framed by centuries-long polemics between Jews and Christians about the meaning of money.

HOW THE JEWISH PROBLEM REFORMATTED AFTER THE HOLOCAUST

In Europe, the aftermath of the debate engaged by Weber and Sombart was, of course, catastrophic. This is not the place to elaborate upon how images and accusations of Jews as antisocial, usurious, and destabilizing elements in the modern economy contributed to the Nazi genocide. The main aspects of this story are familiar to readers because the Holocaust has become a much-discussed subject in world culture for the past sixty years, following the Eichmann trial in Jerusalem in the early 1960s (some scholars have argued persuasively that Holocaust awareness has become part of the "civil religion" of Western culture in this period).[132]

Just a few words will suffice to locate the Holocaust and its aftermath within the context of this discussion about the enduring problem of capital accumulation in relations between Jews and Christians. The origins of modern anti-Semitism can be identified in 1870s Europe, as backlash to the conferral of citizenship rights, particularly in Germany, to Jews. As suggested by the nomenclature, most scholars believe that "modern anti-Semitism" ought to be distinguished from processes of Jew hatred that transpired before modernity. Nobody denies that there is a wealth of evidence pointing to blood libels, expulsions, and other phenomena of Jew hatred in the Middle Ages; but most scholars agree that anti-Semitism became a qualitatively new menace in modern times, thanks to the infusion of racial theory at this 1870s turning point (modern racism grew out of vulgar applications of Darwinist evolutionary theory, and Darwin published his *Origin of the Species* in 1859), as well as the rise of modern media, the activity of political parties, and other new phenomena.

This interpretation about the dangerous novelty of anti-Semitism in the modern period allows that one legacy from ancient and medieval times was determinative. The religious accusation of deicide, the long-propagated theory maintaining that Jews were responsible for the crucifixion of Christ, is the one, enduring and fateful, element in the mix. Without it, there would never have been a sufficient cultural foundation for the Nazis' "Final Solution" of exterminating Jews, no matter how other pressures, motivations, and circumstances exacerbated anti-Semitism in interwar Germany. On this interpretation, modern anti-Semitism exhausted itself after World War

132. Novick, *Holocaust*.

II. Once the repudiation of the deicide accusation picked up authoritative institutional momentum among Christians after the Holocaust, as exemplified by the Second Vatican Council's 1964–1965 Nostra Aetate declaration ("What happened in His passion cannot be charged against all the Jews, without distinction, then alive, nor against the Jews of today"[133]), anti-Semitism lost its mass murderous muscle.

This theory was never foolproof, however. For Jews, it is certainly easier to live in a world when the Catholic Church has ceased accusing them of collective complicity in the murder of Jesus Christ (and this comfort level is enhanced by an unexpected development in Protestantism, which arose in the last sixty years or so, since Israel's 1967 Six-Day War, whereby a major subgroup, the Evangelicals, has displayed philosemitic devotion to the Jewish state and to related Jewish matters). Yet events of the last quarter century, since the collapse of the Israeli-Palestinian Oslo peace process and the eruption of the Second Intifada, have shown how Christian anti-Semitism can regroup and mobilize mass activity in social media, college campuses, and elsewhere in the absence of a formal accusatory writ of deicide. The Second Vatican Council declaration, and related developments, did not forestall the consolidation of a new sort of "Jewish question," this one focused on Israel rather than on the inclusion of Jews in the nation-states of Europe.

Since, for better or worse, we continually revise our understandings of the past in light of contemporary realities, the present configuration of events in North America and Europe in the period of Israel's 2023–2024 Gaza War encourages us to revisit our understanding of anti-Semitism, and its possible foundations. Assuming that Daniel Goldhagen and other commentators correctly judge that masses of Germans in the 1930s and early 1940s were complicit in the mass murder of Jews, among others,[134] might not we recalibrate our evaluation of what was motivating them, in light of decades of experience after the Holocaust? Is Christian anger about the Jews' supposed guilt for the crucifixion really the enduring animus of anti-Semitism? Or is it more judicious to recognize that capitalism always has fluctuating boom and bust periods, and that during the downswings the Christian view of Jewish recalcitrance in economic affairs, as embedded in the Gospels and in a legacy that can discernibly be traced to Jesus' preaching in Galilee, is uniquely portentous? Is it unreasonable to suppose that otherwise sensible, decent Germans rallied around Hitler not because of their thoughts about who killed Jesus, but rather because they had lost jobs and savings in the 1930s Depression and came from a religion which

---

133. Paul VI, *Nostra Aetate*.
134. Goldhagen, *Hitler's Willing Executioners*.

had, from its first days, taught that Jews have malignant dispositions toward other people's jobs and savings?

Though anti-Semitism sweltered on the political fringes of various European countries, controversies about Jewish involvement in the economy remained relatively mute on the continent for decades after the Holocaust. In America, the same situation held true, more or less, but for somewhat different reasons. If, in Europe, post-Holocaust remorse, not to mention the Cold War, set limits to the volume and contents of socioeconomic discussions about the Jews, in America a rather unique arrangement held intact for the half century that elapsed between the World War I Progressive Era we have discussed, the 1960s–1970s period of domestic social unrest, and Israel-related controversy in its 1967 and 1973 wars. Jews made headway in some economic fields, including white-collar professions, but their fame as exemplifications of the "American dream" derived from achievements in cultural spheres and also from the symbiosis between their liberal political temperament and the availability of high-status government positions—particularly in eras of the New Deal, the New Frontier, and the Great Society, when the Democratic party set the tone in Washington and the country. However, rather unlike how their descendants today understand their family pasts, American Jews in this mid-twentieth century period period had no real access to the country's true corridors of power—that is, the inner sanctums of executive management of major corporations. American Jews were "insiders" in cultural and public sector fields and thus susceptible to nasty commentary in these capacities. But, following the ephemeral 1920s-era explosion of Henry Ford's innuendo about Jews running the country, there could be relatively little vituperation about how Jews dominated the economy. This was basically due to anti-Semitism's *success* in America in this period, rather than the absence of it. Jews were emphatically kept out of corporate boardrooms. We turn to that story now.

Jewish Entry in Corporate America

A revealing estimate of how Jews were not perceived as being part of America's corporate establishment before 1967 can be found in an anecdotal, journalistic book about "What It Means to Be a Jew in America," published a few months after the Six-Day War, by Roger Kahn.[135] The Brooklyn-born author, who would find fame a few years later for his adoring *Boys of Summer* account of the Brooklyn Dodgers of the Jackie Robinson era, conducted extensive field research and composed a readable account that was quickly

---

135. Kahn, *Passionate People*.

overlooked, for clear reasons (Israel's Six-Day War in 1967 shifted attention about Jewish affairs, and also Kahn wrote in a politely self-conscious key about Jews, which would feel quaint by the start of the next decade when, coasting on waves of ethnic revivalism in America, writers and popular entertainers like Philip Roth and Woody Allen publicly unveiled scenes of American Jewish life in a comic tone of flamboyant exuberance). Kahn was diffidently careful in his descriptions of American Jewish experiences. His survey of the Jews' nonentry in the country's corporate establishment can be taken as a reliable indication of how the Jews' place in the United States was perceived at the time.

American Jewish business success, Kahn wrote, "is ringed with irony." Jews were thriving in small corporate and industrial enterprises. They were selling "washing machines and manufacturing electric coffee percolators," importing "chateau-bottled wines," and distributing "golf balls guaranteed not to sink" when driven into water hazards. Such Jewish business achievement in America was, the author contended, "considerable"; he surmised that "there may well be more American Jewish millionaires than paupers." In contrast, Kahn accused the corporate establishment of anti-Semitism. "As far as can be learned, there are no Jews on the highest executive levels of Bell Telephone, Standard Oil of New Jersey, U.S. Steel, the Metropolitan Life Insurance Company, or E. I. Dupont," he declared. "There is none near the top of most of the hundred largest American corporations." He cited an anonymous American Jewish Committee spokesman who talked about "executive suite anti-Semitism."[136]

Kahn's ambiguous mention of Ford Motor Company policy toward Jews in the mid-1960s is revealing.[137] Though he broadly blamed anti-Semitism for the exclusion of Jews from top business echelons in the country, his description of the situation at Ford implies that in some places anti-Jewish stereotypes lingered, but they were not really a causal factor in the nexus of Jewish inclusion or exclusion in the 1960s. At Ford, as Kahn saw it, ambitious Jews with business degrees and heady prospects were punishing the company for its notorious history of anti-Semitism associated with company founder Henry Ford, which hit its infamous peak in the 1920s. Kahn noted that Ford's current management deliberately sought to make amends for its past history by forging ties with Israel, in defiance of the Arab boycott, and by scouring both Yeshiva University and Brandeis University for business majors who might opt for an executive-track job offering at the car company. No such promising Jewish student responded to the Ford

---

136. Quotes above drawn from Kahn, *Passionate People*, 178–80.

137. Kahn, *Passionate People*, 180.

company recruitment, prompting Kahn to reflect philosophically that "the disabling effects of bigotry are not easily healed."[138] Meantime, his book quoted a nasty quip from an anonymous Ford executive. Referring to Jews, this manager pronounced, "They're still damn clannish."[139]

In fact, Jewish experiences with Ford Motor Company after the Holocaust and Henry Ford's 1947 death is yet more complicated and convoluted than what is conveyed in Kahn's depiction. They center around the activities of Sidney Weinberg, who became a senior partner at Goldman Sachs in 1930 and subsequently led the investment bank for some three decades, earning the moniker "Mr. Wall Street."[140]

Probably no American Jew in the mid-twentieth century did more than Weinberg to personify and promote Jewish corporate inclusion, often by reformatting and reversing stereotypes of Jewish exclusion. In his career, Weinberg out-Morganed the reputation of J. P. Morgan and outfoxed the memory of Henry Ford, operating as though Jewish corporate success in America depended upon proactively scrambling and erasing legacies of Waspish exclusivity on Wall Street personified by the former, and of dangerous anti-Semitism personified by the latter.

Weinberg had solid ties to FDR's liberal politics in the 1930s. In fact at the height of the Depression, he was Wall Street's sole conduit to a White House inhabited by a president who did not disguise his distaste for bankers' greed. Simultaneously, Weinberg himself embodied many of the symptoms of corporate "bigness," which Progressives like Louis Brandeis had castigated before the Great Depression. Brandeis, it will be recalled, devoted a full piece in his muckraking, pre–World War I series of articles, *Other People's Money and How the Bankers Use It*, to conflicts of interest and other presumed irregularities imposed by interlocking directorate structures, in which investment bankers sat on multiple corporate boards and gained leverage to direct corporate policy at the behest of profit considerations not identical to those of the company's own stockholders, or of the public at large. Ignoring Brandeis's moralistic critique of bigness, Weinberg recognized obvious advantages to be accrued to Goldman Sachs via his own interlocked involvement on numerous corporate boards. On the progressive left, ideological heirs of Brandeis would view this as a Faustian trade-off, whereby a prominent Jewish Wall Street investment bank crossed

---

138. Kahn, *Passionate People*, 181.

139. Kahn, *Passionate People*, 180.

140. The ensuing discussion is based on Cohan, *Money and Power*, 62–84; Ehrlich and Rehfeld, *New Crowd*, 20–30; and Gladwell, "Uses of Adversity."

the street and became fully integrated in corporate America by ingesting the ills of bigness.

Taking the opposite view, today Goldman Sachs views Weinberg's energetic involvement on over thirty corporate boards in this mid-century period as a legitimate business achievement. More than that, the reference to "country club," an obvious metonym for snobby anti-Semitic exclusion, on the bank's website suggests that Goldman Sachs, a banking business, holds regard for the social, as well as business, repercussions of Weinberg's placement on dozens of company boards, as though he himself is a legitimate symbol of how Jews finally arrived in corporate America:

> Few financiers have sat on more corporate boards than Sidney Weinberg (35 directorships). He served as a director of some of America's largest, most prestigious companies, such as General Electric, General Foods, National Dairy (later Kraft), B. F. Goodrich, Ford and Sears Roebuck and Co. Sidney became a highly sought-after director, changing the perception of the duties and responsibilities of corporate board members from the "country club" connotation.[141]

Weinberg, who kept an immigrant trace in his name by pronouncing it "Wein-boig," was a self-made Jewish success story on Wall Street.[142] His life story circulates prominently in the Goldman Sachs histories; in terms of the story of Jewish engagement in Wall Street, it is considered precedent-setting. Weinberg, one study notes, "made it easier for the new breed of self-made Jewish entrepreneurs to follow in his path on Wall Street—a path that led right into the first circle of power."[143]

The son of a struggling Brooklyn liquor dealer, Weinberg's formal education ended at the end of eighth grade at PS 13 (Public School 13) in the borough (he remained loyal to the institution throughout his life). Weinberg was just sixteen years old when the 1907 panic convulsed Wall Street. One day that year, Weinberg took an elevator twenty-five floors to the top of 43 Exchange Place, at the time Manhattan's tallest building. He had worked his way down close to the bottom when he was offered a job at three dollars a week as an assistant to Goldman's janitor. Weinberg cut an unimpressive, pudgy five-foot-four figure that was compared to a Kewpie doll in an oft-cited 1956 *New Yorker* profile.[144] As though in tribute to his humble start at the bank, cleaning spittoons in its basement and brushing

---

141. Goldman Sachs, "Sidney Weinberg."
142. Cohan, *Money and Power*, 65.
143. Ehrlich and Rehfeld, *New Crowd*, 21.
144. Kahn, "Director's Director."

partners' silk hats, he kept a functional office after he made it to the top at Goldman. He lived with his wife, Helen Livingston Weinberg, in a comfortable Scarsdale home from 1923 to the end of his life (in 1969, Goldman Sachs's centennial year). For him, the house was never a mansion. He often treated it as an extension of his office, busily studying corporate reports over the weekend in preparation for board meetings.

In another *New Yorker* profile, published at the grimmest turn of the 2008 financial crisis, Malcolm Gladwell favorably contrasted Weinberg's self-made, rags-to-riches life trajectory to that of the socioeconomic privilege incarnated on the Wasp side of Wall Street by heirs of J. P. Morgan.[145] An astute writer whose analyses often uncover unexpected routes of success in modern life, Gladwell portrayed Weinberg as an outsider who wedged his way into gentile corporate elites by comically accentuating his humble Jewish origins. The schlimazel posturing made him less threatening to gentiles as he climbed up to their status perch. It cheerfully affirmed everyone's understanding of America as a place where even a Jewish klutz could sit on corporate boards. Weinberg, Gladwell notes, "took the subway. . . . [He] would talk about his public school as if it were Princeton, and as a joke he would buy up Phi Beta keys from pawnshops and hand them out to visitors like party favors." Weinberg, Gladwell continues, "thought British and dressed Yiddish."[146] Starting with a janitor's mop on the bottom floor, Weinberg stood stereotypes about Jews on their head in order to reach the top of corporate America.

Weinberg's social climbing strategy identified by Gladwell, and recently explored in broad terms by Harvard Business School professor Laura Haung,[147] is just one part of the story, however. In fact, it can be misleading to think of Weinberg solely as an outsider. The image of a clownish, self-mocking social climber suggests a medieval European Jewish trajectory by which Jews are everlastingly on the margins, performing for empowered gentiles and at best rising from court jesters (who pass around plastic Phi Beta Kappa keys) to court Jews. The Jewish trajectory in America was always more hopefully expectant. While Jews did not become part of the country's corporate establishment until late in the twentieth century, their status beforehand was far from marginalized abasement.

Jews restructured key corporate practices to level the playing field for themselves. They used high-level government appointments, particularly

---

145. Gladwell, "Uses of Adversity."
146. Gladwell, "Uses of Adversity," para. 9, 10.
147. Haung, *Edge*.

in new posts arranged as wartime contingencies, to bypass long-standing obstacles of snobbery and exclusion in elite corporate spheres.

As Jews climbed up in American finance, they de-Yiddishized, in the sense of cropping away high-risk commercial paper trading and security speculation ingrained in the history of banks on the Jewish side of Wall Street. They associated themselves with the steadier side of corporate investment underwriting associated with Morgan's bank. The main traits in Weinberg's career are either not relevant to the insider-outsider typology, or they are as close to the inside as they are to the outside. Far from being Yiddishkeit decoration on over thirty corporate boards, Weinberg had an influential voice on the table, and key corporate practices were molded out of its echoes. As one commentator puts it, "His prescription ranged from the utterly mundane—how many times a corporate board should meet annually and what a meeting agenda should contain, to sensitive matters such as the amount of management bonuses."[148]

Jews who had made a fortune on Wall Street were understood to have operated in shady financial spheres, particularly as stock speculators. In this connection, the best-known portrayal of Weinberg, E. J. Kahn's 1956 *New Yorker* piece, missed the mark by opining that "Weinberg probably comes as close to Bernard Baruch as embodying the popular conception of Bernard Baruch."[149] Baruch, in fact, made his fortune in stock speculation and then mostly retired from Wall Street and undertook extensive self-publicity work to reinvent himself (he was famous at the time of the 1956 *New Yorker* profile owing to his work on the United Nations Atomic Energy Commission, among other things). Baruch never covered up his origins as a speculative trader in the markets, and his autobiography told colorful stories about his Wall Street days; but this memoir clearly relegated them, compared to Baruch's social entrepreneurial work in public service, in later phases of his life.[150] Weinberg, for his part, disavowed the original sin of stock speculation in his Goldman Sachs work. In a revealing pronouncement issued two years before his death, he recapped his career: "I'm an investment banker. I don't shoot craps. If I had been a speculator and taken advantage of what I knew, I could have made five times as much as I have today."[151] J. P. Morgan would have said the same thing about himself, albeit in more refined language. It is not outsider speech.

148. Cohan, *Money and Power*, 71.
149. Kahn, "Director's Director."
150. Baruch, *My Own Story*.
151. Cohan, *Money and Power*, 68.

In public roles at times of war, Weinberg's centripetal movement toward the inside was unmistakable. After America entered World War I, Weinberg enlisted in the navy as a cook and ended up in a naval intelligence office. During World War II he became a high-impact consultant on the War Production Board (WPB), admiringly known as a "body snatcher" who recruited big businessmen for the war effort, including Charles Wilson from General Electric. Despite Weinberg's support for Wendell Wilkie in the 1940 presidential election, the Roosevelt administration retained complete trust in him. With FDR's stamp of approval, Weinberg was sent by the Office of Strategic Services' head, William Donovan, on an errand to the Soviet Union (whose precise purposes have never been determined). In autumn 1946 President Truman awarded Weinberg a medal of merit for his WPB work.[152]

Through his public service work, Weinberg gained acquaintance with the Ford Motor elite in 1947, and within a decade (in August 1956) he became a corporate director of the company after orchestrating its initial public offering (IPO), ending Ford Motor's decades-long run as a private corporation. The episode is a milestone in the story of Jewish adaptation in corporate America. At the height of the 1960s, Ford Motor might have had trouble recruiting young Jewish business majors, but this factoid alone does not fully support a thesis of Jewish estrangement from elite sectors of American business.

Historically, Jews and Christians have used images of one another, many of them mythic and stained by antagonism and prejudice, to fashion a singularly American corporate culture. Up to its IPO in the mid-1950s, Ford Motor evolved in America's economy both as a consummate prototype and as a curious exception, oftentimes operating eerily as a doppelganger mirror image of the Jews' insider-outsider socioeconomic status. In 1916, months before Weinberg became a navy cook, Henry Ford became embroiled in a bitter court battle with the Dodge brothers, John and Horace, who alleged that the company was shortchanging dividends to stockholders. Viewing his own transformative enterprise essentially as a family company, Henry Ford contested the corporate model represented by the Dodge suit on two grounds: he dismissed the economic and social worth of stockholders, calling them "parasites" and "idle drones," and he argued that the business of a modern company was to manufacture for the masses rather than augmenting profits for investors.[153] Ford promoted his infamous anti-Semitic campaign against the Jews for a mix of reasons, none of them completely

---

152. Cohan, *Money and Power*, 78–80.
153. Watts, *People's Tycoon*, 254–57.

adducible, but he expressly identified Jews as being leaders of the stockholding, "parasitic" corporate finance model that he viewed as being antithetical to the true purposes of a modern company (in a similar way, while the full range of motivations undergirding Ford's formal renunciation of anti-Semitism in mid-1927 remains murky, apparently his stereotypical view of Jewish control in finance sectors ranked toward the top of the list since it influenced his concerns about finding investment backing for a new Model A car model after the stoppage of production of the Model T at Highland Park in May 1927).[154] Henry Ford exploited anti-Semitism in order to distance Ford Motor from emerging models of corporate control; in a telling reversal, his grandson Henry Ford II needed Sidney Weinberg to bring Ford Motor into the fold of corporate America by going public in its IPO.

Weinberg first met Henry II in 1947 at a meeting of the Business Advisory Council, an entity operating under the aegis of the Department of Commerce, which the Goldman Sachs banker had helped establish in the late 1930s. With Charlie Wilson as a go-between, Weinberg started operating as a consultant to the Ford family in 1953. Using espionage-like code names in an operation conducted under a strict cloak of secrecy, he brought over fifty proposals for the financial reorganization of the Ford Company and the Ford Foundation. The IPO, the largest of its kind in its time, was announced on November 9, 1955, with Goldman Sachs as one of the underwriters.[155] In view of a number of considerations—(a) Ford Motor's anti-Semitic track record, (b) the company's monumental impact on the shaping of America's landscape and on the structure of the country's manufacturing and consumer sectors, (c) the magnitude of the IPO, and (d) the IPO's validation of Weinberg's strategy of using corporate board membership as a lever for breaking down walls confining Jewish Wall Street—this date can be taken as a turning point portending the inclusion of Jews in corporate America some three decades later.

That said, the story of Jewish entry in America's corporate establishment is fluid and multidimensional, and it cannot be wholly reduced to the exploits of any publicly acclaimed "Mr. Wall Street." Recognizing that causes and effects are often interchangeable in this story and that perceptions are as significant in it as are statistical disclosures, a historian can cite several items that were notable in the process of Jewish inclusion in the corporate establishment by the end of the twentieth century. Some such factors can be listed here in bullet form—they are either *indicators* or *causes* of the Jews' belated inclusion in America's corporate power establishment,

154. Baldwin, *Henry Ford*, 224–40.
155. Cohan, *Money and Power*, 90–92.

starting in the Reagan years. Amplifying on such points could fill volumes, but our subsequent discussion will touch on just a few aspects of the first and last points on this list:

- Jews became prominent in corporate America at times when Wall Street's basic rules were in flux. As innovators it was easier for them to make a fortune and gain social status either in uncharted areas of finance or ones that had heretofore been shadowed by moral dubiety or by practical investment anxiety. The paramount example is Jewish engagement in the leveraged buyouts (LBOs) takeover sphere in the 1980s.

- Corporate entry served as a counternarrative for American Jews in a yin and yang dynamic whereby they demonstrated a "proestablishment" collective identity on Wall Street at a time when antiestablishment Jewish hippies were on full display in the anti-Vietnam movement and in other social causes.

- Several Jews won renown as insightful critics of the financial markets because they themselves were gainfully employed in them as business lawyers, among other things. In the proregulatory tradition of Brandeis, who himself was simultaneously "the people's attorney" and also a successful business lawyer, Jews often positioned themselves as creative regulators who kept a critical eye on the markets while concurrently having insider expertise about their operation, based on their own banking or corporate experience.

- Jews were also "innovators" in terms of criminality in the financial markets. However much this side of the story might serve as fodder for anti-Semitism, I believe it warrants consideration precisely as a measure of how solidly corporate American Jewish individuals and groups became. American Jews—Ivan Boesky in the 1980s, Bernie Madoff in the aftermath of the 2008 crisis—became ultimate symbols of greed and financial criminality in successive periods; their misadventures were preceded by now-forgotten but nonetheless, at the time, much-publicized fraud scandals that featured Jewish businessmen. American Jewish organizational spokesmen naturally feared that once-in-a-generation icons of financial skulduggery like Boesky and Madoff would cause an anti-Semitic backlash, but they did not (what that might possibly mean will engage us in the final sections of this essay).

Junk Bond Jews

Michael Milken (born 1946) grew up without hardship in an upper-middle-class Jewish home in Encino, California, and reportedly displayed his computational and financial skills from the age of ten when he began to help his father, an accountant, keep the books.[156] In the second half of the twentieth century, the process by which Jews changed fundamental terms of Wall Street trading in order to gain a firm position among America's business elite pivots around Milken's career.

His story begins in the late 1960s when he was enrolled as a straitlaced business administration major at the University of California at Berkeley. As an undergraduate, Milken stumbled across the basic concept of junk bonds in a book published in the late 1950s by a Johns Hopkins University–trained economist, W. Braddock Hickman, called *Corporate Bond Quality and Investor Experience*.[157] Braddock's thesis was that it was more profitable, over the long term, to invest in a diverse portfolio of high-risk, low-grade bonds than to put money in top-rated, lower-risk bonds; he appeared to substantiate this unconventional premise via a detailed analysis of corporate bond performance between 1900 and 1943.[158] Milken applied Braddock's academic thesis for practical profit at Drexel Burnham, an investment bank formed in 1971 out of a mix of Jewish and gentile sides of Wall Street (specifically, the bank came out of the merger of an aggressive brokerage house founded in 1935 by Tubby Burnham that was comprised mostly of Jewish traders, and the more stolidly conservative, gentile investment bank, Drexel). When Burnham first approached Drexel, he was informed that three of its two hundred employees were Jewish (Milken, who had been a member of the Jewish fraternity at Berkeley, Sigma Alpha Mu, was one of them).[159] By the mid-1970s, corporate finance activity at Drexel Burnham was headed by Frederick Joseph, a Harvard Business School graduate who had grown up in Boston in an Orthodox Jewish family. Drexel Burnham was barely above water when Joseph came aboard, but he announced a fifteen-year plan to make it as powerful and wealthy as Goldman Sachs.

The prophesy's fulfillment came to depend on Milken, not Joseph. Up to the indictment and prosecution of Milken in the late 1980s on charges of racketeering and fraud, Joseph remained Milken's nominal superior, but Drexel's fortunes were built on the exhausting labors of the junk bond

---

156. The discussion of Milken draws from Stewart, *Den of Thieves*, 51–53.
157. Hickman, *Corporate Bond Quality*.
158. Smith, *Money Wars*, 223–24.
159. Stewart, *Den of Thieves*, 48–67.

wizard from Encino. From 1975, Milken and his underlings operated more or less autonomously at Drexel, enjoying a compensation arrangement by which relatively low base salaries were offset by strong performance incentives, in which Milken's group received 35 percent of profits accrued by their activities, with Milken controlling how this share was to be allocated.

In his career, Milken exhibited fanatical work habits and an uncompromising determination to squeeze every last possible dollar out of each deal. He was a marketing virtuoso who defused tensions engendered by investments in bonds not blessed by high rating approval proffered by the two venerable bond-grading agencies, Moody's and Standard and Poor's. Though they were popularly called "junk bonds," Milken persuaded his investors to think of these financial instruments as "high-yield bonds." During his years of breathtaking financial achievement, Milken can be seen as a Jewish financial dynamo who persuaded markets that major investment returns could be attained while risk is neutralized. Bernie Madoff, of course, later regurgitated and incarnated the same myth; but Milken's story, webbed in voluminous, actual financial activity and in genuine financial innovation, is far more morally nuanced than that of Madoff, who generated wealth by sheer duplicity in a Ponzi scheme (in many minds, Milken's legacy was rightly exonerated by his receipt of a presidential pardon in 2020). Madoff's scandal became "Jewish" because of his own identity and because many of his investment victims were Jewish individuals and organizations. In Milken's more complicated case, the development of junk bond trading created new mechanisms of capital formation for firms, new investment opportunities in general, and also a new field of investment activity for Jews who, for one reason or another, had not operated beforehand as fully engaged players in high-status financial markets. In this (perhaps unique) way, Milken's story belongs simultaneously both to the transformation of American finance and also to the transformation of Jews in America through their inclusion in the country's corporate elite.

Milken jacked junk bond trading up to Brobdingnagian dimensions by operating on three levels: technical, physical, and ethnic. First, his activity at Drexel slipped through regulatory networks due to the high-yield bonds' status as "secondary offerings," i.e., as bonds purchased by Drexel from an original issuer and then reoffered to Milken's own clients in an arrangement that bypassed registration requirements with the Securities and Exchange Commission. Second, Milken's 1978 decision to run his own junk bond outfit on the other coast, at a small Century City office (while he quartered his family in his native Encino, in a home once owned by Clark Gable and Carole Lombard), removed him from long-standing Manhattan assumptions about the unworthiness of low-grade bonds as well as from other subtle, or less subtle, prejudices regarding investment practices on the Jewish side of Wall Street. No doubt, Milken found his comfort zone in California, in an arrangement which suited his workaholic mania (the time zone difference from Wall Street offered an excuse to start his workday at four-thirty in the morning) and which allowed him to surround himself at work with trusted associates, most notably his brother Lowell, a lawyer, who joined the office months after its California relocation. Third, the novelty of Milken's set-up magnetically attracted a group of Jewish (and some gentile) investors who had no use for elite Wall Street norms. These included Saul Steinberg, a financier and raider who had already won control of Reliance Insurance and lost a controversial takeover bid for Chemical Bank, and Meshulam Riklis, originally from Israel, who had made a fortune in America from movie theaters and liquor. Relocation, the advantages of an ethnic subeconomy, familiarity with the intricacies of financial regulation and a willingness to challenge them, not to mention his personal traits (bare-knuckle negotiation style, outrageous work hours, and salesmanship virtuosity)—such were determinants in the exponential growth in junk bond trading, which left Milken himself raking in forty-five million dollars in 1982.

Staggering capital amounts generated in this new sphere inspired thoughts about how junk bond revenue might leverage entry into new fields where yet more money, and corporate power, could be found. The most promising such tributary for junk bond capital was the merger and acquisitions field, particularly corporate company takeovers (called leveraged buyouts, or LBOs, meaning that the acquisition of a corporation is leveraged by borrowed money). As will be recalled, business reporter James Stewart pictures Milken on the eve of this transition into the corporate takeover domain brashly proclaiming, "We're going to tee-up GM, Ford and IBM, and make them cringe."[160] A generation earlier, Sidney Weinberg had proven that a Jewish investment banker could productively sit on corporate boards. Now another American Jew, Michael Milken, was saying that he could own them.

The corporate takeover sphere in the 1980s became heavily manned by Jewish financial professionals, and these figures invented new, unheard-of concepts in mergers and acquisitions. These financiers set examples both of the legitimate limits and also of criminal transgression in a corporate business sphere that is inherently conducive to insider trading. If truth be told, LBOs and related activities are redolent of images and circumstances evocative of a Jewish past of poignant vulnerability and miserable choices—these

---

160. Stewart, *Den of Thieves*, 67.

can be gleaned from the Reagan era's creepy and weird financial terminology regarding so-called "white knight" friendly corporate rescuers (who in some cases never arrived and in other cases wrested control of corporate takeover targets on terms just marginally better than the original extortionate offer proposed by a raider), "greenmail" (essentially bribes proffered to stave off a takeover raider), and the "poison pill" (by which shareholders had a legal option of purchasing a widened share pool to dilute the acquisition share of the raider so as to keep the existing corporate structure afloat, frequently as a Pyrrhic victory). One can imagine that Jewish attorneys and bankers like Martin Lipton who coined these merger and acquisitions (M&A) neologisms sometimes had on their minds pogroms and inquisitions, in which ancestors faced the sobering choice of putting themselves and their children to death or converting under the control of the attacker.[161] Another hypothesis: the high incidence of Jews in this LBO area, including the emergence of some of them, like Milken and Boesky, as fabulously wealthy trading wizards who seemingly never lost, points to tacit cultural assumptions about Jewish experience with risk. In an era when lessons of the Holocaust were circulating for the first time in mass media, starting with the four-part broadcast of television's "Holocaust" miniseries in spring 1978, Jews could recast themselves as survivors who withstood evils whose level of malice trivialized the threat posed by corporate raiders. Not just in the M&A field, this sort of thinking undeniably envelops some successful Jewish financial traders and corporate types in this era (for an example, peruse the autobiography of Leo Melamed, a Holocaust survivor who made his way up, starting as a pork belly trader, in high-risk commodity exchange markets[162]).

Corporate buyouts leveraged by junk bond capital may have been Milken's invention, but just as it is impossible to gauge what parts of his inventiveness might have been "Jewish," the 1980s corporate takeover craze was stimulated by macroeconomic and political factors that well exceeded any single individual's innovation.[163] In a post-Vietnam era plagued by OPEC-backed (Organization of the Petroleum Exporting Countries) oil price hikes, rising interest rates, and inflation, corporate stock was widely undervalued. The bait was there for the taking, and Reagan's 1980 election

---

161. Much in Lipton's activities in the 1980s resuscitated tensions and insights connected to Brandeis's ambiguous situation as the people's attorney and a business lawyer seventy years earlier. The third bullet point in the preceding discussion of Jewish entry in corporate affairs applies to him as much as anyone else. For Lipton: Cole, *M&A Titans*, 153–55; Lipton, "Pills."

162. Melamed, *Escape to the Futures*.

163. The discussion here is based on Stewart, *Den of Thieves*, 97.

victory sent clear signals that the government was not going to muddy the pond. As indication of its anti-regulatory intent, the new administration dropped major antitrust litigation. In the first years of the 1980s, former senior officials from previous Republican administrations were making fortunes on the private side, in M&A activity, without any apparent connection to Milken or any of the other Jewish financial players who had a public profile in LBO activity, and sometimes in insider trading scandals, throughout the decade.

Nonetheless, because banks on the Wasp side of Wall Street were slow to discard stigmatized M&A perceptions, the takeover sphere provided unprecedented opportunity for Jewish entry in corporate America, and Jews took advantage of it. One career representative of the trend belonged to Bruce Wasserstein at First Boston.[164] Wasserstein coheaded M&A and investment banking at this institution from May 1979 until February 1988—that is, through the takeover era. Born in 1947 and raised in Brooklyn's largely Jewish Midwood area (his father had a ribbon business and dabbled in investing, and his maternal grandfather taught at a yeshiva in Eastern Europe), Wasserstein had a prodigal financial career, handling over one thousand deals valued at about two hundred and fifty billion dollars. Just nineteen when he graduated from the University of Michigan, Wasserstein took law and business graduate degrees at Harvard University and practiced law in Manhattan for a spell at Cravath, Swaine & Moore before moving to First Boston's merger group in 1977. Well-educated, the heavyset Wasserstein cut an unusually disheveled figure among neatly cropped investment bankers. Looking like a "shambling academic," he roamed around the office with his tie askew and with untucked shirttails. Since takeover deal profit margins often hinged on make-or-break interpretations of antitrust, disclosure, and other regulatory considerations, a crucial asset contributing to Wasserstein's M&A acumen was his law degree. "What set him apart was his legal training," attested Jim Maher, an investment banking executive and young vice chairman at First Boston.[165]

With his colleague Joseph Perella, Wasserstein aggressively reached out to prospective clients in nationwide marketing campaigns, the aim being to catch up with merger divisions at well-established gentile and Jewish banks, Morgan Stanley and Goldman Sachs. An oft-repeated comment in the Wasserstein-Perella group—"We're not winning clients on a golf course"—aptly captures how making a fortune in M&A was a winning

164. The following discussion on Wasserstein draws from Cole, *M&A Titans*, 80–86; Brewerton, "Bruce Wasserstein Obituary."
165. Cole, *M&A Titans*, 82.

formula for Jews and others who did not have Wasp-white shoes.[166] This was an area with fewer barriers of social prejudice where education, hard work, and intelligence mattered. Soon after leaving First Boston, Wasserstein caught attention working as a consultant to Kohlberg Kravis Roberts (KKR) in the 1989 takeover of RJR Nabisco, often viewed as the decade's archetypal instance of LBO avarice.[167]

More than anything, the 1980s insider trading scandals could be depicted as a Jewish "den of thieves" because of the identities of their dominant characters, Milken and Boesky. The former's background has been mentioned here, and since Boesky (who died in spring 2024) was a much-discussed white-collar criminal, we can be concise about relevant Jewish-related elements in his story. His intimidatingly intense veneer notwithstanding, Boesky was probably the most mediocre financial felon in American Jewish history. His social climbing motivations are tediously explicable.

Madoff, whose Ponzi scheme crimes, when exposed two decades later, had reached yet more biblically prodigious dollar levels, is a more diabolically interesting figure than Boesky. The composure Madoff managed to summon when sitting at a conference table across from Securities and Exchange Commission regulators, who only would have needed to review the details of one of thousands of phonily recorded transactions to pop the Ponzi bubble, has no equivalent in Boesky's career, whose sole instance of rightly calculated composure is to be found in the hiring of a good lawyer at the end of his escapades. These two Jewish uber-crooked financiers belong to different eras, ones separated by technological advances in information, changes in gender norms, and levels of Jewish social advance in America. Boesky's greed appears more brutely macho than that of Madoff's domesticated, gentrified avarice, even though the same unfathomably powerful lust for money power was hidden within the business apparel of both men.

In Boesky's case, the costume was a three-piece black suit, a starched white shirt, and a dangling gold chain. Like other Jewish players in the finance markets, Boesky had been a wrestler in his teenage years, and the way he likened his work as an arbitrageur to his involvement in that sport would raise the eyebrows of any amateur psychologist ("wrestling and arbitrage are both solitary sports in which you live or die by your deeds, and you do it very visibly").[168]

---

166. Cole, *M&A Titans*, 82–83.
167. "Wasserstein Obituary"; Burrough and Helyar, *Barbarians at the Gate*.
168. Stewart, *Den of Thieves*, 41.

Arbitrage had traditionally been a low-risk, moderately profitable pursuit in the financial sphere that depended on exploiting price differentials of transacted items in markets located in different regions and time zones. As new technologies shortened distance and synchronized markets, Boesky (with others) tried to peddle a modified financial activity, "risk arbitrage," as a newly profitable pursuit reliably undertaken by computational wizards and experienced traders who could identify undervalued assets as targets in M&A activity. Boesky published a book to hammer out the point that "risk arbitrage" was a misnomer.[169] He peppered the volume with equations and vapid descriptions and examples so as to show how he had mastered the craft, and turned corporate "merger mania" (his phrase) into a safe, steady investment opportunity for clients who hired him. "Risk arbitrage is not gambling in any sense," proclaimed Boesky. "Done properly, the odds of a risk arbitrage investment are with you, not against you."[170]

As he was writing such lines in this 1985 volume, Boesky was making millions by "parking" money for Milken in tax and regulation avoidance schemes, and packing up briefcases of money to secure illegal information tips from Martin Siegel, an investment banker at Kidder Peabody. "If you studied Ivan's track record, the things he did on his own research were lousy and the things he based on his bribery were terrific," observed Ace Greenberg, a much respected Wall Street figure who was CEO of the Bears Stearns investment bank and brokerage firm during this merger mania period. "It was all horseshit."[171] Boesky claimed to have spent three years writing his treatise, but business writer Jeffrey Madrick, listed in smaller print on the book's inside cover as its editor, was its ghostwriter; the volume seemed suspiciously similar to a 1982 NYU monograph written by a rival arbitrageur, Guy Wyser-Pratte, who called Boesky "Piggy."[172] The book was politely reviewed, but as its author toured seven cities promoting it, media outlets like *Fortune* and *American Lawyer* published doubts about the veracity of Boesky's descriptions regarding his own background, including issues of whether he had spent his high school years fully at an elite Michigan prep school (Cranbrook) and whether he had completed a full undergraduate program at the University of Michigan.

Nonetheless, Boesky's image as a financial genius remained intact in 1986 when he legendarily proclaimed at Berkeley's business school graduation ceremony, "I think greed is healthy. You can be greedy and still feel

169. Boesky, *Merger Mania*.
170. Boesky, *Merger Mania*, 14.
171. Cole, *M&A Titans*, 137.
172. Steward, *Den of Thieves*, 226–27.

good about yourself."[173] A year later, it will be recalled, a reworked version of the quip uttered by Michael Douglas's fictional character Gordon Gekko, in the movie "Wall Street," became the decade's mantra.

Bonded by their lust for power, Milken, a true innovator in the financial markets, worked well with Boesky, a rank imitator. According to Stewart, the first collaboration between the two in an insider trading scheme occurred in January 1985, in a proposed merger deal between Occidental Petroleum and Diamond Shamrock.[174] That proposed deal soured, and for a time Milken owed Boesky several million dollars; but by spring of that year, he had cleared the slate, hiding payments within a busy beehive of transactions and never writing a direct check to Boesky. For Milken, insider trading fraud had limited incentive since he was pulling in millions of dollars from takeover transactions without any necessary reliance on illegal tips (financing one deal related to Storer Communications in this period netted Milken $49.6 million). Still, the partnership with Boesky served multiple purposes for Milken's Drexel outfit at this mid-1980s juncture, and the two concocted what Stewart calls a "sweeping criminal conspiracy." In areas of false public disclosure, tax fraud, market manipulation, and also insider trading, the duo's crimes "meshed to achieve ends more ambitious than anything ever contemplated by the drafters of the securities laws," this author explains.[175] As 1985 rolled along, Milken could raise five billion dollars in a few days to leverage takeover transactions. At his peak, Boesky managed an investment fund that had over three billion dollars in assets, and he had a net worth of over two hundred million dollars.[176]

The Madoff Scandal: Repudiation or Validation of Jewish Inclusion and Success in America's Financial Power System?

After confessing to his two sons, investment manager Bernie Madoff was detained by authorities in mid-December 2008 and subsequently submitted a guilty plea in a Ponzi financial fraud scheme of breathtaking proportions, widely reported as fifty billion dollars (the actual figure of stolen and disappeared wealth was quite lower, though the exact scale of the crime remains disputed).[177] Madoff was seventy at the time of his scheme's exposure. Born

173. Stewart, *Den of Thieves*, 261.
174. Stewart, *Den of Thieves*, 210–19.
175. Stewart, *Den of Thieves*, 219.
176. Stewart, *Den of Thieves*, 222, 328.
177. See Eren, *Bernie Madoff*, 43–44; Cambell, *Madoff Talks*, 180–81. Deducting gains accrued to investors through his Ponzi scheme, Madoff, in prison, referred

in 1938, he grew up mostly in middle-class comfort in Laurelton, Queens, though his Jewish parents faced some rough patches, including the failure of a sporting goods store and iffy behavior on the edge of the financial industry (at one point, his father Ralph, riddled by credit woes, registered his small brokerage firm in his mother's name, Sylvia).[178] A mediocre student, Madoff struggled in school and eventually graduated from Hofstra University, but he is portrayed as having enjoyed some popularity and happiness in these early years, highlighted by his marriage to Ruth Alpern, who had grown up in a more solidly professional, Jewishly observant, home.

Madoff's management of his own brokerage firm dates from his final months at Hofstra. Bernard L. Madoff Investment Securities (BLMIS) engaged in low-status, mostly unregulated dealing in "over-the-counter" (OTC) stock. His forte, even in later years of the Ponzi scheme, was (factually or fictitiously) in the "third market," meaning trading in stocks listed on the New York Stock Exchange among dealers in the OTC markets.[179] Initially, this niche allowed him to bypass more powerful, NYSE, brokerage houses; also, quite usefully, this third market was not on the regulatory radar scheme. That these advantages of the third market were first discerned by Madoff's younger brother, Peter, (who, without partnership title honorifics, worked loyally by his brother's side for forty years and eventually received a ten-year prison term) reinforces an image of Bernie Madoff as a slow-witted con man who applied the entirety of his intelligence to the Ponzi fraud. Historian Michael Berkowitz, who published an article about Jewish dimensions of the Ponzi affair, strikes this chord. He speculates that Ruth (who became a publicly reviled figure but was never prosecuted) was probably the only "brain in the outfit," and Bernie was, categorically, a "stupid bastard."[180]

Such venting about Madoff as an "idiot" glosses as many problems as it solves, however. As pointed out by sociologist Colleen Eren, the author of a fascinating study based on content analysis of media coverage of the Madoff affair in dozens of British and US outlets, these moralistic and dismissive perceptions of Madoff preempt discussion about cultural and economic structures that enable such colossal fraud. "Remarkably, very

---

disingenuously to a total "net" loss of two billion dollars. Commentators estimate that the "net" loss of investors (individuals and institutions), who did not gain from the fraud, could have been twenty billion dollars; among investors who enjoyed an overall gain, over the years, paper losses in the final period when the fraud was exposed also had negative repercussions.

178. Biographical detail here draws from Henriques, *Wizard of Lies*.
179. Henriques, *Wizard of Lies*, 49.
180. Berkowitz, "Madoff Paradox."

little attempt was made or hypotheses offered as to *why* Madoff committed the crime," she observes.[181] Greed, no doubt, is the overwhelmingly correct answer to this *why* question; but there remain vexing secondary questions about Madoff's disposition and capacities, and these need to be unpacked in order to locate the Madoff affair's place in this story about Jewish entry in corporate America.

The sociologist Eren's agenda is to show how excessive media coverage and public discussion about Madoff's villainous character, and also about manifest evidence of SEC incompetence, deflected public attention away from structural issues of monopolistic economic and political power in this 2008 period. This was a time when executives at "too big to fail" investment banks and insurance companies escaped responsibility for their greedy mismanagement, and the average taxpayer was compelled to provide funds which allowed stupendously wealthy financial professionals to avoid the "moral hazard" of paying the price of incompetence in a competitive economy. However, the "why" question about Madoff also has a Jewish component—namely, why was such a monumental fraud perpetrated by a Jewish crook, who victimized so many upstanding Jewish clients?

Evaluation of this question should address a noticeable trend in American corporate and financial sectors from the mid-1970s through the Madoff scandal, a period when technological change and government-sponsored privatization in the United States and elsewhere created new opportunities of entry for ambitious players outside of the Wasp establishment, and also unprecedented "economies of scale" on various levels, including the ability to commit fraud of unprecedented dimension. Up through the 1960s and the divisive Watergate end of the Nixon presidency, episodes of Jewish involvement in white-collar crime tended not to be sensationalized along ethnoreligious lines. Though they sometimes involved millions of dollars, they were not imagined as ranking with the greatest crimes in corporate history. They were prosecuted and judged under conventional assumptions about the efficacy of regulators and the binding nature of fiduciary duty, and they were resoluble in a relatively placid atmosphere, without the sort of vituperative venting and excruciatingly protracted and unsatisfying damages litigation, which colored the aftermath of the Madoff affair.

One of the last fraud scandals in this earlier era involved the collapse of the Penn Central Transportation Company, then America's largest railroad, in June 1970.[182] The railroad had operated 20,530 miles of track in

---

181. Eren, *Bernie Madoff*, 136.

182. Information about the Penn Central affair is drawn from Cohan, *Money and Power*, 151–57; Rubin, *In an Uncertain World*, 73–74.

sixteen states and also in Canada; in summer 1968, Goldman Sachs unsuspectedly sold thirty-five million dollars of Penn Central's commercial paper, regarding this as a solid transaction. Two years later, when the railroad defaulted on eighty-seven million dollars of its short-term commercial paper, Goldman was sued by four railroad investors who charged that the investment bank had withheld pertinent information about the railroad's shaky finances. This occurred not long after Weinberg's death, when Goldman was transitioning under Gus Levy's leadership, and the Penn Central litigation, featuring damages claims for twenty-three million dollars, created "immense anxiety" at the investment bank for over a year.

Goldman was a private partnership, and so its executives theoretically would have been personally accountable were the plaintiffs to be awarded a large share of their demands. The bank, in fact, could not have survived such a resolution (twenty-three million dollars constituted almost half of Goldman's capital). Despite these months of tension, the fraud scandal was noticeably containable. Clearly judicable in terms of existing precedents and accepted norms of dos and don'ts in the markets, the fiduciary breach allegation in the Penn Central matter could be, and was, effectively challenged by Goldman's lawyers. This was not an era when a Jewish financial manager, or an investment bank known as being rooted in Jewish Wall Street, could be castigated as a monstrous financial felon, as a vampire squid, or as a murderously grinning villain, a.k.a. the Joker (as *New York* magazine pictured Madoff on its cover). In fact, ever resilient, Goldman weathered the Penn Central crisis and even squeezed profit from it. "The settlement cost Goldman Sachs less than we eventually made in risk arbitrage trades involving claims in the Penn Central bankruptcy," admitted Robert Rubin, who worked at Goldman Sachs from the mid-1960s in risk arbitrage before going on to higher positions, including his aforementioned term as secretary of the treasury under the Clinton administration.[183]

The late 1970s shift toward vituperative hyperbole in the perception or reality of Jewish corporate fraud can be observed in a leasing services fraud perpetrated by a Jewish-controlled outfit called, of all things, OPM: Other People's Money. (A survey of varying uses of this term—from Brandeis to FDR's first inaugural address, and then to Jerry Steiner's 1989 eponymous play, which two years later reached the silver screen with Danny DeVito and Gregory Peck in lead roles—would uncover fascinating changes in American culture and its perceptions of bankers and corporate activity, from the Gilded Age and the Progressive Era to the deregulated merger mania of the Reagan years.) The OPM leasing services scam played out over a decade,

---

183. Rubin, *In an Uncertain World*, 74.

but the difference between its first (1972–1977) phase, featuring fraudulent loans of some twenty million dollars, and its final (1978–1981) period, when the company bilked $196 million from nineteen lending institutions via misrepresentation, reflects transformations in banking and corporate sectors during the 1970s that were conducive to larger scale fraud. OPM's phony leases centered mostly on mid-1970s computer equipment (mainframes which appear comically humongous and expensive when viewed by eyes accustomed to later, digitalized eras); a major victim of the fraud was Rockwell, then a major aerospace and defense manufacturer.

The main fraud culprits were two brothers-in-law, Mordecai Weissman and Myron Goodman, Orthodox Jews from New York City, who maintained dietary and Sabbath observances at OPM, where there was a mezuzah on each office door. The two were demonstrably committed Jews—Weissman put the OPM business aside in autumn 1973 to serve in the IDF (Israel Defense Forces) during the Yom Kippur War, and Goodman was a trustee at Yeshiva University, to which the OPM crew donated one million dollars, about a third of what it gave to various charitable causes, mostly Jewish.[184] The kernel of the fraud was the use of various forgery and other fraudulent techniques (often colorfully named, e.g., "dipsy doodle" signatures) in order to obtain loans from two or three banks for the same piece of leased equipment. The two main perpetrators, along with some confederates, were convicted in 1981 and 1982 on counts of conspiracy, false disclosure, and wire and mail fraud (Goodman was sentenced to twelve years in prison, Weissman ten). The comically extreme lengths to which the OPM partners went (e.g., beaming flashlights on two sides of a glass desk to forge signatures[185]) in order to forestall what should have been routine exposure of their ever-spiraling fraud, and the underlying crass *chutzpah* and pathological greed of the whole episode, has analogues in the Madoff affair. Similarly, the saga of Jewish entrepreneurs from lower status neighborhoods in the New York boroughs, who adopted fraud so as to quench driving ambitions to realize an American dream of wealth and status, has counterparts in the corporate trading insider trading scandals that unfolded later in the 1980s.

The precise details of the OPM leasing scandal can be found in two full-length accounts.[186] Worth noting here is how OPM represented a shift in business realities and public perception whereby Jewish financial and corporate types came across as monsters of fraud. In its day, reputable media outlets, *The New York Times* and the *Wall Street Journal*, rated OPM as

---

184. Gandossy, *Bad Business*, 6, 18–20.
185. Fenichell, *Other People's Money*, 98–99.
186. Gandossy, *Bad Business*; Fenichell, *Other People's Money*.

one of the largest and worst frauds ever perpetrated in the United States.[187] One of the OPM studies has plastered on its cover, "The Largest Fraud in U.S. Business History."[188] That sort of sensationalism set the stage for the theatrics of the Madoff affair.

The historian Berkowitz hits the target when he complains that the existing literature on Madoff is flawed in that it pays insufficient attention to the previous Boesky-Milken scandal, which also "deeply implicat[ed] Jews," but he runs afoul of the facts when he opines that Madoff "did not possess the ability" of an Ivan Boesky.[189] Hardly a financial innovator on Milken's level, Madoff nonetheless exhibited a readiness to incorporate new, faster technologies in brokerage. This adaptation to computerized trading became part of the con. BLMIS won respect for technological facility and became one of the first firms on the new electronic network, NASDAQ (National Association of Securities Dealers Automated Quotations). Madoff became NASDAQ chairman for three years in the early 1990s. The magnitude of BLMIS trading activity attests also to a capability of sorts, to Madoff's ability to multiply his avarice and manage it on a monumental level. In the 1980s, BLMIS handled 5 percent of all trading on the New York Stock Exchange. By 2004 it had two hundred employees and a reported net worth of four hundred and forty million dollars.[190]

Could any portion of this supposed voluminous activity be attributed to financial management acumen, as opposed to Madoff's criminal talent as a swindler? The answer to that question depends upon when BLMIS initiated its "taking from Peter to pay Paul" Ponzi scheme of providing returns to one investment individual or group by taking funds provided by some other investor. Diana Henriques, *The New York Times* reporter and author of a riveting account of the Madoff affair, speculates that the spiraling Ponzi fraud might have started after the "Black Monday" (October 19, 1987) crash in the markets, meaning that Madoff's particularly crass and straightforward form of fraud took shape right on the heels of the exposure of insider trading crimes executed in the Milken-Boesky field of risk arbitrage. This timeline is not firm, however. Henriques's account notes that dubious or illegal brokerage behavior akin to Ponzi fraud can be identified very early in Madoff's career, including a 1962 episode of pulling money from another

---

187. Gandossy, *Bad Business*, 6.
188. Fenichell, *Other People's Money*.
189. Berkowitz, "Madoff Paradox," 193.
190. Eren, *Bernie Madoff*, 4; Henriques, *Wizard of Lies*, 138.

place to cover nondisclosed losses suffered by clients as a result of an unexpected downswing in the markets.[191]

His Ponzi manipulation apparently well in swing by the end of the 1980s, Madoff conned his clients by describing, in brokerage babble, his investment method as a "split-strike conversion strategy." The con, Henriques explains, hinged on innovations in options trading developed in the 1970s in Chicago's financial markets (a stock option is a contract allowing a buyer the right to buy or sell a stock at a set price for a specified period of time). Madoff claimed to be purchasing for clients a diverse portfolio of stocks, while using options to hedge against possible future price declines.[192] Until the twenty-first century, the purported use of this "split-strike" method turned BLMIS into an investment club for the wealthy—Madoff was peddling unregulated hedge funds, and for the purpose of protecting inexperienced, less affluent investors, regulatory law prohibited hedge fund sale to "non-accredited" investors whose net worth was less than one million dollars. In terms of societal perfidy, Madoff's Ponzi scheme turned a corner in summer 2002 when hedge fund salesmen took a cue from the mutual funds industry and began to market a "fund of hedge funds," by which a pool of small investment institutions (e.g., trade union pension funds) banded together to attain a combined net worth commensurate with the minimum for accredited investors.[193] Since hedge funds, as opposed to regulated mutual funds, remained mostly a high-yield, risky luxury of the wealthy, many of the Ponzi victims were affluent, and Madoff's affair was sometimes depicted with schadenfreude petulance as a scandal of the rich (though he quietly paid brokers semilegal fees for bringing him clients, Madoff cultivated a standoffish, elite boutique sort of image and thereby accentuated BLMIS's reputation as a wealthy investment club). Yet techniques such as the "fund of hedge funds" opened the door to a new, lower class of Ponzi victims. Five years after the fraud's exposure, perhaps a quarter of the fifty-six thousand individuals, from 119 countries, who had filed damage claims were not from the wealthy classes.

Details of how Madoff and a few BLMIS confederates maintained a Potemkin village operation to falsify transaction reports for investors and regulators, and how the SEC botched multiple investigations of Madoff's doings, have become well-known. This is largely because one whistleblower, Harry Markopolos, a portfolio manager from a rival, Boston-based investment house, assertively publicized how regulators ignored his extensively

---

191. Henriques, *Wizard of Lies*, 84–86, 28–29.
192. Henriques, *Wizard of Lies*, 75–77.
193. Henriques, *Wizard of Lies*, 126.

detailed exposures of BLMIS fraud.[194] Also, the SEC subsequently exposed its own miscues in a self-flagellating tome (titled "Investigation of the Failure of the SEC to Uncover Bernard Madoff's Ponzi Scheme").[195]

For our purposes of analyzing how the affair impinged on American Jewish engagement in elite business sectors, we should return to the issue of how Madoff, an utterly villainous figure, had competency of a sort and how that distinguishes his fraud from others we have discussed. Quite unlike the Boesky-Milken LBOs insider trading scandal, Madoff's fraud had readily identifiable victims. Milken and Boesky (the latter was born just a year earlier than Madoff) skyrocketed in the financial world before Madoff because they developed genuine financial innovations like junk bonds. Fatefully, Madoff's ill-begotten success came later. Madoff's Ponzi scheme collapsed because of economic strains caused by the 2008 home mortgages boondoggle; other than that, there was no real causal relation between his fraud and the controversial "too big to fail" government bailouts of investment banks in 2008. The public nonetheless sometimes vented the totality of its wrath about financial fraud at Madoff, thereby creating a perplexing dynamic by which a reprehensible shyster can also be seen as a scapegoat. Had Madoff died earlier, or retired before the age of seventy, who knows what recrimination his Ponzi activity would have caused, if any? Milken's original small cadre of junk bond investors included a disproportionate number of Jews, but that is not really a determinant factor in the fraud. The identities of Milken's victims never became an issue, in fact—as then SEC Chairman John Shad argued, the criminal essence of insider trading is that it undermines public confidence in the integrity of the markets, rather than directly harming investor victims.[196] Madoff's crime was quite different in such respects. If the ethnic angle was, in key ways, incidental for Milken and Boesky, it was altogether determinative for Madoff's fraud. Madoff's Ponzi fraud harmed victims, many of them Jews, some of them quite prominent and very angry Jews.

The Madoff scandal occurred in a period marked by accelerating public frustration about the hypocritical, self-serving, and avaricious behavior of investment banks, and also about mounting income inequality. Compared to the "it's morning again in America" buoyancy of the Reagan years, public sectors in the "too big to fail" era were much less disposed to admire moneymakers on Wall Street, even relatively honest ones.

---

194. Markopolos, *No One Would Listen.*
195. Kotz, "Investigation."
196. Vise and Coll, *Eagle on the Street,* 329–52.

At least in theory, when these ethnic and macro considerations are fused together, a financial fraud scandal on the gargantuan scale of Madoff's Ponzi would appear perilous for Jews. Yet the extent to which the Madoff scandal actually aggravated anti-Semitism is questionable, and circumscribed. An embarrassing, disgraceful *shanda* that neither Jews, nor anyone else, could be proud of, the Madoff affair paradoxically betokens an endpoint, capping American Jewish entry in the corporate and banking establishment.

Owing to the number and prominence of its Jewish victims, to the sheer scale of the Ponzi fraud, and to the way it was publicized in a new social media era of uncensored chat on multiple forums, the Madoff affair was confusing for Jews, to be sure. Yet it was not a perilous catastrophe. The scandal's confusing but contained contribution to anti-Semitism is observable in various commentaries on the Madoff fraud. For instance, Berkowitz's article is apocalyptic in its assessment of the damage caused by Madoff to existing Jewish interests and institutions in the United States and around the globe: "The damage he caused the Jewish community in the United States and worldwide is utterly unprecedented, far worse than the OPEC-led boycotts of Israel and the efforts of self-professed anti-Semites." But the same writer reaches an opposite-sounding conclusion in his discussion of how the Madoff affair impacted anti-Semitism. "In terms of consequences for anti-Semitism," Berkowitz opines, the affair "did not amount to much beyond blather on the internet."[197]

The same sort of inconclusive anxiety about Madoff's damage to the Jews can be found in a book published by one of American Jewry's foremost commentators on anti-Semitism in the period of the scandal, Anti-Defamation League national director, Abe Foxman. A month before the exposure of the Madoff Ponzi, Foxman delivered an address about how "blaming the Jews" for the 2007–2008 financial crisis had worsened anti-Semitism.[198] His 2010 volume *Jews and Money*, filled with grim-sounding chapter headings like "the Madoff Moment," is a follow-up to that address and ostensibly an analysis of how the Ponzi scandal had made a bad situation of mounting anti-Semitism much worse.

To some extent, Foxman's book reinforces such pessimism. "During the months between Madoff's arrest and his sentencing, we saw an incredible flood of anti-Semitic comments on mainstream and extremist Web sites," Foxman declares.[199] However, though rife with graphic and

---

197. Berkowitz, "Madoff Paradox," 202, 194.
198. Eren, *Bernie Madoff*, 52.
199. Foxman, *Jews and Money*, 27.

nasty content, the examples documented in Foxman's book corroborate Berkowitz's dismissive reference to "blather on the internet." The "Bernie Madoff moment," Foxman insists toward the end of his first chapter, "really matters."[200] The remainder of his volume, however, features simplistic summaries of anti-Semitic libels and processes in an array of historical contexts that are not coherently related to myths of Jews and money in the United States or anywhere else; the volume ends with self-aggrandizing descriptions of Foxman's own activity in anti-defamation areas, along with piously histrionic critiques of self-directed Jewish jokes in routines by stand-up comedians like Sarah Silverman.

One barometer of how confused discussion about the religious-ethnic implications of Madoff's fraud became is the concept frequently used to describe it: "affinity fraud." Prima facie, affinity fraud is a cogent idea: one can imagine how an ethnic insider might manipulate his or her own group's particular norms, traditions, and quirks to milk gullible kinsmen investors, not always with nefarious or pernicious intent (witness Jack Black's clever portrayal of a real-life Ponzi criminal, bandleader Jan Lewan, in the Netflix-distributed film, *The Polka King*). Nonetheless, the concept has innumerable interpretative loose ends. Does it refer also to con men impersonators, who merely pretend to belong to a particular group? How exactly are cultural or ethnic groups subsumed within the concept of "affinity"? Is "Jewish" affinity fraud really like (for instance) "African American" affinity fraud? Arguably, the affinity concept simply kicks the can down the road, providing a new catchphrase reference for an impolitic and complicated topic, culture, and white-collar crime. While it lacks analytic rigor and weight, the affinity fraud concept has semilegal status and also some professional footing. The SEC recognizes it on its website, and the internet has numerous listings of attorneys who specialize in affinity fraud; but scholarly discussions of the phenomenon are much harder to find.

The Bernie Madoff scandal had a devastating Jewish dimension. The list of Jewish institutions and individual investors who were victimized by Madoff's fraud reads like a who's who of Jewish life in America at the end of the first decade of the twenty-first century: Yeshiva University, Hadassah, Orthodox day schools in New York and Boston, various Jewish family foundations, Sandy Koufax (America's foremost Jewish athlete), and Elie Wiesel and his Foundation for Humanity.[201] Damages caused to these Jewish victims could be poignantly painful. One example is the American Jewish Congress, a proud American Jewish organization whose origins in the

---

200. Foxman, *Jews and Money*, 31–32.
201. Sales, "Bernie Madoff."

World War I era symbolized processes of democratization in the community. AJ Congress endowments dropped from twenty-four million dollars to three million dollars because of Madoff.[202] Henriques's account highlights connections between Madoff and two New York figures who had high profiles in Jewish organizational and philanthropic circles: attorney Howard Squadron, president of the American Jewish Congress, and Ezra Merkin, a brilliant, erudite figure who donated generously to Yeshiva University and chaired a key committee at the UJA-Federation.[203]

Probably the most devastatingly poignant loss incurred by a prominent Jew featured Holocaust survivor Elie Wiesel, whose foundation sustained losses on the order of $15.2 million.[204] Incensed, Wiesel groused vindictively that Madoff ought to be sent to solitary confinement for the remainder of his life and be forced day and night to view records of victims of his fraud.[205] A telling reflection of the mood of the times, this was nonetheless not the sort of statement Wiesel would have wanted to be remembered as part of his cultural legacy. Sensing dramatic possibilities laden in Wiesel's loss to Madoff, playwright Deb Margolin brought *Imagining Madoff* to the stage; the drama featured an imaginary dialogue between the two. Wiesel threatened to take legal action against what he regarded as "obscene" dramatization; Margolin agreed to modify the identity of the Wiesel-inspired character. Meantime, the media was crassly exploiting the situation's ironies. One *London Times* reporter admitted that he chased Wiesel for an interview because of the "spectacular nature" of a Jewish financier "ripping off the most famous Holocaust survivor."[206]

Still worse, as the sociologist Eren points out, is the rhetoric and logic of the punishment meted to Madoff—one hundred and fifty years (the statutory maximum sentence equivalent to the sum of the eleven criminal counts brought against Madoff). Everyone agrees that Madoff could not have reasonably expected anything other than to end his life in prison; but Eren details double standards in the judication and punishment in the Madoff affair compared to what ensued in other, contemporaneous Ponzi frauds, at least one of which (fanned by Texas sports afficionado Robert Allen Stanford) also reached billion-dollar dimensions. Sentencing Judge Denny Chin's moralistic formulations about Madoff's "extraordinary evil,"[207] the

202. Weiss, "AJ Congress."
203. Henriques, *Wizard of Lies*, 88–89, 110–15.
204. Eren, *Bernie Madoff*, 54.
205. Eren, *Bernie Madoff*, 119–20.
206. Eren, *Bernie Madoff*, 51.
207. Eren, *Bernie Madoff*, 124.

Methuselah-like length of the sentence, and other aspects of the formal, institutional handling and prosecution of the scandal unfolded in a public arena saturated with long-standing, stereotypical "Fagin" or "Shylock" images of the Jews. In this connection, Eren's content study of media reports on Madoff located an unusual incidence of Shakespeare and Dickens references, suggesting that long-standing, prejudicial images of Jews and finance remain in public consciousness in the twenty-first century, and also that they can be nudged toward its forefront by mishaps like Bernie Madoff's Ponzi. As evidence of the lasting imprint of such prejudices, Eren cites one *Boston Review* study of public opinion in the 2007–2008 financial crisis era, conducted by researchers Yoltam Margalit and Neil Malhotra. The study found that a quarter of gentile Americans directly blamed Jews for the Wall Street–inspired meltdown while 38 percent of the respondents claimed that Jews were "a little to blame."[208]

One way of viewing the catastrophic history of anti-Semitism is to view ephemeral explosions of anti-Jewish malice, such as the 1894–1906 Dreyfus affair in France, as a sort of radioactive phenomenon that revives old, hateful ways of thinking about Jews. Such an affair sets new precedents of religious or racial animosity, and it sets the stage for genocidal occurrences that occur further down the road, in subsequent periods of yet heightened socioeconomic stress. Moreover, persons familiar with the rather torturous course taken by Jewish historical research in modern times will recall how scholars trained in the optimistic nineteenth-century frame of the Jewish enlightenment (*Haskalah*) tended, in their own day, to evaluate phenomena like the Dreyfus affair as passing incidents, in subjective interpretations which, in retrospect, reflect considerable wishful thinking. This Haskalah example is a sobering one for any scholar or commentator accustomed to thinking optimistically about American Jewish life: Can anyone authoritatively judge that incidents like the Madoff affair will not have long-term radioactive effects that are not foreseeable in our own time?

That said, my own view is that anti-Semitic closure in the Madoff scandal is the key element in the story, rather than its potential radioactive toxicity. In almost every decade since the era of World War II and the Holocaust, an American Jewish individual or group has captured public attention as an extreme, even quintessential, representation of a chronic problem, or a fundamental tension, of the time. Here is a partial list: Brownsville's Abe Reles and "Murder Inc." symbolizing street crime and juvenile delinquency on the eve of World War II; the "atomic spies," Julius and Ethel Rosenberg, representing nuclear, and patriotic loyalty, tensions as the

---

208. Eren, *Bernie Madoff*, 50–53, 119–49.

Cold War approached its first peak; Jonathan Pollard personifying another issue of patriotic loyalty as America's "special relationship" with Israel was being formed in the 1980s; Boesky and Milken incarnating corporate greed during the Reagan years; Madoff; and yet more recently, sexual predator Jeffrey Epstein becoming the archnemesis of the Me Too era. Such affairs of perceived ultimate evil exhausted themselves in draconic conclusions—that is, in state execution, lengthy prison sentences, or sudden death in a prison cell or on the pavement below a hotel room where a state witness was supposed to be hidden. In some such cases, the Jewish criminal was formally awarded punishments well in excess of what comparable, contemporaneous gentile criminals received in the courts. A double standard against the Jews was institutionally sanctioned.

On the one hand, such conclusions clearly expressed anti-Semitism. On the other hand, they constituted closure, or at least a sanctioned form of expiation crafted to forestall worse future eventualities in Jewish-Christian relations. They emphatically demonstrated that American democracy is a place where transplanted revival of behavioral traits associated with pathological European interaction between Jews and Christians will never be tolerated. In some cases, such as the Rosenbergs and Pollard, American Jews, after some hesitation, protested against double standards. However belatedly, they publicly objected to this dynamic, doubting that enacting exceptionally stiff punishments against transgressor Jews is the best way to reinforce this point about America's exemption from dark dynamics between Jews and Christians. Madoff is a little different solely in this respect: here, self-designated Jewish spokesmen called for excruciating supplements to Madoff's life-term. But the basic dynamic remained the same in all these cases. Though the opportunistic Joseph McCarthy and Roy Cohn, the possessor of an infamously conflicted personal identity, might have set a stage on which Jews could have been held in collective suspicion as subversive communists, the truculent execution of the Rosenbergs erased this grim possibility, allowing Jews to progress in the Cold War era without being under a dark cloud of suspicion about their patriotism. Though the bumptious insensitivity of Pollard's Israeli handlers set a stage upon which pro-Israel work in America might have stirred suspicions of disloyalty, the draconian sentence meted to Pollard brought closure, allowing American Jewish lobbying for a special relationship with Israel to continue within legitimate normative boundaries. Though the OPM scandal, and then Milken and Boesky's insider trading fraud and Madoff's Ponzi scandal, might have revived in America age-old Shylock stereotypes of Jewish malfeasance in finance, the symbolic act of vengeance and expiation inculcated in Madoff's Methuselah-like punishment cleared barriers in a decades-long process of expanding Jewish involvement and success in elite corporate and finance sectors.

THE BIRTH OF THE JEWISH QUESTION IN TWENTY-FIRST CENTURY AMERICA?

This argument about how tensions raised by Jewish success in America's economy, and by corruption scandals centered on Jewish individuals, have been expiated and eliminated by exceptional prosecutions and judgments in the country's legal system points to the philosemitic exceptionalism of American Christianity. In Europe, where Jewish activity through the Holocaust unfolded in a fundamentally anti-Semitic milieu, the relationship between the law and the economy recapitulated conventional understandings of the New Testament. Historically, Christians have understood the Gospel accounts of the crucifixion as implying a dangerous combination of law and Jewish materialism—with the Romans lubricating the process, judicial process worked in tandem with the greedy egoism of the Pharisees and other Jews to yield the unspeakable crime of deicide. On this interpretation, law in the Christian era is to be used to redeem that crime and to punish the Jews for their unrelenting greed and refusal to acknowledge Jesus' messianic status.

In America, as we have seen, the law has functioned in ways far friendlier to Jews. Because the country's cultural system was always founded on an unusually shameless endorsement of capital accumulation, law in America could never have been used to reveal and punish what was imagined to be the unusual materialism of the Jews (this point returns us to the writings of Weber and Sombart, which anticipated the unique circumstance of positively sanctioned American Jewish economic success in the country during the "American Century"). In America, the law functioned to highlight the country's unusually accommodating attitude toward Jewish capitalist enrichment—or stated a bit more accurately, precisely because the law was sometimes so unusually punitive toward Jews, it rescued their American dream.

This situation has very likely changed. Events in coming decades are likely to show how American Jewish criminals and predators in the Madoff-Epstein generation were the last ones whose expiatory sacrifice in judicial process purchased a return to business normalcy for everyone else in the Jewish community. The Jews' socioeconomic status in America is not as stable today as would have been expected a generation ago. Since Donald Trump's 2016–2020 White House term, reports about the rise of anti-Semitic speech acts and physical incidents, many of them grounded in resentment or confusion about American Jewish economic success, have regularly and widely circulated.

In two broad senses it would be anti-empirical to expect continuing placidity and stability with regard to American Jewish economic power. First, surveys of the contemporary scene do not corroborate such optimism, to say the least; second, surveys of Jewish history do not warrant such hopefulness (you do not have to be a Zionist to recognize that prolonged Jewish residence in any diaspora land has always stimulated recycled canards about the Jews' economic activities).

There are specific reasons to expect new patterns of Jewish-Christian interaction, some of them malignant, in America's economic spheres. The first could result from the increasingly conservative, semifundamentalist character of America's special relationship with the Jewish state. Owing to controversies about Israel's military actions, as exemplified by protests in America in response to the 2023–2024 Gaza War, and also to Israel's continuing colonialist control of the West Bank, the mainline liberal Protestant church establishment will at some point become irreversibly unhinged from sympathy for the Jewish state (this trend has been underway for years).

This will leave the Evangelicals as Israel's best friends in the United States, apart from Jewish ex-liberals who will continue to leave the Democratic party for the GOP. The Evangelicals are philosemitic Christian Zionists for reasons that are not likely to abate in years to come. However, as fundamentalists they are the Christian group most likely to read philippic in the Gospels about Jewish (Pharisee) materialistic greed as literal truth applicable also to Jews in the twenty-first century.

Instances of Jewish malfeasance in the economy have increased exposure and widening scale in social media. Crucially, they are becoming less judicable. This means that pressure-release valve mechanisms in legal process, which mitigated damage after episodes like the Madoff Ponzi crime, have reduced relevance, if they have any relevance at all.

In this connection, a useful contrast can be drawn between the Madoff affair and the Purdue Pharma / Sackler family opioid scandal. As detailed in Patrick Radden Keefe's *Empire of Pain*, a family history of the Sacklers,[209] the Purdue Pharma affair seems more maddening and damaging than the Madoff Ponzi in several identifiable ways. Madoff's victims were mainly wealthy investors, and the damage caused by the scandal was (primarily) monetary. Persons victimized by Purdue Pharma opioid products were largely from low-income milieus, and damage caused in the scandal

---

209. Keefe, *Empire of Pain*.

concentrated mostly in the public health sphere, in addiction and death, on a terrifying scale.

Featuring dipsy doodle signatures and Madoff confederates faking computerized transaction records, the ways the OPM crooks and Madoff boondoggled incompetent SEC regulators and other public officials were quite comic. There was nothing humorous in the Sackler crime, however. If there were a Jewish hall of infamy for financial corruption and corporate malpractice, starting with Judas Iscariot and continuing past Ivan Boesky, perhaps nothing would compare to the iniquitousness of the Sackler crime, to the way the family behaved when it mendaciously obtained FDA verification of the supposed nonaddictive character of their drug product and also when, years later, it reversed Purdue Pharma's stance on this cardinal issue in order to forestall fallen revenue from the product's generic marketing.

The point here is not to suggest patronizingly that Americans are particularly susceptible to falling for the old libelous farrago whereby the misbehavior of any individual or small group is presented as being representative of a community as a whole, be it American Jewry or any other ethnoreligious community. Instead, the Sackler scandal seems symptomatic of a new era in which old liberal rules of civility, and faith in good government, have eroded. Those rules remained intact from the New Deal up to Reagan's anti-regulatory administrations (and they are manifestly besieged by the Trump-ist MAGA movement); but Jews have been one of the groups in the country that remained "more liberal" than the sociopolitical consensus. Insofar as it is possible to generalize, it is reasonable to suppose that no less than anyone else, they retained inhibitions about behaving with outright systematic contempt toward government regulation and other public protections. In the Madoff affair, hoodwinking SEC monitors became a central part of the crime, but its technical execution seems to have been improvised, and its spirit was actually cordial. In this regard, the Sackler crime was altogether different, being a fecklessly systematic assault on public protection and health in the name of private profit.

The Sackler crime is a weather vane pointing to a new era. Even when a few individuals did not live up to the liberal ethic's high standards, Jewish realization of the American dream in the twentieth century relied on a liberal ideology of public civility and good government administration. Purdue Pharma opioids were trafficked legally in a realm beyond that ideology. Earlier "Jewish" white-collar scandals transpired firmly within that realm. As in Milken's case, their culprits knew that their products were seen as esoteric "junk" by the public, but more or less they believed that they were contributing to democratic liberty by expanding the potential of free markets.

The protests against Purdue Pharma's crimes also marked a turning point. As exemplified by a much-publicized demonstration at the Guggenheim Museum in NYC in February 2019, these protests were sometimes led by creative artists whose own lives had been endangered by OxyContin.[210] They were staged in esteemed cultural venues where wings had been named in honor of Sackler family philanthropy. A well-warranted exercise in contemporary twenty-first-century "cancel culture," the anti-Sackler protests can also be seen in a wider historical context. They can be seen as an angry reenactment of "calling forth" rituals targeted at individuals who personify antisocial greed, rituals which feature shaming or, in the case of the book of Matthew, individual redemption.

Most importantly, such protest measures designed to obliterate the Sackler name in public space reflect how earlier methods of relieving anxiety about Jewish criminality via extraordinary judiciary process are no longer tenable. The Sackler affair is unlike earlier cases, ones when a Brownsville Jewish gangster cum state witness was simply thrown off the roof, or a Ponzi con man was symbolically put under lock and key for a century and a half. The prosecution of Sackler-Purdue Pharma criminality has been protracted and frustrating and thus devoid of the expiatory functions fulfilled in trials of other notorious American Jewish felons. In summer 2024, the Supreme Court overturned an arrangement by which Purdue Pharma would have paid billions in support of drug treatment programs, while protecting the Sacklers against further litigation.[211] In a close 5–4 decision, the majority objected that the settlement agreement provided the Sackler family more protection than what is allowed under existing bankruptcy law. Though it theoretically left the door open for future litigation against the Sackler culprits, the decision sounded technical and relatively well reasoned, not extraordinarily punitive. For better or worse, American Jews are now living in a new reality, one where their herd is no longer protected by courtrooms that send its black sheep to the moon.

These factors could become important, but nothing casts a pall over the future of American Jewish experience comparable to the accelerating critique of AIPAC, an indictment about the use of private American Jewish capital, and organizational American Jewish capital, in the support of Israeli settler colonialism on the West Bank. In this connection, the 2023–2024 campus protests against Israel's Gaza War were a calling forth ritual more gravely portentous than anything that has happened to global Jewry since the Holocaust.

210. Moynihan, "Guggenheim."
211. Mann, "Supreme Court."

If we are to view these protests as though we are seeing a tableau vivant of Caravaggio's *The Calling of Saint Matthew*, there is no question about the identity of the individual who is being called. American Jewry today is like the bearded, remorseful old Jew from Capernaum in the Caravaggio painting. It is a collective which knows that, like the bearded man, it is thoroughly implicated in colonialism. Like the bearded man, it is a community nervously unsure of whether it can live up to the idealistic challenge inherent in the summons, this time posed not by Jesus but rather by twenty-year-old college students who know hypocrisy when they see it.

How many words do we need to waste in an explanation of why relying on Jewish billionaire alumni of academic institutions to use their philanthropic muscle to oust university presidents who have insufficiently stifled the free speech rights of anti-Zionist students is an obtuse strategy? Is there anything in the unrelentingly volatile history of Jewish-Christian interaction on subjects of capital and power that suggests how this strategy will not create powerful backlash effects, most of them deleterious to objective Jewish interests?

What in the world were American Jews and Israelis thinking over the last generation, following the failure of good-faith peacemaking efforts in the Oslo process, when they believed that they had private capital sufficient to protect themselves, as they supported or implemented settlement policies on the West Bank that were diametrically opposed to the declared democratic intents and purposes of the special relationship between the Jewish state and the United States? Americans were being told that they were paying an extraordinary portion of their tax dollars to support the "only democracy in the Middle East," while Israel's Netanyahu governments massively invested in antidemocratic settler expansion on the West Bank. Until the tactic explosively backfired, these Netanyahu governments even semisecretly funded Hamas's criminal, terroristic regime in Gaza out of a divide and rule strategy whose purpose was to erode prospects for a two-state solution and forestall Jewish settlement withdrawal on the West Bank. American college students occupied campus areas to demonstrate about how none of this makes sense. In response, Jewish big donors compelled university presidents to enact and enforce campus illiberalism, under the threat of dismissal—prestigious commentators, like Robert Reich, former US secretary of labor, worried that such "hounding" (as Reich called it) would fuel anti-Semitism, "based on the perilous stereotype of wealthy Jewish bankers controlling the world."[212]

---

212. Reich, "Academic Freedom."

Illiberal American Jewish philanthropists, like Sheldon Adelson, learned that under the rules of American capitalism, private mega-capital can pretty much do what it wants. What they never learned is that under the age-old rules of Jewish-Christian economic interaction, private Jewish capital cannot always get what it wants.

Going against the grain of a century of diplomatic mediation of the Jewish-Arab conflict in the Middle East, these philanthropists believed that their private capital could bend rules whereby changes on the most sensitive arrangements depend on tacit or express consent given by both sides. They thought that their private capital was enough to support unilateral Jewish action, such as the transfer of America's embassy to Jerusalem. Always an aficionado of private capital, Prime Minister Netanyahu took pages out of Adelson's playbook and boasted to the world about how new diplomatic arrangements—the Abraham Accords, the Saudi Initiative, etc.—would keep Israel safe and secure in the Middle East, without any consideration given to Palestinian statehood aspirations, not to mention daily Palestinian humanitarian needs. Private capital, in this thinking, was the panacea, the sacred cow. Is there anything in the unrelentingly volatile history of interaction between the monotheistic faiths in areas of capital and power that suggests how milking this sacred cow will not create powerful backlash effects, most of them deleterious to objective Jewish interests?

In this thinking, private capital was Don Quixote, Holocaust memorialization was Sancho Panza, and Dulcinea—an old, haggard witch delusionally seen as the romantic fulfillment of a dream—was the West Bank settlement movement. The Jews believed that if they kept dumping funds in Holocaust museums, they would keep the world off-balance about Israel. The maintenance of the special relationship between Israel and the United States on false pretenses, and the colonialist enterprise of the West Bank settlement movement, could always be rationalized and leveraged by endless invocation of the murder of six million European Jews.

Everything in this line of thought was misbegotten. Instead of thinking that their capital and philanthropy was a muscle whose flexing would inculcate particular "lessons" of the Holocaust among gentiles, while also coaxing them to ignore obviously illiberal aspects of Israeli policy, the Jewish billionaires and their organizational confederates might have themselves taken a look at Jewish history, one more nuanced and informed than whatever was comfortably available to them in either AIPAC-sponsored primers on the Middle East conflict or guided tours of the Holocaust Museum in Washington. Nothing in such a review could possibly have justified the idée fixe of the recreant generation of Jews that administered the special relationship between the United States and Israel in the quarter century that elapsed between the failure of the Oslo peace process and the 2023–2024 Gaza War. Nothing in such a review could possibly have warranted the theory that Jews can have long-term success lobbying with a major power on false pretense simply because they have a lot of private capital lying around for targeted campaign donations, for strong-arming university presidents, and for other suchlike measures designed to purchase sympathy.

Many explanations have been, and will be, marshaled to account for the rejuvenation of anti-Semitism, no doubt. For all of us, when we think about this contemporary problem and many others, maybe the best place to start is to wonder what it means when we are called out, by name, by persons of another faith. How far are we supposed to go toward understanding the sensitivities of another religious culture, particularly one which has not always been very sensitive toward us? For me, my own name and all of the identity confusion and moral ambiguity captured on canvas in Caravaggio's painting goes into the way I think about this question.

The part of history written in my own name seems to be saying this: Christians and Jews are never in full accord because the groups have contrasting ideas, or no meaningful ideas at all, about what in this world, or any other world, material success has to do with our innermost faith and yearning.

The entirety of Christian civilization arose out of suspicions about how power brokers from a rival religious group, the Jews, invented pharisaical arguments about the purity of their temple that camouflaged their own egoism and self-interest. This critique is the moral core of the New Testament. If you read the Gospels closely, Jesus, with his disciples echoing his messages, develops neither a clearly consistent argument about his own divinity nor about the necessity of a rupture with Jewish law via the establishment of a new religion. The only incontrovertibly consistent and apprehensible argument in the New Testament derives from its "backward glance" standpoint: when they compiled the record of Jesus' preachings and doings, not too many years after the Jewish hurban catastrophe in the failed revolt against Rome, it was absolutely clear to these founders of Christianity that the Jews endangered and then lost their temple due to the greed and mendacity of their leaders. In the Synoptic Gospels, that is, the scriptural corpus whose turns of phrase and narrative details bespeak one overall story (because the three books, Mark, Matthew, and Luke, are seemingly based on one common document), the pivotal moment occurs when Jesus calls forth a tax collector. He does not summon a Pharisee who doubts his divinity or who wants to argue about the fulfillment or abrogation of Jewish law.

This established the prerogative of the religion that would come. The dilemma of material success versus spiritual integrity became the core issue in Christianity. As the religion's theologians and spokesmen developed approaches to this dilemma, the Jews would everlastingly be under suspicion and serve as a foil. Perhaps, then, the most telling "lesson" of the Holocaust is that nothing can possibly alter this situation. As could be seen in the excesses of social media or anti-Israel protests on college campuses in spring 2024, anti-Semitism persists, decades after the Catholic Church abjured the deicide accusation.

Jews in the passing generation had a choice. Their pro-Israel majority could utilize methods liable to rattle the cage of modernity, and release age-old suspicions about how their professions of devotion to the temple of the modern Jewish state boil down to greed and self-indulgence, to use the words of Matt 23:25. Or they could have refurbished the liberal faith of preceding generations: believing that the universalist idealism of liberalism provides safe zones for the particularist enthusiasms of ethnoreligious subgroups; believing that rational, transparent negotiation diplomacy conducted in good faith, and founded on respect for the national aspirations of other groups, is the foundation of democracy; and believing that democracy can be the only worthy aspiration for any Jewish future in modernity.

Leaders from this passing generation, the Jewish recreants whose names will be remembered solely in ignominy and regret, made their choices. The repercussions of their illiberalism will weigh as a heavy burden on Jewish generations to come.

2

American Schmegegge
Truth, Jews, and Christians

INTRODUCTION: BETWEEN PNYX AND NAZARETH

Let's start with some civics. When you drive to work, when you pay your taxes, when you argue with the county bureaucrats about an extension permit for the porch you want to renovate in your house, when you are drafted into the army (or not), there is a reason why you are likely to have a better, safer, and more prosperous life if, in all these nonprivate realms, you are perceived as operating in spiritually and culturally neutral space. This is because the moment private judgment enters the public realm, you are more susceptible to partial and subjective, or bigoted, value judgments that are shaped out of the self-concerned, not necessarily malicious, preferences of particular religious and cultural groups. In this broad sense of understanding the advantages of public square neutrality, many people in democratic society remain liberals as the twenty-first century approaches middle age.

On the other hand, even though most of these liberals fortunately lack graduate degrees in critical theory and suchlike postmodern fields, they nonetheless understand that "neutrality" is a myth. Even if our public squares remain secularized and neutral in palpable senses, and even though a strong majority of residents in the West profess to prefer living in a democracy, nobody is vigilant about enforcing absolute neutrality in public life. This is either because individuals realize that pure neutrality cannot really exist in a courtroom, in the officiating of a sporting match, or anywhere else in public life, or because they simply do not see the merit of prioritizing liberal vigilantism relative to other concerns they have in life. When was the last time you saw an American go to the mint and return a one-dollar bill because "In God We Trust" is printed on its backside?

The public square neutrality concept has many practical and moral flaws, but it was the best idea that founders of democracy in America and other places could find. There are many other concepts that can be used as the foundation of a successful modern society, and it would be unacceptably *illiberal* for a liberal to deny that religious activists might have a legitimate point when they argue that young people will more successfully deal with challenges of marriage and family life, substance abuse, etc. should their public school education include spiritual instruction of some sort. No liberal could possibly know enough history to make arguments such as "religious legislation, as exemplified by Prohibition in the 1920s, backfires" with full certainty. No liberal could possibly be sufficiently versed in his/her own religious heritage to furnish, with full conviction, arguments about how that heritage truly endorses public square neutrality in twenty-first-century democracy. Out of such considerations we arrive at liberalism's innate irony: to be committed to public square neutrality is a leap of faith.

Why has this leap of faith for liberal democracy been sustainable? How is it possible?

It is possible because the idea of democracy has a place in the world. People who subscribe to it know where it came from. Literally, they can buy a plane ticket and go find its oracle somewhere in the world. Also, democracy, like religion, has a tradition; unlike the case of any particular religion, liberal democratic tradition stretches across cultures and groups and has a reasonably universal appeal.

Religion solved its innate paradox—how could a set of beliefs be "absolutely" true if only one defined group of people subscribed to it—through the idea of revelation. Of course, revelation has spatial coordinates (e.g., Sinai), but these are necessarily parochial; as human society secularized, to some extent, in the eighteenth and nineteenth centuries, imagining that modern political society emanated from the place of one group's revelatory experience became problematically unsustainable.

Modernity organized its politics around the concept of the nation-state. This nation-state model had a plausible measure of sustainability because most, though not all, nations have a perceptibly active ethno-religious majority whose narrative of absolute truth (or at least the sort of powerful truth which makes state power and state violence tolerably acceptable) has a home, some place in the world to which the nation's citizens can trace their moral roots. For this reason, "truth" remained a viable possibility in the minds of citizens of the nineteenth- and twentieth-century nation-state, though its actual efficacy in the inspiration of civil restraint and democratic tolerance can be questioned in view of how this era witnessed the rise of fascism, the maintenance of exploitative colonial regimes, and successive global breakdown in two world wars.

In the new millennium, the twenty-first century opened with the ethos of multiculturalism, one which hypothesized that hybrid, intrafaith formulas could serve as the moral foundation of democratic society. One such formula, "Judeo-Christian civilization," is one of the foci of this essay. Insofar as we are concerned about "truth" remaining a sustainably viable organizing principle in twenty-first-century society, these hybrid formulas are, at best, incoherent and useless and, at worst, pernicious. This is because the multifaith formulas do not provide earnest citizens with a narrative whose core values and home can be found. They have no way of following the choices and preferences inherent in a particular position on a divisive contemporary issue—same sex marriage, pro-choice or pro-life, etc.—back to the "source" and therefore verifying that the particular position coheres with the overall spiritual-moral heritage of their national community. Truth, in other words, has no validation sticker in such a post-nation-state, hybrid political society.

The Judeo-Christian model will receive attention further on, but we can preview it here to elaborate on this particular point. Where is the oracular source of truth in such a hybrid civilization? Jews impute moral authority in their heritage to Jerusalem, but Christians have different ideas of why Jerusalem became important in the transformative late Second Temple period. Christians have enormous spiritual investment in Israel's northern region, Galilee, where Jesus spent most of his life. Jews do not. In fact, spatial coordinates of the Holy Land have been Judaized, favoring Jerusalem over Galilee, in the decades after the Holocaust in a process that badly distorts understandings of Judeo-Christian civilization, an idea which is problematic for many other reasons as well.

The current Jerusalem-centric moral geography of the Holy Land is acutely problematic. For Christians, it is like imagining the life of a young aspiring actress who mortally sacrifices herself in Los Angeles for two years, not getting a big break, after spending the first twenty-five or thirty years of her life in Omaha. Who would say that her life was about California but not Nebraska? I raise this example simply to show how differently Christians and Jews think about the source locales of their value systems, no matter that these two systems have considerable overlap in what Christians, but not Jews, call the Old Testament.

Because morality in these two religions came out of different homes, truth has no identifiable shelter in a modern political society that presumes to be rooted in Judeo-Christian civilization. Truth has no validation sticker that will stop you from getting a parking ticket. In fact, you might deserve a ticket for thinking that truth could be found in such a society to begin with.

In complete contrast, the liberal view of democracy as a secularized concept pivoting on ideas of the neutral public square and church-state separation has an identifiable point of origin: on an Athenian hilltop, the Pnyx. Truth remained sustainable on this model because its adherents who imaginatively climb up to the Pnyx, where Athenians started holding popular assemblies in the fifth century BCE, believe that there was at this source a kernel of universally valid truth. Public debate based on verifiable claims, power sharing, orderly transition of power, an elected representative republic—how much any of this was obtained at the Pnyx is open to debate, but what is significant is that upholders of this democracy narrative believe that it has correct principles at its source. They believe that the subsequent evolution of the story is more or less linear, featuring the elimination of gross contradictions like slavery and the amplification of the original, correct Athenian principles so that formerly marginalized groups come into democracy's tent.

Though the two points are separated physically by just some eight hundred and fifty miles on two (central and eastern) parts of the Mediterranean region, the political distance between the Pnyx and Nazareth is impassable. According to Christian faith, Nazareth—a hilltop town in Galilee where Jesus spent all but the last two or three years of his life—is where spiritual truth and universal morality came to maturation in the divine person of Jesus Christ. The place means nothing to Jews, who never mention it in their Bible, the *Tanakh*. For their part, American Christians have, over the decades, evinced a variety of dispositions toward the New Testament narrative of miraculous deeds and charismatic leadership displayed by Jesus in Galilee areas around his hometown, Nazareth, in his last few years. The dominant Protestant American group in the right-wing pro-Israel lobby, Evangelicals, seems especially interested in the Old Testament prophetic narrative whose spiritual center is Jerusalem, and implicitly derogates Galilee-based New Testament events. But this is by no means a definite rule among Evangelicals, and all groups of American Christians, Protestants and Catholics, exhibit devout affection for Galilee, Jesus' home region. On tourist pilgrimages to Israel, they prefer its northern region. "On average, all Americans like the Galilee region best," observed one academic study, published in 2014 and based on in-depth before/during/after investigation of the experiences of 131 American Christian tourists in Israel.[1]

---

1. Kaell, *Walking Where Jesus Walked*, 138.

Unlike the case at the Pnyx, this admiring orientation toward a moral source can never be translated in a coherent political narrative. When they are struggling to validate their understanding of truth on excruciatingly divisive contemporary issues, like abortion rights, upholders of the public square neutrality model of democracy can go back to the Athenian hilltop. Believers in the Judeo-Christian paradigm of democracy find no such validation on the Galilee hilltop.

The problem is not only that Nazareth means nothing to non-Christians. It is also that the relationship between Holy Land venues and American Christian understandings of modern democracy is extraordinarily complicated. This essay discusses one particular American Protestant orientation toward Galilee, called the "fifth Gospel" approach, which took root after the Civil War and, in retrospect, seems quite compatible with liberal democratic attitudes. But this fifth Gospel orientation exhausted itself around the World War I era. Its pragmatic, relativized view of truth as approximation is diametrically opposed to the literal fundamentalist exactitude of Evangelical Christians a century later. And the fifth Gospel's serenely tranquil acceptance of history is diametrically opposed to the cancel culture radicalism of contemporary progressives, who seek to expunge from the historical record personalities whose ideas and doings are not palatable to their own, politically correct, sensibilities. Thus, even from the parochial Christian standpoint, moral inspiration found at Nazareth and Jesus' Galilee home region has never provided sustainable validation of truth for citizenship purposes in modern democracy.

Trumpism is an accident that was waiting to happen. After World War II and the Holocaust, as soon as energetic influential groups, each acting with morally plausible agendas—Jews, to lobby for Israel; Evangelicals, out of genuine anxiety about the morally adventurous 1960s—reconceptualized American democracy as a Judeo-Christian project, the country was on a collision course. Sooner or later, citizens would begin to cancel, or reject as fake news, anything which was disagreeable and which came their way, thereby recapitulating circumstances at the source of Judeo-Christian civilization two thousand years ago when what was gospel truth to one group was fake news for the other.

Truth, History, and Judeo-Christian Civilization

When measuring the extent to which contemporary society is disposed to be truthful about itself, the surefire indicator is how it relates toward its own past. Nothing in the world is more dangerous than elites whose members view themselves as heirs to ancestors who got away with their crimes.

Through the Vietnam/Watergate era, liberal Americans viewed their life projects through an idealistic prism, believing that their debt to future generations would be paid should they, in their present day, mitigate or redeem the sins of past generations. For the past half century, such idealism has eroded, owing to mechanisms of time-travel atonement. Americans feel unaccountably guiltless in their present because they believe they have the power to go back in time and reform the world of past cultures in line with contemporary twenty-first-century sentiments and values. Many factors can be blamed for this attitude of anachronistic moralism—shoddy work by some historians, cutbacks in humanities study, and so on. But, really. Why have we come to project our politically correct cancel culture onto the past? Why have we stopped viewing our own past through a prism of realistic humanism?

Through the Great Depression and the world wars, many Americans believed that history was meaningless. This attitude sometimes bred misappropriation of energy and resources, but it nonetheless evinced genuine belief in social mobility and in the availability of the American dream for anyone (or at least white heterosexuals) who had strong will, talent, and some good luck. Since the 1960s, in contrast, many Americans have viewed history in selective narcissism, erasing or embracing past events and past individuals insofar as they do or do not accord with their own contemporary, politically correct sensibilities. By the end of the twentieth century, Americans were accustomed to photoshopping their own circumstances and desires on social media and presenting themselves to the world as they wanted to be seen by it—in a fallacious, self-flattering way. In tandem, history was framed anew in social media posts and other public commentary. Innumerable, inconvenient facts of past life were cropped away, and history's scattered, politically correct phenomena (generally attributable to visionaries who were "ahead of their time") are continually appropriated by contemporary narcissists, who look in many directions to find validation for their own personal enthusiasms.

This orientation toward history arose among citizens who felt emboldened in the world's lone superpower. Through the 1940s, prominent Americans professed that "history is bunk" because they viewed their country as a work in progress where mechanisms for social mobility and democratic transformation would buttress the country's future, whatever had happened in its past being irrelevant. America's emergence as a superpower at the end of the twentieth century reshaped this orientation toward the past. Now history was important. By their appropriation of the world's convenient and pleasing parts, elites validated that everything in it was within their aesthetic and moral reach, without any barriers of time or place. The message was that the world had always reinvented itself in ways compatible with the tastes and values of these late twentieth-century American anachronism-mongers.

Today we are connected to our pasts via the methods and logic of a Quentin Tarantino film. History might be filled with vicious or murderous brutes, but we rearrange sequences and tweak the facts to invent past realities wherein justice, envisioned anachronistically in tune with our contemporary, twenty-first century sensibilities, necessarily rules. What exactly is happening on the screen when a malignant white slaveholder is shot in the groin by a self-liberated, righteous ex-slave, as in *Django: Unchained*? It would be useless to propose vapidly that such a scene fabricates history because, as everyone knows, Tarantino doesn't direct realistic documentaries. But what, really, is the point of such politically corrected fantasizing about history?

The point is this: that we have gotten away with all of our daily rotten lies is proven by the fact that we can lie about our past and enjoy it. In Tarantino's footsteps, anyone today can use history to pardon the unspeakable untruths of the present by recreating the past as a lie where social justice reigns. Heritage is a politically correct fantasy. History's purpose is to assuage our unconscionable dissimulation in the present by leading us to believe that the past was governed by precisely the righteous saints we lyingly imagine ourselves to be in our daily lives.

Perhaps the one thing that people from liberal and conservative camps agree upon nowadays is that there is not much truth circulating in the public sphere. From the liberal side, the ascent of falsehood is attributed to authoritarian figures like Donald Trump, who are inveterate liars. While liberals are correct about Trump, the sort of "fact-checking" that goes on anytime Trump confronts Democrats (after the September 2024 Trump-Harris debate, CNN declared righteously that the GOP candidate had lied over thirty times, whereas Vice President Harris had delivered just one untruth[2]) says quite a bit about the manipulative self-image of liberals as self-proclaimed custodians of scientific-rationalist traditions of the Enlightenment, no less than it reflects the political culture of the MAGA movement. On the conservative side, many of Trump's followers understand that he is a circus performer who is not exactly conscientious when it comes to telling the truth, but they tolerate his falsehoods, viewing them instrumentally as a necessary mode of attack on a systematically untrue, rigged establishment

---

2. CNN Politics, "Fact-Checking."

whose continuance is pushing them out of the middle class toward poverty. I myself am on the liberal side of this debate, but looking at the matter fairly, it is sometimes hard to say whether the most dire threat to democracy is posed by the demagoguery of the right or by the sanctimonious condescension of liberals who believe they have a monopoly on the truth.

The crisis facing American democracy—and the political stability of the world as a whole—is not personified by Donald Trump. His buffoonery is symptomatic of the crisis but not its cause. The problem is that the truth was up for grabs for decades before he came along. The story of Trump's adroit use of obnoxious falsehoods, catapulted by his days on *The Apprentice*, is tediously predictable. It is far more interesting and useful to reflect upon the broader moral and cultural sources and dimensions of the truth and information crisis associated with his 2016–2020 term in the White House, and with his possible second term. What does Trump's near-irrepressible popularity say about the way we view truth and lies in our contemporary world and in past worlds that forged our present reality?

This essay explores a series of overlapping claims, all of them based on the assumption that challenges of public integrity in daily life flow, in one way of another, from society's fundamental religious and moral sources. Here are the claims: First, while America idealistically staved off the inevitable for two centuries, truth in its culture became relativized, as happened in other Western cultures, because of its roots in a monotheistic culture that is inherently tense and self-conflicted. At its core, this religious culture hosts an irresoluble information crisis. Western culture is the product of a two thousand-year-old Judeo-Christian information crisis—and so, when new twenty-first-century technologies facilitated vast expansion and acceleration of information flow, this crisis became globally threatening. Second, the vitality of American democracy through the end of World War II is not a tribute to its "Judeo-Christian" moral heritage. Up to the Cold War, American democracy prospered precisely because that heritage was held in abeyance. Conversely, whenever exceptions, setbacks, and betrayals (most glaringly black slavery, but also an array of gender and LGBTQ issues and educational problems) became insufferably acute, there was a corresponding rise in the manipulative use of the Judeo-Christian heritage to rationalize abuses to the country's democratic ethos. Third, the immersion of American society in the Judeo-Christian heritage since the 1960s has unanchored commitments to pragmatic truthfulness in discussions of contemporary reality; it is also responsible for time-travel atonement and other peculiar ways of viewing the past and present.

WHOSE JUDEO-CHRISTIAN CIVILIZATION IS IT?

The concept of "Judeo-Christian civilization" is itself a myth invented by theologians and popular commentators in the 1950s.[3] They projected backwards in time the unusual degree of intra-religious amity experienced in this early Cold War era when Americans had incentive to stress their own positive religiosity, in contrast to the Soviet Union's atheistic Communist system. On the eve of his inauguration in 1952, President-elect Eisenhower highlighted this Cold War motivation, reportedly commenting, "Our form of government has no sense unless it is founded in a deeply felt religious faith, and I don't care what it is. Of course, it is the Judeo-Christian concept, but it must be a religion with all men being created equal."[4] Liberating concentration camps, Eisenhower himself had firsthand knowledge of the Holocaust, but the reason why Americans in the 1950s propagated this cheerful notion of Judeo-Christian civilization is that they were not yet knowledgeable about what anti-Semitism had just wrought in Europe. Nor did they really have pressing reason to learn about the prehistory of the Holocaust, about the blood libels and expulsions, about the persecution of Jews in the Crusades and the Inquisition. This was simply because these anti-Semitic atrocities happened outside of North America.

Paradoxically, just as it seems absurd for any person with a minimally reasonable education in world history to talk about "Judeo-Christian" civilization in view of the oft-gruesome relations between members of the two faiths over the centuries, it has also sometimes been perfectly reasonable for Americans, through the present, to use the term in earnest. Before the end of the twentieth century, Americans had reason to believe that what was exceptional about their country's past was actually the historical norm.

By the end of World War II, it seemed as though Jews had penetrated to the core of power and beauty in the country. Bess Myerson, a twenty-one-year-old Jewish woman from an immigrant family in the Bronx, became Miss America in September 1945. Just some three weeks earlier, the country celebrated V-J Day, its triumph in the Pacific clinched by the activities of J. Robert Oppenheimer, a middle-aged Jewish theoretical physicist from a better-established immigrant family in Manhattan. Oppenheimer had directed the secret Manhattan Project for the development of the atom bomb in Los Alamos, New Mexico.

---

3. Silk, "Notes."
4. Henry, "'And I Don't Care,'" 38.

To survey the history of post–World War II Jewish inclusion in the United States from these two symbolic points of origin, Myerson and Oppenheimer, would be laborious. In classrooms in Israel over the past decade, I have abbreviated this long story by alluding to the family histories of the two presidential candidates in 2016, an election most Americans would regard as an unusually fateful one. As though it were testimony to how deeply integrated Jews have become in the country's corridors of power, both candidates, Donald Trump and Hillary Clinton, have Jewish sons-in-law (Ivanka Trump leads a fully Jewish life, as a convert; also Trump's rival in the 2024 race, which was swinging feverishly toward its November outcome when I wrote these words, Kamala Harris, is married to a Jewish man, Doug Emhoff, who actively organized initiatives against anti-Semitism when Harris served as vice president under Joe Biden).

When you dig a little deeper into such symbolic milestones, you usually find that they are more multidimensionally complex than they seem. A few examples: both Myerson and Oppenheimer had quite complicated public-political careers after their 1945 heyday; and the family of Marc Mezvinsky, Chelsea Clinton's husband, includes an uncle who was an outspoken anti-Zionist and a bitter antagonist of organized parts of the American Jewry's pro-Israel majority until his death in 2022.[5] Nonetheless, the examples cited here suffice as indications of how, in past decades, Jews have climbed to the pinnacle of America's establishment and of how success and power in the country has often featured Jewish-Christian cooperation. Such partnership includes intimate family life, society's most sensitive sphere. It is safe to say that most Americans view this Jewish success story as a congruous outcome of their national culture's foundation in the Bible, whose Hebraic Old Testament complements its Christian New Testament. Why shouldn't they think of themselves as belonging to Judeo-Christian civilization?

So be it. Many of us have reservations about associating the term "civilization" with anything that has happened over the past decade in America, a period darkly clouded by the rise of Trump's MAGA movement, by devil-may-care partisanship in both houses of Congress, and by the Supreme Court's grossly derelict indifference toward a woman's fundamental right to decide about her own body, and also toward the application of constitutional norms of checks and balances to the executive branch. Most threatening, from the Jewish standpoint, is the sheer incivility of Trump's leadership style—for two hundred and fifty years, Jews in modernity have been drawn toward political systems committed to inclusive norms of civility. Still, let's grant that powerful counterarguments, such as Trump's apparently

---

5. Levin, *Our Palestine Question*, 177–78; Radosh, "Tale of Two Mezvinskys."

supportive attitude toward his daughter's Jewish family, overturn any point of suspicion regarding present and future Jewish-Christian relations in the United States. Still, assuming that things are going swimmingly between these two religious groups and are likely to remain in this salubrious state in America for decades to come, what are we really saying when we view tolerable, or even excellent, relations between these two groups as being a healthy outgrowth of Judeo-Christian civilization?

We are saying that we do not understand the foundations, implications, and expiration date of American exceptionalism. In reality, the two religious groups have a tense heritage of prevarication; the history of relations between them comes down to the creative or destructive management of lies, or half-truths. Through the 1960s, what kept America detached from the lugubrious history of the West was that the Christian-Jewish history of mutual defamation and endless untruth never exactly took root in the colonies and in the evolving culture of the young republic. That is to say, Judeo-Christian civilization never really assembled itself in the United States, much to the relief of fair-minded persons from both these groups. The absence of a Judeo-Christian foundation in America contributed to the country's democratic culture in two ways.

First, Americans may never have lied *less* than anyone else, but up through the Vietnam-Watergate era, they did not lie as artfully well as other peoples. Up to the 1970s, lying in America was not the execution of public policy by untruthful means. Because lying was not an embedded component of national culture, a number of romantic notions which would have raised hackles elsewhere, first and foremost the idea of the "American dream," retained authentic inspirational power in the minds of many newcomers and veteran citizens of the country. American earnestness had its drawbacks, to be sure. Americans' bluntly self-interested character, and their complete lack of cultural pretentiousness, rendered them lousy travelers, wrote Mark Twain in his *Innocents Abroad* (published a few years after the end of the Civil War). After World War I, Fitzgerald's *The Great Gatsby* explored how capitalist prosperity overwhelmed romantic yearning and sincerity. In the mid-1950s, Graham Greene's *The Quiet American* suggested that owing to their ineptitude for artifice, Americans were lousy spies; this novel, like *Gatsby*, showed how Americans could leave behind a lot of debris, even when they were not specious con artists.[6] Still, such defects were tolerable; Americans, and anyone in contact with them, benefited from the gullible sincerity that pervaded the country's national culture, at least in matters pertaining to white heterosexuals.

6. Twain, *Innocents*; Fitzgerald, *Great Gatsby*; Greene, *Quiet American*.

The transformation after the 1960s was quite steep. It can be argued, of course, that all ambitious nations institutionalize lying at some point. In fact, perhaps the only noteworthy thing about the American case is that the country's adoption of constant hucksterism occurred *just one* generation before technological innovation endowed lying with new multiplier effects. One wonders about what the world would be like today had digital technology revolutionized in the mid-1960s rather than 1993 (the year when the first internet browser went into public use). In the mid-1960s American legislators, reared on an ethos of can-do idealistic practicality, pushed through landmark civil rights legislation, as well as a liberal-minded open-door Immigration and Nationality Act. In 1993, by contrast, Americans had a new rising class of heroes. Barry Bonds, Lance Armstrong, and Monica Lewinsky were well on their way (the first was a newly traded member of the San Francisco Giants and hit forty-six homers; the second was at the peak of his pre-cancer career, winning the Union Cycliste Internationale World Championship; the third was newly enrolled in an undergraduate program at a college in Oregon). Within a few years, each name would symbolize how the new era of big lies reached its first, pre-Trumpian, peak.

Americans had accumulated two or three decades of experience with unadulterated mendacity by the time the internet highway opened in 1993. The timing of this convergence of cultural transformation with information technology innovation meant that the World Wide Web was destined to be covered in sleaze.

In early 2023, the Pornhub pornographic site had monthly traffic of nearly two billion visits, and it made the top fifteen rankings for website visits.[7] Meantime, social media giants like Facebook routinely face litigation on charges of spreading misinformation and hate speech. But what would have happened had the internet taken off during the first window in the mid-1960s, when truth-telling was still a public norm, of sorts, in the United States? Would what passed for carnality on television in the late 1960s have held back the way sex got onto the internet? Would a fully clothed website, LoveAmericanStyle.com, hold a top fifteen traffic ranking today, in lieu of Pornhub? In the early 1970s, the period when Woodward and Bernstein at the *Washington Post* exposed the Watergate scandal, journalism was perceived as a public trust. Had internet evolved in that earlier era, would news and information have better-tempered conveyance in virtual reality today? Maybe WalterCronkite.com, managed by upstanding graduates of public policy and truth in journalism degree programs, would have the top ten internet traffic spot held nowadays by Reddit.

7. Routely, "Ranked."

Second, the absence of Judeo-Christian civilization in America up to the end of the twentieth century was very good for the Jews. Ironically, it meant that there was relatively little anti-Semitism in the country. True, commentators in America started to talk about such a civilization in the 1950s. These discussions, however, tended to be blandly antiseptic. They were not always predicated on specific images of one group held in the minds of members of the other group.

In America's pre-prevarication era, the most explicit statement about a Judeo-Christian civilization in the country came in the mid-1950s in a book published by Will Herberg, a Jewish thinker who started his career as a Marxist but ended up as a religious conservative.[8] The title of the book, *Protestant-Catholic-Jew*, roundly evoked such a civilization, but the volume's main point is that Americans had mostly secularized. As Herberg saw it, they took in religion like they took in farina—blandly, in small bowls. Far from having a religious civilization, the closest thing in America to a spiritual creed which united Christians and Jews was belief in the American way of life.

Only after the 1960s—only after Jews, Christians, and everyone else in America took up the habit of lying obsessively—was it possible for spokespeople from these two big religious groups to talk publicly about how much they loved one another and about how about they had proceeded and flourished in American democracy thanks to their mutual civilization. America's Judeo-Christian civilization did not become an axiomatic big deal until the mid-1970s, after Israel's controversial conquests in the 1967 Six-Day War and after its confusing setbacks in the 1973 Yom Kippur War. It was in this period when America and Israel first cultivated a "special relationship" that remains intact, albeit in a newly shaky way after the spring 2024 anti-Zionist campus protests. Before the 1960s, when Christians and Jews in the United States were still relatively honest about how they felt toward one another, there was no such special relationship between Israel and the United States. The two countries had an alliance, more or less a diplomatically regular one, albeit far too stingy in the provision of security assistance to Israel for the Jewish state to survive over the long term.[9] From its inception, the sole indisputable truth of the special relationship is that a major upgrade of security assistance to Israel after the 1967–1973 period was necessary to forestall the annihilation of the Jewish state. Otherwise, the special relationship has not won distinction for its truthfulness.

---

8. Herberg, *Protestant-Catholic-Jew*.
9. Little, "Making of a Special Relationship"; Lazarowitz, "Different Approaches."

In view of chicanery's overall assault on American culture in the past half century, it could not have been otherwise. Nonetheless, even in its general setting of public policy deceit, the special relationship has its own highlights and oddities. A strange fact of American sociopolitical history is that Jesus is the only Jew who has been honored in the country more than Benjamin Netanyahu. The first is known to every believing Christian in the world as the son of God, whereas the second is regarded widely around the world as a son of a bitch. To date, the Israeli prime minister who will be remembered in opprobrium in Jewish history as a shameless wizard of lies, and who will need to avoid entry in some 124 countries should the International Criminal Court (ICC) issue war crime arrest warrants against him,[10] has addressed a joint session of the US Congress four times, one more time than anyone else (Churchill won the honor three times).

The special relationship came into being in the mid-1970s, just as Israel embarked on its colonialist project of erecting illiberal, illegal settlements in territories won in the 1967 Six-Day War.[11] The rationale for the special relationship's consolidation was that Israel deserved disproportionately generous aid on the grounds that it was the "only democracy in the Middle East"—that this rationale was articulated exactly as Israel embarked on its illiberal settlement misadventure bears witness to the untruthful spirit of the era as a whole. Before the 1967 war, when it was a smaller and less complicated (albeit much beleaguered) country, Israel had a less blemished democracy, particularly in the two- or three-year interval before the Six-Day War when it lifted military government restrictions on its Arab citizens. But in this earlier period, nobody seriously cited its democracy as a warrant justifying a special relationship.

It was only after the special relationship's inception that America's paramount fundamentalist group, Christian Evangelicals, proclaimed unqualified love for the Jewish state and became a powerful pro-Israel lobby force (including support for the settlements) and also the leading gentile charity giver to the Jewish state.[12] This Evangelical Zionism is founded on a lie. Far from unqualified love, the Evangelicals attach very long strings to their lobbying and philanthropy for Israel—these strings, in fact, reach the sky. The Evangelicals' expectation is that the conversion of 144,000 Jews will turn the tide in a fateful showdown with the antichrist, after the supernatural rapture wherein Jesus' followers have risen to the clouds.

---

10. Weeks after this book was drafted, the ICC issued these arrest warrants, infuriating Netanyahu's right-wing base constituency in Israel. See Landau, "Bibi Netanyahu."
11. Rubinstein, *Mi la-H*; Shafat, *Gush Emunim*.
12. Ariel, *Unusual Relationship*; Carenen, *Fervent Embrace*.

Meantime some liberal Protestants, who understandably criticize antidemocratic Israeli settler colonialism on the West Bank, have endorsed various anti-Zionist lies, including exaggerated attributions of genocide to Israel's 2023–2024 Gaza War, and also deceptions propagated by the BDS (Boycott, Divestment, Sanctions) movement regarding demands for a Palestinian right of return whose camouflaged agenda is the overturning of the Jewish statehood project.[13] That is to say, both Israel's philosemitic supporters in America and its most judicious gentile critics have either succumbed to, or contributed toward, ongoing dynamics of falsehood in the special relationship.

The sketch given thus far is too dark. Of course, innumerable idealistic instincts and enthusiasms, among Jews, Christians, and others, are embroiled in the special relationship's perpetuation. Without exception, liberal Democrats who have held power in the Oval Office since the special relationship's inception displayed genuine special commitment toward the Jewish state (this is true even in the case of Jimmy Carter, who was more adamantly critical of Israel's settlement policies than were his successors). This component of personal, presidential affection for Israel bred unforgettable episodes, such as President Clinton's eulogy at Yitzhak Rabin's funeral and the elderly President Biden's immediate, energetic response on behalf of Israel security after Hamas's October 7, 2023, attacks. This basic, visceral sympathy for the Jewish state displayed by US presidents (including Republicans, from Eisenhower to Trump) reflects the way millions of Christian Americans, surely still a strong majority of this community, feel about the Jewish state, both in principle and also as a meaningful practical response to the Holocaust.

What I am addressing here is the way US-Israel relations were ideologically packaged after the 1970s, during a half century when public culture cannot be credited with maintaining a high degree of honesty. Carter, Clinton, Obama, and Biden—that is, all liberal US presidents—displayed genuine, personally felt commitment for Israel, but they also obliged sacred cow rituals and conventions in the special relationship, such as the taboo against applying genuine pressure in opposition to the illiberal West Bank settlements. Some of them, like Obama, who for a few years jousted with a Netanyahu government over a settlement building freeze, were not thrilled about this taboo, but they all heeded it. The result is that Israel has become a noticeably *less liberal* democracy during the half century of the special

13. For a survey of different views about the intentions of BDS supporters and the validity of their claims, see Halbfinger and Wines, "Is B.D.S. Anti-Semitic?" For a mainstream American Jewish organizational contention about the untruth of the Gaza War genocide accusation, see American Jewish Committee, "5 Reasons."

relationship. This outcome is crushingly disappointing to liberal-minded Israelis and Palestinians who had fervently hoped to live, and to raise their children, in a relatively peaceful environment framed within a two-state solution, however imperfect and unsatisfying such a solution will necessarily be for both sides.

The special relationship, in sum, has done many good things for Israel, primarily in the conferral of security assistance required for its survival. But this does not mean that the way it consolidated in policy formulas optimized affairs for Jews and Arabs in the Middle East. Far from it. Special relationship ideology is flawed because it came into being in a post-1960s era that was far too receptive toward shibboleth rationalization of public policy.

Lying about Israel in America, and elsewhere, goes round and round in vicious circles. The anti-Israel college protests of spring 2024 were a telling exemplification of how lying in American culture has become a kind of pathological dialectic. The first time significant untruths that underlie the US-Israel special relationship were publicly and widely exposed, the truth-telling was done by young people who were propagating a big lie of their own, accusing Israel of perpetrating genocide on the Gaza Strip.

The ubiquity of lies about Israel and Palestinians, and of lies generally in American culture, can be traced back to myths and misconceptions in interpretations of Judeo-Christian civilization. On the whole, the idea of such civilization gained credence in America after World War II, and Jews and Christians in the country imagine that they treat one another well, and collaborate in pro-Israel policy, because of its heritage. In fact if such civilization exists, its heritage is that Jews are suspicious or contemptuous toward Christians, and Christians are dangerously hostile toward Jews, sometimes murderously so. Insofar as Jews and Christians in America have related positively toward one another and have also enacted many idealistic measures for Israel—and in my work as a historian, I have tried to chronicle many such inspiring exchanges between the two groups in America and in collaborative policy toward Israel—it has been *despite* the legacy of "Judeo-Christian civilization," not because of it.

Why does this topic of Judeo-Christian civilization seem so confounding? In this essay, as in its two companion pieces in this volume, I propose that such mysteries are best addressed by going way back to the source, to the days of Jesus in Galilee.

Peter's Confession at Caesarea Philippi as an Alternative Fact

Judeo-Christian relations are in everlasting crisis about truth and falsehood. The core of the crisis, of course, is the mystery of Jesus' nature, as God or mortal. The battleground for debates about whether perceptions of Jesus constitute divine annunciation, or fake news, is Galilee, the northern region of today's Israel, where Jesus spent the first three decades of his life before setting out on his earth-changing three-year mission, which also unfolded mostly in Galilee, though some of its key episodes, culminating in the crucifixion in Jerusalem, occurred outside of the region.

Galilee was the most challenging area in the country for manifestations of, or claims about, Jesus' divinity since many of its inhabitants knew him as Joseph the carpenter's son (Matt 13:55). The New Testament conveys no descriptions of Jesus' childhood in Nazareth (a nondescript town on a hill located in the middle of Galilee, roughly halfway between the Sea of Galilee to the east and the Mediterranean coastline to the west), but some unauthorized information about his Galilee youth can be gleaned from noncanonical writings.[14] This canonical issue, featuring a division between sanctioned, sacred New Testament tidings and what was, in antiquity, the equivalent of dark web data about Jesus (known by scholars as "Lost Scriptures," or the Pseudepigrapha), is one major aspect of the information crisis about Jesus' life and nature, but we will set it aside here.

The most awesomely mysterious episodes in Jesus' life, his birth in Bethlehem and his martyrdom on the cross (we might also include the Bar Mitzvah–like scene of the twelve-year-old Jesus in the Jerusalem temple, recorded in Luke 2:41–52) occurred outside of his home region of Galilee. The Gospels are not always consistent in their explanation of why these occurrences transpired outside of Galilee. As to the nativity, for instance, Matthew (Matt 2:1) records flatly that Joseph and Mary were in Bethlehem when Jesus was born; Luke provides new details, suggesting that Joseph and Mary planned to have the birth in Galilee, but the Roman Emperor Caesar Augustus ordered a census of Jews, and since Joseph descended from King David, he was required to register in Bethlehem (Luke 2:1–6).

Looking at the New Testament from the standpoint of a non-Christian, it seems plausible to hypothesize that the most awesome occurrences in Jesus' life were more conveniently located outside of the Galilee region where residents had known and thought of him as a mortal youth. New Testament passages (Matt 11:23; Mark 6:1–6) that hint about incredulity among Galileans, in Capernaum or Nazareth, regarding Jesus' preaching or unearthly

---

14. Ehrman, *Lost Scriptures*; Foster, *Apocryphal Gospels*.

powers, support this supposition—that is, it might have been easier for Jesus' followers to chronicle his messianic activities outside of Galilee, owing to homegrown skepticism in Nazareth, Bethsaida, Capernaum, and other northern locales. But this does not mean that Jesus' mission was tranquilly uncontroversial outside of Galilee. In fact, Jesus' experiences in non-Galilee venues raise acute dilemmas about truth-telling, personal integrity, and human loyalty. Such dilemmas and challenges are illustrated by the description of Peter's three denials of Christ following the Last Supper, as recorded in all four Gospels, and also by the story of Judas Iscariot's betrayal of Jesus.

Perhaps more than any other recorded happenings in history, the Bethlehem and Jerusalem chapters in Jesus' life and death resonate in world culture. But Galilee nonetheless stands out as the venue where monotheism fractured, owing to the contentiously debated mystery of Jesus' nature. Though the Gospels' chroniclers are inconclusive about whether Jesus intended to reform ("fulfill") Judaism or replace it, their records of his mission in Galilee make it clear that he rejected as duplicity observances in what we today call Judaism. Christianity institutionalized this skepticism, thereby ensuring that a "heritage" constituted as an amalgam of the West's first two major monotheistic religions must have a core of unyielding mutual suspicion and disbelief.

Whatever his truest intention, Jesus showed his disciples a pathway on which they could righteously break away from Judaism on the grounds that its priestly elites were untruthful hypocrites whose ritualistic observances were detestably crass. When this pathway was later selected, Jesus' uncompromising quarrel with fellow Jews in Galilee was institutionalized in formal Christian ritual designed as an alternative to Judaism.

The paramount instance in which Jesus' preaching was readily interpreted by followers as a statement about how the two religions use words and rituals for differing purposes—about how what is truth in one religion is an alternative fact for the other—is the Lord's Prayer. The prayer's inclusion at the heart of the Sermon on the Mount attests to how Christianity's awesomely impressive moral cornerstone also has beguilingly complicated sociopolitical implications. The same sermon that is renowned for its inclusive appeal to all classes of society also authorizes and solidifies Christianity's departure from Judaism.

To state the matter in contemporary terms, Jesus tells his followers not to become social media friends with the Jews because Judaism is a fallen faith whose rituals are supervised by priestly elites whose sole concern is how many "likes" they will get. Christian prayer (as exemplified by the Lord's Prayer, whose text is transcribed in the Sermon on the Mount section, Matt 6:1–13, that we are citing here) is private, spiritual, and truthful, whereas Jewish prayer is social, selfish, and false. "And when you pray," instructs Jesus' sermon, "do not be like the hypocrites [Jewish worshipers], for they love to pray standing in the synagogues and on the street corners to be seen by others" (Matt 6:5). Jesus condemns Jewish almsgiving on identical grounds, saying that the Jews' charity works are spiritually false because they are undertaken by persons who merely "want to be honored by others" (Matt 6:2). This line of attack accelerates in Matt 23, where Jesus reprimands the Jews' religious leaders, the Pharisees, calling them a "brood of vipers" condemned to hell (Matt 23:33). The accusations again focus on the spiritual untruth of Judaism, whose leaders "make their phylacteries wide and the tassels on their garments long" for the purpose of attracting notice (Matt 23:5). Fulminating about Pharisee hypocrisy, Jesus summarizes, "Everything they do is done for people to see" (Matt 23:5).

How the root of Judeo-Christianity is a crisis about the credibility of information can be seen yet more clearly when we look at the events of Jesus' mission in Galilee from the Jewish standpoint. That his miraculous works in Galilee irked disdain and incredulity among the region's solidly rooted Jews is suggested by the number of instances where Jesus' wondrous deeds do not apply to Jews at all, or occur at the geographical edges of the region or beyond its borders—east of the Jordan in the Decapolis, or north of Galilee in today's Lebanon. Two examples of Jesus executing miracles to followers (or servants of followers) who were not part of Galilee's Jewish majority are the ministration done at the request of the Roman centurion (Matt 8:5–13) and Jesus' healing of the demon-possessed daughter of a Canaanite woman (Matt 15:21–28; Mark 7:24–30).

The latter incident is particularly interesting. Jesus' initial, crudely phrased, refusal of the woman's request ("It is not right to take the children's bread and toss it to the dogs," Matt 15:26) suggests his retention of a Jewish parochial attitude inculcated by a young life spent entirely in a remote, rural region like Galilee. Working through this instinctive recoil, Jesus relents and exorcizes the woman's daughter. Read by believing Christians, the passage's account of his reversal is clear and compelling: Jesus is won over by the woman's powerful demonstration of faith, and he says so. When considered outside of this standpoint of Christian belief, the episode takes on a different meaning. It implies that Jesus' original intention was to reveal his divinity via miracle-making among his own (Galilee) Jewish population, but its members proved to be an unrelentingly skeptical audience. Exactly in this encounter with the Canaanite woman, it seems, Jesus is deciding to extend the range of his mission beyond what we today call Judaism (parenthetically, I keep using this phrase, "what we today call Judaism," because in the late Second Temple period, ethnonational identity was not separated from religious belief, unlike situations familiar to modern minds).

This interpretation of a turning point, of sorts, in Jesus' mission accords with the general view proposed by nonfundamentalist New Testament scholars, including Christians. On this interpretation, key parts of the Synoptic Gospels, particularly in the book of Matthew, were written toward the end of the first century by scribes who were not in full agreement about whether Jesus viewed himself as an in-house reformer, whose ministrations were designed mostly or primarily for Jews, or whether he recruited disciples with the specific agenda of their spreading a new faith among gentiles.[15] The healing incident with the Canaanite woman can be read either way. Significantly, it occurs north of Galilee, in the Tyre and Sidon area (today's Lebanon), where word of Jesus' miraculous intents or powers had presumably spread. The locale here is a crucial component of Jesus' ambivalence about healing gentiles. As though he is guided by an invisible hand that has knowledge of how his healing charisma will have better effect outside of a region inhabited by skeptical Galilee Jews who have known him all his life as a carpenter's son, Jesus acts against his own instincts and takes the demon out of the body of the Canaanite girl. That the miracle is an exorcism coheres with an interpretation which sees this incident as a dress rehearsal for Christian missions among gentiles—symbolically, by healing the gentile girl, Jesus also seems to by ripping Jewish parochialism out of his own soul.

Though it is more complicated in that it involves two thousand swine and two unruly demons, another exorcism sequence suggestively occurs outside of Galilee, in the Decapolis area described by Matthew (8:28) as the "region of the Gadarenes." If its intention is also to rehearse embryonic Christianity's power outside the provincial confines of Jewish Galilee, the swine miracle apparently has mixed results (the Gospels record that the whole fearful town implored Jesus to leave the region: Matt 8:32–34; Mark 5:14–17; and Luke 8:34–37); but on the line of interpretation we are following here, the important point is the experimentation with miracle-doing outside Galilee areas that were soaked in Jewish skepticism.

Of course, Jesus won followers among Galilee's Jewish population. However, if we follow a conspicuous example, that of the fisherman from Capernaum, we move yet closer to the convulsive shock center out of which Christianity erupted, from Judaism. Capernaum, discussed in more detail in another chapter, was a town lipping a northwest stretch of the Sea of Galilee where Jesus (apparently) kept a home in the period of his mission. Saint Peter, nee Simon Peter, the most prominent fisherman convert, was

---

15. See Saldarini, *Community*; Overman, *Matthew's Gospel*; Kampen, *Matthew*.

from nearby Bethsaida, but he was apparently a familiar figure at his mother-in-law's home in Capernaum. As indicated by the post–Last Supper story of the three denials, Simon Peter remained, to the end, poignantly aware of the sociopolitical risks incurred by becoming a Jesus devotee. Responding to Jesus' query at Caesarea Philippi, Peter, in contradistinction to other disciples, recognizes his leader's identity as "Christ, the Son of the living God" and so is rewarded with the keys to heaven and the privilege of building up Jesus' church upon a rock at the site (Matt 16:13–20). Once again, for our purposes, the important feature of this famous sequence (Peter's confession of Christ) is its locale, Caesarea Philippi. Appropriately, the locale identified in the New Testament as the foundation for Jesus' church is both within and without Galilee, at an arcadian rocky stream area known today as Banias, just south of Lebanon at the end of contemporary Israel's Upper Galilee border, also on the edge of the Golan Heights.

This site was known in ancient times as Paneas, after the Greek god of the wild, Pan.[16] Its reputation as Galilee's pagan northern edge would have been well-known to the writers of the book of Matthew. One of Herod's sons, Phillip the Tetrarch, was entranced by this site, where a Jordan River tributary gently flows; in 14 CE, Phillip named his renovation project in honor of Emperor Augustus (the "Philippi" was added to distinguish the site from another Caesarea, an important Herodian city located on the Mediterranean coast). The Caesarea Philippi area had been known for its Pan-related fertility cults, and it is sometimes suggested that its reputation struck Gospel writers as being compatible with the description of the birth of a new church (more prosaically, scholars have speculated that composers of the Matthew Gospel dwelled not far from Caesarea Philippi and thus described familiar turf when they recorded Peter's confession sequence).

I think that there was a pointed political motive underlying the selection of Caesarea Philippi as the site of the ultimate act of "replacement theology" (or supersessionism) whereby the revelation of Jesus' messianic nature, coupled with the Jews' refusal to acknowledge it, is seen as requiring the insertion of New Testament prophecy as the substitute for the invalidated acts of Old Testament prophets, like Moses.[17] If, as many scholars have proposed, the book of Matthew was compiled by scribes who were physically close to Caesarea Philippi and who wrote a decade or two before the end of the first century, when the disastrous culmination of the Jews' revolt against Rome (66–70 CE) was a recent memory, they would have viewed this Upper Galilee locale as the place where the Jews' hope for sovereignty

---

16. Information here is drawn from Wilson, *Caesarea Philippi*.
17. Silver, *Galilee, 47 BCE to 1260 CE*, 82–87.

in their Eretz Israel homeland was symbolically and humiliatingly extinguished by the Romans. After the Jewish revolt was crushed (apart from the holdout fortress in the south, Masada) and as the victorious Roman commander Vespasian sailed toward Greece, his son Titus chose Caesarea Philippi for gladiatorial circus victory celebrations. According to the historian Flavius Josephus, dozens of defeated Jewish rebels were tossed to "wild animals" at Caesarea Philippi in a punitive ritual designed to symbolize how Jewish aspirations for political control in the land had been annihilated.[18] Since Caesarea Philippi was thus branded as a symbol of the Jews' lost religious-political kingdom, it was an ideal place for Christianity's founding group, comprised of Jesus' followers, to depict the ritualistic enactment of Christianity's severance from Judaism by the building of a church (*ekklesia*) at Caesarea Philippi.

The fact that the New Testament's Galilee miracles are reported as having occurred in marginalized or high-charged circumstances and locales has ironic resonance today. The Hermon Stream (Banias) Nature Reserve belongs to the sovereign territory of the Jewish state, but when I wrote this section, access to this historic Caesarea Philippi site was closed to Israeli tourists and to Christian visitors from overseas. Some one hundred thousand residents in the broad Upper Galilee area had been evacuated, and this entire region was subjected to daily bombardment emanating from Hezbollah in Lebanon.

Caesarea Philippi's symbolically fraught character exemplifies how the core of Judeo-Christian civilization is a *communication* crisis. Everyone in the cultural world shaped out of monotheism knows that Jesus came from Galilee and performed most of his miracles there before moving on to his excruciating act of martyrdom in Jerusalem. Yet the New Testament was composed by backsliding Jews—that is, newly (or soon-to-be) declared enthusiasts for a new faith based on Jesus. These writers naturally wanted their chronicles to have credibility in the eyes of Jews, particularly Galilean Jews from whom Jesus emerged and toward whom he originally directed his mission. Yet the Galilean Jews had displayed incredulity toward the selfsame miracles which were to be showcased in the Gospels as demonstrations of Jesus supernatural divinity.

This was simultaneously a supremely inconvenient and perfectly convenient situation. To have put the Galilee miracles in a straightforward frame of documentary realism would (presumably) have raised hackles among the once-intended audience of Jesus' mission. On the other hand, it was imperative to "shame" the Galilean Jews (who became, metonymically,

18. Josephus, J.W. 7. 23–24.

"Pharisees") in the Gospels because the consolidation of Jesus' preaching and worldly experience in a new religion, severed from Judaism, would have made much less sense had his Galilee Jewish home audience been seen as enthusiastically embracing him as a new Jewish prophet in a long line of prophets.

As you will know, and as anyone would tell you, the crux of the separation between Judaism and Christianity is a difference of opinion about the nature of Jesus Christ as the messiah and Son of God, or not. However, the Christian resolution of this argument with Judaism was a long time coming—its ostensible resolution, at the Council of Nicaea convened by Emperor Constantine, came about two hundred and fifty years, a quarter of a millennium, after the composition of the Gospel of Matthew. Much New Testament scholarship suggests that the main lines of this solution, known to everyone today in lands shaped out of monotheistic culture, were either not really known or were not uniformly accepted by the groups which composed key parts of the Synoptic Gospels. That is to say, at the core of monotheism's fracture, when canonical texts of Christianity were in composition, the crisis was neither metaphysical (pertaining to Jesus' true nature) nor existential (pertaining to what we would call today the "religious identity" of Jesus' disciples and documentarians). Instead, the crisis was communicative. The crisis featured a search for a way to express "the" truth, or "a" truth, about Jesus' preaching and deeds that would simultaneously retain credibility among the people who had really known him (or their descendants) but also invalidate the morality and spirituality of these people without supplying any plausible rationale for their incredulity—that is, without delving into metaphysical sophistry about the cause of this incredulity. In these senses, the nucleus of Judeo-Christian civilization is inherently unstable, its supernatural essence being tethered to, and untethered from, one identifiable place. Jesus is shown as performing his religion-changing miracles in Galilee where he grew up, but when you closely review the Gospel records, and bear in mind how their composers had to bypass and concurrently highlight phenomena of homegrown skepticism about Jesus, it is possible to surmise why he is not exactly seen as enacting miracles in the heart of Galilee.

Jews, of course, have struggled for two thousand years, trying to forge an adequate response to the information crisis posed by the New Testament narrative of Jesus' miraculous activity in Galilee.

Practically speaking, the separate, Jerusalem-centered, deicide accusation of Jewish responsibility for the crucifixion caused more trouble for Jews over the centuries. Of course, Jewish apologetics regarding deicide were never effective (how could they have been, given the balance of power between the two religious groups following Constantine's policy of Christianizing the Roman empire?), and this futility, combined with many other factors, produced the Holocaust. From a strictly communications standpoint, however, Jerusalem-area events leading to the crucifixion were easier for Jews to talk about. This was because they unfolded in a trial format; thus once, as non-Christians, you eliminated the issue of Jesus' divinity, the issue could be discussed as a legal matter. Up to the Second Vatican Council process (1962–1965), which relieved Jews of collective responsibility for deicide, books written by Jews in the apologetic "we didn't kill your God" mode proliferated. Their production was habitual since erudite Jews shared a motivation of displaying their skills as defenders of their people.

Even after the Holocaust when there was much less left to defend, and it did not really matter anymore whether gentiles were listening, this habit remained intact, at least up to the time of the Vatican's Second Council. A very late example is a 1968 book written in Hebrew, *The Trial and Death of Jesus Christ*, authored by Haim Cohn.[19] The author, whose career pinnacle was a twenty-plus-year term as an Israeli supreme court justice, had an energetic life, crossing from one pole to the other in many dimensions of twentieth-century Jewish life.[20] German born, as a teenager Cohn studied in Jerusalem's unusually pro-Zionist yeshiva, Merkaz Harav, but he ended up as an adamant opponent of the brand of religious legislation and right-wing politics that is associated with disciples of the father-son team that ran this yeshiva. During Israel's first years, Cohn worked as its attorney general, and leftists sometimes regarded him as an authoritarian security czar; but Cohn actually turned out to be a liberal champion of civil rights. This all amounted to an impressive resume, but it does little to explain why Cohn would produce a Hebrew apologetic contending that the Romans, not the Sanhedrin, were responsible for the crucifixion, given that the book's main reader audience was comprised of Jews who needed no argumentation to accept its premises. The answer to this riddle seems clear. Historically, when Jews discussed Christianity, they tended to choose the wrong subjects, and they easily fell into the habit of preaching to the choir—that is, they rehashed arguments about these ill-chosen topics which sounded valid only to Jews and philosemites, who were predisposed to accept them.

Metaphysically, deicide is a difficult, even oxymoronically difficult, concept to fathom. However, never being drawn to cosmic claims of Jesus' identity, Jews and many others never found it very hard to discuss this topic,

---

19. After a few years, this book came out in an English translation. Cohn, *Trial and Death*.

20. Information here is drawn from Cohn, *Mavo Ishi*.

deicide. In contrast, the issue of Jesus' wondrous deeds in Galilee often kept Jews tongue-tied for three reasons. First, of course, the everlasting balance of power between Christians and Jews made it impolitic to say that the Gospels lie about the miracles; in inquisitorial periods, it was suicidally lethal for a Jew to develop this argument. Second, from the Jewish standpoint, the issue is not the unreality of the miracles. Instead, the problem is that a critical mass of Jews, an amount sufficient to serve as the foundational kernel for the rise of a new, rival religion, were apparently credulous about the illusions perpetrated by Jesus and his followers. Third, in the premodern world, apologetics designed to refute a rival religion's claims about messianic divinity did not require denials about reported supernatural occurrence (in other words, the issue was not whether extraordinary, unnatural events happened but rather whether they bore witness to divine visitation on earth).

Taken together, these factors cast a communicative spell on Jews. In the Middle Ages, even when they were writing in their own (non-Latin) languages and describing Jesus' activities and language in a bitterly intemperate fashion, Jews chose not to deny the supernatural character of Jesus' deeds in Galilee. The important example here is a text called *Sefer Toledot Yeshu* (The Book of the Life of Jesus), which circulated as dozens of manuscripts in various languages (including Aramaic, Hebrew, Arabic, Yiddish, and Ladino), apparently from the eleventh century.[21] Rather than straightforwardly refuting Gospel reports of Jesus' wondrous deeds, *Toledot Yeshu* depicted them as evil sorcery.

As modernity took shape in the nineteenth century, emerging out of the semisecularized eighteenth century era of the Enlightenment, Jewish commentators tended to follow trends in liberal Protestant theology that concentrated on the life of the historical Jesus, almost to the point of ignoring that Christian religious belief had always depended upon there being a supernatural component in that life, responsible for extraordinary miraculous occurrences in Jesus' home region. By "ignore," we are not saying that liberal theologians had nothing to say about the miracles—it is more accurate to say that they had little to say in support of the wondrous supernaturalism of the Galilee occurrences. Albert Schweitzer's 1906 study, *The Quest for the Historical Jesus*, is filled with examples of liberal Protestant commentators proffering natural explanations of the miracles, based on the argument that they were unusual but not impossible happenings.[22] Among Jews, the parallel is the naturalist explanations given by semisecularized

---

21. Schafer et al., *Toledot Yeshu*.
22. Schweitzer, *Quest*.

commentators, such as Reform rabbis, regarding Old Testament miracles wrought by Hebrew prophets. However, for Jewish commentators the transposition of this naturalist approach in discussions of the New Testament was rather awkward, so nineteenth-century liberal theology among these two groups often developed on separate tracks. To say that the Red Sea parted and that two thousand swine fell into the Sea of Galilee because of naturally explicable friction in tectonic plates draws a parallel between Moses and Jesus that is flattering neither to Jews nor Christians.

Outside of the liberal Protestant movement on the continent, some semisecularized commentators of Catholic ancestry also promoted demystified explanations of Jesus' ministry in Galilee. The most significant example here is Ernest Renan's best-selling 1863 *Life of Jesus*, which presented a psychological approach to the Galilee events wherein Jesus, seemingly more than anyone else, is conscious of how they might not really be supernatural.[23] For Jewish commentators, who were acutely conscious of early rumblings of a newly modern, and dangerous, brand of anti-Semitism, Renan's psychological realism approach was a red hot potato. When it came to sensitive Christian matters, the latitude enjoyed by an esteemed gentile Semitics scholar who had been educated by priests was rather wider than that available to Jewish commentators, and members of this latter group were loathe to publish anything that might be interpreted as suggesting that Jesus was a con man. Thus, Abraham Geiger, probably mid-nineteenth-century Europe's most prominent Reform rabbi and a commentator deeply invested in what would be called today anti-defamation, Jewish self-defense work, publicly upbraided Renan for his earthly characterization of Jesus' work and motivations. He wondered about how Renan could possibly have shown Jesus exercising "very low morality" in various Galilee episodes.[24] That a liberal Jewish commentator chastised a respected Christian scholar for displaying irreverence about Jesus in a book of immense popularity among gentile readers shows how Judeo-Christian civilization rejuvenated in modern times in the same, medieval cast as a non-dialogue unfolding on separate tracks wherein the most liberal-minded commentators from the two groups groped fruitlessly for points of tangency.

Once they had determined that disquisition about Jesus' character, or about the "real" nature of his extraordinary activities in Galilee, was risky or useless, nineteenth-century Jewish commentators focused on the topic of his followers in the region.[25] Why would they conceivably have forsworn

---

23. Renan, *Life of Jesus*.
24. Geiger, *Judaism*, 129.
25. The analysis here follows Silver, *Galilee, 1538–1949*, 187–92.

their Jewish religious culture and switched allegiances to the Jesus movement? Exactly as their liberal Protestant peers had done when they furnished answers to the mystery of the historical Jesus, these liberal Jewish commentators resolved the riddle they had chosen by means of anachronism. As Schweitzer detailed, the Christian commentators dressed up Jesus in line with their nineteenth-century bourgeois concerns and sensibilities; similarly, the Jewish commentators, who were worrying about Jesus' Jewish followers rather than the nature of their leader and his wondrous deeds, dressed up Galilee in line with their concerns and sensibilities, as modernizing nineteenth-century European Jews.

Specifically, what, at the time, was on the mind of a Reform rabbi like Geiger, and also the secularized Jewish historian Heinrich Graetz, was the influx of traditional Jews from East Europe, pejoratively known as *Ostjuden*, in Central Europe. Not long after the midpoint of the nineteenth century, Geiger, Graetz, and many other liberal European Jews worried that the arrival of masses of Ostjuden would foment anti-Semitism in the newly emerging state of Germany and other lands in central-west Europe (in another decade or two, well-established Jews in the United States would rehash this concern).[26] By modern Western standards, the East European Jews were uneducated and uncouth; so Jewish communal leaders worried that Ostjuden would either be susceptible to the demagoguery of missionaries and other gentile elements and assimilate, or they would remain Orthodox and thereby provide ammunition to anti-Semites who were arguing that Jews were a primitively antisocial group, one that was incompetent to contribute to the society and economy of a modern state.

Geiger estimated that the tragedy of Judaism's inability to forestall schism and Christianity's rise could be inferred from the plight of the Ostjuden in his own day.[27] Like the Ostjuden, Galileans were uneducated, uncouth country Jews who had just one Jewishly viable option—just as Geiger's contemporary agenda was to extend Reform rabbinical influence over the Ostjuden, he argued that Jews in Galilee would not have lost their identity and set the stage for Christianity's emergence had they abided by the well-reasoned leadership of Jerusalem's priestly elite, the Pharisees (whom Geiger unabashedly depicted as an early version of modernity's Reform rabbinate).

Geiger thus resolved the mystery of monotheism's fracture by depicting Galilee's Jews in 30 CE as though they were Ostjuden in Germany in the second half of the nineteenth century. The region's "lower class of people,"

---

26. Aschheim, *Brothers and Strangers*.
27. Geiger, *Judaism*, 129–40.

who were ignorantly susceptible to attestations of wonder and miracle, became Jesus' first followers, whereas the "educated and intelligent were not attracted to him." Galilee's uneducated Jews were "inclined to rebellion" and easily swayed by eschatological preachers who announced that "this world was breaking down, and a new world, the future world, would soon appear."[28] The historian Graetz, who bitterly argued with Geiger about many other issues, chimed in.[29] When he accounted for Christianity's rise, Graetz drew distinctions between constructive Jewish culture in Judea and the unstable, vulnerable country culture of ignorant Jews in Galilee—this distinction conveyed obvious echoes of mid-nineteenth-century polemics in which Westernized Jews kept a distance from the Ostjuden. Provincial Galilee, wrote Graetz, was "far behind Judea in mental attainment and knowledge of the law." Nazareth-raised Jesus encountered a Jewish environment devoid of the "lively interchange of religious thought" characteristic of the temple setting in Jerusalem.[30] From this Jewish standpoint, the problem posed by the breach between Judaism and Christianity had virtually nothing to do with the character of Jesus and everything to do with the presumed uneducated, provincial character of Jews in Galilee.

In the nineteenth century, liberal Christian theologians wrote and reflected on the basis of different premises. They produced a remarkable array of biographies of the historical Jesus, casting him in an illogically expansive number of guises. This trend has continued into the twenty-first century, during what some commentators call the "third" quest for the historical Jesus conducted by Christian commentators (the second phase, led by the German New Testament scholar, Rudolph Bultmann, who died in 1976, focused on textual-theological questions, avoiding biographical discussion of Jesus); there is still a lively market for academic and popular books that cast Jesus as a shaman, a rabbi, a Jewish political zealot, and many other things. The only common denominator on this post-Holocaust third quest, suggests scholar John Meir, is its axiomatic understanding that Jesus was a Jew.[31]

This Christian consensus about Jesus' Jewishness is good news for the Jews. Still, it would be a stretch to say that post-Holocaust philosemitic developments in the liberal Christian quest for the historical Jesus have really promoted interfaith understanding in a revitalized North America–based Judeo-Christian civilization. From the earliest reports of the resurrection

---

28. Geiger, *Judaism*, 138.
29. Graetz, *History of the Jews*, 149–61.
30. Graetz, *History of the Jews*, 149.
31. Eddy and Beilby, *Historical Jesus*, 48.

to the present, Jewish and Christian discussions of the core issue of this presumed civilization, i.e., monotheism's fracture owing to conflicting impressions of Jesus' activity in Galilee, have proceeded on separate tracks.

In recent decades, Christian scholars of the New Testament have turned to the topic that monopolized nineteenth-century Jewish discussions about monotheism's fracture—namely, the character of Galilee's Jewish population in Jesus' time. Moving into a dizzying array of fields—anthropology, literary theory, critical geography, history (specifically the "primitive rebel" research strand associated with E. J. Hobsbawm), and more than anything else, archaeology—they have produced an impressive corpus of work delineating circumstances in northern Palestine's economics, society, and politics.[32] This work will be required reading for future generations of scholars and nonspecialists who ruminate about the Jewish-Christian fracture. Meantime, in step with the centuries-long exegetical tango, Israeli scholars almost utterly ignore this scholarly corpus produced by gentile New Testament scholars. Their interest in late antiquity Galilee attaches to other topics, ranging from circumstances and developments in the region during the early phase of the 66–70 CE revolt against Rome, to the early Talmudic (Tannaitic) culture that took shape in Galilee toward the end of the second century, several decades after the composition of the New Testament Gospels.

As exemplified by the writings of David Flusser (1917–2000), a Hebrew University of Jerusalem scholar, Jewish scholarship in the post-Holocaust era on Jesus and the Christian-Jewish breach has featured textual-based research centered on the premise that Jesus' preaching drew heavily, if not entirely, on extant beliefs, sayings, and practices in Jewish culture in this late Second Temple period.[33] Bypassing Gospel reports of Jesus' miraculous doings in Galilee, this approach assumes that there was nothing especially unusual or original in the Jesus phase of Christianity's emergence. Recapitulating a long-standing view in Jewish scholarship about Jesus (earlier propounded, for instance, in Joseph Klausner's influential 1922 volume, *Jesus of Nazareth: His Life, Times and Teaching*[34]), leading post-Holocaust Jewish scholars on New Testament issues associate the rise of Christianity with the doings and writings of Paul the apostle in a period after the crucifixion, in places far from Jesus' home region. Whatever its merits, this approach endorses an indifferent or monochromatic attitude toward a wealth of

---

32. See Horsley and Hanson, *Bandits*; Freyne, *Galilee*; and Strange, "First Century Galilee."

33. Flusser, *Sage from Galilee*.

34. Klausner, *Jesus of Nazareth*.

material in the Synoptic Gospels that is fraught with suggestions, tensions, and approaches regarding the breach between Judaism and Christianity.

An arresting example of such bypassing of the Galilee Synoptic Gospel narrative in discussion of the Judaism-Christianity breach is Paula Fredriksen's 2018 book, *When Christians Were Jews: The First Generation*.[35] This is an engagingly readable book packed with important information about embryonic Christianity. The author, professor emeritus at Boston University who has also taught as a distinguished visiting professor at the Hebrew University (and who is, according to internet chatter, a Jewish convert from Catholicism), circumvents dramatic Galilee events in Jesus' life that hundreds of millions of people would identify as primary or significant causal parts of the sequence leading to Jesus' followers' formal identification as Christians. It seems like a counterintuitive feat, but the book has as sturdy evidentiary foundation as can be managed (at least, in a volume designed for a mixed academic and general audience) once the Synoptic Gospels are deprioritized. Fredriksen leans hard on the book of John, whose geography often substitutes Jerusalem for Galilee. As Jewish and philosemitic scholarship regarding the New Testament invariably does, her book overlooks the extraordinariness of Galilee events (at least as judged from Christian standpoints) and instead highlights how Jewish culture envelops everything in narratives about Jesus' preaching and mission and about his early followers. In this sense, and many others, *When Christians Were Jews* is Jerusalem-centric. It is part of a post-Holocaust process by which Galilee has been semideliberately written out of history, apart from Jewish-inflected eras and developments relevant to Zionist priorities in Israeli educational, tourist, and park administration policy.

Where Does Judeo-Christian Civilization Come From?

Since antiquity, Galilee has been a tricky subject for historical remembrance for reasons that subsume the Jewish-Christian dispute about the nature of Jesus' identity but go beyond them. As showcased in the aforementioned 1922 Jesus biography produced by another Hebrew University scholar, Joseph Klausner, it is impossible to separate hermetically discussion of Jesus' Galilee mission and his final Jerusalem ordeal from early percolations in the Jews' revolt against Rome, which erupted in 66 CE, roughly the length of Jesus' own lifetime after the crucifixion. As Klausner interpreted it, Jesus' biography belongs to the context of Jewish messianism and its ebbs and flows

---

35. Fredriksen, *When Christians Were Jews*.

in these final decades of the Second Temple period.[36] He believed that this messianism had two tracks, one spiritual, the other political. His preaching identifiably based upon the sayings and outlooks of earlier Jewish teachers, Jesus directed his followers toward the first, eschatological, track. Klausner was an ardent Jewish nationalist (his right-wing zealotry impeded his career advancement at the Hebrew University in this British Mandate period, a time when a mildly socialist, Labor Zionist approach dominated the political culture of pre-state Israel), and he was thus apt to emphasize antagonism between the two religions, at least after Paul (on Klausner's view) corrupted, popularized, and disseminated the new Christian creed in Jesus' name. Yet Klausner's highlighting of the messianic, unruly Jewish Second Temple context is shared by scholars of different ideological temperaments.

For instance, writing in an early twenty-first-century American milieu where Jewish-Christian amity is fashionable, Reza Aslan published a decade ago the aforementioned bestselling Jesus biography whose thesis is that Jesus was a political Jew from the zealot branch of the anti-Roman rebellion.[37] As, I suspect, many readers realize after they put down Aslan's well-turned book, this thesis is overdrawn and incompatible with many of our ideas about Jews and early Christians. Nonetheless, it is significant that a well-received book about Jesus draws an inviolable link between his earthly career and the Jews' anti-Rome revolt, exactly as scholars of very different dispositions, like Klausner, had done before Aslan.

This link further problematizes Jesus' story in Galilee and Galilee history as a whole, however. The link, in fact, is the prime reason why Galilee history became the "Greatest Story Never Told" and why it is nonsensical to talk about foundations of "Judeo-Christian civilization." Such a civilization cannot be said to be rooted in any particular place. For that reason, and many others, for as long as there have been relations between Jews and Christians, they have drowned in an information crisis. It is a relationship wherein absolute truth can never be told, or accepted.

The sole meaningful primary source about Second Temple Judaism, its messianic variants, and the Jewish revolt against Rome are the writings of Flavius Josephus, known during the early phase of his life (before he "went Roman") as Yosef ben Mattityahu.[38] Belonging to a conservative, well-adjusted Jerusalem priestly elite, Josephus was equivocal about the anti-Rome revolt. He nonetheless ended up commanding its early Galilee

---

36. Klausner, *Jesus of Nazareth*.

37. Aslan, *Zealot*.

38. For the primary sources, see Josephus, *Jewish War*; Mason, *Flavius Joseph*. For Josephus's life and its Galilee phase, see Cohen, *Josephus in Galilee*; Rajak, *Josephus*.

portion. This stint culminated in the Romans' devastating siege at a hilltop village, Jotapata (known today as Yodfat), where Josephus self-interestedly violated a suicide pact forged with Jewish partisans under his command and surrendered to the Romans, who ended up appreciating and lucratively rewarding his efforts as a chronicler of the revolt and of other episodes in Jewish history (with uncanny precision, Josephus's shamelessly self-promotional account of how he joined the enemy after the debacle at Jotapata reverses the moral logic of the Jewish zealots' last stand in 73 CE at the Dead Sea fortress, Masada, whose sole description is to be found in Josephus's most important book, *The Jewish War*).

Josephus's writing is riddled with class bias, personal grudges, obsequious winks to his Roman patrons, and self-justification. Quantifying subjects of fundamental importance regarding what happened in the revolt, and also in Jesus' experiences, such as the number of Jewish inhabitants in Galilee, he outrageously exaggerates numbers. On the other hand, when he quantifies subjects known to his own eyes, and of direct importance to his own exploits, he can be remarkably accurate. Israeli military historians and archaeologists, for instance, have almost fully verified Josephus's record of the number of Jewish fortresses in Galilee, and they have also found evidence possibly supportive of the large number of Jewish Galilee towns and villages, 204, cited by him.[39] In short, while there is an awful lot of "fake news" in Josephus, there is also a considerable amount of reliable writing on crucial subjects about which the author had direct knowledge, or special interest.

Josephus's writing is its own information crisis, and proportions of falsehood and truth in this chaotic corpus have been measured quite differently over the ages. One extreme example in the pro-Josephus camp is American: the case of Selah Merrill, an ordained Congregational minister from Connecticut who served, on and off, as American consul in Jerusalem for a quarter century (ending in 1907) in a diplomatic role that was sometimes marred by controversy (some regarded him as an anti-Semite).[40] Merrill was a Josephus devotee who compiled a collection of his writings. In his 1885 booklet, *Galilee in the Time of Christ*, Merrill adopted a fundamentalist view of Josephus, insisting that every word written by this historian is true.[41] That judgment is humorously wide of the mark, but there are nonetheless many reasons why Josephus's writing is indispensable, even though it itself constitutes an information crisis.

39. Avi-Yonah, "Missing Fortress"; Aviam and Richardson, "Josephus' Galilee."
40. Goldman, "Holy Land Appropriated."
41. Merrill, *Galilee*.

For one thing, Josephus represents the sole documentary source for topics that are staples in the West's understanding of monotheistic culture. An example is his discussion of the three known subgroups among Jews in this Second Temple period: Pharisees, Sadducees, and Essenes. As often happens with Josephus, this description seems incomplete (scholars in recent generations have engaged a fascinating debate about whether there were more factions than these three groups; in fact, following a suggestion made by a prolific rabbinic Judaism scholar, Jacob Neusner, they have wondered whether, in view of the intense factionalism, it is even plausible to refer to one "Judaism" in this period).[42] On the other hand, Josephus's account of the three factions has an appealing ring of personalized authenticity since he details how he himself, in his teens, spent three years experimenting with lifestyle options offered by the three groups.

Generally, scholars who have spent much of their careers researching Josephus observe that he rarely invents details out of whole cloth.[43]

For our purposes, Josephus's writing is noteworthy owing to the reception it won over the centuries. This subject has been expertly analyzed by Oxford University scholar Martin Goodman.[44] He shows that Josephus, whose *Jewish War* opportunistically exonerated his Roman patrons, future emperors Vespasian and Titus, of responsibility for the burning of the Second Temple, has generally been treated suspiciously, as a scurrilous turncoat, by Jews. However, Goodman notes, this suspicion or hostility sometimes abated—Jews who wrote as part of ideological movements which were dependent upon the largesse of imperial powers, as in the example of nineteenth-century "enlightened Jews" (Maskilim) in Central and Eastern Europe, tended to appreciate the dilemmas faced by Josephus, and they identified nuances and perhaps subterranean criticisms of his Roman patrons in his writings.

On the other side, as their religious civilization consolidated, Christian commentators found much cause for enthusiasm when they perused Josephus's *Jewish War*. For them, the book's luridly vivid descriptions of the temple's destruction were seen as ratification of Jesus' prophecies in the Gospels. They also approved of *The Jewish War*'s moralistic theme, holding that Jews in the first decades of the first century forfeited God's favor owing to their recalcitrant intemperance. Goodman suggests that the reason why Josephus's writing circulated prominently over the ages was because of this

---

42. Kampen, *Matthew Within*.

43. Cohen, *Josephus in Galilee*, 38. See also Martin Goodman's introduction in Josephus, *Jewish War*, xxvii.

44. See Goodman, *Jewish War*.

evaluation about its compatibility with Christian prophecy. This judgment seems reasonable. It means that in *both* foundational texts regarding the period of monotheism's fracture, the Synoptic Gospels and Josephus's *Jewish War*, what is agreeable to Christians is antagonistic to Jews; the reception of both writings depended on this dynamic whereby what was happy truth for one religion was miserable falsehood for the other.

Both writings—that is, Josephus's history and the New Testament Gospels—pivot on presumably eyewitness documentation of core events in Galilee. Mirroring fluctuating inconsistencies in the different Gospels' record of particular events, Josephus released two accounts of the Jewish revolt in Galilee, the historical subject best known to him. These are the *Jewish War* and an autobiographical fragment, *The Life of Josephus* (also known simply as *Vita*).[45] The two works were written in different phases in the Romanized period of Josephus's life; manifest variations in the contents of these two writings stem from oscillations in the author's agenda and in his degree of concern about whether his information would be palatable to different subgroups of readers, Jewish and gentile. *The Jewish War* tends to frame the author's leadership in the revolt in Galilee as a Jewishly patriotic endeavor in a heroic struggle between two worthy antagonists (though in many ways Josephus undermines this frame). In contrast, the Galilee parts in *Life* project a sense of preordained Jewish failure. In *Life*, the author seems to be assigned the role of damage control; devoid of hostility to the Roman enemy, the text almost casts Josephus as a double agent.

In both writings, Josephus's tall tales about his own cleverness and courage strain credulity.[46] He leaps into boats moored at the sea of Galilee, creates a shell façade of a floating flotilla on this lake to fool and intimidate enemies, forces dastardly rivals to amputate their own limbs, and so on (it bears mention that his rivals in these James Bond–like exploits are mostly Jews, not Romans). Readers surely respond differently to the author's descriptions of his own wondrous exploits in Galilee. The situation parallels that of a Jewish reader of Jesus' miracles: if you are not with the program ministered by Josephus's text, much of its information about its hero looks blatantly far-fetched (in fact, in Josephus's case the protagonist comes across as an opportunist and a coward in episodes like the end of the Jotapata siege).

Crucially, in both core texts about the period of monotheism's fracture, different tranches of information serve different audiences addressed by the protagonist. In the Gospels, Jesus can sometimes be seen purveying

---

45. Josephus, *Jewish War*; Mason, *Flavius Josephus*.
46. Silver, *Galilee, 47 BCE to 1260 CE*, 34–45.

information to disciples which is, at least for the time being, beyond the ken of Galilee's rural masses. The New Testament's moral core, the Sermon on the Mount, seems to bifurcate, with disciples sitting close to Jesus in a circle as though they are privy to quietly dispensed messages while a larger audience lines up and down the hill, it never being quite clear what parts of the sermon, some of them imposing inhuman moral and practical burdens among followers, are heard or supposed to be heard by whom. In an interpretation credited to Protestant theologian William Wrede (who died in 1906), parts of the Synoptic Gospels, especially the book of Mark, hinge on a "messianic secret," meaning that the revelation of Jesus' true identity is being temporarily withheld from everyone in Galilee (not to mention later readers of Scripture), other than his disciples.[47] Josephus's work has its own secrets, starting with the never-resolved issue of what he was trying to accomplish as a rebel leader in Galilee; but, more important are its information tranches and the way they parallel polyphony in the New Testament.

In many ways, the information crisis in Judeo-Christian civilization stems from a Hellenistic geography whereby mysterious secrets belong to the rural periphery, whereas the city is the home of plain truth. The tranches we are following in these canonical texts contribute to this geography. In Josephus, rural populations nominally under his command are described as "Galileans," and they are inherently untrustworthy.[48] In his two writings about the rebellion in the region, Josephus frequently pictures himself demagogically defusing the dangerous hostility of the Galileans in orations filled with half-truths and empty promises. Soon after he extracts himself from the lethal clutches of the ignorant rural masses, Josephus adopts a very different communicative style with elites in the region's two cities, Tiberias and Sepphoris, whose members, like himself, harbored reservations about the revolt. Of course, in the Gospels no such bluntly extreme dichotomy is drawn between speech designated for the rural masses in Galilee and "messianic secret" speech purveyed to elite disciples, but Jesus' preaching and communications are nonetheless multilayered in tune with distinctions between elites and rural masses in ways comparable to the tranches in Josephus's writing. In fact, communication in some passages of Josephus and of the New Testament seems to be directed at the same group of gullible "Galileans."

This should suffice as discussion of how dialogue layering, geography, class bias, authorial motivation and reliability, and many other factors contributed to a crisis of information transmission and destabilized the core

---

47. Wrede, *Messianic Secret*.
48. Zeitlin, "Who Were the Galileans?"

of Judeo-Christian relations. To live in a civilization molded out of those relations is to never be sure of truth.

After the two climactic events in Judea, the crucifixion and the hurban destruction of the Second Temple, Galilee lost its place in history. With that, Judeo-Christian civilization lost its geographic core. Christianity consolidated elsewhere, moving its church from Caesarea Philippi to Rome.

When Christianity returned to Jesus' home region, its settlement in it was ephemeral and uncertain. Around 135 CE, groups of Jews fled from Judea after the failure of a second anti-Rome revolt (the Bar Kokhba revolt) and established an embryonic proto-Talmudic community in Galilee, led by scholarly *Tannaim*, a group of religious teachers. In this period, up to Constantine's revolutionary Christianizing policy in the mid-fourth century, apparently few Christians dwelled in Galilee.[49] There are reports of Christian pilgrimages reaching Galilee sites as early as 333 CE (the "Bordeaux Pilgrim"), and Constantine and his heirs seem to have invested in building up sites in places like Nazareth and Capernaum, reportedly in concert with a Jewish apostate from Tiberias known as Count Joseph. Have traces of early Byzantine rule in Galilee, layered upon sites in Capernaum and elsewhere where Jesus and his followers lived, prayed, and visited, ever been found? This question is bitterly disputed by scholars and clerics (Franciscans, some of whom became involved in archaeological work, are prominent in the "pro" group that argues for the discernibility of the Jesus movement in identified Galilee spots).

Byzantine rule hosted Christian settlement in Galilee, particularly on its western side, according to Israeli archaeologist Mordechai Aviam.[50] This Christian period ended calamitously in 636 CE largely because an energetic, competent Byzantine ruler, Heraclius, grew old, focused his energy on a campaign to reconquer Jerusalem from the Persians, and ignored the rise of Islamic faith and military power. Muslim forces swept into Palestine, and although they were apparently outnumbered in a scale of four to one, these fighters drove Christianity from Galilee and the Holy Land at the Battle of Yarmuk, a decisive clash conducted in a riverbed area connecting Galilee and the Golan Heights (today it is a zone of dispute between Israel and Syria and is monitored by the United Nations). Not for the last time, a phase of Christian rule ended in Galilee with Christian soldiers slaughtered on a cliff. The medieval Islamic geographer, Yaqut al-Hawami, reported

---

49. Taylor, *Christians*.
50. Aviam, "Christian Galilee."

that eighty thousand Christian fighters perished at a ravine later called Al Wakusah, a name referring to the "breaking up" of Christianity.[51]

The second time Christian rule downsized in the Holy Land because a decisive battle in Galilee ended with Christian soldiers scrambling around a mountain occurred in 1187 at the Battle of Hattin, where the Crusaders were vanquished by Ayyubid forces led by the legendary Islamic hero, Saladin. Famous accounts of this fateful battle stress the miscalculations of the Crusader ruler Guy of Lusignan, a relative newcomer to the Holy Land (to some extent, his errant leadership reprised the story of Yarmuk half a millennium earlier, though Heraclius was a much more imposing figure than Guy).[52] Launching an attack march from a compound at Sepphoris, Guy ignored the counsel of a wiser, more experienced Crusader, Raymond III, prince of Galilee; the incompetent king neglected the provision of water for his troops, who battled in fierce early-July heat and were demoralized and dehydrated before Saladin's soldiers relieved their misery. This time, instead of tumbling down from a cliff, Christian hopes for Holy Land restoration died with soldiers vainly running up a mountain, with Muslim cavalry chopping them down.

After Hattin, Jerusalem was lost to the Christians, but Crusader rule continued for another seventy-five years, now limited to the Galilee north, its base being the Acre harbor (pronounced "Akko" in Israel today) on the Mediterranean coast. The Crusader Acre kingdom constitutes a fascinating chapter in history, but its rich complexities are mostly occluded today, owing to the repugnance felt in the West toward the violently colonialist, anti-Muslim animus of the Crusader enterprise as a whole. This attitude is reflected in the monumental biography of France's King Louis IX published in 1996 by Jacques Le Goff.[53] Louis IX, a luminary figure of Christian medieval Europe (he was the only French monarch canonized as a saint), led the Seventh Crusade (1248–1254), a turbulent misadventure which culminated in the Capetian monarch's capture in Mansourah, Egypt. After having emptied France's treasury for ransom payment, Louis remained in Acre for a few years in a penitent phase whose transformative character is detailed by chroniclers, particularly the king's liege Jean de Joinville, and whose impact on King Louis IX's subsequent rule in France, and on European reevaluation of the Crusades as a whole, is readily discernible.[54] However, in a scholarly version of cancel culture, Le Goff peremptorily dismisses Saint Louis's Acre

---

51. Silver, *Galilee, 47 BCE to 1260 CE*, 190–204.
52. France, *Hattin*.
53. Le Goff, *Saint Louis*.
54. Joinville, *Memoirs*.

contrition, his words reinforcing how Galilee history has been lost, for an array of reasons, and remains the "Greatest Story Never Told." "For all their efforts, the crusaders ultimately left only the ruins of imposing monuments, notably in Jerusalem and Acre," opines this biographer.[55]

The short-lived, but colorful and energetic, Acre kingdom left a much greater mark than Le Goff presumes. This can be seen today by tourists on a visit to Acre, a cluttered but enticing place whose old city is designated as a UNESCO world heritage site; and Acre tours can be supplemented by visits to inland sites in rural Galilee, such as the Montfort castle, an imposing relic in a verdant, secluded hilly area which attests to the Teutonic Order's Holy Land activity during this second Crusader Kingdom period.[56] Still, in terms of the centuries-long aftermath of Jesus' three-year ministry, Galilee's Christian legacy is confusing and ambiguous.

This is symbolized by the Horns of Hattin, the site of the Crusaders' ill-fated 1187 battle. According to one legend, as discussed in an 1863 Holy Land travel memoir published by a Scottish general practitioner, a Wesleyan, Dr. Fergus Ferguson, the Horns of Hattin is "supposed to be . . . the eminence on which Christ delivered the greatest discourse ever preached, the Sermon on the Mount."[57] A more familiar designation for the sermon's delivery is the Mount of Beatitudes, on the Korazim plateau, where a Franciscan chapel (built in the 1930s) stands today. Nonetheless, the Horns of Hattin tradition is thought provoking: precisely on the spot where Christians have believed Jesus sermonized and proclaimed, "Blessed are the peacemakers" (Matt 5:9), the Crusaders waged and lost a terrifying battle some 1,155 years later. Confusing, no?

How you interpret the meaning of this Hattin tradition depends on how much weight you accord to contradictory parts of the book of Matthew. Should the peacemaker blessing (Matt 5:9) have the prerogative? If so, what is to be done with the warriors-of-Christ passage, "Whoever wants to be my disciple must deny themselves and take up their cross and follow me" (Matt 16:24), which was cited by Crusader recruiters, such as Bernard of Clairvaux, as a sanction for "holy war" ideology? In short, the Horns of Hattin tradition cited by Fergus Ferguson is one of many consequences bequeathed by the information crisis stirred by Galilee's canonical texts. Rising out of the unstable core of Judeo-Christian civilization, a hilltop cited by some as the arena of antiquity's most renowned anti-war message also hosted one of the Middle Ages' most violent and climactic battles.

55. Le Goff, *Saint Louis*, 144.
56. Boas, *Montfort*.
57. Ferguson, *Sacred Scenes*, 297.

For Jews, Galilee slipped in and out of their history. The region is where significant groups in Judaism's history regrouped after traumatic events. Before modernity, this happened twice. The first time followed the catastrophic end of the Bar Kokhba rebellion when the Romans enforced punitive *gezerot* (or *shemad*) decrees in Judea and Tannaim resettled in Galilee, where they compiled the early part of the Talmud known as the Mishnah. The second instance occurred after the Spanish Inquisition's brutal expulsion of Jews when, in the sixteenth century, a group of mystical Kabbalists settled in a town on a Galilee mountaintop, Safed. Major texts and religious streams in Judaism emanated from these two Galilee periods separated by some thirteen hundred years, one being not just the Mishnah but one of two versions of the Talmud, known under the misnomer, the Jerusalem Talmud (scholars assume that it was mostly compiled in Galilee's Tiberias), and another being the Lurianic stream of Kabbalah associated with Isaac Luria (1534–1572; Luria is known as Ha'ari).

Integral components of Judaism, such texts and ideological streams are points of pride for Jews, who are well aware of their Galilean settings. Nonetheless, as is the case for Christians, Galilee has had an unstable and rather incoherent place in Jewish historical consciousness.

The Tannaitic period, lasting in Galilee for about a century after a founding assembly in 138 CE in a nondescript village, Usha, is distinguished by figures like Judah Hanasi, the Jewish patriarch who forged various accommodations with the Romans and also redacted the Mishnah, and Tannaitic scholars like Shimon bar Yochai (known as Rashbi), a militant mystic whose memory is evoked annually at a huge *hillula* ceremony at his reported tomb on Meron, near Safed. Orthodox Jews, and other Jews who study Talmud, have deep knowledge of the Mishnah and the Tannaitic culture that produced it, but this Tannaitic phase in Galilee has never had a firm place on the Jewish historical narrative. Almost all Jews, apart from strongly observant Orthodox (Haredim), are invested in this narrative whose theme is exile and return, and which stipulates that Jews were cast from their land for "two thousand years" following the failed rebellion against Rome (that is, the 66–70 CE revolt described by Josephus). Israel's anthem, *Hatikvah*, refers to this two-thousand-year exilic period, as do innumerable other authoritative references to the Jewish history timeline in Israel and elsewhere. This exile and return chronology means that Tannaitic Galilee is written out of history, more or less in an official fashion. State-sponsored Israeli songs and symbols pivot on this concept of the ingathering of exiles who have not had a homeland since the Jews lost sovereignty in Eretz Israel, no later than the Bar Kokhba rebellion.

The status of Safed Kabbalah is rather different.[58] Perhaps the closest parallel to its unstable place in Jewish memory is the way Christians have reevaluated the legacy of the Crusader period as spiritual heroism or shameful colonialism, though the trajectory of revisions in these Jewish and Christian cases is different. Kabbalah today is extremely popular, of course, both among religiously invested Jews in Israel and overseas, and also among gentiles and nonobservant Jews (not religiously knowledgeable Jews) in the diaspora.[59] Over the past century, Kabbalah and associated forms of Jewish mysticism have attained (or regained) canonical status as a full-fledged part of normative Judaism. This century-long process whereby Kabbalah's status was positively reevaluated, within academia and well beyond it, is associated with a German-born Hebrew University scholar, Gershom Scholem. Learned, religious Jews have always engaged Kabbalah (usually at relatively advanced stages of their scholarly growth, owing to Kabbalah's extensive engagement with issues of sex and spirituality). However, starting in the late eighteenth century and through the Holocaust, modernizing Jews aggressively relegated Kabbalah. They dismissed it as irrational derangement, and even as a possible barrier impeding Jewish integration as citizens in modern nation-states. Largely for this reason, the Zionist movement, starting in its state-building, pioneering phase through the end of the British Mandate, ignored Safed. Even today, some seventy-five years after Israel's establishment, the town has neglected infrastructure and somewhat chaotic administration (I write as a resident of the town).

Supplementing the anti-mystical rationalism and prejudices of modernizing enlightened Jewish *Maskilim* in the nineteenth century, many forces contribute to the instability of Safed Kabbalah on the Jewish historical narrative. One factor worthy of note is ongoing confusion about Kabbalah's place relative to other religious cultures, such as Islamic Sufism and, more apposite to this discussion about Judeo-Christian civilization, Christianity. Most, though not all, of the roughly two hundred thousand Orthodox participants in the hillula at Meron, Israel's largest annual public event, dress up and view themselves as traditionalists whose observances, including this pilgrimage to Rashbi's tomb, insulate themselves from contaminating gentile influences in modernity. Anyone not versed in nuances of world religion and Israeli life would apprehend the hillula as a "very Jewish" event. In actual fact, unlike the other two foundational blocks of Judaism, Torah and Talmud, Kabbalah consolidated partly out of interaction with

---

58. Silver, *Galilee, 1538–1949*, 7–88. For a critical overview of Kabbalah scholarship, see Huss, *She'alt kiyuma*.

59. Myers, *Kabbalah*.

Christianity. Gentile influences on Jewish mysticism can be discerned both on a folkloristic level (e.g., Kabbalistic veneration of tomb sites) and also in a long roster of mystical concepts. Popularly seen as being very Jewish, Kabbalah is actually the component in Judaism that developed in unusually rich and complicated interactions with Christianity, and other gentile spiritual influences.

Kabbalah consolidated powerfully in the Lurianic stream of sixteenth-century Safed. Nonetheless, the current generation of Jewish mysticism scholars follow Kabbalah's migration throughout many Mediterranean locales, and beyond them, in early modernity.

Owing to such considerations, Safed Kabbalah's place on the Jewish history narrative is bright but unanchored. This circumstance almost seems designed. It befits a spiritual ideology that stresses the continual movement of mutually interactive orbs, *sephirot*, wherein sparks of redemptive light glimmer now and then in a broken world that was wrought by mishaps in the creational moment of contracting light, *tsimtsum*.

The historical reputation of sixteenth-century Kabbalistic Safed has flip-flopped, moving from its unwarranted derogation through the 1960s to its fashionably trendy status today. This down-to-up pattern reverses the timing and arc of the Crusader Acre kingdom's reputation.

Jews and Christians (or the ancestors of people who adopted these religious labels) first met in sustained encounter in Galilee, not Jerusalem. The foundational texts which describe this encounter are responsible for a prolonged information crisis. When we refer to Judeo-Christian foundations of Western civilization, we are alluding more to that crisis than to anything else that might possibly have consolidated over time in coherent and constructive relations between Jews and Christians.

It simplifies matters, and of course it is not wrong to say that monotheism fractured because of a difference of opinion among Christians and Jews about the true identity of Jesus Christ. Yet, as we all know, arguments have diverse ways of expressing themselves. Often it is not the factual crux of the disagreement but the way it is expressed which breaks hearts, separates siblings for decades, dissolves marriages, and even causes countries to go to war. While the argument about Jesus' messianism is fundamental in Western civilization, there is no necessary reason why monotheism's fracture could not have been denominational rather than semi-apocalyptic. Rather than its catastrophic culmination (at least for the present) in the Holocaust, the fracture, theoretically, might have expressed itself in the semi-amicable way religious denominations interact with one another in the United States today, or in the way the three Jewish factions (Pharisee, Sadducee, Essene) coexisted before the Second Temple hurban. This denominational option was excluded because of the information crisis, because there was no way that a rough baseline of truth could be extracted from canonical documentation about the first century's transformative events.

Branded as the venue where truth was lost in the information crisis, Galilee could never gain stable footing in history. Its most successful rulers understood that their power rested not on the monopolization of truth but rather on the artfully manipulative juggling of historical narratives. A striking example of Galilean empowerment via the use of alternative facts is the rule of the Druze prince, Emir Fakhr al-Din, in the region and beyond it in the 1620s, not long after Kabbalistic Safed lost its creative energy. Fakhr invented stories about how the Druze descended from French crusaders; he also spread false promises about how he would lead a Druze crusade to recapture Jerusalem for Western Christianity.[60] Such falsehoods thrilled notables in Medici courts in Tuscany, where Fakhr had regrouped as a temporary exile in an early phase of his career, and the support garnered by his dissimulation propelled Fakhr to a uniquely successful political career in Galilee (the early seventeenth century counts as the only time since late antiquity when the region was governed by a figure not connected to one of the three monotheistic religions).

Parenthetically, the ironic unreality of Galilee history can be seen from the third monotheistic angle, Islamic history, which we are not addressing in this essay. Muslim warriors fought and won a series of history-changing battles in the region—against the Byzantines at Yarmuk in 636, against the Crusaders at Hattin in 1187, against the Mongols at Ayn Jalut in 1260, and against Napoleon's French invasion, at Acre, in 1799. However, Galilee's place today on the "Islamic" narrative of history features the region's central role in a military-political debacle, the 1948 Palestinian *Nakba* (catastrophe), which culminated in the mass exodus of some seven hundred thousand Palestinian Arabs. The Galilean Nakba is a particularly poignant part of the overall story both because it utterly altered the region's demographic balance (on the eve of the November 1947 UN Partition resolution, 169,500 Muslim Arabs were a clear majority of Galilee's 241,000 residents[61]) and also because a late episode of the 1948 fighting, the sixty-hour implementation in late October of an Israeli military operation called Hiram, constitutes the clearest instance of a deliberate Palestinian expulsion policy in the war.

Of course, the facts of 1948 events and policies like Operation Hiram remain in bitter dispute among pro-Israel and pro-Palestinian camps. This gap between Israel's "Independence War" narrative and the Palestinian

---

60. Gorton, *Renaissance Emir*.
61. Silver, *Galilee, 1538–1949*, 312.

Nakba narrative applies to many parts of the country. Many people believe that the most emotionally fraught, and diplomatically entangled, locale in the Israeli-Palestinian dispute is Jerusalem. However, when it comes to sorting out truth and falsehood regarding the mass Palestinian exodus—a clarification with weighty political implications pertaining, among other things, to the Palestinian demand for a right of refugee return, which is for Zionists a nonstarter—the most disputed part of the country is Galilee.

This fact is reflected in the writing of Benny Morris, the most authoritative historian on the topic of Nakba refugee flight. In one collection of Morris's writings, the title (in Hebrew), *Correcting a Mistake*, and the centerpiece essay, relate to revisions in our understanding of the extent to which Operation Hiram was really an exercise in compulsory expulsion.[62] Morris, who adopted a darker interpretation of Israel's intents in this military operation after identifying fallacious details in the testimony of a high-ranking army officer, Moshe Carmel, seems to be suggesting that vital secrets of the Israeli-Palestinian dispute would be unlocked were we to be certain about what is true and what is false in reports about fighting in the Galilee panhandle in late October 1948. Responding to this surmise, anyone familiar not just with the contentiousness of Palestinian-Israeli debates over events in the 1948 war, but also with Galilee's everlasting propensity to fan crises in information dissemination, would say, "Good luck with that."

Finally, I might note that I have written this section about how, historically, the cradle of Judeo-Christian civilization, Galilee, is clouded by information confusion while in a present moment of enormous information confusion. Israel has fought a war in the south, in Gaza, for close to a year. To date, this war has not reached a satisfactory conclusion. Over a hundred kidnapped hostages, presumably half of them alive (at least), remain in hellish underground tunnels built and manned by Hamas.

If you are a liberal in Israel, you believe unreservedly that an agreement for the hostages' release, and for an end to the Gaza War, has not been reached due to Prime Minister Netanyahu's own political interests. Specifically, the stumbling block is Netanyahu's desire to keep his coalition (which includes racist war hawks) intact and thus defer his own trial on charges which include bribe-taking and breach of trust. Then again, if you are a liberal in Israel, you are probably co-opted by the country's decades-long, illegal, illiberal, and colonialist occupation on the West Bank. So if you are an Israeli liberal, instead of recognizing that our conflict in Gaza was caused, as much as anything, by our right-wing government's manipulative policy agenda of avoiding a two-state solution that might have grown out of

---

62. Morris, *Tikun ta-ut*, 141–49.

years-long collaboration with the relatively moderate Palestinian Authority administration on the West Bank, you spend all day grousing about how the only remaining problem in Jewish history, which will soon enter its 5785th calendar year, is Benjamin Netanyahu (much as liberal Democrats in America avoid serious discussion about true economic reform that would hurt their own wallets by imagining that the only thing wrong on heaven and earth is Donald Trump). That is to say, throughout this year-long Gaza War information crisis, Israeli citizens, who are exceptionally proficient in social media and high-tech spheres, have had limited understanding of what has really happened in our lives. They, we, are also increasingly doubtful about the endgame: should the worst happen to us tomorrow, we wonder whether we would die while still holding on to a reasonable handful of moral idealism.

More than any liberal Israeli would tell you, a year of being accused of genocide in Gaza has taken a heavy emotional toll. Neither myself nor genuinely thoughtful people here believe that this genocide accusation has serious evidentiary basis. But neither myself nor genuinely thoughtful people here really believe that Israel did anything close to what needed to be done over the past generation to avoid political and moral quandaries caused by Hamas's brutal attack on October 7, 2023. We are all recreants.

Last week, the brunt of violence in this year-long, multifront war moved to the north, to Galilee where I live. Most residents in Galilee's border kibbutzim, villages, and towns evacuated their homes a few days after the October 7 events on the other side of the country. They—about one hundred thousand persons—have spent the past year in temporary lodgings quite far from their homes on the Galilee border. Meantime, Hezbollah fired missiles at their homes with impunity. Several of these border communities are now scorched-earth memories, their homes pounded into rubble. The worst place, where 80 percent of the dwellings are decimated,[63] is Kibbutz Manara, where I lived for two or three years while I served as a lone soldier in the Israeli army in the mid-1980s.

That was not long after Israel's First Lebanon War, and I spent a few months in uniform in what later became known as the "security zone" on the Lebanon side of the Upper Galilee border. I remember Lebanon as being politically anarchic and geophysically beautiful, even more stunning than Galilee on the Israeli side (now and then over the years I have daydreamed about getting an invitation to lecture at the American University of Beirut, but that would be suicidal). When I was a soldier in southern Lebanon, Hezbollah had not yet come into being, and our enemy was a secular Shiite

---

63. Gilad, "Ben-Gurion."

group called Amal (which still ekes out a political and military existence). Meantime, Israel's expedient alliance with a Christian militia called the South Lebanon Army (SLA) was running strong; as an awkwardly conspicuous American Jewish immigrant soldier in the IDF unit's base near Marjayoun, I sometimes shot the breeze with SLA fighters about whether Larry Bird was better than Magic Johnson (this was, and remains, perhaps the world's most irresoluble argument apart from Middle East controversies).

Years later, in 2000, when Israel withdrew its forces from the so-called security zone in Southern Lebanon, SLA soldiers were sitting ducks for reprisals launched by Hezbollah, a ruthless and vindictive organization. So Israel absorbed hundreds of SLA veterans, resettling them on our side of the border reasonably close to Lebanon, the country from which they were forced to flee. For my part, though I have lived in several places in Galilee, I have never drifted too far from Manara, a mountaintop kibbutz that mesmerized me in my early twenties as a mix of the hilly landscape at Cornell University, where I had just done an undergraduate degree, and the oldtime Labor Zionist *halutz* pioneering ideals I admire. So, as things turned out, several of my neighbors in the Safed neighborhood where I am writing these lines are resettled SLA veterans. They are quiet but good-natured Lebanese Christians who keep a reasonably adjusted, low-key lifestyle in Israel. Last night, when I was preparing to write these paragraphs, there were several missile alarms in our neighborhood. The booming of intercepted missiles rattled windows and sounded uncomfortably close. So this morning I went over and spoke to some of these Lebanese neighbors. Will there be a big war? I asked. What about the shards we find in our backyards from intercepted missiles? Do you think we'll be evacuated? How frightened should we be? They shrugged their shoulders and smiled.

Sometimes I wonder about what would happen if this miserable year ends in a less than optimal way—and how can it not, in view of the monstrous egoists in Israel's elected government and with Trump licking his chops a few weeks before the November elections in the United States? Who will continue what Josephus started? Will there be anyone left to document and explain how the illiberal spirit of a recreant Jewish generation deserves to be left behind in the rubble it created after Hamas gave history a nasty push? Or how, on the Gaza border if not (for the time being) the Galilee border, liberal-spirited Jews, some of whom had taken affirmative steps in favor of rapprochement with Palestinians, were raped, taken hostage, and killed by Hamas, a terror group that exploited utterly misbegotten Israeli policy. Deprioritizing security on Israel's southern and northern peripheries, areas within the country's internationally accepted pre-1967 borders, this policy had its own peculiar objectives. It now sees the world this way:

Ultranationalist, racist Jews should thrive on West Bank settlements. Sara Netanyahu should enjoy her Fifth Avenue perks and keep humiliating her husband's political rivals, while the couple's obnoxious son tans himself, under expensive Israeli security protection, on a Miami beach, shirking IDF reserve service.

Over the past quarter century, this period when I have taught in public colleges in the north, Israel took many proactive steps to shrink the pool of humanities-trained scholars who research and reflect about our country's plight, its relations with Islam, its relations with Christianity, or its relations with Americans, from a broadly humanist perspective. The state-funded academic institutions in Galilee do not have bona fide humanities departments. I am feeling very lonely and a little frightened. From a professional standpoint, maybe the best thing that could happen here in weeks ahead would be a Hezbollah victory. In the end, the chances that Teheran would establish humanities studies, of some sort, in northern Palestine are not lower than the chances that an Israeli government, staffed by racist schnooks like Itamar Ben-Gvir and Bezalel Smotrich, would establish a genuine university here in Galilee, a pluralistic institution where Jews, Christians, and Muslims might engage genuine discussions about the history of their shared monotheistic culture. Nothing here, nothing there, hatred everywhere. Maybe the worst thing that could happen is for us to win this war and solidify our ultranationalist ways in this region, allowing me to keep drawing my monthly salary as the last historian in Galilee.

ISRAEL'S PUBLIC RELATIONS CRISIS AND THE RISE OF THE JUDEO-CHRISTIAN MODEL

The turning point in American and world perception of Israel occurred in 1982, during Israel's First Lebanon War. For the first time, television viewers in the West witnessed images that jarred Israel's long-standing reputation as a plucky David fighting purely defensive wars, fending off menacing, Goliath-like, Arab states.

Because it could be packaged as just redress for the Holocaust, this reputation was widely popular among Christians in the West. Along with a slingshot of Cold War strategic arguments, this plucky David branding was useful in lobbying for political and charitable support for Israel.

The reputation was jostled a little by the sequence of 1967 and 1973 wars—in 1967 because Israel's victory outsized the modest dimensions of its branding as David; in 1973 because the grueling Yom Kippur War turned into a major event in the Cold War during which America went on

DEFCON 3, the highest peacetime alert, and so this affair evoked a different set of biblical associations, like the apocalyptic book of Daniel. Then came the rise to power of the right-wing Likud party in Israel in 1977 and the country's massive project of establishing illiberal settlements in occupied territories, particularly the Gaza Strip and the West Bank. For liberals in North America and Europe, alarm bells were going off, but these were muffled for a few years thanks to the peace accord between Israel and Egypt. The Israel-Egypt peace accord actually arose out of Egyptian leader Anwar Sadat's courageous visit to Jerusalem in late 1977, and it was brokered skillfully by the Carter administration; but it signified assent to the "land for peace" formula from Menachem Begin's right-wing government and therefore endowed Israel with a few more years of grace devoid of outright suspicion among liberals in the West.

The casus belli of Israel's 1982 Lebanon War was clear. Subsequent controversies in Israel about how Begin had opted for a war of choice, defying the country's long-standing *ein breira* (no choice) policy of taking up arms purely in self-defense, reflect "inside baseball"–type oddities of internal Israeli political culture, and they can be misleading (the peculiarities arise from the rivalry between what were then Zionism's two main political camps, the fading Labor Zionist establishment and Begin's ascending Revisionist Zionist stream known as Likud). The objective reality was that Southern Lebanon had become a stronghold of the Fatah faction of Yasser Arafat's PLO (Palestine Liberation Organization), and it was being used as a launching pad for terrorist rocket strikes against civilian areas in Israel's Upper Galilee region, just south of the Lebanon-Israel border. From the mid-1970s until the Begin government launched the Lebanon War in 1982, the symbol of unprovoked rocket attack unleashed by Fatah, a Palestinian nationalist force, was the Israeli border town Kiryat Shmona, just as the same town has, for the last year, been the symbol of unprovoked missile attacks unleashed by Hezbollah, a Shiite Muslim Lebanese organization.

Israel's 1982 Lebanon War was mishandled by its Likud-led government, primarily owing to Defense Minister Ariel Sharon's deceptions and his grandiose ambition to rearrange the balance of power in Lebanon in favor of Israel-friendly Phalangists, a political party representing Maronite Christians. Many people around the world remember the catastrophic end of the war. Its horrific conclusion was a massacre of residents in Palestinian refugee camps, Sabra and Shatila, by Phalangists who were outraged by the Syrian-directed assassination of their leader, Bashir Gemayel (an Israeli state commission of inquiry subsequently found that Sharon bore indirect responsibility for this atrocity). Today, many of us in Israel are apprehensive that another Likud-led government could lead us toward another catastrophic military misadventure in Lebanon in weeks ahead. This anxiety might be warranted because the extremist politicians in Netanyahu's current government are far less publicly accountable than were the right-wingers in Begin's cabinet at the time of the First Lebanon War (like Begin himself, many of those 1980s Likud politicians viewed themselves as law and order liberals, never acknowledging that their settlement expansion policies badly undercut this self-image).

For our purposes here, from a public relations standpoint, the relevant part of the 1982 Lebanon War's legacy is not Israel's internal, inside baseball, bickering about wars of choice and wars of no choice. Nor is it even the potent, but ephemeral, global pushback following the Sabra and Shatila massacre. The turning point was the nightly broadcasts of Israeli bombardment and associated military actions during the siege on Beirut. It did not really matter that Israel's war policy—insofar as it could be differentiated from Sharon's bombastic political scheming with the Maronites—had plausible rationale. The First Lebanon War even yielded a victory, of sorts, for Israel, as Arafat's PLO forces were booted out of Lebanon and forced to relocate in Tunis. What mattered was the optics, and they were toxic. Prowling around and ravaging Beirut, Israel now became Goliath, in front of an increasingly suspicious world television audience.

It seems odd, in retrospect, that Israel's global public relations *hasbara* (a Hebrew term for pro-Israeli advocacy) crisis did not begin a decade earlier in the aftermath of the 1973 Yom Kippur War. OPEC punished the Nixon administration for its airlift support of Israel during this Yom Kippur War by manipulating oil supply and prices so that Americans in the mid-1970s found themselves waiting in long lines at gas stations. Those of us who are old enough to remember this episode know that the gas lines were a pretty serious irritant. They were ingeniously crafted by oil sheikhs out of an agenda of coercing Americans to believe that their huge Cold War advantage over the Soviet Union, a boisterous consumer sector, could dissipate if they kept supporting the Jewish state. Nobody in America bought into this agenda, however. The potential hasbara crisis was avoided.

Israeli diplomacy in the mid-1970s was crafted by Prime Minister Yitzhak Rabin. Rabin had won accolades as chief of staff of Israel's army during the Six-Day War. He understood America's sociopolitical realities thanks to his term as Israel's ambassador in Washington after that 1967 conflict, and before the Yom Kippur War crisis. Rabin's first round as Israel's prime minister in the mid-1970s was far from a huge success. But unlike his Likud successors, from Begin to Netanyahu today, Rabin understood that settlement expansion in the post-1967 occupied territories was a cancerous affliction to the spirit and rationale of the Israel-US special relationship; he judiciously managed the land for peace formula by withdrawing IDF troops from part of the Sinai Peninsula, thereby setting the stage for Sadat's peace initiative a few years later at the end of the 1970s.

Israel was never a saintly democracy before 1982. For instance, its 1956 Sinai War was hardly a "no choice" (*ein breira*) defensive measure, though Labor Zionist spinmeisters in David Ben-Gurion's government got many to believe that it was. But Israel never faced a genuine public relations crisis because its Labor Party governments were mostly willing to abide by liberal-spirited rules of international diplomacy.[64] This was either because they genuinely believed in these rules (as seems to be the case with prime ministers like Moshe Sharett, Levi Eshkol, and also Rabin, certainly with regard to his second, early 1990s, term that ended in his assassination) or because they were crafty, capable politicians who understood how Israel's long-term interests would be served by heeding those rules, even though they themselves had little patience for Western liberal attitudes toward the Jewish state, believing that they often camouflaged anti-Semitism (David Ben-Gurion and Golda Meir fit this mold; Shimon Peres is unusual in that he fits both of the categories mentioned here).

Most significantly, Labor Zionism's attitude toward settlements in the post-1967 territories was never broadly enthusiastic. Following some early fumbling after the 1973 war, a tumultuous period when the first iteration of the settlement movement, Gush Emunim, swung into motion, most Labor politicians identified as opponents of the settlement movement.[65] Likud, which has by and large held power in Israel since Begin's 1977 election, changed this situation. The party's wholesale support for the settlements set Israel on a collision course with liberal world opinion. The accident that was waiting to happen occurred five years after Begin's first electoral victory, and the crash scene, from a public relations standpoint, was on millions of television screens where the IDF's 1982 siege on Beirut was broadcast, from mid-June 1982 to August 21, 1982.

When they forge alliances, Americans are more agreeable toward partners who fight fairly than they are toward partners who fight strategically. That is the reason why the pro-Israel hasbara lobby had to kick into high gear after the Beirut siege controversy in 1982 and then, with renewed vigor, after the eruption of the First Intifada Palestinian uprising in the occupied territories in late 1987. At such moments, Americans were

64. Some recent scholarship, focused on the Eisenhower pre-1967 Six-Day War period, has given this long-accepted claim some pushback, particularly with regard to a brutal IDF reprisal raid at Qibya in 1953. Aridan, *Advocating for Israel*, 135–64; Hixson, *Israel's Armor*, 90–101.

65. Gorenberg, *Accidental Empire*.

confronted with disturbing evidence of Israeli bullying behavior. In such times, the public relations branch of the pro-Israel establishment had to devise new explanatory approaches that extenuated the bombardment of a major Middle East city, Beirut, as well as the incarceration of stone-throwing Palestinian youths in the Intifada. Most importantly, it was incumbent upon these hasbara spinmeisters to persuade the American public that the violent excesses of the Israel-Arab conflict (no matter who is to blame for them) are not really connected to the profound spiritual and moral forces that bind Israel and the United States in a special relationship.

In contrast, the demise of the Cold War at the end of the 1980s did not create such pressures, even though decades of pro-Israel lobbying had stressed how the Jewish state was a Free World democratic stronghold in the Middle East, which staved off Communist domination in the region. From the standpoint of mainstream America, how strategic considerations are recalibrated in keeping with changing global circumstances is a policy matter for the experts, whereas nightly television images (or, in today's climate, constant social media chatter) portraying an ally as a nasty bully is a punch in the gut.

This is the background to the hasbara paradigm shift after the 1982 Lebanon War controversy. Its promoters understood that what had brought the IDF to besiege Beirut was rather more complicated than the monochromatic portrait drawn by the anti-Israel blame throwers, just as pro-Israel activists today know that what brought about the 2023–2024 Gaza crisis was much more complicated than the monochromatic portrait of genocidal Israeli colonialism depicted by the anti-Zionists in social media and in college campus protests. These two cases are separated by forty years, but the problem is the same. Then, as in the situation today, pro-Israel advocates had no choice other than to acknowledge that the strong ("special") relationship between the United States and the Jewish state, whose strategic dimensions cannot be squandered if Israel is to survive, could not be sustained under existing hasbara rules of explanation.

Nobody knows what will happen regarding this second, contemporary, hasbara dilemma, but we are following in this section and the next one how the first, Reagan era, challenges bred a new myth, the concept of Judeo-Christian civilization. Later sections in this essay will discuss how the myth's circulation in the Israel lobbying context and beyond it is both a symptom and a cause of a perilous information crisis that has led to this current moment, when America seems poised to reelect an unconscionable liar as president.

The Multipurpose Theory of American Democracy's Hebraic Roots

After its hesitant, bland debut in the 1950s, the myth of Judeo-Christian civilization circulated powerfully after the mid-1980s because it was harnessed to a pro-Israel lobbying agenda, unlike the earlier case of Herberg's *Protestant-Catholic-Jew*. The myth's reincarnation transpired in 1983 in a smartly argued book, *Israel in the Mind of America*, authored by Peter Grose.[66] The son of a history professor, Grose had worked for years as a foreign correspondent for *The New York Times*, delivering copy from hot spots like Saigon and Moscow and winning praise as a "quiet, calm, judicious" journalist cut in the cloth of *The New York Times* professionalism of this era. Some five years before he produced his book about Judeo-Christian civilization and pro-Zionist outlooks in America, Grose quit journalism and cultivated strong ties in the country's foreign policy establishment. He served for a stint at the State Department under Secretary of State Cyrus Vance during the Carter administration, before moving on to the Council on Foreign Relations (after the release of his 1983 book, he served as managing editor and executive editor of the *Foreign Affairs* journal for a decade).[67]

The fact that such a prestigious figure gave this pro-Israel version of the Judeo-Christian civilization idea its initial push was significant. It would not have gained traction had respected yet lower-ranking figures shouldered the theory in the immediate aftermath of the 1982 Lebanon War crisis. This supposition is supported by the story of Moshe Davis, a Conservative rabbi, Jewish communal activist, and knowledgeable historian of American Judaism who gained an academic position at the Hebrew University of Jerusalem and had a key role in the establishment of its Institute of Contemporary Jewry. From the late 1970s, Davis sponsored and edited a series of volumes, called *With Eyes Toward Zion*, which promulgated most of the propositions that appear in Grose's volume;[68] but the series lacked the foreign policy gravitas that was wrapped up within the covers of *Israel in the Mind of America*, and it was much less influential. Grose, it bears mention, was well aware of documentary material collected in the *With Eyes* project, and he opened the footnote sources section of *Israel in the Mind of America* with praise for Moshe Davis, as "a man of immense energy."[69]

---

66. Grose, *Israel*.
67. Biographical information drawn from Risen, "Peter Grose."
68. Davis, *Scholars Colloquium*; Davis, *Themes and Sources*.
69. Grose, *Israel*, 319.

"Liking it or not, Americans who are willing to look see something of themselves in Israel," proclaimed Grose at the end of his book. "As the Judaic heritage flowed through the minds of America's early settlers and helped to shape the American republic, so Israel restored adopted the vision and values of the American dream. Each, the United States and Israel, grafted the heritage of the other onto itself."[70] As expounded by Grose, and subsequently elaborated in volumes produced by academics like Shalom Goldman, and also by publicists like Michael Oren who were connected to the Israel-American Jewish foreign policy elite, the Judeo-Christian heritage theory insists that Old Testament, Hebraic influences heavily shaped the development of America's democracy.[71] Puritan founders of the pre-1776 colonies typically viewed themselves as Protestant versions of the biblical Israelite exodus narrative of liberation from slavery and national restoration in a promised land. This Hebraic influence permeated well beyond the Puritans, whose religious zeal tends to confuse secularized contemporary Americans.

More than is realized today, a mid-eighteenth-century education for a proper gentleman often included familiarity with Jewish Scripture and the Hebrew language. For this reason, the founders of American democracy attired, or tried to attire, the new country in Hebraic symbols and concepts. A favorite example in this connection, which is rehashed at the start of Grose's book, is Benjamin Franklin's proposal at the 1776 Continental Congress for a Great Seal picturing Moses lifting his wand to divide the Red Sea, while waters wash over the pharaoh in his chariot.[72] A similar, intellectually more interesting, example is the Yale insignia: the Hebrew words "Urim Ve-Thummim," which was interpreted by the university's founders as meaning the "Christian Truth"—the insignia brands Judeo-Christian interaction in a cornerstone institution of American culture.[73]

Yale furnishes more evidence for this Hebraic America theory. In a 2004 volume, *God's Sacred Tongue: Hebrew and the American Imagination*, which is a scholarly brushup of Grose's theories but also a similarly engaging, readable book, Goldman elaborates on the career of Ezra Stiles, a Congregationalist theologian and early president (1778–1795) at Yale College, depicting it as a stellar example of Hebraic philosemitism in the new country's evolving democratic culture. Among many other Old Testament–inflected episodes in Stiles's term at Yale, he wrote the college's 1778

---

70. Grose, *Israel*, 316.
71. Goldman, *God's Sacred Tongue*; Oren, *Power, Faith and Fantasy*.
72. Grose, *Israel*, 5.
73. Goldman, *God's Sacred Tongue*, 13–14.

inaugural address in Hebrew, a language he had been studying in earnest for the preceding decade.[74]

Writers in this Judeo-Christian heritage school furnish a long roster of examples along these lines, and they need not be rehearsed here. The most famous, or notorious, example is a map project sponsored by Davis in the *With Eyes Toward Zion* framework. The maps delineate how place names in New England and elsewhere in America often draw from biblical sites and episodes, and from Hebrew.[75] In the pro-Israel lobbying world, Davis's Hebraic map matches Edmund Burke's aesthetic criteria of the sublime. The map might not strike skeptical gentiles as being very pretty, and it may never have propelled a single one of them toward pro-Israel conversion, but it is nonetheless a striking visual testimony to industrious pro-Israel advocacy. At the very least, it helped my Israeli children feel at home during summer visits to New England ("Salem," well now that's "shalom," probably an abbreviation for "Jerusalem," I would tell them, before they asked about when we could stop for pizza).

Much can be said in favor of the Davis-Grose Judeo-Christian paradigm. To this day, it serves as one of two broad frames within which American-Israel interaction is understood. When people say that Congress traditionally supports Israel for cultural reasons, or that Bill Clinton and Joe Biden displayed visceral sympathy for Israel, they basically mean that Americans have a philosemitic, positive disposition toward the Jewish state. This disposition, in turn, is rooted in Sunday school instruction or church sermons where the Israelite Old Testament is revered as an element of America's spiritual-moral tradition, complementing the New Testament's revelations about Jesus' messianic coming. Starting with the popularity of nineteenth-century enthusiasts who advocated Jewish national restoration (these zealots included an American Jew in the Jacksonian period, Mordecai Noah, and a Christian evangelist later in the century, William Blackstone; you can find information about such figures in Grose's book, and others written in its spirit), there is a wealth of evidence indicating that what developed into the Zionist program has always won grassroots support among "ordinary" Americans. Crunch time displays of American support for the Zionist program—from the 1922 Lodge-Fish Resolution in both houses on Capitol Hill in favor of the British Mandate in Palestine, through America's immediate recognition of Ben-Gurion's Jewish statehood declaration in May 1948, and continuing with American support in material, political,

---

74. Goldman, *God's Sacred Tongue*, 56–73.

75. Davis, *America*. For an example of such a map, apparently crafted for early education purposes, see Davis and Davis, *Land of Our Fathers*.

and other senses for Israel during a series of wartime crises through the present one, on the Gaza Strip—could never be explained were it not for a widespread cultural disposition in the United States favorable to Jewish nationalism, and its ambitions in the Jews' biblical homeland.

Moreover, the other broad frame through which US-Israel relations are viewed, one which stresses the pro-Israel "Jewish lobby" (largely the AIPAC organization) and its use of noncultural tactics such as campaign donations for pro-Israel candidates, is not diametrically opposed to the Judeo-Christian cultural model. This point is worth stressing because the corrosive rhetoric used by scholars who deploy this "lobby" paradigm, such as John Mearsheimer and Stephen Walt in their 2007 book *The Israel Lobby*, has a zero-sum, "it's our theory or theirs," feel.[76] Philanthropic muscle and campaign donations go very far in American politics, but there still appear to be limits to their power. Were politicians not aware that pro-Israel politics enjoy support among constituents, they would not always open the door to lobbyists. That might sound naïve—after all, gun control is popular with a majority of Americans, but policy in its spirit is stifled by a lobby group, the NRA. But the important point is that the "cultural" explanation, implying that many Americans know something about the Bible and associate it with support for Israeli security and its democracy, is always lurking around in any analysis of US-Israel interaction, even in the case of scholars and other commentators who are critical of the relationship between the two countries and who believe that it is sustained undemocratically by brute power politics. That is, the "cultural" model is usually correct, to some extent.

Generally, when people think about and discuss Israel and the Middle East, they have little patience for the analytic Manicheanism of scholars who believe that the US-Israel relationship is either the product of lobbyists' special pleading and pressure tactics or that it expresses philosemitic affection for the Jewish state grounded in the Bible education of many Americans. Lots of stuff gets packed into pro and con discussions of Israel—the Holocaust, impressions stirred by the latest Netflix series about the Mossad, Gigi Hadid or Gal Gadot, images of Palestinian suffering on the Gaza Strip or of kidnapped Israelis in Gaza—and staples of the two paradigms we have mentioned, Biblical Hebraism on the Davis-Grose model and campaign donations on the Mearsheimer-Walt model, are not always prominent parts of the mix.

All that said, the argumentation popularized by Peter Grose is deeply flawed, and its perpetuation in the twenty-first century, a period shadowed by the crushing disappointment of the failure of the 1990s Oslo peace

---

76. Mearsheimer and Walt, *Israel Lobby*.

process, is causing more problems than it solves. Grose took his cue from Moshe Davis, who as a scholar was expertly informed about how American Jews have experimented with various apologetic and public relations strategies since the community's birth in North America in the middle of the seventeenth century. These two figures, Grose and Davis, essentially grafted one apologetic rhetoric upon another and ended up with a dubiously multipurpose concept of Hebraic America.

For as long as Jews have seriously researched their history in North America, they have commented upon how Hebraic, Old Testament influences permeated through the political culture of the thirteen colonies and then in the early republic. Oscar Straus, the first president of the American Jewish Historical Society (which was founded in 1892), researched and wrote about Old Testament imagery and influences among Puritan leaders, and also in election day sermons and other aspects of the public culture of the colonies. Straus, whose family made a fortune from Macy's and who became the first American Jew to become a cabinet secretary (under Theodore Roosevelt), peddled this idea about Hebraic influences on the evolution of American democracy in an 1885 publication entitled *The Origin of the Republican Form of Government in the United States of America*.[77] This was a century before Peter Grose. The idea never really gained currency among scholars of America's founding documents and experiences—in years before Straus's 1926 death, prominent American historians like Carl Becker were busily tracing the roots of the Declaration of Independence to natural rights doctrines developed by gentile thinkers on the continent (neither the Old Testament nor any other Jewish referent is cited in Becker's 1922 book on the subject).[78]

Nonetheless, the notion that America's democracy grew out of Old Testament sources cast a long spell over American Jews of various persuasions. One example is Milton Konvitz, a Safed-born rabbi's son who became a constitutional and labor law professor at Cornell University. Konvitz expounded on this theory in a 1978 book, *Judaism and the American Idea*.[79] Writing five years before Grose, Konvitz's agenda was to carve out a prestigious intellectual-cultural place for American Jews in the period of the Bicentennial celebrations. Other American Jews used this concept of Hebraic contributions and components in American democracy for a variety of purposes. For example, under Straus's tutelage, research and writing at the new American Jewish Historical Society was first undertaken in the

77. Straus, *Origin of the Republican Form*.
78. Becker, *Declaration of Independence*.
79. Konvitz, *Judaism*.

1890s, a period when the mass influx of Jewish immigrants from Eastern Europe was causing backlash. At this time, restriction-minded nativists publicly aired anti-Semitic innuendo about how Jewish newcomers were supposedly unfit to contribute as citizens to a democracy. In such a setting, self-appointed Jewish stewards like Straus had strong incentive to develop arguments implying that America's democracy itself was an outgrowth of ancient Israelite culture.

When the same idea is put to several different argumentative purposes, it is likely to be stretched to the breaking point.

As it happened, Grose and his epigoni never really explained why Americans whose democratic outlooks drew from Hebraic sources would necessarily endorse Zionism's political project of bringing Jews back to the biblical homeland. The evidence they marshaled on this point seemed static. Grose, for example, lavished nine pages on the story of Mordecai Noah (1785–1851), leaning heavily on a soon-to-be published manuscript version of Jonathan Sarna's important biography of Noah.[80] Noah's schemes for Jewish national restoration, not just in the biblical Holy Land, attracted attention in the Jacksonian period of democratic ferment, but this response was largely the result of the evangelical temper of the Second Great Awakening. Noah's story thus attests to the popularity of adventurous Jewish ideas in a period of religious revival. It is hard to determine what exactly Noah's proto-Zionist, Hebraic example has to do with the popularity of Zionism in later phases of America's democracy, such as the secularized Roaring Twenties (when early stirrings of the Arab-Jewish conflict, in riots that occurred at the end of the decade, posed challenges utterly unlike anything Noah's audience a century earlier could have imagined).

Plenty of Americans whose youthful education was, like that of Ezra Stiles, immersed in the Old Testament displayed tepid or antagonistic attitudes toward nineteenth-century, messianic-tempered Jewish restoration ideas, or toward the much more politicized twentieth-century variant, Zionism. In fact, many such Americans were Jewish, and several of these Jews were ordained rabbis in American Judaism's progressive streams. Moshe Davis, whose most important scholarly work addressed the rise of Conservative Judaism, was cognizant of these facts, which comprise the Achilles' heel in the transplant of the Hebraic America theory in the pro-Israel hasbara context.[81]

I admired Professor Davis, who was the first American Jew to submit a doctoral dissertation at the Hebrew University of Jerusalem, but I have never

---

80. Grose, *Israel*, 13–22; Sarna, *Jacksonian Jew*.
81. Davis, *Emergence*.

been a fan of this variant of Judeo-Christian civilization theory. He was an elderly man, his impresario traits mostly cocooned, when I was summoned to his Jerusalem apartment when I was starting off as a doctoral student at the same university. At his own initiative, Professor Davis explained to me that the *With Eyes Toward Zion* series had hasbara intents. The comment honorably reflected an aging man's Jewish idealism, however problematic it might have been from an academic standpoint—I ignored it and wrote my dissertation in a different key.

Jewish public relations apologetics come with their own shelf life. They can backfire when they are used after their expiration date. I remember trying to garner a sense of Professor Davis's perspective on this point. For instance, as we noticed in the previous essay, depicting Puritans as Protestant Hebrews is not necessarily "good for the Jews"—in his attack on Max Weber's thesis about the capitalist spirit, Werner Sombart used this view of Puritans to reinforce his own stereotypical ideas about the Jews' supposed hyped-up involvement in capital accumulation. What exactly is the point of mapping Hebraic place names in New England? I explained to Professor Davis that I had family in a Washington, DC, suburb where street names were named after Native Americans, but nobody ever imagined that this attested to healthy symbiosis between American democracy and Native American culture. The comment was rude and drew no response.

In the early 1980s, when Peter Grose wrote his book, he would not have expected serious pushback after he applied findings about Hebraic influences in the 1776 revolutionary era to controversies about America's support for the Jewish state, a few years before the 1987 intifada. Despite the public relations and moral setbacks of the First Lebanon War, Israel was still widely thought of as a nation of immigrants which nursed a growing, vibrant democracy, essentially as a later, miniature version of the United States. The syllogism—the birth of America's democracy owes something to the Old Testament; both America and Israel are Free World democracies; Americans are culturally disposed to act as pro-Israel philosemites—has many holes in it, but they would not have seemed so gaping at the time when Grose repackaged the Judeo-Christian thesis for hasbara purposes. He cannot be blamed for the fact that subsequent illiberal developments in Israel, first and foremost the expanding presence and powers of the settlement movement, rendered aspects of his theory outdated.

The blemish in his theory is not its failure to foresee the future. Instead, its defect is that it is not inherently liberal, despite the optimistic hues of its presentation and its rhetoric about democratic symbiosis between America and the Jewish state. The revival of the Judeo-Christian theory for Zionist hasbara purposes in the Reagan era stressed the *religious* roots of American appreciation of the Jewish state. There are many, and they are important topics of discussions for historians. For instance, cued by the Davis-Grose theory about how Bible-loving Americans are often drawn toward Zionism, scholars like Yaakov Ariel produced important studies of fervent American Evangelical support for the Jewish state.[82]

In political lobbying and in philanthropy, Evangelicals operate as Christian Zionists, their efforts sometimes outmatching those of Jewish pro-Israel groups. However, these Fundamentalist Christians are a profoundly illiberal element in the America-Israel nexus that reformatted after the 1967 Six-Day War. The Evangelical vision of the modern state whereby more religion suffuses the public square, with some spaces in that square allotted for faiths other than Christianity, had appeal to many Jewish neoconservatives and moderate liberals during the Reagan years, and after them. But they are at variance with the classic idea of church-state separation, which has been upheld by generations of Jewish liberals and gentile liberals in America. And Evangelical positions on specific topics like LGBTQ, abortion, and Islam are repugnant to liberals, Jews, and others.

Evangelical Christian Zionism exemplifies how the religious roots of American sympathy for Jewish nationalism in the biblical homeland can generate a mass ferment of activity that is not necessarily supportive of liberal democracy. In fact, a strong argument can be made holding that the Evangelicals, who support Jewish settlement expansion on the West Bank and whose ideas about rapture and messianic dispensation seem to be predicated upon the outbreak of apocalyptic war in Jerusalem and elsewhere in the Middle East, have given Israel a push in a theocratic, militant, and antidemocratic direction. Quite confusingly, Grose's book and other studies published under its theoretical aegis present the America-Israel relationship as a liberal democratic progression whereby the Jews helped bring democracy to America in 1776 and Americans have helped bring democracy to the Jewish state after 1948. This premise was not wholly true when Grose published his book; thanks to the Evangelicals and many other factors, it has been dramatically undermined in the twenty-first century.

This can be seen as melancholy vindication for my lousy behavior during my dinner with Professor Davis. Hasbara has a shelf life, and it can be toxic when applied after its expiration date.

Belatedly, pro-Israel writers who work with avowed or semi-avowed hasbara intents have acknowledged this truth. In the past decade, they have produced works that reverse the premise of the Grose-Davis school, arguing that Israel was founded on a nation-state model designed to prioritize

---

82. Ariel, *Unusual Relationship*.

the rights of a particular group (the Jews), whereas America's universalist paradigm of a state for all its citizens is dissimilar in design and execution. Daniel Gordis's 2019 volume, *We Stand Divided: The Rift Between American Jews and Israel*, is a good example of such argumentation.[83] Its approach can be commended for candor; but such books will seem unsatisfying to liberals in America, Jews and gentiles, who are wondering whether taxpayer money ought to support state systems which do not treat all their citizens equally and fairly, and who view locution such as "preferential democracy" as being oxymoronic, at least insofar as the preferences are going to a state's empowered majority. All the snap, crackle, and pop in Gordis's smartly marketed booklet goes off with the purpose of calming American Jews who are worried about how Israel seems to be increasingly illiberal and discriminatory toward its Palestinian citizens who live within the pre-1967 Green Line (the author deliberately downplays what happens to Palestinians who are under occupation on the West Bank). In fact, as demonstrated by the eruption of anti-Zionist campus protests four years later, liberal Jews in Gordis's audience had lots to worry about. Worse than their misbegotten neoconservative political agenda, publications like Gordis's 2019 volume commit intellectual and spiritual injustice, unjustifiably narrowing the tense complexity of Judeo-Christian interaction. They overturn premises of the Judeo-Christian civilization model developed by figures like Moshe Davis and Peter Grose, but they retain its parochialism. Even when it is stood upside down by pro-Israel apologists like Gordis, the model is an outrageous exercise in Jewish narcissism and Jewish hubris.

When distinguished American historians like David Hollinger complain that they simply cannot take Jewish studies writing very seriously, they are undoubtedly thinking about works written with conspicuous public relations agendas, such as ones shaped around the American Hebraism concept we have been following.[84] Such works comically overrate Jewish involvement in history. With regard to our topic of experiences in the biblical Holy Land and their legacy in a possible Judeo-Christian civilization, a non-parochial methodology might have much to reveal about how Americans in different periods have thought about sources of their morality, about history in general, and about whether truth is absolute or relativized and reducible to facts and alternative facts. What we desperately need, in short, is a method that will help us figure out whether contemporary American schmegegge is preordained in the Bible.

83. Gordis, *We Stand Divided*.
84. Hollinger, "Communalist and Dispersionist."

In lieu of contributing to such a discussion, Jewish and other pro-Israel scholars and commentators have bowdlerized surveys of the Holy Land's past, researching and writing as though the only evidentiary matter that can be brought up for consideration is what suits pro-Israel lobbying. They have written at length about Americans and the Holy Land without mentioning Jesus Christ. They have written at length about American democracy and the Hebraic Old Testament while ignoring the topic of American democracy and the Christian New Testament. They have written at length about Jerusalem and said nothing about Galilee. They have written about Judeo-Christian civilization as though it is Judaic and not also Christian.

We return now to Galilee and to how nineteenth-century Americans related to the region. Our hypothesis is that the static, worshipful attitude they displayed toward the Holy Land, an orientation that has been called the "fifth Gospel," represents a significant phase in American thinking about history and truth. This reverential attitude toward history was overturned by the pressure of secular forces in the twentieth century. By the twenty-first century, Americans reversed the view of history inculcated in the fifth Gospel: rather than surrendering themselves to history in the Holy Land region where it was frozen and sacred, they insisted that history surrender itself to their own contemporary, politically correct sensibilities.

THE FIFTH GOSPEL

In the United States, campus protests against the 2023–2024 Gaza War, and other contemporary debates about Israeli and Palestinian affairs, are an outgrowth of prolonged American interest in the historic "Holy Land" region, throughout its successive Ottoman, British, and Israeli periods. This fascination found new, palpable forms of expression in the mid-nineteenth century owing to technological advances such as steamship travel, political stabilization in the Middle East following the Crimean War (1853–1856), and post–Civil War economic reconsolidation in America leading to Gilded Age prosperity.[85]

For well-placed Americans, travel to Ottoman Palestine became an alluring possibility in this era. Viewers of Steven Spielberg's film *Lincoln* will remember its late scene in which the president expresses a desire to make a Holy Land tour, and some scholars believe that Lincoln really staged such a conversation shortly before his April 1865 assassination (and two of his Union comrades, Ulysses S. Grant and William Seward,

---

85. Vogel, *To See*.

later toured Ottoman Palestine).⁸⁶ In this postbellum period, one scholar notes, "middle-class lay people in increasing numbers, as well as wealthier public figures such as politicians, generals and authors, made pilgrimages to Palestine that would have previously been impossible."⁸⁷ For Americans who lacked the wherewithal to make the journey, new visual representation technologies facilitated what we would today call "virtual" tours of late Ottoman Palestine. For example, using a high-tech dual lens camera called a "stereoscope," the photograph imagery firm Underwood and Underwood offered one such virtual tour in 1914.⁸⁸ Also, conventional Holy Land travel books flourished in America's publication scene—some five hundred Holy Land pilgrimage travel books were published in the United States between the 1840s and the interwar period of the 1920s and 1930s.⁸⁹

What scholars have described as "Holy Land mania" in America from the 1840s through the 1920s has been analyzed from various standpoints, including tourism, missionary activity, and visual arts. For our purposes, however, the trend's theological foundations bear emphasis because they reflect a phase in America's orientation toward the past, and toward truth. The surge of Holy Land interest in the 1840s-1920s was underpinned by a readily identifiable religious ideology, Protestantism's "fifth Gospel."

The term fifth Gospel, implying that Holy Land travel reports are meaningful testimonials, a kind of fifth Gospel supplement to the New Testament's four Gospels, circulated early in postbellum writing when steamship travel made Ottoman Palestine much more accessible to American Christians. For instance, the term can be found in one of the early memoirs, published in 1878, discussed later in this section.⁹⁰

Fifth Gospel ideology constituted an accepted norm in American religion through the Civil War and Gilded Age eras.⁹¹ In the colonial and early Republic periods (through the Second Great Awakening), a Hebraic emphasis weighed on the way Americans thought about the Bible and the land it came from, as aforementioned authors (Davis, Grose, Goldman, Oren) have discussed at length. In contrast, a New Testament approach consolidated as early as the 1830s and dominated discursive and travel practices regarding "the Land and the Book" (as W. M. Thomson called

---

86. Vogel, *To See*, 41.
87. Rogers, *Inventing*, 21–22.
88. Hurlblut and Kent, *Palestine*.
89. Rogers, *Inventing*, 7.
90. Schaff, *Through Bible Lands*, 14–15.
91. Silver, *Galilee, 1538–1949*, 221–22.

it[92]) through the 1920s. By the start of the postbellum 1870s, the central components of the fifth Gospel's creed hinged tightly together. They were (a) atemporality,[93] (b) the outdoors' spiritual frontier, and (c) a sense of presence. Formulated less concisely, these tenets were that (a) the Holy Land is a timeless museum whose ancient truths are preserved in the daily practices of its current population; (b) religion is an outdoor phenomenon; and (c) neither in textual exegesis nor in pilgrimage tour is fundamentalist fastidiousness about the meaning of particular words or the designation of specific sites desirable, and the fifth Gospel's purpose is to afford a modern Christian a "sense of presence" in the Holy Land, bringing him or her closer to Jesus.

W. M. Thomson's *The Land and the Book* is the premier antebellum exemplar of American Protestantism's fifth Gospel movement.[94] Thomson based his 1858 book on a tour undertaken in the Holy Land, starting from Lebanon in the north, a year earlier; his exploration's itinerary attests to its investment in the New Testament narrative. *The Land and the Book*, by far the most impactful of some five hundred Holy Land pilgrimage books published in North America between the 1840s and the 1930s, devotes roughly five hundred out of seven hundred of its pages to the country's northern regions.

Thomson, the son of a Presbyterian minister, came from Ohio and graduated from Miami University in that state. Thomson became a missionary in the Middle East, hanging his shingle in Lebanon, where he founded a boys school in Beirut in 1835. His experience in the region won recognition and respect and boosted the credibility and authority of *The Land and the Book*, a text with numerous illustrative drawings that was deliberately designed for a wide readership. Several times, the narrator offhandedly informed his readers that this was his twentieth visit to a particular locale. *The Land and the Book* became a publishing event, reaching sales figures in England unmatched by any American book other than *Uncle Tom's Cabin*

---

92. Thomson, *Land*.

93. Readers may notice similarity between what is identified here as "atemporality" and phenomena analyzed as "orientalism" by Edward Said (Said, *Orientalism*). Fifth Gospel approaches denied historical agency to Middle East inhabitants, in keeping with Hegelian and other European ideological prejudices toward the "east"; and Said's persuasive association of these ideologies with nineteenth-century colonialism has been hugely influential. Yet in the context of American Protestantism's evolution, the fifth Gospel's pragmatic orientation in holy space is most readily associated with the religion's liberal branches—it is the antithetical, fundamentalist approach of the Evangelicals that can be associated with Israeli settlement colonialism on post-1967 territories.

94. Thomson, *Land*.

and going through thirty editions while in print well into the twentieth century. In America, the book remained familiar for decades as a Sunday school prize.[95]

The fifth Gospel was a theology of outdoor travel. "A large part of these pages was actually written in the open country, on sea shore or sacred lake, on hill side or mountain top," Thomson explained. "That blessed Book," he added, referring especially to the New Testament, "wears the same air of country life; and He who came from heaven to earth for man's redemption loved not the city." In the volume's most enthused and exhortative passage, describing the author's entry into the Galilee region from Acre on the coast, Thomson reiterates, "The Bible is not a city book." Christianity's messages are best fathomed in open-air locales where Jesus preached and worked miracles: "He who would bring his spirit most happily into communion with this divine Teacher must follow him afield, must sit on the mountain side and hear him preach ... must walk with him from village to village."[96]

The fifth Gospel bequeathed to its practitioners, Holy Land pilgrims in Galilee's open spaces, enhanced insight about biblical texts and also about nature itself. As Thomson explained, "The divine Architect constructed this country after a model, infolding in itself, unfolding to the world." The Holy Land's features "are still preserved unchanged, to teach the same great truths to every successive generation."[97]

Thomson's text brims with acerbic comments. In them, the chatty author explains to readers why sleeping in tents is preferable to accepting hospitality in flea-ridden, malodorous Arab homes. Yet, beholden to the fifth Gospel theory of atemporality, Thomson, like other American Protestants in this era, could not roundly condemn the Holy Land's indigenous peoples since they were believed to preserve facets of society relevant to Jesus' era and to Hebraic periods before it.

Being a missionary, the author was invested in saving the souls of indigenous peoples whose behavior and life patterns he vehemently upbraided. Owing to Ottoman Palestine's legal and sociopolitical circumstances, this conversionist motivation was mostly stifled (three or four years after the publication of *The Land and the Book*, Thomson initiated a process that culminated in the American mission's most serious organizational achievement in the region, the establishment of the American University of Beirut, originally called the Syrian Protestant College[98]). The Ohio native's

---

95. Davis, *Landscape*, 45; Vogel, *To See*, 105.
96. Thomson, *Land*, 327.
97. Thomson, *Land*, 340–41.
98. Anderson, *American University*, 3–6; Dodge, *American University*, 12.

antagonism toward Muslims was sometimes slightly restrained in descriptions of agriculturally settled fellaheen.

After a quarter century in the Middle East, Thomson's knowledge of contemporary Arab affairs was unusual, certainly by American standards. Thomson sometimes did not share with readers the products of energetic anthropological-demographic investigations of Muslim society he carried out over the years. In Upper Galilee's Huleh valley, for instance, he refers to how he had compiled a list of thirty-two Arab villages but does not share their names. In a more agreeable mood, he sometimes allowed his writing to diverge from its Bible-centrism; so *The Land and the Book* includes interesting details about Shiite Arabs in today's Upper Galilee in Israel and Lebanon (called *Metawelies* by Thomson), and Syrian Alawites (*Nusairieh*), who responded cagily to the American's attempt to measure their connection to Christianity.[99]

Throughout his book, Thomson vituperated furiously about Bedouins, referring to their proclivity for plunder and murder and detailing incidents where his party survived only because Thomson had previously bribed local sheikhs to furnish them protection. Thomson rebuked earlier Holy Land travelers like the Swiss Johann Ludwig Burckhardt for having soft-pedaled reports about Bedouins in their books. Beyond the view of Bedouins as a terror threat to travelers, Thomson condemned local Bedouin culture as a whole. The men "tyrannize over women" while they "lounge idly and lazily about the tent, smoke, drink coffee and play games of hazard." They are "execrably filthy and foul-mouthed, totally uneducated and supremely proud."[100]

Such bigotry was voluble, but to stress it here would distract attention away from the fifth Gospel's distinctive mix of empiricism and romanticism and, more generally, from the way the American Christians apprehended the Holy Land just before photography facilitated heightened degrees of realism. Thomson's book, with its multiple illustrations, conveyed considerable documentation about several aspects of Palestine's Arab society, including one extended section devoted to its leisure and hospitality culture, male and female dress, and footwear (this passage consists of seven drawings spread over eight pages).[101] This encyclopedic method was warranted because of the fifth Gospel's belief in the timelessness of the Holy Land. A visitor looking at its contemporary Arabs witnessed sandals and headdress used in the Second Temple period. Nothing had changed in time. The words in the

---

99. Thomson, *Land*, 191–92, 226–27, 253.

100. Thomson, *Land*, 369, 383.

101. Thomson, *Land*, 113–21.

following quotation about apparel apply to the way fifth Gospel witnesses like Thomson looked at everything in the Holy Land, from insects to olive presses: "The ancient Hebrew costume is thought to have resembled, more or less closely, the Oriental dress of our day."[102]

An interesting parallel to the mix of anti-Arab prejudice and romanticism about how Palestine's indigenous people's preserve the spirit and culture of Jesus' time can be found in Mark Twain's famous postbellum travel book, *The Innocents Abroad, or the New Pilgrims' Progress* (1869). Twain, like Thomson, wrote vituperatively about many aspects of Arab culture, as in a passage at Caesarea Philippi where he explodes with disdain: "Would you suppose that an American mother could sit for an hour, with her child in her arms, and let a hundred flies roost upon its eyes all that time undisturbed."[103] On the other hand, it is sometimes forgotten that a stratum of earnest Christian testimonial is laden within the rollicking satire of Twain's record of his group's journeys in Europe and the Middle East. Interestingly, Twain's notoriously irreverent book records the author's epiphany at Caesarea Philippi, the site of Peter's confession and also the place where Twain upbraided the insalubrious filth of the Arab mother and child: "It seems curious enough to us to be standing on ground that was once actually pressed by the feet of the Saviour," Twain reflected. "The situation is suggestive of a reality and a tangibility that seem at variance with the vagueness and mystery and ghostliness that one naturally attaches to the character of a god."[104] In a volume whose plotline stretches between restless, unsophisticated American travelers unable to spend more than two hours at the Paris Exposition, and a Holy Land climax wherein the hard-boiled American capitalists choose to save one Napoleon and thereby never fulfill their trip's paramount objective of sailing on Jesus' Sea of Galilee, this Caesarea Philippi passage is extraordinary. It must have warmed the hearts of Twain's publishers and their colleagues who were investing in the postbellum boom business of Holy Land travel.

In fact, Mark Twain preached the fifth Gospel. His postbellum view of Holy Land atemporality is taken straight out of the pages of Thomson's much more religiously invested antebellum book. Twain wrote that Arabs were the "lineal descendants" of the Israelites. When you visit the Holy Land, Twain testified, "the scenery of the Bible is about you—the same people, in the same flowing robes, and in sandals, cross your path."[105]

102. Thomson, *Land*, 116.
103. Twain, *Innocents*, 473.
104. Twain, *Innocents*, 472.
105. Twain, *Innocents*, 465–67.

Whereas fifth Gospel perspectives sometimes incubated, and are not always fully prominent, in antebellum books like Thomson's, they are conspicuous and virtually canonical in Holy Land travel books published in the Gilded Age and through the 1920s. We can briefly point to fifth Gospel ideology in three representative travel books produced by persons of stature in American Protestantism from the 1870s to the 1920s.

Philip Schaff, a Swiss-born and German-educated theologian who held posts at important American seminaries and gained renown as a church historian, traveled to Palestine in late 1876, following the death of a daughter, and published his *Through Bible Lands* two years later. "Palestine has not inaptly been called the Fifth Gospel," declared Schaff. Jerusalem repelled him as the "most desecrated spot on earth," whereas New Testament locales, particularly Nazareth with its "pleasing appearance," thrilled him.[106] Standing atop a hill close to the small village where Jesus spent his boyhood, Schaff imagined that he was peering at "the future highway of the gospel of peace to all mankind." At this summit, Schaff bore witness to the "astounding" truth: "Jesus of Nazareth is the central miracle of history."[107]

A generation later, in 1908, Henry van Dyke published his tellingly titled *Out-of-Doors in the Holy Land*, an outspoken text that proclaims the main tenets of the fifth Gospel with catechistic explicitness. Born in Pennsylvania a decade before the Civil War, van Dyke was a more Americanized character than Schaff. Before his tent-pitching visit to the Holy Land, van Dyke had been involved in groundbreaking liturgical projects for the Presbyterians; later, in 1913, he received an ambassadorial appointment from Woodrow Wilson. The testimonials in his travel book suggest a kind of supersession travel itinerary by which Galilee's New Testament landscape replaces Old Testament Judea: "It was not here [Jerusalem] that Jesus found the men and women who believed in Him and loved Him, but in the quiet villages, among the green fields, by the peaceful lake-shores." Moving north in late Ottoman Palestine, van Dyke believed that he was leaving behind an Old Testament landscape of war and heading to the New Testament region where peacemakers were blessed ("Going from Samaria into Galilee is like passing from the Old Testament to the New"). Nazareth, van Dyke affirmed, "is distinctly the most attractive little city we have seen in Palestine."[108]

Van Dyke's view from a Nazareth hilltop reprised Schaff's utopian gaze from the same place. "City on a hill" phraseology, of course, has New Testament roots in the Sermon on the Mount (Matt 5:14), but in American

---

106. Schaff, *Through Bible Lands*, 14, 232, 323.
107. Schaff, *Through Bible Lands*, 321.
108. Van Dyke, *Out-of-Doors*, 35, 104.

Protestant history, the phrase is commonly associated with John Winthrop and the Puritans' identification with the Old Testament's exodus and promised land narrative. In the fifth Gospel, American Protestantism's utopian aspirations relocated firmly in the locale of Jesus' sermon and the New Testament narrative. On the Nazareth hilltop, the American pilgrim, van Dyke, imagined that a portal opened to a "spirit world" conducive of communion with Jesus and a devotional state of grace: "On this hilltop," proclaimed van Dyke, the boy Jesus "could watch the creeping caravans of Arabian merchants, and the glittering legions of Roman soldiers, and the slow files of Jewish pilgrims." On this city on a hill, the modern pilgrim might sense what Jesus beheld, "the spirit world, where there is no night, nor weariness, nor sin, nor death."[109]

Third, and finally, a striking example of the fifth Gospel's durability is the presence of its main tenets in a volume published in 1927 by Harry Emerson Fosdick, *A Pilgrimage to Palestine*. Fosdick wrote his Holy Land travel book under quite different circumstances since British Mandatory rule after the Great War had replaced the Ottoman regime. Unlike the two aforementioned Gilded Age visitors, who imagined imperialistically that Turkish-Islamic rule would be swept aside by Christian Europe, Fosdick confronted the post–Balfour Declaration prospect of a third national-religious group, the Jews, turning Palestine into their own national home; he was deeply ambivalent about how Zionist pioneers he observed were laboring to that end.[110] Fosdick, an iconic liberal figure (Martin Luther King Jr. called him the twentieth century's foremost preacher[111]), was in a turbulent phase of his career when he made the trip to Palestine. In response to the outcry caused by his pro-modernist sermon, "Shall the Fundamentalists Win?," he had left his pulpit at the First Presbyterian Church in Manhattan; at the time of his 1927 pilgrimage, Fosdick was reformatting professionally under Baptist auspices.

Such global and personal developments distinguished between this third visit and those of the two predecessors, Schaff and van Dyke, but Fosdick remained wedded to the prevailing frontier ethos of the fifth Gospel. "One impression stands out clearly in Palestine," he declared. "It is only the out-of-doors that matters much. Almost everything that men have put under a roof they have spoiled for the intelligent visitor." To be sure, under conditions of British rule in the country, "conditions as to sanitation are infinitely better," wrote Fosdick; but he nonetheless avoided built-up areas.

109. Van Dyke, *Out-of-Doors*, 116.
110. Robins, "Cultural Zionism"; Fosdick, *Living*, 86–87.
111. Lupfer, "100 Years Later."

The fifth Gospel penchant for pitching tents and climbing hills held strong. "Nothing in Palestine under a roof is much worth seeing and nothing in Palestine out of doors is not worth seeing," Fosdick concluded, his epigram attesting to a century of frontier spirit in American religion and to its experiential, fifth Gospel, Holy Land orientation.[112]

In Fosdick's outlook, the ravages of World War I drained American Protestantism of any pro-Hebraic strains that might have lingered from the Puritan era. As far as he was concerned, the bellicose Hebrew God belonged morally to another, uncivilized era: "The Hebrews, with their tribal god who stood for them against all others and backed them up in any assault and battery upon another folk, shared the current theology of all ancient nations."[113] In truth, beholden to the fifth Gospel's atemporal view of the Holy Land, Fosdick believed that all the country's landscapes, those known from the Old Testament and also Galilean stretches familiar in the New Testament drama of Jesus, were nonmodern, out of time. The bellicosity he found in the Old Testament repulsed him, whereas he identified with the Sermon on the Mount's endorsement of peacemakers; but everywhere, in its Hebraic and Jesus-related parts, the landscape was primitive and unchanging. In Nazareth, after the First World War, the progressive Fosdick attested to Holy Land atemporality exactly as the missionary Thomson had paid witness to it a few years before the Civil War. "So little have village houses changed that many a residence in Nazareth would remind him [Jesus] of the home he lived in," reflected Fosdick. "Many a custom and conversation" in contemporary Nazareth," he added, "would be familiar to the returning Jesus now."[114]

How can we account for the fact that American Protestantism's theologically cohesive approach to the Holy Land, the fifth Gospel, reached its peak during the Gilded Age, a period notorious in American history for venal corruption, when robber barons like Andrew Carnegie co-opted religious terminology and when the sermons of prominent preachers like Henry Ward Beecher were suspected of snuggling complacently with the interests of their churches' wealthy patrons?[115] In fact, the careers of the most ethically scrupulous characters referenced in a discussion of the fifth Gospel depended on the largesse and legacy of the big business trusts—an example is John D. Rockefeller Jr. spreading a safety net for Harry Emerson

---

112. Fosdick, *Pilgrimage*, 19, 99, 20.
113. Fosdick, *Pilgrimage*, 79.
114. Fosdick, *Pilgrimage*, 80.
115. Marty, *Righteous Empire*, 166–76.

Fosdick at the Park Avenue Baptist Church when the minister faced professional turmoil in the mid-1920s.[116]

The fifth Gospel worshiped at the Gilded Age's materialistic altar in at least two ways. It provided an overseas smokescreen of pious experiential authenticity useful to Americans as they pursued their avaricious agendas at home, and it served as an advertisement for travel junkets that lined the pockets of businessmen who had invested in the growing tourism field.

There are many other ways of understanding the fifth Gospel, however. One possibility is the global biblical criticism frame. Secularized trends in the search for the historical Jesus, which gained headway in Europe via books published by figures like David Friedrich Strauss and Ernest Renan, prompted prominent American Protestant figures, such as Henry Ward Beecher, to revisit Jesus' story.

Another analytic frame is inner dynamics in American Christianity and their overseas repercussions. Antebellum mobilization against Catholic immigrants, such as Know Nothing Party activity, influenced Americans when they went overseas, exacerbating skeptical feelings held by Protestant travelers toward Holy Land sites controlled by Catholic forces, particularly in Jerusalem. In sharp contrast to the situation in the holy city, key village settings and sites of Jesus' story in Galilee, such as Capernaum and Caesarea Philippi, were not identified definitively by theologians and scientists (whose roles were conflated in a mid-nineteenth-century scholarly field known ambiguously as "biblical geography"). This meant that American Protestant travelers had much to investigate in northern reaches of the country, far from places like Jerusalem where Eastern Orthodox and Catholic investments in relics and holy sites repulsed them as unholy fetishism.

On the other hand, the demographic surge of Catholic populations in the United States from the mid-nineteenth century onward, overcoming nativist resistance, created magnetically complicated, attraction and repulsion, dynamics among the majority Protestant group. On their positive side, some Protestant spokesmen and creative artists displayed a mildly amenable disposition toward Catholic organizational hierarchy and toward Catholic theories of sacred space and objects.[117] This moderate Catholicization process among some Protestant subgroups provides one explanation for the fifth Gospel's compromise formula, "a sense of presence," which straddled between Calvinism's traditional hostility toward the sacralization of objects and Catholic devotion in designated spaces.

---

116. Fosdick, *Living*, 177–80.
117. Schwain, *Signs of Grace*, 13–41.

Another analytic frame is the frontier. Much as it provoked Mark Twain's satirical imprecation, frontier posturing of the sort exemplified by W. C. Prime's *Tent Life in the Holy Land* (1857) constituted a significant part of fifth Gospel dealings with the Holy Land.[118] It prioritized Galilee's New Testament areas since they were reminiscent of the American West. In contrast, in the era of the frontier's closure, Jerusalem-based, Old Testament city imagery resonated less sonorously as Americans, in their own country, drifted massively toward urban locales of questionable moral status.

Finally, we should briefly discuss how new illustration technologies constitute a final analytic frame for understanding the fifth Gospel. Technological innovation that brought the Holy Land to Americans tended to highlight the New Testament narrative. In particular, new illustration techniques, which made their impressive debut some fifteen years before the Civil War with the 1843–1846 production of Harper's *Illuminated Bible*, showcased New Testament images, particularly ones connected to Jesus.[119] In general, explaining why American Protestants might have had a special stake in the Jesus story might seem like gratuitous tautology, but we should nonetheless point to the main lines of an argument about why new Holy Land pictorial possibilities tended to hone in on Christ rather than Old Testament Jerusalem sites like the Tower of David, which were also eminently representational in drawing or photography.

In an engaging "visual history" of modern Christianity, David Morgan proposes that Protestants reject Catholic beliefs regarding divine presence in particular spaces and objects. Instead, they frame their views about distinctions between spirit and matter in temporal, not spatial, terms, while tending to view all inspiring physical presences as signs rather than actual tokens of divinity.[120] Morgan's thought-provoking discussion may not wholly apply to nineteenth-century American Protestants, however. Members of this group brought to the Holy Land both unusually expansive spatial frames of reference, coming from a rapidly growing, large frontier nation, and they also had an unusual temporal perspective because they came from a young country, a national infant compared to the ancient Holy Land.

Often thought of as an unusual, iconoclastic book, Mark Twain's *Innocents Abroad* is quite characteristic of how Americans related to space and time on visits to the Holy Land. In the spatial realm, Twain regards everything in the Holy Land as being comically and disarmingly small, whereas

---

118. Prime, *Tent Life*.
119. Morgan, *Protestants*, 61–65.
120. Morgan, *Forge of Vision*.

in the temporal realm he unrealistically dismisses the factor of time, á la the fifth Gospel's principle of atemporality.

Twain's spatial shock in the Holy Land is a well-known motif in *Innocents Abroad*.[121] In the Bekaa Valley (Valley of Lebanon), he feigns astonishment about how grapes are "excellent" but regular-sized, whereas he had been taught by children's picture books to expect grapes of "monstrous" dimensions swinging on poles. The future author of *Life on the Mississippi* seems unable to understand how the famed Jordan River can be so puny ("When I was a boy I somehow got the impression that the River Jordan was four thousand miles long and thirty-five miles wide. It is only ninety miles long"). In one instance, when Twain compares the dimensions of the "solemn, sailless, tintless" Sea of Galilee to his beloved Lake Tahoe ("the celebrated Sea of Galilee is not so large a sea as Lake Tahoe by a great deal"), his humor is so harsh that it almost implies a supersession geography, substituting the majestic, flourishing dimensions of North America for miniscule, desiccated Ottoman Palestine.[122]

New illustrative dealings with the Holy Land became possible to Americans precisely in an era when they had enhanced incentive to re-embrace Jesus. The devastation of the Civil War, and also Reconstruction era efforts in its aftermath, intensified interest in the New Testament narrative of resurrection. Crosscurrents in the postbellum period—the tough swim between the Scylla of forgiveness toward ex-Confederates and the Charybdis of the victor's righteous pride in its manly victory and its muscular agenda of physically reconstructing war-torn areas—created anxiety in gender realms of religion. Were Christians worshiping a feminine creed of love and mercy or a manly faith of righteous power? This particular question had pertinence in the Gilded Age partly because its most popular novel, Lew Wallace's *Ben-Hur: A Tale of the Christ*, conveyed a number of mother- or female-oriented solutions to dilemmas of reconciliation and salvation that troubled Americans after the Civil War.[123] In the last year of the nineteenth century, a Protestant weekly, *Outlook*, asked a number of American clergymen whether ancient and modern artistic depictions of Jesus' visage satisfied their idea of a "strong face." Most of the seventeen published replies answered in the negative; in many of these cases, the gist was an objection to the overly female cast in such artistic representation, though respondents

---

121. Vogel, *To See*, 69–77.
122. Twain, *Innocents*, 441, 596, 507.
123. Shamir, "Encounters."

also found other reasons to complain (three of them, a rabbi, a Unitarian, and an Episcopalian, chided Jesus art for underplaying his Jewishness).[124]

The impact of new illustrative and media technologies on American perceptions of sacred space and the Middle East is a topic of continuing scholarly investigation and ongoing controversy,[125] but two broad areas of particular pertinence to the fifth Gospel can be cited here with some confidence. First, because depictions of Jesus stirred huge public interest and won the patronage of leading businessmen (as exemplified by John Wanamaker's boosterism of Jesus paintings rendered by J. James Tissot) and because such artwork was increasingly accessible in mass reproduction, Protestant commentators had no choice but to ruminate about the topic of Jesus art, and seek creative compromises.[126]

The popularity of Jesus art is related to the fifth Gospel both as a symptomatic expression and as a causal determinant of American Protestantism's release from the chokehold of Calvinist prohibitions over the course of the nineteenth century. Literally and figuratively, Henry Ward Beecher's *The Life of Jesus, the Christ* (1871) illustrates this point. This popular book contained a chapter in which the author proffered arguments about why Jesus can never be rendered satisfactorily in art, but its frontpiece and contents featured illustrations of him.[127]

Second, the falling costs of illustrations, and the rapid growth of pictorial technology, in the Gilded Age both enhanced the atemporality plank of the fifth Gospel and also challenged and potentially compromised it. On the one hand, innovative Holy Land presentation and illustrative processes offered new vicarious experiential possibilities. American Christians who stayed at home could become partial witnesses in the fifth Gospel either by visiting Holy Land theme parks, the most famous example being the Palestine Park near Lake Chautauqua, or by perusing photographs, as in the case of a remarkable 1894 volume, *Earthly Footsteps of the Man of Galilee*, which warrants classification as the emblematic pictorial version of the fifth Gospel.[128] Many of this book's five hundred original photographs seem to have a design of portraying local Arabs in a premodern frame, thereby affirming the fifth Gospel vision of a timeless Holy Land whose current occupants resembled inhabitants of the Second Temple era. But the fifth Gospel's atemporality was an extremely unrealistic proposition, and photography is

---

124. Morgan, *Protestants*, 298–300.
125. McAlister, *Epic Encounters*.
126. Schwain, *Signs of Grace*, 3.
127. Beecher, *Life of Jesus*, 134–35.
128. Vogel, *To See*, 2; Bain et al., *Earthly Footsteps*.

inherently realistic and powerful; the creators of *Earthly Footsteps* seemed to understand that they had no power to control whether readers would view photographed Arabs within a Second Temple frame of reference or whether they would perceive these Arabs in many other possible ways. Such lack of control frustrated them, as seems to be exemplified by the peptic bigotry in this volume's caption descriptions of Palestine's Arabs.[129]

As illustrated by Harry Emerson Fosdick's Holy Land visit, by the end of the 1920s—a new "postbellum" era defined in global terms—Americans articulated lingering devotion to the fifth Gospel. But their appreciation of Holy Land and Bible topics was splintering along fundamentalist and liberal lines. As the twentieth century progressed and the balance of power between these two groups fluctuated, with the first (known today as Evangelicals) gaining prominence after events like the 1967 Six-Day War in Israel, the Jerusalem-based, Old Testament narrative often regained traction in the "American mind." We have already cited one of many examples: in the early twenty-first century, leading scholars found sources (e.g., the Gospel of John, the least Galilean Gospel) which enabled them to discuss the rise of Christianity in the Holy Land almost wholly within a Jerusalem setting, keeping Jesus' Galilee out of the picture. Such a Hebraic, Old Testament approach returns to spiritual priorities in America that lasted through the colonial period to the Second Great Awakening, but it reverses the fifth Gospel orientation of the Civil War era through the Gilded Age and the 1920s, when prominent American Protestant pilgrims, along with widely popular Holy Land picture books like *Earthly Footsteps*, followed in Jesus' path, striding mostly within the Galilean New Testament narrative.

From the Fifth Gospel to Evangelical Schmegegge

The fifth Gospel practice of outdoor pilgrimage in the presumably timeless Holy Land lasted through the 1920s, but its earnest latitudinarianism was ill-fitted to the decade's new circumstances. A new spiritual reality was created by American Protestantism's liberal-fundamentalist split in this dry decade when Prohibition stirred speakeasy cynicism and church righteousness, and when debates about Darwinism, science, and faith flared at the Scopes Monkey Trial.

Hostile to indoor, organized church hierarchies and committed to a nonliteral reading of Scripture whereby spiritual seekers sought approximate communion with Jesus, to have a "sense of his presence" rather than to arrive at the precise sites of supernatural events, the fifth Gospel attracted

---

129. Davis, *Landscape*, 77–89.

liberal streams of American Protestantism through the 1920s, as the Fosdick example suggests. Fundamentalist approaches toward Scripture and the Holy Land were gaining ground, however. The long-standing liberal Protestant objection to literal readings of the Bible was losing traction in a decade which, despite its "roaring" reputation, had a darkly tribal underside of anti-immigrant and antiblack prejudice.

In fact the historian John Higham, who died in 2003, labeled the decade the "tribal twenties" but left the stage before he could have recognized how many of its traits foreshadow dynamics in Trump's MAGA movement.[130] Membership estimates of the Ku Klux Klan in this 1920s decade range from two and a half million to eight million, with four million seemingly the most likely figure. Some two hundred thousand Klansmen participated in a 1923 rally in Kokomo, Indiana, and seventy-five members of the House of Representatives are believed to have owed their elections in this decade to the Klan.[131] KKK members were Protestants.

Before the Civil War, as part of a process whereby liberal Protestantism shook away Calvinist fatalism in favor of a warmer, more inclusive form of worship of Jesus, antislavery preachers like Henry Ward Beecher jettisoned literal readings of the Bible because some of its portions were illiberal and ill-fitted to the challenges of modern life.[132] In particular, parts of the Bible appeared to sanction slavery. Such biblical sanction was not really a stumbling block for the fundamentalists, who reorganized during the 1920s, laying foundations for Evangelicalism's major role in the Republican Party and US politics today. *Moody Monthly*, a leading fundamentalist outlet of the time, was ambivalent about the KKK, sometimes declaring that "the religion of Ku Kluxism is not the religion of Jesus Christ" but also acknowledging that fundamentalism shared many items on the Klan's agenda. "While fundamentalists expressed some qualms about working with the Klan, Klansmen and women had no problems seeking alliances with fundamentalists," observes Matthew Avery Sutton, in his history of American Evangelicalism.[133]

Fundamentalism's growth in the 1920s was chaperoned by pastors like Baptist leader William Bell Riley, who established the World's Christian Fundamentals Association in 1919, and also by newly spiritualized businessmen like Lyman Stewart, a Civil War veteran and oil wildcatter who sold his business to John D. Rockefeller's Standard Oil before striking

---

130. Higham, *Strangers in the Land*, 264–99.
131. Pietrusza, "Ku Klux Klan."
132. Applegate, *Most Famous Man*.
133. Sutton, *American Apocalypse*, 129.

"black gold" in California and making a fortune from his own Union Oil Company. Rockefeller became a patron of liberal American Protestantism (as exemplified by the Manhattan Riverside Church he built for Fosdick), while Stewart's philanthropy championed fundamentalist projects, including a twelve-volume book project. Drawn toward premillennial ideas about the rapture and apocalyptic war ushering in Jesus' one-thousand-year reign, Stewart funded projects like the republication of *Jesus Is Coming* by William Blackstone, whose name has been mentioned earlier as the sponsor of an 1891 petition to US President Benjamin Harrison for Jewish restoration in Ottoman Palestine.[134]

In the 1920s, premillennialism's messianic irrationalism worried ministers and theologians from American Protestantism's liberal wing. Shailer Mathews, for instance, issued prophetic warnings about Evangelicalism's antidemocratic implications. "Partly because of the war [World War I], partly because of the extensive circulation of its literature, partly because of its literalistic appeal to the Bible, partly because of the lack of theological education on the part of active Christian workers, premillenarianism is a danger," Matthews warned.[135] As a bridge between, on one side, the fifth Gospel precept of atemporality and, on the other side, contemporary Evangelical activism dedicated to radically transforming Middle East realities, this 1920s period was transitional. The premillennialists and other fundamentalists were substituting a literal approach for the fifth Gospel's relatively relaxed "sense of presence" orientation toward sacred space and sacred words; but they were not yet prepared to sponsor radical attempts to transform contemporary Holy Land realities according to a messianic agenda.

Zionism in the pre-1948 British Mandate era had little attraction for the fundamentalists. In fact, as Caitlin Carenen shows in her 2012 study of American Protestantism and Israel, the Evangelicals kept a distance from Jewish nationalism and Israel before the Jewish state took control over an undivided Jerusalem in the 1967 Six-Day War, before religious Zionism gained a strong foothold in Israeli politics, and before the territorial expansionist Likud party rose to power in the late 1970s. Before these turning points, the secular, socialist-inclined character of Zionism repulsed the American Evangelicals.[136]

In lieu of Christian Zionism, a major trend within American Protestantism's fundamentalist branch between the world wars was anti-Semitism.

---

134. Sutton, *American Apocalypse*, 82–90.
135. Sutton, *American Apocalypse*, 94.
136. Carenen, *Fervent Embrace*.

During the Depression, for instance, William Bell Riley blamed the Jews for America's economic crisis, just as he believed that Jews were responsible for the breakdown of the globe's post–World War I political order. According to Sutton, Riley "praised Hitler in 1934 for clamping down on supposed Jewish communism, which excited 'the wrath of all Jews and of deceived Gentiles throughout the world.'"[137]

Meantime, conservative Christians were using new interwar technologies to disseminate their messages in America. One Los Angeles preacher, Charles Fuller, began radio broadcasting in 1924. Twelve years later, he had a coast-to-coast fundamentalist radio program, the *Old Fashioned Revival Hour*; by the end of World War II, the program reached an audience of twenty million.[138]

Whether or not the messiah was waiting in the wings, the stage for twenty-first-century Evangelical Christian Zionist schmegegge was set by such developments within American Christianity before the Holocaust and Israel's establishment. The road between the fifth Gospel's reverential modesty and its nonliteral flexibility in approaches to space and Scripture, on the one hand, and the fundamentalism of late twentieth-century premillennial Evangelicalism, its activist intervention in Israel's colonialist projects in the post-1967 territories, and its investment in radical alteration of the Holy Land's present and future, on the other hand, is very long. But we have cited here main stretches, up to the Holocaust and Israel's establishment in 1948.

FROM HISTORY IS BUNK TO FAKE NEWS: THE TIMELINE OF AMERICAN SCHMEGEGGE

The story of history, truth, and falsehood in American politics and culture over the last century has identifiable bookends. The starting point is the World War I era, when Henry Ford declared that "history is more or less bunk," and the endpoint, for now, is Donald Trump's repeated use of the term "fake news" during his 2016–2020 term in the White House. The utterances are separated by a century.

Ford reportedly delivered his rejection of history in a 1916 interview with a journalist from the *Chicago Tribune*, who had inserted a reference to Napoleon in their conversation. His response warrants quotation:

> What do we care about what they did 500 or 1,000 years ago? I don't know whether Napoleon did or did not try to get across

---

137. Sutton, *American Apocalypse*, 127.

138. Sutton, *American Apocalypse*, 122–23.

and I don't care. It means nothing to me. History is more or less bunk. It's tradition. We don't want tradition. We want to live in the present and the only history that is worth a tinker's dam is the history we make today.[139]

Ford's views about history were under public scrutiny because in late 1915 he had sponsored a Peace Ship journey to Europe with the intention of ending what was then known as the Great War.[140] His inspiration for this venture came from Rosika Schwimmer, a Hungarian Jewish pacifist who, before Ford, had tried to use the International Congress of Women to promote her passionate belief in the power of international mediation to bring the brutal conflict to an end (a contemporary Jew who had a background unlike Schwimmer's, but who shared this naïve but endearing confidence in neutral mediation, was Oscar Straus). Ford was lambasted for ignoring centuries of enmity and rivalry that were propelling Europeans and others into mass slaughter. This was a valid charge, but a strong case can be made that the same accusation could also be applied to many planks in the Fourteen Points that was promulgated two years later by President Woodrow Wilson, formerly a professor and president at Princeton University who had authored books about history.

Amazed by Ford's irreverence about history, the *Chicago Tribune* editorialized about how he was an "ignorant idealist." A prickly, proud man, the car manufacturer struck back, launching a sensational million-dollar libel lawsuit against the newspaper. On July 14, 1919, Ford took the stand for cross-examination in the trial, held in a sleepy hamlet, Mount Clemens, just some twenty miles from Detroit, the cradle of Ford's unmatched popularity as an American hero.

Ford was questioned on the stand for eight days. He testified that the American Revolution occurred in 1812. Benedict Arnold, he stated, was a writer, and he defined treason as "anything against the government." Ballyhoo, Ford believed, is a "blackguard or something of that nature," the Monroe Doctrine is a "big-brother act," and a mobile army is "a large army, mobilized." The media mocked Ford's performance, demeaning him as a "country-store philosopher."[141]

After you read the newspaper reports of how Ford sat on the stand, "lowering his eyes when he wants to think" and "rubbing his hand across his long jaw, a rural gesture," the next natural step is to view the YouTube clip of the scowl on Donald Trump's face when President Obama roasted

139. Watts, *People's Tycoon*, 265–71; Hirst, "Henry Ford."
140. Kraft, *Peace Ship*.
141. Watts, *People's Tycoon*, 268.

the star of Celebrity Apprentice at the 2011 White House Correspondents' Dinner.[142] Crusted in racial, regional, and other stereotypes, such episodes raise the cardinal question of information crises: Whose knowledge counts? Addressing this question, liberals typically have reasonable answers but also display low emotional intelligence—not a winning combination.

After being drubbed and humiliated by the *Chicago Tribune* and the libel trial, Ford lashed back. The victims were the Jewish people, who were blamed for all the world's problems in a rehashing of the forged czarist anti-Semitic tract, *The Protocols of the Elders of Zion*. The anti-Semitic vitriol was circulated in Ford's *Dearborn Independent* journal for seven years, starting in spring 1920 (it was stopped after an aggrieved American Jewish attorney, Aaron Sapiro, whose work as a farm cooperative organizer in California had been libeled in the *Independent*, took a page out of Ford's own playbook and initiated a million-dollar damages claim against the car manufacturer).[143]

After being drubbed and humiliated by Obama at the Correspondents' Dinner, Trump lashed back. The victims have been American Constitutional democracy, public decency, and everyone in the world, and the extent of the damage done to them remains to be seen.

According to the British newspaper, *The Independent*, Trump's first use of the term "fake news" occurred in his twitter feed in December 2016, almost exactly a century after Ford derided history as bunk. During his first term, Trump used this phrase, "fake news," close to two thousand times.[144] Ford spent decades privately regretting his 1916 over-stated rejection of history—twenty years after the ill-fated *Chicago Tribune* interview, he issued a clarification, insisting that his reference was to historians, not history ("They wrote what they wanted us to believe, glorifying some conqueror or leader of something like that").[145] Trump, in contrast, unrepentantly takes ownership for the phrase *fake news*. "I call the fake news now corrupt news because fake news isn't tough enough," he said in the Oval Office in 2019. "And I'm the one that came up with the term. I'm very proud of it, but I think I'm gonna switch it to corrupt news." A few months before the 2020 election, Trump had made 20,055 false or misleading claims, an average of twenty-three per day (as documented by the *Washington Post*'s fact-checker database).[146] Then, after he lost the November balloting, he lyingly called the election a lie, and his

---

142. Watts, *People's Tycoon*, 269; CNN, "Watch Obama Roast Trump."
143. Baldwin, *Henry Ford*.
144. Woodward, "Fake News."
145. Hirst, "Did Henry Ford."
146. Woodward, "Fake News."

incitement about untruth in American democracy prompted thousands of followers to stage the January 6 attack on Capitol Hill.

In this essay I am defining American schmegegge as the prominent cultural phenomenon of what others have called the "American Century," which is properly defined as having lasted from 1921 to 2021, rather than the first year of the twentieth and twenty-first centuries (if you remember the elementary school joke "How long was the Hundred Years War?" then you have known for a long time that what historians regard as a "century" can have rather loose dates). The starting and ending dates allude to two events that symbolize the limits of American idealism and power (in the century between them, Americans did everything they could to exceed these limits, pouting in the end about how everything is a lie instead of acknowledging the futility and arrogance of those efforts). In November 1921, America hosted the Washington Naval Conference, in which it and eight other countries (conspicuously, Germany was not one of them) discussed disarmament plans. Partly because of what preceded it (i.e., President Wilson's failure to win congressional approval for participation in the League of Nations, the linchpin of his Versailles Treaty diplomacy) but mostly because of what came after it, the Naval Conference was a mixed success, at best. At the end of August 2021, the United States ended its twenty-year engagement in Afghanistan in a chaotically organized and executed withdrawal of its troops. Partly because of what came before it—that is, the undertaking of the Second Iraq War under false pretenses and the abject failure to steward democratic transition in Iraq and de-Talibanization in Afghanistan—but mostly because of all the rot and ruin that is destined to unfold in the next seventy-five years of the twenty-first century, the Afghanistan War was a mixed success, at best.

The first (1921) event was held at a Jazz Age time of economic prosperity, inventive ingenuity, and social enthusiasm, when America's global transition from a debtor to creditor nation marked the start of the American Century. The second (2021) event, marked the end of a post–Cold War period when America's Free World leadership and triumph over the Soviet Bloc inaugurated a period when it operated as the world's sole superpower. The 2021 Afghanistan withdrawal symbolizes how the challenge posed to America by Al-Qaeda's brutal and unprovoked attack on September 11, 2001—the opportunity to create a new world order of democratization, economic fairness, and environmental awareness—had not been met. What, other than Osama bin Laden's capture and execution, had been accomplished in America's prodigious Middle East military efforts, which ended ingloriously in the August 2021 Afghan pullout? Because there is no surefire answer to this demoralizing question, the event can be regarded as the end of the American Century.

Schmegegge is a word used by my grandmother, a cheerful, loquacious woman who belonged to the last generation of my family that was fluent in Yiddish. She used the term to describe crazy nonsense. I will define it a bit more analytically in a second, but if my years as a classroom lecturer have taught me anything, it is that people get a better grasp of what you are talking about when you give some examples, in lieu of abstract, pretentious definitions. So here is a sampling of American schmegegge. The examples are not listed chronologically, but they are all from the second half of the century when, after incubating from 1921 to 1971, schmegegge erupted in its full glory:

- The 18.5-minute blank space in President Nixon's Watergate tape, attributed to a gaffe made by his secretary, Rose Mary Woods.
- Whatever was on Mark McGwire's mind on September 8, 1998, as he trotted the bases after hitting his 62nd home run, breaking Babe Ruth's single season record, with steroids juicing through his body.
- Whatever was on President Clinton's mind during his January 28, 1998, declaration, "I did not have sexual relations with that woman."
- The establishment of the Livestrong Foundation in 1997, under the inspiration of cyclist champion Lance Armstrong, who confessed to illegal doping in an Oprah Winfrey interview in 2013.
- President Donald Trump's April 2020 suggestion that disinfectant injection might be a cure for the Coronavirus. And everything else that Trump says and does.
- The contents of Secretary of State Colin Powell's February 5, 2003, speech to the United Nations Security Council, outlining the rationale for the Iraq War, which began a month and a half later.

Schmegegge is a state of blatant falsehood brought on by selective, unrealistic orientations toward the past, present, and future. Ford, who did not believe in the past, and Trump, who does not believe in the present, represent the progression that produces this state. First, a culture (or a person) denies the relevance of the past out of unjustified confidence in its ability to create a better or perfect future out of can-do, optimistic work in the present. Then, in an intermediate step, a culture (or person) confronts the bitterly disappointing fact that a vastly improved, or utopian, future will never arrive. So, third, a culture (or person) seeks relief from a confusing or unpleasant present by calling it fake news or by believing it can be fixed by time-travel reform of the past. Throughout this three-stage progression, the state of schmegegge is articulated by constant falsehood.

Schmegegge arises out of the myth of Judeo-Christian civilization. Schmegegge would not have become the outcome of centuries-long experimentation with democracy were it not for the fact that a harmoniously inclusive political culture molded out of monotheism is a contradiction in terms. Christianity and Judaism are necessarily in conflict with one another (we have left Islam out of this discussion, but I am sure that its inclusion would, on the whole, strengthen the premises and conclusions of this essay). Because these two monotheistic faiths arose in an information crisis, deliberate efforts to infuse them in the public sphere are doomed to exacerbate preexisting confusions about public accountability, and also to create new sorts of information crises.

Christianity and Judaism forged their dysfunctional fraternal relationship in a region, Galilee, that resisted realistic documentation at the time of monotheism's fracture. After the resurrection and the Second Temple hurban destruction, both religions found a number of reasons to downplay the heritage of the place where they first encountered one another. Innumerable national and ideological movements have a geographically identifiable "lost Eden" origin story, but Judeo-Christian civilization was lost in space from the start—one side locating itself in diasporic exile, the other shuffling around its capital from Jerusalem to Rome. This means that when a self-proclaimed Judeo-Christian civilization finds itself seeped in falsehood and corruption, as America does today, it would have no place to go to, even were it to be able, collectively, to go back to the blackboard. It stays suspended in the increasingly ugly chatter of virtual reality, and it relates to the past in astonishingly self-centered and eccentric ways.

Finally, schmegegge generates "cunning of history" ironies, that is, its powers and ascendance do not become apprehensible in a timely fashion to concerned citizens who would rather not live in a polity whose leaders tell them to ingest bleach during a pandemic, which wages wars on false pretense, and whose entertainment and sports heroes are repeatedly exposed as con artists.

In the example we have discussed, the American Jewish community promoted Judeo-Christian concepts in the expectation that they would usefully dissolve controversies that have swirled around Israel since the 1967 Six-Day War. The use of these concepts might have notched some passing tactical gains, mitigating this or that Intifada controversy, but the utilization of religious-based ideas in political lobbying, in oblivious disregard of their toxic volatility over a torturous two-thousand-year experience of diaspora life, was a crucial strategic blunder for the American Jewish community, which will spend the next generation trying to mitigate its repercussions.

After the 1967 Six-Day War, American Jews had a choice. They could spend the next half century pounding away at Christian guilt for the Holocaust and hammering away about how American democracy owes much to the Old Testament, and is therefore a partnership venture in Judeo-Christian civilization. Or they might have found a different way of supporting Israel, under the aegis of a special relationship with the United States—one way or another, this option would have necessitated a different, non-indulgent, orientation toward Israel's illiberal colonialist behavior in occupied territories since the special relationship has been intensely developed, and marketed to the public, as a partnership between two democracies. American Jewry as an organized collective chose the first option. Belatedly, American Jews are realizing that what protects them in a complicated modern democracy has nothing to do with a Yale College president dabbling with the Old Testament and Hebrew two hundred and fifty years ago, or Benjamin Franklin toying with the idea of using an image of Moses at the Red Sea to brand the new nation.

A much wiser starting point for American Jewish politics, and for discussions with Christians about Israel or any other subject, would be Thomas Jefferson's *The Life and Morals of Jesus of Nazareth* (1820), the so-called Jefferson Bible, which excises supernatural references in Gospel descriptions of Jesus' Galilee mission and other subjects. Conscious of all the tensions and complications that arise from the use of sacred Scripture as foundational texts in modern society, the founders of American democracy sought to keep it separate from the lachrymose history of Jewish-Christian relations and also from Christianity's own post-Reformation history of internal schisms and tensions.

It is worth remembering that the rise of American schmegegge along this century-long timeline had nonreligious sources as well, and we survey some of them in subsequent sections.

ECONOMIC DETERMINANTS OF SCHMEGEGE

Probably the most potent nonreligious engine of untruth in American life was the rise of corporate power from the late nineteenth century. The information crisis caused by corporatism played out in two phases: the first in Progressive Era anxiety about monopolistic trusts and the second in finance babble from the late twentieth century to the present, a period when an ever-increasing share of national wealth has been accrued from rent and capital investment rather than from labor and industrial production.

The origins of corporate schmegegge stretch to the late nineteenth-century Gilded Age, when the concentration of wealth on an iniquitous scale comparable to today's situation sparked public outcry about "robber barons."[147] The robber barons, it was believed, had the power to manipulate political processes and the legal system, and thereby hold plainspoken truth hostage to their own interests. The gross, corrupt excesses of this business elite inspired some brilliant critical commentary, both among Progressive journalists (dubbed "muckrakers" by President Theodore Roosevelt in 1906) and also scholars like Thorstein Veblen, who published his *Theory of the Leisure Class* in 1899.[148]

Well-known concepts evoked in this commentary, such as Veblen's analysis of "conspicuous consumption," applied mostly to the realm of social manners and are thus not apposite to our discussion of systematically institutionalized falsehood in American life. Why people behave in ways crudely offensive to Anglo-Saxon propriety, and whether they can be conspicuously rich and also good Christians, is an interesting riddle, addressed both by academics (witness Max Weber's booklet, discussed in another essay in this book) and by the late nineteenth-century robber barons themselves (witness Andrew Carnegie's article "The Gospel of Wealth," originally published in 1889[149]). But there is a difference between bad manners and fake news. Parvenus who act grossly can be ignored or admired (as happened when half the electorate voted Donald Trump into power in 2016, after hearing a taped recording of him aping about how women are always there for his groping). In contrast, presidents who set national policy on the basis of what they declare to be "alternative facts" pose a different sort of challenge, one pertaining to the dimension of truth and democracy rather than the realm of manners and politics.

This distinction was not entirely lost to the muckrakers and Progressives who criticized extreme concentrations of wealth from the Gilded Age through the Great Depression. Their critique often straddled between the muckrakers' moralistic attacks on the robber barons, and the Progressives' stated commitments to expert administration and scientific management. Ida Tarbell, the journalist famed for her exposé of the Standard Oil monopoly's predatory behavior in articles published in *McClure's* between 1902 and 1904, predicated her critique of Rockefeller on an accusation whose

---

147. Josephson, *Robber Barons*.
148. Veblen, *Theory of the Leisure Class*.
149. Carnegie, *His Autobiography and Essay*.

status is indefinite since it is footed both in the sphere of social impropriety and also the realm of criminal illegality.[150]

The only time Tarbell ever saw Rockefeller in person was in a church, and she articulated a positive estimate of the oil tycoon's character, opining that "there was no more faithful Baptist in Cleveland than he. . . . He was simple and frugal in his habits. . . . He gave much time to the training of his children, seeking to develop in them his own habits of economy and charity."[151] This implied that the problem posed by Rockefeller's oil trust was not behavioral, but Tarbell's analysis never really detached itself from a moralistic critique. She argued that rebates Rockefeller received from railroad lines eager to convey Standard Oil freight violated the trains' classification as "common carriers"—it was never particularly clear whether the railroads were being charged with illegally violating statutory bans of preferential treatment for particular classes of customers, or whether Tarbell's idea was that the railroads were a national project obligated morally to operate as a public trust offering nondiscriminatory service to all users.

To date, the one instance when America's political system offered voters a genuine array of choices on issues of corporate power was the 1912 presidential elections.[152] The incumbent, Republican William Howard Taft, had broken up some trusts during the previous four years, but he lurched rightward, adopting a pro-business approach. Taft vied against the Democratic candidate, Woodrow Wilson, who won the election and proceeded to sign the 1913 Revenue Act for a federal income tax, and to strengthen antitrust law via the 1914 Clayton Antitrust Act and the establishment of the Federal Trade Commission. Wilson ran in the 1912 elections on a "New Freedom" platform whose aggressive anti-monopoly outlook came from his confidante on economic matters, Louis Brandeis, the "people's attorney." A zealous opponent of corporate power, what he derisively called "bigness,"[153] Brandeis's radical plans to break up monopolies across the economy were well beyond the political wherewithal of any president, but Brandeis's outlook nonetheless warrants mention in this discussion of corporatism's contribution to public falsehood.

As much as any other twentieth-century public activist, Brandeis operated effectively to de-schmegegge business affairs in the country, demanding and devising procedures for corporate disclosure whose

---

150. Tarbell, *History*; Weinberg, *Taking*.

151. Weinberg, *Taking*, 82.

152. Information about the 1912 elections is drawn from Mowry, *Era of Theodore Roosevelt*; Cooper, *Warrior*; Goodwin, *Bully Pulpit*.

153. Brandeis, *Curse of Bigness*.

enforcement later became the responsibility of new regulatory agencies like the Securites and Exchange Commission.[154] In his pre–World War I polemic, *Other People's Money*, Brandeis remarked, "Sunlight is said to be the best of disinfectants."[155] In the ensuing century, this call for corporate transparency was overwhelmed by a culture of business non-accountability.

This outcome was preordained by the unfolding of the 1912 election. Wilson won, but the liberal economics philosophy enshrined by the balloting belonged not to the president-elect's advisor, Louis Brandeis, but rather to the third party ("Bull Moose") candidate, Theodore Roosevelt, who mounted a dramatic but unsuccessful bid to return to the White House (like Trump during the 2024 campaign, Roosevelt was the target of an assassination attempt while stumping on the election trail in 1912). Roosevelt's idea was that the determination of what counted as a criminal monopoly or a good trust ought to be determined at the discretion of the executive branch.

Unlike most other Western democracies, American politics never hosted a serious, socialist-spirited labor party, and its antitrust law eroded over time, becoming, as the historian Richard Hofstadter lamented in the mid-1960s, one of the "faded passions of American reform."[156] This meant that Roosevelt's Square Deal philosophy in the 1912 election gained traction and, more or less, became the accepted standard. It gives presidents tremendous latitude to decide what can reasonably be deemed admissible or inadmissible bank or corporate behavior.

Prima facie, the problem raised by the adoption of this plank of Roosevelt's Square Deal pivots on the character and quality of the president himself or herself. But this has not really proven to be the case, as shown by the 2007–2008 financial meltdown. As a frustrated public observed during this crisis, the undue latitude given to the president by this Bull Moose rule of executive discretion can be abused both by conservative Republican presidents, like George W. Bush, and also by liberal Democrats, like Barack Obama—the administrations of both men arbitrarily provided bailout money to some (but not all) faltering investment banks based on bogus theories like "too big to fail," or sanctioned the unconscionable provision of fat bonuses to executives from these banks whose rescue depended on taxpayer money.[157]

Not the personal character or declared political philosophy of the executive but rather the same conceptual confusion that lingered after

---

154. McCraw, *Prophets of Regulation*, 153–210.
155. Brandeis, *Other People's Money*, 92.
156. Hofstadter, *Paranoid Style*, 188–238.
157. Suskind, *Confidence Men*; Sorkin, *Too Big to Fail*.

the muckraker-Progressive period brought the country into a state of schmegegge corporatism by the end of the twentieth century. The Roosevelt rule of executive decision implies that corporate transparency is a behavioral issue of good manners or bad manners. It is up to the White House to decide whether corporate executives have made a good-faith effort to be accountable toward their investors or to the public. A different approach holds that protection against corporate duplicity is an inviolable legal right held by citizens.

Having discussed why the topic of business truth or falsehood should be seen in relatively strict legal terms, rather than behavioral ones, we can pinpoint the starting line in the ascent of corporate chicanery in the United States. It is the Sherman Antitrust Act of 1890, whose ostensibly clear and resolute language outlawing combinations that restrain trade between states or with foreign nations proved susceptible to manipulation by power elites. Far more devastating than thousands of Trump's insulting and untrue tweets from the Oval Office, the egregious, class-biased twisting of the language of the Sherman Act (regarding "restraints of trade") for the purpose of clamping down on labor unions up to the World War I era was a devastating blow to public truth in America. True, these abusive interpretations were corrected by the 1914 Clayton Act, which exempted labor unions from prosecution on "restraint of trade" grounds (and incidentally legislated proposals broached by Brandeis in his *Other People's Money* polemic, such as his call for limiting interlocking directorate arrangements). Nonetheless, in the business sphere, the Sherman statute set a chilling precedent of the use of the law to say one thing and mean another.

Schmegegge-speak about business affairs became routinized by President Trump, but rather than exemplifying his well-known prevarication about the success, or lack thereof, of his companies, it suffices here to cite two cases in which the court testimony of an era's emblematic business leader exposed the hapless inability of the country's legal system to enforce truth-telling among corporate executives. These two instances of antitrust prosecutions, one against Rockefeller's Standard Oil monopoly and the other against Bill Gates's Microsoft monopoly, display some uncanny affinities, as legal scholars have recognized.[158] Standard Oil's unfair railroad rebate arrangements stifled industrial innovation, such as the development of pipelines, prosecutors charged; similarly, according to prosecutors in the late 1990s investigation, Microsoft's "bundling" of its Internet Explorer software with its Windows operating system stifled competition against other web browsers and thereby impeded innovation.

158. Flynn, "Standard Oil and Microsoft."

In 1888, owing to a New York Senate committee investigation of Standard Oil's monopoly, Rockefeller was summoned to testify in a New York City Superior Court hearing room. His obfuscation reached its acme in an exchange with Committee Counsel Roger Pryor, who was trying to clarify Rockefeller's part in an oil and railroad combination in Pennsylvania seventeen years earlier called the South Improvement Company. Pryor fumbled his words and asked Rockefeller about whether he had been involved in the Southern Improvement Company; Rockefeller craftily exploited this innocent malapropism, amazing the courtroom by denying his widely known involvement in this early, postbellum exercise in oil monopolization. He never showed remorse about how he had exploited a prosecutor's mistaken annunciation ("Southern" for "South") in order to dodge public accountability for the formative part of his career. "I was quiet and self-controlled," Rockefeller proudly affirmed, recalling this court appearance. "It was not part of my duty as a witness to volunteer testimony. While they thought they were leading me into a trap, I let them go into the trap themselves."[159]

Gates, for his part, was reportedly vulnerable to antitrust prosecution owing to a 1995 memo he drafted and circulated to Microsoft colleagues, warning about the damage to the company that would be caused should Netscape's browser system gain traction in the market. Proceedings in *United States v. Microsoft Corporation* began in May 1998 under the direction of Judge Thomas Penfield Jackson of the US District Court for the District of Columbia. Gates's videotaped deposition remains accessible on YouTube and is a classic exercise in splitting-hair evasion about terms like "compete."[160] Gates repeatedly pulled the "I don't remember" card. Media reports referred to Gates's evasiveness and claimed that Judge Jackson chuckled over Gates's dodgeball gamesmanship when shown a transcript of the record.[161]

During the first quarter of 2024, Americans earned $3.7 trillion from interest and dividends.[162] This figure is higher than the gross national product (GNP) of India in 2022, which was recorded as $3.385 trillion. So, every three months Americans are earning from investments wealth roughly equivalent to all of the goods and services produced and rendered in a year by the most populated country of the world.

Official US agencies still insist that Americans work for a living, but their wan, carefully parsed accounts of where income comes from in the

---

159. Chernow, *Titan*, 295–96.
160. See Gates, "Deposition Highlights."
161. Heilemann, *Pride Before the Fall*; Auletta, *World War 3.0*.
162. Uberti, "Americans."

United States make clear that the richest people in the richest country in the world are solidifying their elite status by talking to brokers, studying the markets, and investing (whether or not they are going to work each day is an extracurricular matter). Here, for instance, is how the Congressional Budget Office relates to the issue: "For most households, labor income makes up the bulk of their income. But among households at the top of the distribution, capital gains constitute a greater portion of income before transfers and taxes than they do for other households" (this quote is from November 2023, relating to US household income in 2020).[163]

Regarding what really matters to them—social status, lifestyle enhancement, improving their children's future—members of the highest income brackets in the United States are not communicating in plain speech. Instead, protecting and expanding their income, they are speaking in the dialect of the financial markets, using esoteric technical terms and sloppy metaphors in discussions that are entirely concerned about private gain and have nothing to do with communality and public interest. Here is how a Merrill Lynch Capital Market Outlook forecast (September 2024) expressed itself, mixing buffaloes with Magnificent Seven cohorts:

> In July, as global Equity volatility picked up, we referenced an analogy, characterizing the market environment to a buffalo. Less attractive than a bull, given its heavier and disheveled nature, it "roams" more erratically instead of "charging" in one direction, lacking dominant catalysts like those present in a bull market. . . . Importantly, earnings strength continued to broaden beyond the Magnificent 7 cohort. While some metrics underwhelmed, overall, the latest data suggests that a durable earnings uptrend is underway.[164]

Translated, I think this says the following: your broker does not have a clue as to what market indicators he (she) ought to look for, and the markets are erratically moving in many directions; but mostly the investment climate is pretty good, and most special measurements used by financial experts point to big investment returns, though some of them do not warrant such investment optimism. Good luck.

A wealth of political science research shows that what Trump supporters in the MAGA movement, and others, suspect is true: in terms of attracting the attention of politicians and influencing legislation, among other things, the wealthy elites are really running a country whose democratic system has over the past generation or two taken on plutocratic

---

163. Habib et al., "Distribution."
164. Merrill Lynch, "Chief Investment Office."

characteristics.[165] In turn, when they are thinking and reaching decisions about what really matters to them, members of the elites who run the country are not speaking a plainly apprehensible language based on values of community, mutual understanding, and mutual empowerment. Instead they are speaking a specialized tongue for financial mandarins that has no words for public interest and power-sharing and that bathes its speakers in bubbles of self-concerned expectation, leaving it for others, who don't have money to burn, to try to figure out which bubbles are likely to burst.

More precisely, the elites are speaking two languages in a communication world of greed and guilt. Because they spend their private time conversing in the esoteric language of the market whose only meanings are personal enrichment, they spend their public time conversing in the politically correct language of social inclusion and public improvement. This forked-tongue circumstance is one reason why masses of people who still work for their income do not listen to the judgments and warnings of the elites when they are speaking in their politically correct public language, even when those cautions and admonitions on matters of public health, or the environment, seem to be correct. Everyone knows which language, political correctness or finance speak, is favored by the elites. Everyone knows that they prattle vacuously about transgender bathrooms, whereas they are very serious about finding meaning in the esoteric utterances of finance-speak regarding how "most metrics used by the Magnificent 7 mean that a durable earnings uptrend is underway."[166]

So much for the corporate and financial reasons why truth became a vanishing resource as the American Century progressed.

URBANIZATION, IMMIGRATION, AND SCHMEGEGGE

Some demographic and migratory reasons are worth noting, as well. Americans know about Turner's Thesis, concerning the closure of the frontier at the end of the nineteenth century. They recognize that myths and sentimentalization increasingly colored the way they (or their parents and grandparents) thought about the middle and western parts of the country as the twentieth century progressed. Americans, Turner argued, had historically moved westward to discover and develop truth about their own national identity. As the nineteenth century closed, this compelled Americans of

---

165. Hacker and Pierson, *Winner-Take-All*; Bartels, *Unequal Democracy*; Turchin, *Elites*.

166. Merrill Lynch, "Chief Investment Office."

spiritually restless character to look for identity frontiers in new places—we have seen how this trend played out in the Holy Land through the "outdoors" ethos of the fifth Gospel.

The first decades of the twentieth century witnessed many important demographic-migratory trends in America, including the movement of blacks from southern states to northern ones and the arrival of masses of immigrants. But probably the single most significant event was the movement of innumerable Americans from rural farm areas and lifestyles to cities. Urbanization, in all national settings, fosters myths about lost rural life. In America's case, the dominant myth, cowboy images of the Wild West, was perhaps atypically muscularized and romanticized. Its activist, shoot and annihilate anything that stands in the way, character inculcated a particular orientation toward the past among members of the post–World War II baby boom generation.

Baby boomers were the last Americans who idolized John Wayne and really enjoyed Westerns. Before they became young adults responsible for children and careers, they escaped from reality in a violent and aggressive reimagining of the past where the victims (Native Americans) were blamed for the genocide that extinguished them, and the past was glorified in an astonishing exercise of romanticized colonialism. Everyone knew that in reality the towns of the Wild West were dreary, if sometimes rowdy, stopping points for cattle rustlers whose lives were tedious, dirty, and enervating; and everyone loved Westerns, which had very little to do with this reality.

As much as from any other source, contemporary rituals and attitudes of time-travel atonement and political correctness emanated out of the rise and fall of the Western. The turning point, it seems to me, was the 1990 film *Dances with Wolves*, which won the Academy Award for Best Picture, along with six other Oscars. Kevin Costner's movie was released at the end of the Cold War, when Americans were basking in triumph while harboring an inchoate sense of the absurdity of having lived for some forty years in a world divided between white hats and black hats. *Dances with Wolves* was an early, widely impactful example of what became a familiar cultural motif—reversing the roles of good guys and bad guys when we think about the past. The simplistic Manicheanism remained, it was just that where there had been only light, there was now only darkness, and vice versa. Political correctness assaults nuance, and time-travel atonement leapfrogs over gray areas in the present and past.

The people who invented these methods ate a lot of popcorn, watching Westerns up until the end of the baby boom generation in the mid-1960s. After revolutionary turbulence in the 1960s made it impossible for them, as young adults, to overlook evidence of how the foundation of their comfortable present lives was land expropriation and genocide, they were hardly in a position to give back their land or even think very deeply about the mass murder of Native Americans. Instead, they reshuffled the white hats and black hats, atoning for their present by reimagining how their past had been reimagined to begin with, in Westerns.

In the 1890s, the Americans' domestic, western frontier closed, but a generation later, in the 1920s, the country closed its global frontier, passing in Congress two successive anti-immigration bills in 1921 and 1924 (the Emergency Quota Act and the Immigration Act). After the Civil War, the country's immigration laws discriminated against Asians, but this was an exception. After minimal regulatory standards were imposed by the Immigration Act of 1882, and until the gates were closed during the "tribal twenties," America was an exceptionally generous and inclusive country, for whites. Its policies and activities in this sphere underpinned genuinely inspiring visions of the American dream and also recalibrated symbols of the country's civil religion, making (for instance) the Statue of Liberty a national icon for a country of immigrants and their descendants.

The flip side to this ennobling story can be found in the period between the mid-1920s and the mid-1960s. Essentially, for forty years, until the 1965 Immigration and Nationality Act repealed mechanisms enacted in the spirit of 1920s nativism (i.e., the national quota origins system), America became a country "for people like us," where the baseline was white, Western-Northern European; America suspended the Ellis Island vision whereby it was coming to be seen as a land of increasing white ethnic diversity. This happened because the 1920s restrictive acts were aimed against immigrants from Southern and Eastern Europe but allowed entry for Western-Northern Europeans who presumably came from the same white Anglo-Saxon stock as America's elite.

No less than the domestic demographic swing from farm country to cities, America's changing immigration scene in the twentieth century through the mid-1960s set the stage for the peculiarities in the way Americans view the past, and lie about the present, in the schmegegge era of Trump's impending reelection.

Reverential or respectful attitudes toward the past come from two broad sources. One is religion, and a Holy Land, offshore example of how faith shapes views about the past and present has been surveyed here. The other is family life. In America, generation gap phenomena can be attributed to a number of causes—political ferment, differences in the economic careers of parents and children, and so on. But it is customary to imagine that the most volatile version of the phenomena arises in newcomer families wherein immigrant parents warily watch the Americanization of their children, their suspiciousness being grounded in cultural-religious considerations as well as their (the parents') own ambivalence about their own native homelands.

That there is much truth to this view of generation gap volatility in immigrant families can be inferred from the durable popularity of movies and television shows which revolve around the tension between parents' foreign-oriented sensitivities and their offspring's desires and capacities to make it big in America (the fate of the children's career success, or matrimonial wishes, hangs in the air in these dramas). In fact, the history of mass entertainment in America throughout the past century can be told by using two benchmarks: one being the first movie "talkie," *The Jazz Singer* (1927), a soapy, sentimental depiction of whether the son of an immigrant cantor will fulfill his untraditional, un-Jewish, dream of becoming a jazz singer; the second being recent films and television streaming series, like Aziz Ansari's *Master of None* (first aired in 2015), whose heroes deal with gaps between their Americanized lifestyles and the foreignness of their parents, whether they are from India, as in Ansari's case, or some other, usually non-European, place.

This way of looking at immigration and culture can be misleading, however. As Tolstoy observed, all unhappy families are miserable in their own way; so it can be injudicious to generalize about how generation gap tensions arise in immigrant families. Nonetheless, I suggest that our way of thinking about this topic is wrongly inverted in a few ways. The children of immigrants often reject the foreign world of their parents; all of us who grew up in mixed American neighborhoods can remember families enlivened (or marred) by arguments and other types of volatility that arose out of this dynamic. However, even when they exaggeratedly "reject" the foreign ways of their elders, immigrant children retain levels of realism and knowledge about the pasts represented by their parents. They may reject their parents' religion, or not want to hear stories about their overseas homelands, but such children retain levels of fluency in the foreign languages of their family homes, they are accustomed to eating foreign foods, and their sense of humor, their attitudes about privacy and intimacy, and so on are shaped largely out of the overseas cultures which were imported into their American homes by their parents.

I raise these pedestrian points in order to introduce another way of thinking about why Americans at the end of the twentieth century began to cultivate noticeably lax attitudes toward the truth, along with extraordinarily aggressive, "cancel culture," annihilationist attitudes toward people who do not behave like them, or toward aspects of the past that are not to their liking. Many Americans through World War II grew up in the homes of immigrant families. Their attitudes toward "the past," which for all children is molded largely out of what they understand about their parents' background and upbringing, was fundamentally realistic. For them, the past was a place immediately perceptible in the foreign accent of their parents, in food that was on the table, and by the way people dressed in private. The past might be "rejected" by such immigrant children, but it could never be the subject of outlandish reimaginings where black was white and white was black. This immigrant background preserved levels of realism in American orientations toward space and time through the 1960s—because of immigration restrictions that had held intact since the 1920s, the 1960s can be seen as the start of a period when many mature Americans had grown up in homes that did not have an immigrant presence at all (the effects of the 1965 act liberalizing immigration policy would not be felt for another generation or two, after new norms of public chicanery and time-travel atonement were already locked into place around the start of the twenty-first century).

First proposed in 1938 by Marcus Lee Hansen, a sociological rule about immigrant heritage, holding that what the son wishes to forget the grandson wishes to remember, elucidates elements in the process which led to America's slide toward truthless realities.[167] In family homes during the 1960s era of semirevolutionary tumult, children belonged to Hansen's third generation. As in my own Jewish case, these third-generation children were born to assimilated, American-born parents; they occasionally heard mostly lost foreign languages like Yiddish from their largely Americanized grandparents, and they occasionally ate relatively exotic foods in their grandparents' city apartments but not in their own suburban homes. As Hansen recognized, for such third-generation children, the return to the family's "tradition" can be a natural act of rebellion against the Americanized ways of parents; but it is necessarily an imaginary rebellion because third-generation Americans lack firm grounding in their families' immigrant past. They lack a cultural skill set that would enable them to be realistic about what they think they are embracing.

I have some familiarity with American Jewish literature, and I think that readers familiar with this or other ethicized subgenres of American literature will recognize how the dynamics we are surveying here find expression in the world of letters. The first (immigrant) generation writes about the journey to America and settlement in it, in a mode of naïve romantic realism. The second-generation writer bitterly (and sometimes comically, as in the case of an author like Philip Roth) rejects the foreignness of immigrant parents while managing to evoke powerfully and realistically how

167. Hansen, "Problem."

that foreignness lingered in his or her childhood home. Authors from the third-generation return to the past and foreign lands of their grandparents (often, in the case of American Jewish writing, to the Holocaust or to East European shtetl settings), imaginatively recreating worlds with which they have no direct, intimate knowledge. Though it sometimes keeps the reader's attention, at least as a nod in deference to the author's earnestness, the deliberately crafted historical realism of the third generation feels contrived. In contrast, second-generation writers like Roth chew on the scenery of their immigrant family homes, ridicule it, contrive plotline romances with gentile *shiksas* expressive of their desire to flee from the family's traditional past, and produce novels with quite higher degrees of realism compared to their successors in the Hansen's Law generation.

Dynamics of immigrant culture in twentieth-century America created a window that opened for a few decades after the 1960s, beckoning many third-generation young people who were disposed to investigate their families' past traditions but who lacked resources and skills that are needed to undertake these journeys with some degree of realism. The most influential mass culture productions which inspired moralistic time travel undertaken in keeping with Hansen's Law—for example, the 1977 television miniseries *Roots* based on Alex Haley's 1976 novel, or the Holocaust television miniseries from 1978—were presented as realistic renderings of atrocious pasts, and there is no reason to be cynical about the educational intents of writers and television producers who generated these products. In retrospect, however, much in the plot, characterization, and historical detail of such productions makes one blanch—they are more valuable as testimony to the way issues like slavery or anti-Semitism were seen in the 1970s than as reliable imagined documentation of the historical issues themselves. Teenagers who grew up watching such 1970s miniseries productions had strong incentive to think moralistically about the past and to yearn to retrospectively repair its wrongs; but the television productions offered no pathways toward a realistic confrontation with the past, and their third-generation viewers lacked cultural skills needed for such realistic confrontation.

SCHMEGEGGE AND RELIGIOUS ANTI-MODERNISM

Ethnic revivalism in the 1960s sprawled in many different directions. For our purposes, an especially apposite trend is the anti-modernist backlash it spawned, particularly in Judaism and Christianity.

If we grant that it had ever existed in America, Judeo-Christian civilization made a huge comeback from the 1970s onward. Increasing members of these faiths became involved in neotraditional, fervently religious streams, either as fundamentalist-tempered, born-again Christians or in the parallel Jewish movement often known as "Teshuvah," a term that literally means repentance or return and usually refers to secular, or not particularly observant, Jews who undergo a process of becoming Orthodox (the most ritualistically strict, ultra-Orthodox alternative for such newly religious Jews is called Haredi, plural Haredim).

Despite all the reservations and criticisms articulated in earlier sections of this essay, I think it is fair to say that "Judeo-Christian civilization" has consolidated over the past half century in America. At least, this is true in a few senses. First, Israel has become a leading public affairs topic and a disproportionately favored recipient of US political and financial assistance. Second, public sphere spaces and rituals (e.g., Hanukkah menorahs beside Christmas trees) regularly evoke Jewish-Christian interactivity. And third, various social trends, such as the aforementioned phenomenon of celebrity power-couple intermarriage (which is an elite twist of the broad trend of Jewish intermarriage, which demographic surveys, published since the late 1980s, indicate are on a scale of about 50 percent[168]), reflect intimate bonds of trust between members from the two religious groups. The problem is explaining why the rise or rebirth of Judeo-Christian civilization has not enhanced the credibility of American public life and has instead contributed to increasingly confused, untruthful sociopolitical affairs in the country.

Religiosity upgraded its presence in American life as part of a broad cultural backlash to the perceived hippie licentiousness of the 1960s, to fractures in traditional family structure, and to transformations in the gender sphere. Within this post-1960s backlash, rapidly growing, neofundamentalist streams within Judaism and Christianity started enacting lifestyles expressly contemptuous of modernity itself. Teshuvah Jews and Evangelicals were very busy. On the Christian side, they built huge churches. They produced televangelist programs. They adopted Israel as a paramount concern, throwing their substantial political weight in lobbying for the Jewish state's policies, including (or especially) illiberal ones in post-1967 occupied territories. On the Jewish side, they created new ultra-Orthodox Jewish neighborhoods in the NYC metropolitan area and many other places. Even as anti-Zionists, they joined Israeli cabinets and used their newfound political leverage to fund handouts for Haredi families, yeshivas, and, increasingly, West Bank Orthodox communities. The Teshuvah Jews and Evangelicals

---

168. Pew Research Center, "Portrait."

invested prodigious resources for one purpose: to replace a sinful present with a righteously imagined past and to usher in a messianic future. This last messianic goal tends to be more pronounced among Evangelicals than among Haredim, but it is on the agendas of both groups; as shown by authors like Gershon Gorenberg and Yaakov Ariel, it explains the bizarre, and frightening, cooperation between Haredim and Evangelicals on Jerusalem's Temple Mount, in favor of the construction of a Third Temple.[169]

Fundamentalist contempt for the present became a make-or-break component of politics within two countries representative of Judeo-Christian civilization: the United States and Israel. Certainly if you are Donald Trump, or any other Republican, you cannot be elected president in America unless you curry favor with the Evangelicals. If you are a right-wing politician in Israel (and almost all electorally significant politicians in Israel for the past generation have been right-wing), you cannot become prime minister unless you curry favor with the Haredim. Currying such favor in both places means that the rise or rebirth of Judeo-Christian civilization since the 1970s has translated as the construction of more antidemocratic settlements on the West Bank. In the Jewish Israeli case, it means that increasing numbers of Jews, Haredim, will shirk army service, depend economically on government subsidies, and most fatefully, lack elementary and secondary school instruction in topics like mathematics and English, and thus not have knowledge and skills necessary for constructive citizenship awareness and adjustment in modern life. In the Christian case, it means increasingly noisy opposition to science instruction in subjects like evolution in public schools, or to the use of various challenging classics of world literature in classrooms. In both Jewish and Christian cases, fundamentalist groups impeded the implementation of reasonable public health policies during the Covid pandemic. Because Haredi and Evangelical constituencies are indispensable for Republican or Likud power brokers, advances in areas of women's rights and LGBTQ rights that seemed impregnable not too many years ago are now under threat in these two centers of Judeo-Christian civilization, the United States and Israel.

None of this matters with regard to the one question we have been asking here—namely, why has truth receded tragicomically in public life and been replaced by nonsensical schmegegge? A key piece of the puzzle is that the renewal of Judeo-Christian religiosity has brought to the fore, in America and other places, zealous groups which insist that the present is meaningless, that it is better to live in an imagined past than in the present,

---

169. Gorenberg, *End of Days*; Ariel, *Unusual Relationship*, 198–213.

and that the imminent future will be supernaturally and messianically transformed.

These born-again fundamentalist movements within Judaism and Christianity were largely third-generation, Hansen's Law, phenomena. In Judaism, the Teshuvah movement first became visible toward the end of the 1970s, and its anti-modernism was manifestly a response to the perceived lecherous excesses of 1960s activism.[170] The nucleus of Judaism's neo-Orthodox returnee movement was comprised of disillusioned young American Jews who were in their mid-to-late twenties and bitter about their hippie experiences. They drifted into Jerusalem, where spiritually enterprising rabbis, especially Mordecai Goldstein and Noah Weinberg, created a new type of religious institution for them: Teshuvah yeshivas like Ohr Sameah and Aish Hatorah that catered to religiously ignorant but spiritually eager teshuvah returnees. "The choice seemed to be the drug scene in New York city or a mid-west commune. . . . [But] the normal hippie rock scene: organic food and the rejection of the values of the United States wasn't for me. So I decided to go to Israel and see what would happen," one of these American Jewish migrants to Jerusalem, a Teshuvah returnee, told Janet Aviad, who published an early, important study of the birth of the Teshuvah movement. As of the mid-1980s, some fifty-five hundred returnees from overseas, mostly American Jews, had studied in Israeli yeshivot, and thirty-five hundred of them apparently remained in the country for extended periods.[171]

They were joined by Israeli counterparts, mostly young men in their late twenties who had grown up in homes that mixed secularism and Jewish traditionalism but were not rigidly observant Orthodox.[172] The backgrounds and motivations of these Israelis were not identical to those of the American Jewish Teshuvah returnees. Many of them were IDF veterans who had been startled or traumatized by the 1973 Yom Kippur conflict, a war whose early setbacks in the Sinai Peninsula and Golan Heights were painfully confusing for a young generation that had been persuaded of Israel's invincibility due to the Six-Day War triumph just some six years before. Teshuvah's emergence within Judaism by the end of the twentieth century was a perfect storm spinning out of many other factors (the missionary-like activism of the Chabad movement, Israel-state subsidies for Orthodox returnees within the non-European, *Mizrahi*, Jewish population under the inspiration of the "Shas" political party, and more), but it suffices to mention here that the

---

170. Aviad, *Return to Judaism*.
171. Aviad, *Return to Judaism*, 5.
172. Beit-Hallahmi, *Despair and Deliverance*; Meislish, *Hazara b'teshuva*.

Teshuvah takeoff of Jewish fundamentalism shaped itself in an anti-modern guise as a rebuttal to the flower-power modernism of 1960s radicalism.

But it was not exactly a rebuttal. The hippie was the doppelganger, not the nemesis, of the Jewish neo-Orthodox returnee. Both displayed profound suspicion toward the "establishment"; both assumed that no truth was to be found in the present. In terms of understanding the roots of schmegegge, this doppelganger affinity is crucial: starting in the 1960s, within Judaism (and there are parallels in Christianity, as we will note below) the most innovative modernist movements and anti-modernist movements have evinced radical skepticism about the credibility of the public sphere and assumed that it is largely or wholly untruthful.

The important difference between the 1960s Jewish hippie and the Teshuvah returnee, and the reason why only the latter has proliferated through the present, has to do with orientations toward the past. Nobody doubts that the drug-taking, wildly creative music, and political protests constituted a radically adventurous hippie lifestyle; but the 1960s activists were not particularly radical when they thought about where they came from and how that might relate to where they could go in the future. Those who were Jewish would never have taken the breathtakingly radical step of thinking that they might dress up, and presumably act, as their ancestors had in order to bring about a better future. This step was taken by the born-again, religious anti-modernists alone.

Think of Jimi Hendrix playing the "Star-Spangled Banner" at Woodstock, an iconic 1960s moment. Parts of his costume loosely evoked an abstract Arcadian past, not necessarily an American one; much in the sound and look of his presence pointed to an anti-establishment future. Relatively little in this presence referenced ethnic (black, in this example) difference. In sharp contrast, the Jewish Teshuvah returnee lives in denial of the present, imagining that his or her life replicates a traditional Jewish past and is hermetically separated from impure goyish cultures. In such respects, the time-traveling religious anti-modernists are the true radicals. Together with the Evangelicals, the Teshuvah returnees have done more than anyone else to ensure that dimensions of time, space, and truth would fly in rapturous confusion, in a state of schmegegge, in the post-1970s era of resurgent Judeo-Christian civilization.

Teshuvah radicalism draws from many sources—too many, in fact, to dip into here. The common denominator uniting all of them is that Teshuvah's core concept, return, is a myth. The ultra-Orthodox Jews you see in Borough Park or Bnei Brak have something in common with Haredim who were killed in Europe during the Holocaust and with their pre-Holocaust ancestors who dwelled in East European shtetls. But lines of discontinuity between these present and past groups are as significant as the professed faith and adopted lifestyle that unites them; as I think even gentile visitors to Israel, or to Brooklyn, are aware, the late medieval, Polish-looking fashion of such contemporary Orthodox Jews probably has very little to do with the way Old Testament Jews looked, or prayed. What we call Orthodox Jews today are the prominent anti-modernists in Judaism, but paradoxically, they are an invented product of modernity (this sentence might sound complicated or counterintuitive, but when you think of it, all contemporary anti-modern movements are themselves responses to modernity that could have only come about in modern times). Before the late eighteenth-century process called, by Jewish historians, "the exit from the ghetto," there were no Orthodox Jews in the world (just as there were no "secular" Jews before modernity).

The make-believe playacting, outright ignorance, and *chutzpah* of neo-Orthodox Jews who profess to be "returning" to the "real" Judaism that has "always" existed attests to how Teshuvah is sometimes a Hansen's Law phenomenon. If the core Teshuvah group had not been third-generation American Jews who soared into Jerusalem on the wings of a bad LSD trip, the ensuing decades of Orthodoxy's consolidation in the Jewish world might have passed by a bit differently. These original Jewish returnees lacked cultural tools which might have been used to carve out a more discriminating attitude toward the born-again *bubbe-meise* Jewish missionary indoctrination that washed over them at Yeshiva Ohr Sameah, or early Chabad houses. They were like a twenty-year-old African American in the late 1970s walking into a NAACP office thinking he is an updated Kunta Kinte.

This Hansen's Law factor should not be overestimated, however, because Teshuvah has, in Israel and beyond it, drawn in tens of thousands of Jewishly sophisticated Ashkenazi and Mizrahi Jews. The main reason why Teshuvah has become a prominent part of the schmegegge myth of escaping or correcting the present via time-travel atonement in the past is Israel itself.

State support in Israel for yeshiva study, as well as for Haredi shirking of elementary citizen requirements in educational, security, and other spheres, goes part of the way toward explaining why the Jewish state is responsible for Haredi schmegegge. But the main factor is the way Zionism, even in its early phases which were overwhelmingly secular, viewed Jewish redemption in the present and future as being dependent upon national relocation in an ancient land. A highly activist ideology, Zionism is in many ways backward looking; and much more than comparable nationalist ideologies, it has encouraged make-believe reenactments of imagined pasts in the daily present. Consider one comparison. With considerable fanfare stirred by charismatic Europeans like Lord Byron, Greek nationalism consolidated some seventy years before Herzl convened the first Zionist Congress, but when was the last time you saw anyone in Athens going to work in a *himation* and philosophizing like Socrates?

The tipping point in the story we are telling here was when Zionism's activism penetrated the Jewish group that was pronouncedly anti-modern and also anti-Zionist. As the first decades of the twentieth century progressed before the Holocaust, the world's important organized ultra-Orthodox groups, such as the Agudath Yisrael party, rejected Zionism, arguing that the project of restoring Jews in their biblical homeland was God's work and that mortals who undertook it were false messiahs who sacrilegiously "pushed for the end of days" (*dehikat haketz*). When viewed as a contrast to the first Zionist Congresses, where some Orthodox Jewish delegates iconoclastically defied this *dehikat haketz* rule that was conventionally and widely upheld in their community, the situation today in Israel is breathtaking.[173] In fact, many commentators believe that the future of the country belongs to Haredim who have become hyped-up right-wing nationalists (there is a term for this group, *Hardalim*).

Brought into the world by Zionism's ambiguous orientations toward the past, present, and future, the Hardalim are Israel's paramount contemporary contribution to the phenomenon we have surveyed here. Anti-modernists who believe that everything in the present, outside of their secluded communities, is impure and untruthful, Hardalim are nonetheless deeply involved in (or implicated in) the most divisive contemporary issues in the Jewish state, such as its colonialist, antidemocratic settlement movement. Believing that the present is a lie and that it is preferable to live in a re-enacted Jewish past, the Hardalim fuel the consternation of young secular Jews in North America and Europe, who have furiously protested Israel's 2023–2024 Gaza War and who believe that the presentation of Israel as a Jewish democratic state is a lie. For utterly different reasons, anti-modernist Teshuvah Jews who live in an imagined past, and young secular Jews who live in an Americanized present and who know very little about the Jewish past, believe that liberal visions of the Jewish state are utterly misguided. They are an improbable but powerful alliance consecrated by the belief that there is not, at present, any truth to be found in the Jewish part of Judeo-Christian civilization.

In American Christianity, the path to schmegegge paved by the Evangelicals follows many of the stages we have just traced in the Teshuvah,

---

173. Transformations in religious Zionism have never been suitably surveyed. For the early situation at the first Zionist Congresses, see Klausner, *Opozitsyah*. A recent overview, aimed at popular audiences in Israel, is Sheleg, *Hahut*.

Jewish American-Israel case. Unlike the case of Teshuvah, Evangelical Zionism has a foundational text, Hal Lindsey's *Late Great Planet Earth*, which was published in 1970 and which, according to *The New York Times*, became the best-selling nonfiction volume of the decade. *The Late Great Planet Earth* opened a new, Israeli, window through which conservative American Christians could articulate objections to liberal sociopolitical events of the 1960s. Just as the rabbis who opened Teshuvah yeshivas in Jerusalem would have attested, Lindsey mentioned that he had lectured on college campuses where he found that young people were disaffected by "what they consider materialistic, hypocritical and prejudiced elements within our American culture." One chapter in *The Late Great Planet Earth* described the rapture as "the ultimate trip," and the book was sprinkled with anecdotes touting premillennialism as an antidote for hippie culture.[174]

Sociologically, there is much in the profile of pro-Israel Evangelicals, through the present day, that recapitulates the third-generation characteristics of young American Jews in the early 1980s who jump-started the Teshuvah movement. As described by Zev Chafets in a smart, snappy 2007 book about such Evangelicals, *A Match Made in Heaven*, many of them who come on pilgrimage to Israel are surprisingly low key. Christian tourists in Galilee and Jerusalem are Americans with tough luck stories who are drawn to Evangelicalism because of the way it boosts their morale, self-esteem, and self-discipline as they struggle to get their lives together, Chafets observed.[175] Modest-level hopes for spiritual self-improvement, not grandiose dreams of the rapture, bring such American Evangelicals to Israel.

The question then becomes, why are such low-key laymen drawn to the apocalyptic politics of Evangelical Zionist preachers like John Hagee, who breathlessly reports in his end-of-the-world books about how he has brought Benjamin Netanyahu to his Cornerstone Church in San Antonio in order to discuss Iran's nuclear threat in sermon performances beamed into ninety million homes in one hundred countries?[176] A similar question is this: What is on the minds of readers of the *Left Behind* series of premillennial dispensationalist novels, which came out between 1995 and 2007 and reached sixty-five million readers, with some of the books hitting the top of *The New York Times* bestseller lists?[177] Parts of the answers to these questions are difficult for secularized persons to deal with since it is very hard for them to understand how Evangelicals and fellow travelers might

---

174. Lindsey, *Late Great Planet Earth*, 183, 135–36.
175. Chafets, *Match Made in Heaven*.
176. Hagee, *Jerusalem Countdown*.
177. Wilkinson, "*Left Behind* Series."

seriously believe in cloud-ascension rapture. But I think that liberal skeptics and fundamentalist believers can roughly concur that the precondition of any answer is Israel.

A century ago, when the last pilgrims in the fifth Gospel movement toured the Holy Land, they had no reason to believe in scenarios of its radical transformation. As far as they were concerned, the Holy Land's past was its present, and sacred space was out of time. A century later, liberal Protestants and Evangelicals have witnessed how Zionism radically changed the temper and practical circumstances of Jerusalem, Galilee, and the rest of the Holy Land. In particular, Jerusalem's reunification (or what Judeo-Christian narratives, but not Islamic ones, would regard as its reunification) in the 1967 Six-Day War, along with Israel's possession of Old Testament sites like Hebron, taught such Christians that Holy Land space is far from timeless. Instead, it is eminently transformable.

Such recognition is a crucial piece in the puzzle of time-travel atonement. A hundred years ago, American Christians humbly toured the Holy Land, quietly looking for a ballpark "sense of presence" of where Jesus had lived and preached. Their pilgrimages actually had very little to do with progressive politics (Fosdick's fifth Gospel tour is not the reason why Martin Luther King Jr. regarded him as the twentieth century's foremost preacher). On the other hand, the moderate, accommodating temper of the fifth Gospel could never have become incorporated in militant political fanaticism about particular spaces. A century later, Evangelicals like John Hagee proactively manipulate Middle East politics, encouraging the Netanyahu governments to tempt apocalypse by toughening Israel's stances toward Teheran, among other things. They are truly Christian Zionists in this respect. Just as Zionist activism inspired Teshuvah returnees to shake off Orthodoxy's traditional passivity toward affairs in the Jewish homeland, Eretz Israel, it has also inspired Evangelicals to believe in the state of Israel's integral role in schemes of the messianic rapture.

By his active participation in America's transfer of its Israel embassy to Jerusalem, under the sponsorship of the first Trump administration, the Evangelical leader Hagee gave a strong boost to Israeli unilateralism.[178] This is the idea that major changes in the status quo of the Israel-Arab conflict can be initiated without any semblance of Palestinian consent. The unilateral diplomacy approach, enthusiastically championed by Netanyahu before the October 7, 2023, catastrophe, has been disastrous for Israel. Among many other things, it lowered the Jewish state's moral high ground after Hamas's brutal, criminal attack. What options were left to the Palestinians,

---

178. Goldberg, "Grotesque Spectacle."

after Israel and America negated diplomacy as a means of resolving their claims and grievances? Whereas Teshuvah returnees made zealous lifestyle and identity choices without having in their possession cultural tools useful for judicious discernment, Evangelicals willfully meddle in Middle East politics on the basis of prejudicial suppositions about Islam, not even wanting to hone cultural skills needed for understanding local needs and sensitivities that are outside the orbit of their understanding of Judeo-Christian civilization.

Teshuvah and pro-Israel Evangelicalism are profoundly antidemocratic phenomena. The secret to Netanyahu's longevity in Israeli politics and on the world stage is the alliance forged between his Likud party and Israel's Haredi religious parties. The origins of this coalition are to be found in Menachem Begin's governments, from 1977 to the end of the First Lebanon War. The coalition has been going strong since Netanyahu's debut as prime minister in 1996, when he was elected, in the aftermath of Yitzhak Rabin's assassination, on the basis of a platform opposing the Oslo peace process.

In September 1997, shortly after Netanyahu's election, a poll conducted by Dr. Roby Nathanson, from the Israeli Institute for Economic and Social Research, found that not a single Haredi respondent supported withdrawal from the occupied territories (half of secular respondents supported territorial withdrawal in the peace framework).[179] Other polls indicated extraordinarily high levels of Haredi opposition to branches of Israel's democratic system, including its judicial branch. One poll, conducted in spring 1988 by the Israeli Institute for Economic and Social Research, which surveyed sixteen hundred young people, twelve hundred of them Jewish, from the ages of fifteen to twenty-one, found that 72 percent of young Israelis had confidence in the country's judicial system. But just a third of Haredi young people indicated in this poll that they had faith in Israel's judicial system (the figure would be even lower today because Haredi hatred of the court system has grown, owing to questions raised by the High Court in recent years regarding existing arrangements of IDF service deferral for the ultra-Orthodox).[180]

Because it is a more familiar subject for English-language readers, we will not review here data about Evangelical illiberalism in the United States. The details would only distract attention from the main point.

In the late 1970s, when the Teshuvah movement was taking shape and when Evangelicals were strengthening connections with Menachem Begin's government in Israel, pro-Israel hasbara spinmeisters came up with the idea

179. Ilan, *Haredim*, 26.
180. Ilan, *Haredim*, 59.

of playing the Judeo-Christian card. They wrote books, and they drafted AIPAC talking points to convince policymakers and the public that highlighting the religious basis of the American-Israel relationship was good for democracy. Democracy, they insisted, had foundations in Judeo-Christian civilization. Their ideas about Judeo-Christian civilization? Schmegegge. Their neoconservative project of promoting enhanced religiosity in the public square and relegating long-standing liberal Jewish commitment to the separation of church and state? Schmegegge with sprinkles. And the reality that has been created out of the rise of Evangelicalism as a key factor in American politics and the rise of Haredi parties as crucial partners in Israeli government coalitions? Schmegegge with sprinkles and fudge sauce.

Whenever it is in the public square, Judeo-Christian civilization is a threat to democracy in America and to the survival of Israel as a liberal Jewish state.

3

What Was Rabbi Jose Thinking?

Colonialism, Jews, and Christians

(For J. S.)

INTRODUCTION: WHAT DOES THE TALMUD SAY ABOUT COLONIALISM AND EXILE?

Two thousand years ago, or thereabouts, Jews enacted anti-colonialist campaigns against the Romans, launching two revolts in their Holy Land, the first in 66–70 CE and the second several decades later, 132–135 CE. Both ended in disaster. The Second Temple went up in flames after the first rebellion, and according to tradition, the Jews' exile in diaspora lands began in the aftermath of the second uprising, known as the Bar Kokhba rebellion. On this traditional view, or what can be called the "Jewish narrative," Jewish anti-colonialism bred two thousand years of cursed exile (since Israel was established as a sovereign Jewish state in 1948, the computation is wrong by almost two hundred years, but Jews can be excused for being bad at math whenever we are thinking about our own maiming).

Jewish religion and experience transitioned in this period. Before the anti-colonial rebellions, "Judaism" constituted a temple-based cult in Jerusalem. This cult had been inspired by divine revelation at Sinai and its transcription in the Hebrew Bible (the Tanakh); it featured a priestly elite and sacrificial pilgrimages and rites. After the calamitous two rebellions against the Roman empire, this Jerusalem temple cult was replaced by devotion to a supplemental Oral Law, transcribed in the Talmud. Toward the end of the third century, some one hundred and fifty years after the Bar Kokhba fiasco, this Talmud-based Judaism was interpreted and applied by a new rabbinical elite.

The Jewish narrative is inconsistent about the role of the Holy Land, Eretz Israel, in this transformation. Jews have always believed that the failure of these two anti-colonial revolts spelled diasporic exile, meaning that the new form of rabbinic, Talmudic-based Judaism developed outside of the ancestral homeland. In modern Jewish nationalism, Zionism, the Talmud is virtually synonymous with exile. The generation of secularized, socialist-leaning, pioneering Zionists (*halutzim*, in the nationalist lingo) which created kibbutz colonies and laid the foundation of a Jewish state roughly a century ago, more or less when Western-styled modernization in the country under the British Mandate supplanted Ottoman Turkish rule, coined slogans to underscore this view of history. David Ben-Gurion, who became Israel's first prime minister, talked about Zionism as a bridge between the Tanakh (the Hebrew Bible) and the Palmach (a militia of idealistic halutzim, which fought effectively in Israel's 1948 War of Independence). The rhyme suggests that the "medieval" entirety of Jewish history, spanning between Bar Kokhba's second failed rebellion and the early Zionist "Aliyot" immigration waves before and after World War I has little relevance. The rabbis' Talmudic form of Judaism bred submissive, vulnerable Jews who were crushed and decimated by the Crusades, the Inquisition, and the Holocaust. The Talmud, on this classic Zionist interpretation, ranks as prime cause and poignant symptom of the Jews' exilic vulnerability. Developed outside of the Jews' own historic homeland, the Talmud symbolizes Jewish rootlessness and powerless lack of political sovereignty.

This Jewish narrative is riddled by loose ends and internal contradictions. *All* of its problems stem from the fact that Jewish consciousness is ridiculously inconsistent in the way it relates to colonial power. The spectacle witnessed by an astonished world in spring 2024—idealistic young Jews on college campuses protesting against alleged Israeli genocide on the Gaza Strip while Israelis talked about the war as the most just one in their history, and about their military, the Israel Defense Forces (IDF), as the most moral army on earth—is not ugly happenstance. It was scripted over two thousand years, preordained as though written by history's central casting talent agency.

To simplify matters, it can be useful to think about "the Jewish narrative" as having two mutually inconsistent frames, a political one and a religious one. Through the political frame, as we have just seen, the Talmud is viewed negatively, as the cardinal symbol of Jewish rootlessness and weakness. The religious frame is rather more complex, owing to its creative use of historical myths and its much more sophisticated way of thinking about how Jewish minorities can, and ought to, relate to colonial power. We turn to this frame now.

Unlike its political counterpart, this religious narrative acknowledges the historical fact that the origins of the new, Talmudic, model are to be found in the Jews' historic homeland, Eretz Israel. According to its Jewish rebirth story, in the calamitous aftermath of the first anti-Roman revolt, a rabbinical leader (part of a group known as Tannaim), Yohanan ben Zakkai, cleverly wrested permission from the Romans to launch a religious academy at Yavne, a locale positioned in what is now central Israel. Ben-Zakkai's maneuver combined spiritual defiance and formal, practical submission. By reformatting their identity as Judaism, a religion, in lieu of the Jewish national sovereignty model that had just been embroiled in the anti-colonial rebellion, Ben-Zakkai and fellow Tannaim allowed the Romans to believe that the few pocket enclaves of Jews which remained in the country could not pose a political threat. Rather than anti-colonial guerilseparated, they would be populated by religious scholars engaged in the compilation of what later became known as the Talmud, a sprawling written conversation about religious observance and communal rules.

The Ben-Zakkai story highlights two serious glitches in the way Jews have seen their history through the other, political, frame. First, Jews have always understood that the origins of what became Talmudic Judaism are to be found in Eretz Israel, in the Ben-Zakkai/Yavne story. Second, one of the two versions of the Talmud is known as the Palestinian, or Jerusalem, Talmud, implying that its protracted composition, over many decades, transpired in the Jews' homeland, Eretz Israel (in fact, the "Jerusalem Talmud" title was a marketing ploy which gave precedence to the most spiritually charged city in the country, but this version of the Jews' Oral Law was compiled mostly in the Galilee city of Tiberias).

Such glitches arose in ways Jews thought about their political history because when they moved into modern times, the Talmud, as a symbol of medieval Judaism, seemed obstructive to an array of political agendas. Modern Jews often thought about their political identities in diametrically opposite ways, but the one thing they agreed on was that the Talmud was a problem. As nation-states arose in Europe in the nineteenth century, gentiles typically derided the Talmud as a medieval document whose antisocial ethos of Jewish separatism belied the professions of liberal, assimilated Jews who desired to integrate as loyal, patriotic citizens in France, Germany, Russia, and other countries. This view won a serious degree of sublimated acceptance among modernizing Jews, both in the nineteenth-century Jewish Enlightenment movement, the Haskalah, and the liberal religious stream, Reform Judaism. Then, when some Jews abandoned the dream of integration in the modern nation-states of Europe and adopted nationalism via the Zionist movement, formally organized by Theodor Herzl at the end of the nineteenth century, they degraded Talmudic Judaism essentially for the opposite reason. For these secular Zionists, the rabbis' prodigious Talmudic effort was anathema precisely because it enabled a durable form of Jewish life in exile, outside of Eretz Israel.

For these reasons, relatively few people understand that one the most significant discussions engaged by Jews about colonialism before our own postmodern times, prior to the contemporary debate about Israel, transpired early in Talmudic times, in the era of the Tannaim, in Eretz Israel.

In truth, Jews were never dispersed as a mass bloc from their homeland after the failed Bar Kokhba revolt—how exactly would that have worked, from a techno-administrative standpoint, in the middle of the second century CE? Regrouping, many fled from the country's Judean heartland, where the Romans enforced harsh punitive measures (known, by Jews, as *gezerot*, or *shemad*, decrees), to Galilee, which, most historians agree, had remained relatively quiet during the Bar Kokhba revolt and was thus less susceptible to persecutory Roman retaliation.[1] Over two hundred thousand Jews, or about 75 percent of the region's total population, dwelled in Galilee for many decades in this Tannaitic period, following the Bar Kokhba debacle.[2] We are talking about Jewish relocation within Eretz Israel, not exile, and this relocation has a well-documented origins story. According to the Talmudic commentary (*midrash*) on the Song of Songs (*Shir Hashirim Rabbah* 2:5), prominent Tannaim, led by Rabbi Judah bar Ilai and including Rabbi Meir and Rabbi Shimon bar Yochai (known as Rashbi), gathered at a Galilee village, Usha, a small locale (near today's Arab town, Shfaram) that would not have been subject to much Roman monitoring.[3] This happened in 138 CE, and the Tannaim, whose name literally means "teachers," issued a religious and educational proclamation proclamation saying, according to this midrash, "whoever has studied, let him come and teach, and whoever has not studied, let him come and learn."[4]

This Usha proclamation marked a turning point in Jewish history. Congregating in Galilee towns like Sepphoris, and led by Judah Hanasi, whose heyday stretched between 175–220 CE, the Tannaim compiled the Mishnah, which became the first part of the Talmud. Yet Usha's preeminent

---

1. For scholarship about the status of Galilee during the Bar Kokhba revolt, see the bibliography in Oppenheimer, *Ha-galil*, 30n1.
2. Goodman, *State and Society*, 32.
3. Silver, *Galilee, 47 BCE to 1260 CE*, 103–8.
4. *Shir Hashirim Rabbah* 2:5:3.

role in the refashioning of Jewish experience in a centuries-long Talmudic era was nudged aside, to the point where most Jews in the world today would probably not recognize the event and place-name. This is largely due to the aforementioned prejudices about the Talmud, which remain prevalent today among secular Jews in Israel and the United States.

There is one other reason why the Jews' Talmudic debate about colonialism lost resonance in history. The early consolidation of Talmud in Galilee was one response to the calamities in Jerusalem caused by the Jews' anti-Roman rebelliousness. Another response, the rise of Christianity in the same Galilee region, turned into a nuisance for Jews on many different levels. Tannaim regrouped in Usha just one generation after disciples in the Jesus movement, located (many scholars believe) in nearby Galilee locales, sat down to compile New Testament canon, like the book of Matthew; this made second-century Galilee a nettlesome venue in Jewish memory.

How exactly the Jews lived in Tiberias, Sepphoris, and other Galilee locales under Roman authority, from Usha in the mid-first century and through the advent of the Byzantine Christian era in Palestine in the mid-fourth century, remains open to question. Israeli scholarship on the topic has a self-contradictory agenda. It is pulled in one direction by the myth of sudden, mass exilic Jewish dispersion after the Bar Kokhba revolt (on this myth, the resumption of Jewish sovereignty in 1948 after a two-thousand-year hiatus makes Israel's establishment an exceptional, perhaps unique, event in history). But it is pushed in a different direction by the maddening conflict with the Palestinians whose durability incentivizes Zionist-tempered historians to emphasize how Jews maintained collective presences in Eretz Israel over the ages, in messianic expectation of eventual nationalist restoration in the land. As decades passed after 1948, the image of Jewish abandonment of Eretz Israel after the Roman rebellions became a liability in the confrontation with another national group, the Palestinians, whose claim of centuries-long settlement in the country appeared to have strong empirical footing. Hence, Israeli historians were drawn increasingly to the second pole in this push-and-pull dynamic by which Jewish national meaning was ascribed to the experience of Jewish communities that remained in Eretz Israel after the Bar Kokhba revolt, starting with the Tannaitic era in Galilee after Usha. As suggested in the work of Israeli historians like Aharon Oppenheimer, Jews maintained semisovereign autonomy in Galilee in this late Roman period, whose pinnacle was the term of the patriarch (*nasi*) Judah Hanasi.[5] Judah exercised powerful spiritual authority, as the Tannaim reconstituted the *Sanhedrin* rabbinical council. In fact, Judah became the

---

5. Oppenheimer, *Yehuda Ha-nasi*.

redactor of the Mishnah. Meantime, he undertook a series of sociopolitical steps, facilitating (for example) land purchases by Jews and also entertaining symbolic measures (including a proposal for the annulment of the Tisha B'Av mourning fast, commemorating the destruction of the Jerusalem temple) whose gist was an expectation of bona fide Jewish national revival in a reconstructed, Tannaitic proto-Talmudic, community in Galilee. So suggests this brand of Israeli-Zionist historical scholarship.

Outside Israel, some Jewish historians have similarly identified a viable socioeconomic infrastructure of Jewish life in second-century Galilee. They paint a provocative, counterintuitive portrait of Jewish revival in Eretz Israel after the calamitous anti-Roman rebellions. For instance, relying largely on the discerning use of Talmudic materials, Oxford University scholar Martin Goodman refers to thriving Jewish economic activity, based on olive production, in Galilee under Roman rule.[6] His analysis imputes cultural viability to Jewish life in Galilee, based on the Aramaic language as well as Hebrew. Tellingly, the Jewish sources used by Goodman impute Jewish cultural dominance in this setting, suggesting that gentile conversion to Judaism was a phenomenon sufficiently significant to annoy Roman officials.

In contrast, Columbia University scholar Seth Schwartz believes that Tannaitic scholars comprised an isolated, uninfluential enclave through the second and third centuries.[7] On his view, Judaism in this period was in utter disarray following the hurban destruction of its Second Temple foundations. Jewish Galileans were demonstrably drawn to Roman-pagan identity sources in lieu of what, in this context, we anachronistically call Judaism, Schwartz writes. Pointing out that they were written centuries later by sages who were typically based in far-off Babylonia and who, bereft of any commitment to historical veracity, utilized references to Tannaim instrumentally, to illustrate religious principles, Schwartz eschews the use of Talmudic materials by historians. He also doubts that Israeli archaeological excavations in Galilee have furnished persuasive evidence of an infrastructure, centered on synagogues or other spiritual-communal institutions, which might have supported Jewish cultural revival in Galilee in this period. Whereas Goodman's reliance on Talmudic materials led him to sprinkle his account with hints of gentile admiration for Judaism's transformation and revival in this Sanhedrin-patriarchate Galilean setting, Schwartz argues that the overwhelming cultural trend was in the opposite direction, as Romanizing Jews cultivated a cult of zodiacs, animal symbols, and other emblems

6. Goodman, *State and Society*.
7. Schwartz, *Imperialism and Jewish Society*.

of paganism or Hellenism. The pro-Roman, assimilatory implications of mosaics and other decorative expressions that can be seen today on display at Tzippori and several other excavated sites in Galilee have been roundly ignored, or unpersuasively mitigated, by Israeli archaeologists and historians, Schwartz pungently argues.

This scholarly debate about Roman-controlled Galilee in the Tannaitic era is relatively amicable. Despite the obvious divergence of their methodologies and conclusions, Jewish scholars like Goodman and Schwartz do not really present themselves as antagonists. In general, the story of Jewish accommodation, or continued resistance, to Roman colonial control after the two failed rebellions has largely been overlooked in scholarship, owing to the predominance enjoyed by the story of Christianity's rise and consolidation. Yet there are reasons to expect that this intensive focus on the story of relations between Jews and early Christians will abate in decades to come, and commentators will become newly interested in how Jews related to Roman power in Palestine between the failure of their two anti-colonial rebellions and the Christianization of the Roman Empire in the fourth century CE era of Constantine.

Frustratingly, there is a dearth of Tannaitic documentation of Jewish encounters with such early Christians, who are called *minim* in the sources, the early followers of Jesus, who is called Jesus ben Pantera in these Jewish records (not all scholars agree that minim is a special reference to Christians).[8] There are a few suggestive but inconclusive records of such encounters in two Galilee locales north of Nazareth: Kfar Semai and Kfar Sikhnin (Sakhnin). Meantime, urgency in discussions about Jesus' own Jewish background has abated among New Testament scholars who relate to Galilee in the late Roman period. As noted earlier, the most recent "third wave" of scholarly inquiry about the historical Jesus culminated in an "emphatic reaffirmation of the Jewishness of Jesus," observed John Meir, a Catholic priest and prominent scholar of early Christianity.[9] For such reasons, we can anticipate a turn in interest, moving from the problem of Jews and early Christians in this Galilean setting toward the issue of Jews and colonialism in the Mishnaic period.

One Talmudic account retroactively captures the Jews' dilemma with colonialism in the late Roman period, following the two failed rebellions.[10] The account features a discussion between two Tannaitic interlocutors

---

8. Kimmelman, "Identifying Jews and Christians"; Miller, "Minnim."
9. Eddy and Beilby, *Historical Jesus*, 48.
10. Avi-Yonah, *Jews*, 65; this account can be found in the Babylonian Talmud, b. Shabbat 33b.

about the Romans. One is the aforementioned leader of the Usha convocation, Rabbi Judah bar Ilai, and the other is Rabbi Shimon bar Yochai, Rashbi, who has become in Israel one of the most revered Jewish personalities in the whole compass of history spanning between the Second Temple hurban catastrophe and the present. Advocating a policy of Jewish accommodation with Roman colonialism, Rabbi Judah proclaims, "How pleasing are the actions of the Romans." The Romans, he explains, build "marketplaces, bridges and bathhouses" for the land's residents.[11] Rashbi, the anti-colonialist, dismisses this argument. Denying that the Romans are committed to their subjects' welfare, Rashbi castigates their projects and policies as self-interested exploitation. The Romans set up markets to profit from sex trafficking; they build bathhouses for their own luxury; and they erect bridges to fleece travelers with toll fees, opines Rashbi.

The uncompromising militancy retrospectively imputed to Rashbi in this exchange contravenes stereotypes of medieval rabbis as submissive accommodators in exilic lands who passively awaited the messiah's arrival. Laden within Rashbi's anti-Roman remark is recognition of colonialism's overall iniquitous hypocrisy. In fact, the recorded discussion suggests that *anti-colonialism* retained a substantive niche in Talmudic culture.

In general, traits in Rashbi's militant personality make him popular with many groups in contemporary Israel, which is becoming both more religiously observant and also more bellicosely nationalist.[12] Rashbi was an outspoken advocate of the Tannaitic project of reconstituting Jewish identity in Galilee, after the hurban in Jerusalem. He proclaimed, "When a man is banished from Judea to Galilee . . . this cannot really be called exile."[13] In Galilee, Rashbi insisted that Tannaim devote themselves exclusively to religious study. If they were they to sow and plow the fields, he pointedly asked, "What will become of Torah?"[14] Tannaitic sages probably supported themselves by working in various trades, but Rashbi previewed the contemporary position of ultra-Orthodox Haredim in Israel, who announce that "Torah" is their sole trade (*Torato Umanuto*) and thus shun daily work and also army service.

On the other hand, Rashbi was a militant anti-colonialist activist. In a tale repeated with some variations in different Talmudic accounts, Rashbi faced Roman persecution, owing to his outspoken criticism of colonial

---

11. B. Shabbat 33b.
12. Silver, *Galilee, 47 BCE to 1260 CE*, 124–34.
13. Oppenheimer, *Ha-galil*, 53.
14. B. Berakhot 35b:7.

exploitation, as exemplified in the exchange with Rabbi Judah.[15] Fearing for his life (particularly the possibility that his loquacious wife might betray his whereabouts to the Romans), Rashbi and his son, Eleazar ben Shimon, hid in a Galilee cave for thirteen years, before emerging to effect various wondrous deeds. Most famously, in his subsequent career, Rashbi won renown for purifying Tiberias, the town on the Sea of Galilee coast that had long been repellent to spiritually scrupulous Jews because King Herod's son, Herod Antipas, had sacrilegiously built it atop tomb sites.

Rashbi's prodigious discipline and marvelous restorative powers, his mix of political militancy and zealousness about religious study, have a larger-than-life quality. It is little surprise that he became a favorite topic in mystical streams of Jewish culture known as Kabbalah. In truth, many of the Tannaitic rabbis have magical attributes in Talmudic accounts, and some of them could conceivably have become the main protagonist in Kabbalistic lore; but Shimon bar Yochai is preeminent thanks to his starring role in *Sefer Ha-Zohar* (Book of Splendor), the cornerstone of Kabbalistic belief whose authorship is apocryphally attributed to Rashbi himself. Actually, the *Zohar* was composed in late-thirteenth-century Spain by Moses de Leon, who drew inspiration from the way the Tannaim regrouped in Galilee and saved Judaism after the Romans crushed Jewish rebels and destroyed the Jerusalem temple.[16] With the Christian *Reconquista* picking up steam on the Iberian Peninsula, Leon and fellow Kabbalists found comfort in framing their exposition of Jewish mystical belief around a story of Rashbi and fellow Tannaim roaming around Galilee, ultimately delivering messianic revelation to Jews, unperturbed by Roman rule in the land. According to Arthur Green, author of a *Guide to the Zohar*, Rashbi figures as a Jewishly credible alternative to Jesus in this cornerstone Kabbalistic text. "The tale of a great holy man, Rabbi Shimon bar Yohai, followed by a group of faithful disciples as he wanders about the Holy Land, especially the Galilee, has a familiar ring to it," Green writes.[17] Like Christianity, the mystical branch of Judaism, Kabbalah, uses the Galilee landscape to tell a story about a charismatic leader's spiritual resistance to colonial power, the Romans.

Rashbi, or his tomb on the Meron hilltop adjacent to Safed, is the focal point of Israel's largest annual event, the *hillula* celebration held on the folkloristic Lag BaOmer holiday, late in the spring. Attended by masses of mystical-minded Orthodox Jews, the hillula pilgrimage to Rashbi's tomb, and late-night prayer vigils at this site, are mystical expressions crafted in

---

15. Levine, "R. Simeon b. Yochai."
16. Silver, *Galilee, 1538–1949*, 7–14.
17. Green, *Guide to the Zohar*, 90–91.

line with promises and possibilities uncovered in Kabbalah study. But Lag BaOmer celebrations in Israel are also regarded as commemoration of the Bar Kokhba revolt against the Romans. And while they are notoriously disassociated from modern political activity, it is impossible to overlook how the messianic mystics who throng Meron on Lag BaOmer are there in homage to a militant rabbi who, according to a legend that is palpably real to them, spent thirteen years in a Galilee cave due to his opposition to colonial Roman power. In this sense, Jewish mysticism is "anti-colonialist," as is another Galilee-based creed, Christianity.

What about the other extreme in the Talmudic debate about Roman power, that of the accommodationist Rabbi Judah bar Ilai? His pragmatic, compromising orientation toward Roman rulers is associated with the Tannaitic era's House of Shammai, a religious scholarly school whose interpretations of holy commandments focused on the practical results of actions, rather than their perpetrators' actual intentions. This is a philosophy that wants life to go along efficaciously, without extraneous fussing over subjective variables such as personal or collective honor. Politely, the Talmud casts Rabbi Judah as a bit of a dolt, at least in comparison to Tannaitic intellectual giants like Rabbi Meir (who objected to the mediocrity of functionaries in the evolving patriarchate and insisted that Jewish communal power belonged solely to serious religious scholars).[18] Damning him with faint praise, the Talmud casts Rabbi Judah as a "wise sage when he wanted to be."[19] This phrase conveys traces of the way his interlocutor, Rashbi, must have seen Rabbi Judah during the famous exchange, as a second-rate opportunist.

I want to cast the spotlight on the mysteriously silent third man in this Rashbi/Rabbi Judah discussion about Roman power. On the Talmudic account, a third Tanna, Rabbi Jose ben Halafta "remained silent" as Rashbi and Rabbi Judah exchanged their extreme pro and con views about the Romans.[20] This is a curiously noncommunicative posture, just as the high price paid by Rabbi Jose for his nonparticipation participation in this debate is curious. The Roman "monarchy," this Talmudic passage records, gained knowledge of the debate. In addition to emplacing a death warrant on Rashbi, the Romans also banished Rabbi Jose to Sepphoris, presumably on the grounds that he had tacitly condoned Rashbi's subversive peroration.

From what we know about Rabbi Jose, this banishment constituted a homecoming, rather than exile, since the Tanna came from the Galilee town, today's Tzippori. Rabbi Jose's name appears frequently in the Mishnah—the

---

18. Lau, *Hakhamim*, 75–77.
19. Lau, *Hakhamim*, 76.
20. B. Shabbat 33b.

Talmudic text's redactor, Judah Hanasi, lavishes praise upon the pious Jose. Jose's background brims with suggestions of a defiant attitude toward officious Roman power. He was ordained as a rabbi in defiance of Roman rulings. In fact, the mentor who conferred this rabbinical *semikhah* (ordination) to Jose, Rabbi Judah ben Bava, was an anti-colonialist whose martyrdom (with nine others) is commemorated annually by Jews, in poems recited on Yom Kippur and Tisha B'Av. According to legend, while ordaining Rabbi Jose and several other Tannaitic luminaries (including Rashbi, Rabbi Meir, and Judah Hanasi), Judah ben Bava was spotted by Hadrian's soldiers. Using his own body to shield his students, figures later responsible for Judaism's Mishnaic revival, Rabbi Judah ben Bava was mutilated by three hundred Roman iron spears.

Talmudic politics on this issue of Roman colonialism is thus Janus-faced. On the one hand, the prominent figure in the Usha founding event of the Tannaitic campaign in Galilee to save Judaism, Rabbi Judah bar Ilai, was a "pro-colonialist" accommodationist who valued the benefits of a Roman administration which had destroyed Jewish national sovereignty. On the other hand, the anti-colonial martyrdom of Rabbi Judah ben Bava can be regarded as the origins story of the Tannaitic revival, since the sacrifice saved the lives of revered rabbis who are known as the "restorers of the law." Having, years before, been ordained by one anti-Roman martyr, Rabbi Jose listened in silence as Rashbi harangued about Roman oppression. What really was on the mind of this third man as he listened to Rashbi and Rabbi Judah bar Ilai exchange views about Rome? What was Rabbi Jose thinking?

PRO-ISRAEL, ANTI-ISRAEL, AND THE THIRD WAY

One of history's mysteries is whether there is a viable third perspective on colonialism, one which keeps a healthy distance from violently mind-messing dynamics that unfold between the colonizers and the colonized. For Jews, this mystery traces the whole arc of their journey of exile and return, beginning in late antiquity with two disastrous revolts against the Roman empire, and continuing in our present time when American Jews and Israelis are accused of complicity in genocidal colonialism, allegedly perpetrated by the Jewish state under the patronage of neocolonialist American foreign policy.

The third-perspective mystery is far from an exclusive Jewish issue, however. Wherever there are arguments about colonialism, there are always "third way" moderates to be found who try to wriggle away from the zero-sum gridlock in which the colonialists and anti-colonialists are trapped.

In today's Jewish drama, yearning for a third way option belongs to American Jewish organizations like J Street and Israeli organizations like Breaking the Silence. Such left-wing groups adhere to a patriotically Jewish position (which is called "pro-Israel" or "Zionist," depending upon what time zone you are in) while proactively opposing colonialist modes of Israeli power, specifically those forged beyond the 1967 Green Line borders by Jewish settlers. Because they hold beliefs which everyone else views as being inherently contradictory—that Israel is a democracy which provides its non-Jewish citizens a reasonable measure of liberty and opportunity while it is also a colonialist outrage in terms of its oppressive policies toward Palestinians who dwell beyond the 1967 borders—these organizations walk precariously on a tightrope between groups that hold an all-or-nothing view of the Israeli-Palestinian conflict.

On one side of them are anti-Zionist activists, many of them young Jews who were active in spring 2024 college campus protests about Israel's Gaza War. These anti-Zionists subscribe to the postcolonial studies thesis about how colonialism ineluctably breeds genocide. Ostensibly, this thesis is corroborated by the excruciating death toll, forty thousand as of this writing, of Palestinians subsequent to Hamas's October 7, 2023, attack across Israel's southern border.

On the other side, Israelis, including centrist and left-leaning ones who profess to abhor the Netanyahu government's policies, overwhelmingly view the country's war on Hamas in Gaza as a rightful response to the Islamic organization's horrific October 7 attacks. Since Israel pulled its settlements out of Gaza in 2005 and Hamas subsequently invested its energy in building underground tunnels for a future offensive against the Jewish state, and periodically lobbed missiles into Israel's southern locales such as the town of Sderot prior to the October 7 offensive, the colonialism accusation sounds like a long stretch, to Israeli ears. In fact, on the mainstream Israeli view, the "genocide" charge is viewed as outright anti-Semitism.

Israelis were so bruised and benumbed by the October 7, 2023, attack that nobody in the country could relate empathetically to Palestinian deaths incurred in the Israel Defense Forces' war on the Gaza Strip. Even excusing such deaths as "collateral damage" seemed unduly apologetic in this mainstream view. Israelis, by and large, believe that Hamas is widely supported in Gaza, and there are strong reasons to believe that this is so. With this focus, Israelis are reluctant to differentiate between the death of a Hamas combatant on the Strip and that of a local resident. As far as the mainstream Israeli is concerned, the IDF is the "most moral army on earth," and it has made a reasonable effort to forewarn Gaza residents of impending operations.

As far as exponentially expanding anti-Zionist groups on the global left are concerned, Israel's failure to respect distinctions between Hamas fighters and civilian Palestinian residents is colonialism in spirit. And it is genocide when translated into military policy.

For Israel, Palestinian deaths in the Gaza War count for almost nothing. For Israel's critics, they are evidence of genocide. The question is whether a third perspective could retain credibility while pointing out how these two views are objectionably extreme and distorted.

Israel's ambiguous diplomatic and moral status in the early twenty-first century reformats the ambiguous civil and political status held by individual Jews a century earlier in European countries. That is, anti-Semitism has survived, as have the Jews; but they both have been rebooted in a postmodern era where relativism holds sway, as opposed to the rubric of modernity that stayed intact up to the world wars, in which liberalism was (supposedly) the dominant mode of thought. Today, nobody who is honestly attached to the era's postmodernist ethos can award absolute truth points to Israelis when they profess to be fighting in Gaza out of self-defense, or to Palestinians when they accuse Israel of genocide. Each side has its narrative which is equally true ("equally" may not be the precise term to use here because "truth," on the relativist view, is immeasurable, but the point is clear—in the postmodern world, everyone has a story to tell).

Despite the salutary strain of interpretive caution embedded in this postmodern view, one which theoretically holds that nobody has an absolute hold on truth, the Jews, as a collective congregated in Israel, remain the world's most upbraided and excoriated group. Its wartime policy in Gaza provoked far more outcry and remonstration on college campuses than did any other country's warfare in past decades, including America's fighting in Iraq and Afghanistan, Russia's war in the Ukraine, and Syria's civil war.

The same thing can be said about the "Jewish problem" in pre-Holocaust Europe. Before the Holocaust, the prevailing understanding on the continent was that Enlightenment concepts of liberal rights pertained to all groups, including Jews who, west of Russia, won formal emancipation in all countries by the 1870s (and, in many places, before that decade). Nonetheless, the Jews, whose problem at that time was powerlessness, remained the continent's most vehemently abused group. Similarly, Israel, whose main problem today—at least according to those who accuse it of genocide—is its excessive power, has become a uniquely lambasted entity in forums like the United Nations and the International Court of Justice. In one era, universal liberalism was a red herring for the Jews. Today, multicultural relativism is a Trojan horse stuffed with danger for Israel.

Young people who took part on the campus protests about Israel's Gaza War have been taught to think about Israel as the "world's last colonial power." Their protests might have lacked widespread popularity in America, but they reflect an upsurge in anti-Israel sentiment. Positioned on the political left, anti-Zionism now has a firm niche in the American political spectrum. This marks a political paradigm shift. For decades after Israel's founding, when feelings of guilt about the Holocaust ran high, anti-Zionism was viewed as a marginal, political deviation perpetrated mostly by crackpots, either self-hating Jews or outright anti-Semites.[21]

As a measure of how far we have come, this last point warrants elaboration. In the 1950s, anti-Zionism was not part of legitimate discourse in America. After World War II, the vast majority of Jews in the country rejected it—the term "self-hating Jew" was developed by researchers like Kurt Lewin in reference to Jews who thought that a sovereign state in the Middle East was a bad response to the Holocaust.[22] Since most Americans after the Holocaust believed that Israelis deserved a fair shot, anti-Zionism went nowhere. Today, repackaged as a critique of American-backed Jewish colonialism in the Middle East, anti-Zionism can gain (and has gained) substantive footing in America. Its legitimacy has transnational foundations, and from the Jewish standpoint, anti-Zionism's ascendance is a self-inflicted wound, perhaps a mortal one. Ultimately, anti-Zionism's legitimacy is buoyed by the reality that close to a majority of Israelis tacitly or avowedly believe that the anti-colonialist critique applies, to some extent, to one important facet of their country's experience—namely its establishment of Jewish settlements in lands conquered during the 1967 Six-Day War.

For the past quarter century, after the collapse of the 1990s Oslo peace process, Israeli leftists have been out of breath. Cravenly, they have not opposed the way the Netanyahu-led Israeli right exploited Oslo's failure, camouflaging the illiberal, often violent, behavior of West Bank settlers and manipulatively deflecting anybody's criticism of anything in Israel as "anti-Semitism." Still, whereas liberal moderates and more adamant leftists have dwindled in size (today they might not constitute more than a third of Israel's Jewish population), and have been quiescent recreants for an entire political generation, their interpretation of Israel's behavior on post-1967 territories dovetails with aspects of the anti-colonialist critique of

---

21. Kolsky, *Jews Against Zionism*; Levin, *Our Palestine Question*; Alterman, *We Are Not One*, 39, 77.

22. Lewin, *Resolving Social Conflicts*, 186–201.

Israel, vented in college protests and in other forums in North America and Europe. Overseas anti-Zionists are much more strident, and sometimes astoundingly ignorant, in their criticism of Israel than are self-critical, weary, genuinely experienced liberals who live in the Jewish state; but the semantic and moral affinities in the way Israel's liberal left talks about the West Bank settlements, as "conquest" (*kibosh*, in Hebrew), and the way young anti-Zionists in America talk generally about Israel are undeniable.

To be sure, this similarity has its limits. Relatively few Israelis, either from the liberal left-center or the Likud-led right, would appreciate the thrust of the comparison we have just drawn. I do not write in the voice of Israel's political mainstream, but in fairness to it, we should mention that in the embattled realities of 2023–2024, most Israelis, including centrist liberals, were sickened by the spectacle of progressive North American Jews who identify as feminists and who condemned Israel's putative genocide while downplaying what happened to Israeli women who were raped, killed, and kidnapped by Hamas on October 7. Israelis were disgusted by American Jews who view themselves as socialists and who rationalize Palestinian terror, portraying it as part of a worldwide "resistance" struggle against capitalist exploitation. For most Israelis, listening to Bernie Sanders and Naomi Klein (two North American Jewish leftists whose work and activities in many other contexts have considerable appeal to many liberal Israelis, myself included) excoriate what they described as Israel's genocidal policies in Gaza brings to mind the opportunistic palaver of assimilated Sephardic Jews in fifteenth-century Spain who prattled about the imputed misanthropy of the Talmud for the bemused titillation of the Inquisition.[23] A harsh traditional term for such Jews is *moser*—a moser (or moiser) is a communal renegade who, for self-interested reasons, tells hostile gentiles what they want to hear about the Jews in ways that endanger Jewish lives.

My agenda in this essay, however, is not to defend the mainstream Israeli view. My purpose is not to expound upon how anti-Zionist Americans and liberal Israelis are unlike one another, despite commonalities in their critique of the West Bank settlements. Instead, I want to explore in this essay whether an intelligible third way can be wedged between the anti-Zionist critique of Israeli colonialism, which has suddenly gained traction in North America and Europe, and the mainstream Israel denial of "colonialism" as an applicable description of Israeli experience. In an era when *all* political discussion is stridently polarized, is there an overall viewpoint

---

23. Sanders, "Naomi Klein." The Israel discussion begins at 16:40. At 18:00 Klein describes Israel's Gaza War as the "most violent example" of shock doctrine policies she described in her book. At 19:00, Sanders accuses Israel of "clear and very systematic destruction of Gazan society."

about the Jewish state that acknowledges the legitimacy of both camps, while upholding policies conducive of reasonable futures for Israelis and Palestinians? Could the relationship between Zionism and anti-Zionism ever become *civil*? Could such civility serve as a model for third way resolution of other disputes—abortion, gun control, immigration policy—that are now ripping the fabric of global democracy? Relating to this last question, readers who are well informed about the intractability of Israel's conflicts in the Muslim Middle East, might say "good luck with that." Nonetheless, I believe that many of them would agree that this attempt to penetrate the private thoughts of Rabbi Jose, and apply them to contemporary conundrums about Jewish affairs, is not a moot exercise. The Holocaust happened *just one lifetime* ago; so what is the alternative? To allow the Zionism versus anti-Zionism argument to become increasingly uncivil and violent?

The debate about Israeli colonialism is emphatically not a disguised anti-Semitic maneuver. The discussion about Israel's allegedly colonialist practices raises new challenges for Jews, and it can be (and often is) expediently co-opted by anti-Semites; but this does not mean that the logic and structure laden within the discussion is anti-Semitic. The discussion's logic and structure is recognizable in many conversations about colonialism, most of them applying to contexts that have relatively little, or nothing, to do with Jewish issues. Debates about Israel typically become overwrought and stray into realms of stereotypical baiting, in which contestants implicitly or explicitly start making essentialist, and ultimately indefensible, claims about Jewish nationalists (Zionists) or Palestinian nationalists. Nevertheless, in political and moral senses, this is a legitimate conversation about colonialism. It is a discussion about whether Israeli policy, particularly after the 1967 war conquests, has taken the Jewish state in illiberal directions that are inconsistent with its own democratic self-image, and with the liberal branding that has been a mainstay in lobbying for the disproportionately generous support which Israel receives from the United States.

From Zionism as the Fifth Freedom to Zionism as Genocide

Israel's current predicaments, featuring its war against Hamas on the Gaza Strip and its confrontation with Iran and its Lebanese proxy, Hezbollah, on the border between Israel's Upper Galilee and Lebanon, have sparked a confusing swell of allegations about colonialism. This was inevitable because the Jewish state has been entangled in a murky web of historical paradigms since its establishment in 1948. Its supporters have never been able to cut through that web by explaining where Israel stands in a post–World War II era when—apart from apologetic analyses contrived by conservatives like Niall Ferguson[24]—colonialism is rightfully considered a menace to democratic liberty.

For a passing generation of overseas Jews and philosemitic Christians, persons who grew up before the 1967 Six-Day War in homes where the Nazi genocide of Jews had haunting prominence, the creation of the Jewish state a few years after the end of World War II was seen as an extension of the Allies' battle against evil, antidemocratic forces—these were jingoistic Japan, Fascist Italy, and in particular, Nazi Germany. It took a few years for this perception to take root. The view's delayed consolidation was caused by an ephemeral, but deeply confusing, set of circumstances that persisted for a few years after the conclusion of World War II. In the final years of the British Mandate in Palestine (which lasted from 1920 to 1948), Zionists fought against the English, demanding that Palestine's lame-duck rulers open the country's doors to Jewish immigrants, largely Holocaust survivors who were then called, antiseptically, displaced persons. This campaign had violent, embittering moments. They included the bombing of British administrative offices at Jerusalem's King David Hotel by a right-wing Zionist group (the *Irgun*). At times the Zionists flamboyantly distanced themselves from the heroic view of Britain as a key player in the fight against Nazism. For instance, on the *Exodus*, a boat freighted with Holocaust survivors whose entry in Palestine's coastal waters was notoriously blocked by the British, and then sent to Germany, outraged Jewish passengers waved flags and posters on which swastikas were superimposed on the Union Jack.[25]

Once Britain left Palestine and such perplexing images faded from memory, it became possible to package Israel's establishment as a morally appropriate extension of the Allied fight in World War II, since the enemy, Nazi Germany, had sought the wholesale decimation of Jews, and Israel's establishment represented Jewish collective rebirth. The American Jewish writer Leon Uris showed how this view of Israel as an inspiring fulfillment of the Allied fight for the Four Freedoms could penetrate to the core of Western consciousness, and even far beyond it (the unsuspecting Uris even became a hero to anti-Soviet Jewish dissidents).[26] Just a few years after Uris's novel *Exodus* became a bestseller, the Eichmann trial in Jerusalem cleared fifteen years of cloudy thinking about the Holocaust; this trial solidified a view of Israel as a democratically justifiable remedy to one of history's most

---

24. Ferguson, *Empire*.
25. Halamish, *Exodus Affair*.
26. Silver, *Our Exodus*.

diabolical crimes.[27] On this view, the stifling of Palestinian national aspirations was often obscured, owing to colonialist racism that had a sublimated or semi-active presence among activists and writers who were in the Allied camp, and who thought of themselves as staunch upholders of democratic liberty (Uris's novel, for instance, was blatantly prejudicial, and when the director of the *Exodus* film, Otto Preminger, infused its script with some hopeful images of Arab-Jewish power-sharing, Uris stomped out of the movie project). After 1948, a few significant figures in America's media and power establishment (I. F. Stone, Dorothy Thompson) poured some castor oil into the pro-Israel cocktail.[28] Despite the monumental efficacy of efforts like Uris's *Exodus* to simply dispose of the Palestinian problem, not everyone could toss aside reports circulated by mavericks like Stone, since some seven hundred thousand Palestinians had turned into displaced refugees during the 1948 war. Whenever evidence of injustice to Palestinians could not be hidden or ignored during the first couple of decades of Israel's existence, it was regarded as proportionately acceptable collateral damage that was offset by the historic redress of anti-Semitism facilitated by the establishment of the Jewish state. Israel was seen as a shining triumph for democracy and as invaluable recompense for centuries of anti-Semitic persecution and the Nazi crime.

A concise way of thinking about how Israel became glued to the heroic World War II triumph narrative is this: up until the late 1980s First Intifada, when the colonialist legacy of Israel's Six-Day War triumph first became widely evident in the West, nobody remembered the confusing images of swastikas on the Union Jack that were photoshopped by Holocaust survivors on the *Exodus* boat. In contrast, when they entered Israel's main Holocaust museum, Yad Vashem, visitors were deeply moved by photographs and explanations of how the Palestinian leader, the Mufti of Jerusalem (Haj Amin al-Husseini), had spent the war years in Berlin, organizing and lobbying for the Nazis. Imagine how such images affected early middle-aged visitors, Americans (Jews and gentiles) who visited Yad Vashem in, say, the early 1970s. How could they have not come away thinking that the Israelis were fighting an aftergrowth of the evil their parents had mobilized to defeat during World War II?

The weightiest intellectual theories about World War II and the Holocaust that circulated in these pre-1967 years added gravitas to the conventional way of thinking about Israel as an extension of the Allies' democratic

---

27. Lipstadt, *Eichmann Trial*.

28. For discussions of criticisms of Israel in this early period voiced by well-placed gentile Americans, see Linfield, *Lion's Den*, 229–61; Alterman, *We Are Not One*, 53–54; Levin, *Our Palestine Question*, 116–17; Hixson, *Israel's Armor*, 99–101.

triumph. In effect, the era's most trenchant intellectuals (some of whom were not really fans of Zionism) solidified the image of Israel as what we will call here the "Fifth Freedom"—in addition to the four freedoms identified during World War II by Churchill and Roosevelt, Israel's establishment constituted a Fifth Freedom (for Jews, freedom from anti-Semitism; generally, freedom from hatred). The work of Hannah Arendt, one of the thinkers who, fairly or not, became prominently associated in the Cold War with the Free World's fight against "totalitarianism," is a revealing case in point.[29] Arendt, a Jew who fled Germany after the Nazi rise to power, was a courageous but complicated person whose views on Zionism, Jewish behavior in death camps, the Eichmann trial, and other subjects hardly won widespread approbation among Jews. Inadvertently, the main thrust of her work proved useful to the mainstream pro-Israel view. Her writings contextualized colonialism in a way conducive to thinking about the Jewish state as part of the solution, not the problem.

Arendt's most important study, *The Origins of Totalitarianism* (1951), analyzed how colonialism inspired or refurbished an array of prejudices, including anti-Semitism, and in the right circumstances, molded them as totalitarianism.[30] Whether or not Arendt would have liked it, parts of this paradigm could be co-opted by defenders of Israel, who viewed it as a Fifth Freedom nemesis of totalitarianism (this perception's rationale was enhanced as the Cold War progressed in the 1950s and Arab states, such as Nasser's Egypt, tilted toward the Soviet camp). In contrast, nothing in Arendt's colonialism/totalitarianism paradigm was helpful to pro-Palestinian activists who wanted to explain to the West how Arabs in the Middle East thought of colonialism as a minatory force that had victimized them, owing to causal dynamics and historical processes that were quite unlike ones highlighted in Arendt's book.

As it turned out, when Jewish settlements in the post-1967 occupied territories, and the rise of PLO terror and resistance, unavoidably compelled commentators to discuss colonialism in the Israeli context, right-wing neocons extracted manipulative capital from totalitarianism theories championed by Arendt and others (readers who are skeptical or curious about this point can examine the mid-1970s case of Norman Podhoretz, one of American Jewry's precedent-setting, prominent neocons; using America's UN Ambassador Daniel Patrick Moynihan as his *shofar* mouthpiece, Podhoretz framed objections to the UN's controversial "Zionism is

---

29. For background about Arendt and her views on Zionism, see Linfield, *Lion's Den*, 17–79.

30. Arendt, *Origins*.

racism" resolution as a fight against Soviet totalitarianism[31]). In this same 1970s era, intellectuals like Edward Said had to develop new conceptual models to reconfigure terms in discussion of colonialism so that Palestinians might win an invitation to the debate (such reframing was promoted by Said's landmark 1978 volume *Orientalism*).[32]

For three decades, the Fifth Freedom view of Israel was powerful. The view held strong through the 1970s, but it was positioned to snap irretrievably in the 1980s for a number of reasons. First, the new right-wing Israeli power structure, which first arose when the Likud party, led by Menachem Begin, won Israel's 1977 national elections, embarked on a massive project of erecting illegal, illiberal settlements on the West Bank and Gaza Strip (Likud's determination in this respect was fortified, not diminished, when Anwar Sadat and Jimmy Carter compelled the reluctant Menachem Begin to sign the Israel-Egypt peace deal, which required Israel's withdrawal from the Sinai Peninsula). The mechanics of this settlement movement—the creation of a dual legal system discriminatorily advantageous to the settlers, land grabs sanctioned by partisan Israeli bureaucrats and judges, the operation of a Jewish terror underground, and so on—permanently undermined the benign paternalism stance adopted by Israeli publicists for years after the 1967 war.[33]

For the first several years of Israel's occupation of post-1967 locales like the West Bank and Gaza Strip, influential writers and activists in its center-left establishment sometimes jumped ship and joined the messianic-tinged Greater Israel movement. This movement, then called Gush Emunim, was founded on the idea that Jews have unassailable spiritual and historical rights to settle in the disputed territories, which were then called by members in this evolving pro-settler camp (and by almost everyone in Israel today) "Judea and Samaria."[34] Others developed "white man's burden" sorts of explanations to apologetically justify Israel's continuing occupation on the West Bank and Gaza. One such apologetic referred to how Defense Minister Moshe Dayan "opened bridges" after the Six-Day War so that

---

31. Troy, *Moynihan's Moment*.

32. Scholars who have different overall assessments about Edward Said agree about how he filled a gap because rules in American public commentary were not conducive to the sounding of a pro-Palestinian viewpoint through the 1970s. See, for instance Alterman, *We Are Not One*, 242–43; and Muravchik, *Making David into Goliath*, 98–123. Implicitly, Levin's recent discussion of efforts made by figures like Fayez Sayegh to break through this culture wall during Israel's early, pre-1967, period accentuates the singularity of Said's situation and achievement in the 1970s (Levin, *Our Palestine Question*, 110–52).

33. Zertal and Eldar, *Lords of the Land*.

34. Rubinstein, *Mi la-H*; Shafat, *Gush Emunim*.

residents of these conquered areas could visit relatives in Jordan and within Israel's pre-1967 borders (the border between pre-1967 Israel and disputed territories conquered in the Six-Dar Way is called the Green Line).[35]

Inaugurated by the Zionist movement's founder, Theodor Herzl, in his 1902 utopian novel, *Alteneuland*, this was a traditional line of Zionist argumentation. Herzl and his followers depicted Jewish nationalism as a kind of benign colonialism that would bring socioeconomic benefits to the land's Arabs. In the end, the land's indigenous residents would realize that they had no tangible interest in opposing Jewish newcomers.[36]

The 1967 conquests imposed new, vexing challenges to this line of thinking. Members of the old Labor Zionist establishment who remained liberal realized that Israel was now responsible for the lives of so many Palestinians that it would take an awful lot of Zionist-induced prosperity for West Bank and Gaza residents to withhold resentment about the Jews' administrative and political power over their lives. Even were such trickle-down prosperity to sway some Palestinian hearts, these liberals reasoned, how could Israel possibly maintain a Jewish majority if democratic rights were to be awarded to these Palestinian groups?[37] These were good questions, but up to the 1990s Oslo peace process, most Israeli liberals clung tenaciously to Herzl's model of benign colonialism. Hence, through the 1980s, Israeli commentators who refused to view colonialism as a genuine problem for Zionism but also kept a distance from the messianic, irredentist Greater Israel pro-settlement movement, viewed the post-1967 territories as a mixed blessing (Shabtai Teveth, a biographer and confidante of Labor Zionist icons like Ben-Gurion and Dayan, titled an early book about the occupation in this vein, calling it *The Cursed Blessing*).

This apologetic Zionist white-man's-burden view utterly lost credibility after Likud took the reins in Israel, and launched its aggressive settlement policy. Some prominent leaders of the original, Gush Emunim, settlement group, figures like Hanan Porat (a man whose family had lived in the Gush Etzion area of the West Bank before Jewish enclaves in it were decimated during the 1948 war), did not articulate avowedly chauvinistic attitudes toward West Bank Palestinians, and refrained from discussion of population

---

35. Teveth, *Cursed Blessing*. An array of factual claims in Teveth's apologetic account were overturned in subsequent scholarship, such as Raz, *Bride and the Dowry*.

36. Silver, *Zionism*, 186–207; Herzl, *Old-New Land*.

37. On the Israeli liberal-left, the first systematic critique of the post-1967 occupation framed around such questions came from Aryeh (Luba) Eliav who, tellingly, lost his post as the Labor Party's secretary-general when he published his views. Eliav, *Eretz Hatzvi*.

transfer agendas.³⁸ Still, after the late 1970s, nobody could pretend that settlers, even relatively moderate ones, were creating enclaves like Elon Moreh near crowded Palestinian areas for the benefit of these non-Jewish residents.

Israel's general loss of international credibility in the 1980s made it harder for the Jewish state to maintain its counter-empirical position about colonialism. A nationalist movement whose fulfillment necessitated the dispossession of seven hundred thousand persons, Zionism has since 1948 tried to have its cake and eat it too by denying that this fact of its history means that it really has to confront the issue of colonialism. By and large, this stance did not strike people as being counterintuitive during what can, reasonably, be called Israel's heroic period in the 1950s and early 1960s. In this pre-1967 period, the Jewish state absorbed hundreds of thousands of immigrants from Iraq, Morocco, Egypt, Poland, Romania, and many other lands; it faced recurring *fedayeen* terror attacks on its borders; against all odds, it stabilized its economy; and it built a democratic infrastructure which, a few years ahead of the Six-Day War, became substantively inclusive toward Arab citizens thanks to the dismantling of a military government that had governed their lives.

The Fifth Freedom view of Israel collapsed about a decade after the 1967 Six-Day War. In the 1980s, it will be recalled, ordinary folks in America and elsewhere watched Israeli soldiers bombard Beirut during the First Lebanon War. They heard about how Israel deployed an American Jew, Jonathan Pollard, to spy on its foremost ally, the United States. Most importantly, they saw how Israel's foolhardy, self-defeating occupation of the Gaza Strip and West Bank had, to some extent, democratized Palestinian nationalism.³⁹ During the First Intifada uprising, in the late 1980s, Palestinian youths on the West Bank and Gaza Strip threw rocks at Israeli tanks in what looked like to many observers, in America and elsewhere, legitimate civil disobedience against a colonial occupier. Suddenly, Palestinian nationalism looked more like Lexington and Concord in 1775 than the terror scene at the 1972 Munich Olympics (we use this analogy advisedly since, in this late 1980s period, leading drop-outs from the old pro-Israel coalition in America were liberal Protestants from the mainline churches for whom 1776 and the American Revolution is the reference point in discussions about colonialism). Israel had been telling the world that PLO terror, which had been excruciatingly lethal and globalized in the 1970s, was the gist of Palestinian nationalism. Ironically, Israel's sole accomplishment

---

38. Huberman, *Hanan Porat*.

39. For an overview of rising American Jewish disenchantment with Israel in this period, see Rosenthal, *Irreconcilable*.

in its ill-managed 1982 Lebanon War, the banishment of Yasser Arafat's core PLO group to Tunis, backfired. During the First Intifada, the power vacuum in the occupied territories was filled by these brave, stone-throwing Palestinian teenagers. To many in the West, these youngsters looked like freedom fighters from a cohesive national collective, not fang-toothed terrorists representative of nothing, as Israel propagandistically depicted them as being (up to the 1990s Oslo peace process years, Israel routinely denied that Palestinians constituted a real nation).

Had it not been for the sprawling array of mishaps in the 1980s, Israel might have withstood the fallout in its prestige and popularity caused by the First Intifada. Crucially, Begin's pro-settlement governments forged fawning alliances with ultra-Orthodox political parties, and these Haredi politicians kept sponsoring "Who Is a Jew" legislative proposals whose adoption would have delegitimized conversion rituals integral to the non-Orthodox, Reform and Conservative, streams of American Judaism.[40] This meant that the core group of the pro-Israel lobby, modern-minded American Jews (mostly liberal Democrats), was unprecedentedly demoralized exactly at the wrong moment. Just when increasing numbers of Americans were coming to see the Jewish state as a colonialist aberration in the modern world, Israel's key constituency in the United States bristled for reasons that had nothing to do with this developing discussion about colonialism.

To be sure, several prominent American Jews who had heretofore been reticent or acutely defensive about Israel and related issues—A. M. Rosenthal, who had just stepped down as executive editor of *The New York Times* when the Palestinian uprising began, and Woody Allen, who had just finished filming one of his better movies, *Hannah and Her Sisters*—published devastating condemnations of IDF violence against unarmed Palestinians during the Intifada.[41] Nonetheless, what really agitated liberal American Jews in this 1980s decade was not the injustice served to Palestinians by Israel's colonialist occupation in post-1967 territories. Instead, what hit them in the gut was the insult to their non-Orthodox Jewish observances perpetrated by Who Is a Jew legislative proposals in Israel's parliament, the Knesset.[42] It did not matter that Who Is a Jew bills, if legislated, would have affected the identity status of no more than a handful of converted Jews who intended to immigrate to Israel from America. Hundreds of prominent

---

40. The Who Is a Jew controversy had been percolating for years before it exploded in the post-1977 Likud era of Israeli politics. Kraines, *Impossible Dilemma*.

41. Rosenthal, *Irreconcilable*, 99–102.

42. One well-informed commentator reported that American Jewry issued a "virtual declaration of war" against Israel's government during the most heated round of the Who Is a Jew controversy. Goldberg, *Jewish Power*, 337.

American Jewish organizational leaders shuttled to Jerusalem to browbeat Israel's leading politicians, Yitzhak Shamir (Likud) and Shimon Peres (Labor), and threaten the withdrawal of philanthropic support should the Who Is a Jew bills be legislated.[43] To this day, no comparable delegation of high-ranking American Jewish leaders has ever flown to Jerusalem to question Israel's leadership about Zionism's colonial occupation in post-1967 territories.

Looking at the matter from a sheer tactical standpoint, members of the pro-Israel camp would have most prudently invested their resources in this period had they engaged proactively with the fallout in Israel's popularity caused by the First Intifada. Nobody knew it at the time, but the Oslo peace process in the 1990s would radically alter political alignments within Israel, as well as terms in the relationship between American Jews and Israel. Before this sea change, American Jews had compelling reasons to listen to *both* the left and right sides of Israel's political spectrum. The left was categorically correct when it argued that the continued development of the colonialist, illiberal settlement movement on the West Bank and Gaza Strip would render the main plank of American Jewry's pro-Israel work meaningless. How long could you argue that Israel warrants disproportionately munificent assistance from the United States on the grounds that it is the "only democracy in the Middle East" when hundreds of thousands of Palestinians in the occupied territories lack fundamental civil liberties, while Jewish settlers profit from legal and socioeconomic discrimination in these same areas? The political right, too, had something to say. The glorification of Palestinian nationalism during the First Intifada had repugnantly objectionable aspects. Palestinian schoolchildren in Gaza and elsewhere were (and remain) saturated by malevolent, inciteful educational materials—when Benjamin Netanyahu raised this point later in the 1990s, it was one of the more persuasive planks in his campaign against the Oslo peace accords. Also, the power vacuum in the territories created by the PLO's exile was filled not only by young Lexington and Concord–like Muslim Minutemen who bravely threw rocks at the occupier's tanks. Intransigent, violent groups were also filling the gap. In particular, this First Intifada period was when Hamas, an Islamic fundamentalist organization whose covenant referred to the Holocaust as a Zionist ploy and belligerently denied Israel's right to exist, began to capture hearts and minds in Gaza.

In other words, then, like now, Palestinian nationalism warranted genuine consideration, not glorification. American Jews were fatefully slow to grasp this fundamental point. In the 1970s, their organizational

---

43. Goldberg, *Jewish Power*, 337–40; Cardin, *Shoshana*, 90–99.

mainstream utterly ostracized a liberal group, called Breira, for advocating dialogue about Palestinian rights (including talks with the PLO), no matter that leading members of this short-lived organization were highly respected rabbis, academics, and communal activists.[44] When measured in pace with the high-speed volatility of Israel's geopolitical circumstances, a veritable eternity then passed. For decades, liberals, American Jews and gentiles, have vacuously upheld slogans about a two-state solution; but sloganeering aside, how often have you seen an organized faction in the pro-Israel community *really* fashion its activities out of recognition that the individual and national rights of Palestinians in the occupied territories will remain disrespected so long as illiberal Jewish settlers live beside them, largely for the purpose of frustrating their statehood aspirations? When an organized American Jewish group that upholds this viewpoint (J Street) belatedly gained footing on the edge of the community's mainstream, it was thirty-five years after Breira's founding!

What would have happened had American Jews challenged the glorification of Palestinian nationalism during the First Intifada by adopting a realistic, rather than a propagandistic and unduly partisan and ethnocentric, attitude? What would have happened had, in the late 1980s, their organizational mainstream proclaimed that Palestinian nationalism deserves its place in the sun, but anti-Semitic educational incitement and Hamas do not? Thirty-five years after the First Intifada, would American Jews be dealing with college student protestors on campuses who wear keffiyehs, chant "from the river to the sea," and celebrate Hamas, as though an organization which kidnapped hundreds of unassuming civilians—including the elderly, mothers, and small children—and committed other atrocities on October 7, 2023, warrants recognition as freedom-seeking resistance to Zionist colonialism?

The Fifth Freedom view of Israel lost footing for another reason. Under circumstances that congealed in the final decades of the twentieth century, the World War II–based outlook on Israel was supplanted by a different historical paradigm: postcolonialism. Father Time played a part in this transition, of course. By the 1980s and 1990s, increasingly fewer observers of Middle East politics were persons whose outlooks on history had been forged by direct experience, of some sort, with the Allied fight against Nazism during World War II.

Migratory and technological factors contributed to the paradigm shift. Major Western cities like London were dramatically more cosmopolitan in

---

44. For Breira, see Wertheimer, "Breaking the Taboo." For a survey comparing Breira to other American Jewish organizations, see Levin, *Our Palestine Question*, 186–217.

the last years of the twentieth century than they had been several decades before, in years after World War II. Largely, the demographic changes featured immigrants from formerly colonized lands drifting toward what had been the metropole. Had you visited London in the 1950s, when physical evidence of the blitz remained in view and white British, scrambling to rebuild their lives, monopolized the urban landscape, you would have concluded that the fight against Nazi aggression constituted the century's paramount struggle. Had you visited the city in the 1990s, and witnessed a far more diverse setting where Indian, Pakistani, Bangladeshi, and many other immigrant groups scrambled to make new lives for themselves, you would have concluded that decolonization constituted the century's premier phenomenon.

The explosion of information technologies from this 1990s period through the present also contributed to the trend. For all its drawbacks, social media has democratized political discourse, bringing into the discussion innumerably more users who are descendants of persons whose political outlook was framed by experience with colonialism than users for whom the issue of Holocaust and anti-Semitism, and the drama of Israel's birth, is the paramount political frame.

THE ALGERIAN PRECEDENT

The postcolonial paradigm's foundation is the Algerian War of Independence, an armed confrontation between France and the Algerian National Liberation Front (FLN) that lasted from 1954 to 1962, culminating in Algerian independence. The FLN campaign is regarded as a late, landmark, anti-colonial struggle. In truth, the FLN's triumph did not really usher in a happy ending for anyone. In its wake, some eight hundred or nine hundred thousand pieds-noirs—that is, 80–90 percent of the country's French/European population—fled to France.[45] In the 1990s, as the popularity of an Islamic group (the Islamic Salvation Front) surged, the country plunged into civil war that was not really resolved when Abdelaziz Bouteflika seized power in an election widely regarded as being rigged (thanks to several convenient constitutional changes, Bouteflika kept control of the country for twenty years). Despite its imperfect outcomes, the FLN struggle was lionized for many understandable reasons.

The film about the crucial phase (1954–1957) of the anti-colonialist campaign, *The Battle of Algiers*, rivetingly puts the confrontation in a David

---

45. McDougall, *History*, 231.

versus Goliath frame.[46] Though it was directed by an outsider, an Italian, Gillo Pontecorvo, the movie was filmed on location, with persons who had been involved in the fighting stepping in as actors. In its best frames, the film creates an uncanny documentary effect, as though the viewer is seeing the historical events transpire in real time. Among several unnerving scenes, the film shows French officers, called to Algeria for anti-terror pacification work, speaking candidly about how the colonialist power's use of brutal torture and mass murder is the only way to ensure a measure of security and some sort of future for the pieds-noirs. These officers, who look "real," are suave cynics. Complementing the incendiary pronouncements issued by Jean-Paul Sartre or Frantz Fanon, the disturbing image struck by the movie's army officers, as executioners who never shed their dashing French style, has, for generations of youthful idealists, vivified and validated the main premise of postcolonial theory: however much it disguises itself with the trimmings of Western civilization, the outcomes of colonial rule are torture and genocide.

More than a movie mythologized the FLN campaign, however. In the 1950s, the world was weary of war, but hundreds of millions of persons around the globe—in Africa, Asia, South America, and elsewhere—harbored acute grievances about colonialism's myriad crimes.[47] In the decolonized, emerging nations, the FLN victory sublimely closed a circle. France's Napoleonic Wars constituted the first time when democratic ideals of modernity, liberty, equality, and fraternity had been deputized in the service of brutal conquest; Algeria was where the decolonization struggle climactically buried the democratic West's hypocrisy once and for all.

The farcically self-defeating equivocation in France's leadership on the Algerian issue, personified by Charles de Gaulle's zigzags, was telling. Two world wars had drained from the West's Enlightenment philosophies their pretense of universal benevolence. Frankfurt School theorists and others argued that Enlightenment universalism was really a Trojan horse conveying power-lust and racist extermination, and their teaching was impactful.[48] Suddenly, public policy in places like Vietnam that was marketed in the name of global objectives (i.e., "Communist containment") lacked legitimacy. De Gaulle was not a philosopher, but his flip-flops on Algeria ratified the intellectual retreat from Enlightenment universalism, which eventually ushered in our own era of postmodernity. When he belatedly concluded that anti-FLN pacification measures conducted for the pieds-noirs and

---

46. Pontecorvo, *Battle of Algiers*.
47. Jansen and Osterhammel, *Decolonization*.
48. Adorno and Horkheimer, *Dialectic of Enlightenment*.

continued French rule could not possibly be justified by appeals to the greater good, De Gaulle essentially admitted that colonialism is selective morality that sacrifices the welfare of masses in order to sustain the privileges of empowered minority enclaves.

In the West, colonialism's jig was up. This became vividly clear in the mid-1950s, several years before the FLN exhausted France. The ill-fated exercise in neocolonialist tomfoolery in Egypt attempted by France and England, in concert with Israel, in response to Gamal Abdel Nasser's policy of nationalizing the Suez Canal, was overturned by Western public opinion (among other things, England tore down Anthony Eden's government for its part in the 1956 Sinai Campaign).[49]

It bears mention that Israel's main international ally in this period was France, not the United States. Though this alliance was ephemeral, it endowed Israel with crucial strategic assets, including its widely reported nuclear arms facility in Dimona;[50] this alliance also cast the Jewish state on the illiberal, unpopular, losing side of the global decolonization struggle. The one era when France found Israel to be particularly useful arose when it was trying to stave off a terror-soaked insurrection of Muslims in a Middle East setting, in Algeria, in the days of the FLN revolt.

To be sure, Israeli officials who cultivated French ties in the 1950s, particularly a young Shimon Peres (then a defense ministry official empowered by Ben-Gurion's patronage), did not consciously view their doings as reinforcement of Western colonialism. Not without cause, Israel's leadership in this period believed that hostile Arab states, led by Egypt, would launch a "second round" of attacks to repeal the results of the 1948 war. Since Nasser was busily fortifying Egypt's army with weapons proffered by the Kremlin's proxies in Eastern Europe, Israel's leadership could articulate its part with England and France in the semiconspiratorial 1956 Sinai Campaign as part of the Free World's showdown with totalitarian Soviet Communism.

Such explication sounded disingenuous in the West, however. The Eisenhower White House, embroiled in a reelection campaign and outraged after being kept in the dark by the Jewish state and the two European democracies, understood that the Sinai exercise in neocolonialism undermined the moral legitimacy of the West's objections to Communist authoritarian expansionism, especially at a time when Soviet tanks and troops poured into Hungary to quell its liberation movement. Almost seventy years before anti-colonialist protestors staged takeover protests on

---

49. For the 1956 war, from Israel's standpoint, see Golani, *Israel in Search*; Bar-On, *Gates of Gaza*.

50. Cohen, *Israel and the Bomb*, 57–58.

American college campuses in protest against Israel's Gaza War, the White House precipitated a noisy public standoff with Jerusalem, demanding that Ben-Gurion's government remove IDF soldiers from the Gaza Strip, as well as from the Sinai Peninsula.[51] Eisenhower's Secretary of State, John Foster Dulles, sometimes spoke about "Zionism expansionism" in a censorious cadence that previewed the tone of the spring 2024 campus condemnations of Israel. Dulles was much more mildly spoken than these campus protestors (the young comedian, Carol Burnett, raised hackles on television when she wondered how anyone could possibly be seduced by the boringly methodical secretary of state),[52] and sociopolitical conditions in Gaza changed over the decades. But the larger analytic point remains intact. Israel lost the New Left because of its conquests in the Six-Day War, and that 1967 event vastly complicated the Jewish state's status as a liberal democracy. Nonetheless, to say that the post-1967 occupation of territories initiated debate about Zionism and colonialism is not an historically accurate judgment; and this myth is manipulated, both on the left and the right, to advance innumerable agendas.

Owing to its extraordinarily complex and vulnerable geopolitical circumstances, Israel became entangled in controversies about colonialism in years right after its founding, in the 1950s. Also in the 1920s and 1930s, in Zionism's pre-state "Yishuv" period (*Yishuv* is a term used to describe Jewish communities in the country before 1948), Palestinian nationalists quite successfully put debates about the country in a colonialist frame. They did so, for example, during a major 1936–1939 uprising. In this pre-1948 rebellion, Palestinian guerillas gunned down both British and Jewish targets, objecting that the Mandate's immigration and land purchase policies were opening the door to Zionist colonialist control of the country (the Jews, for their part, argued that liberal immigration to Palestine, in a period when America's "golden door" was shut to Jewish refugees and Nazi persecution was intensifying in Europe, was a survival imperative; in 1939, the British mollified Arab anger by throttling Zionist immigration and land purchase in its White Paper policy)[53].

Exactly at this time, Palestinian nationalism prepped and forecasted the fundamental precept of postcolonial studies, regarding genocide. This happened when the historian George Antonius published his *Arab Awakening* (1939) and concluded in the book's last lines that the escalating Jewish-Arab conflict was a lethal zero-sum situation. "No room can be made in

---

51. Aridan, *Advocating for Israel*, 135–64; Hixson, *Israel's Armor*, 106–12.
52. Wilsey, *God's Cold Warrior*.
53. Kessler, *Palestine 1936*.

Palestine for a second nation except by dislodging or exterminating the nation in possession," proclaimed Antonius.[54]

In other words, the Talmud's documentation of the debate between Rashbi and Rabbi Judah about challenges posed by Roman rule in Palestine in late antiquity is just an early step in the Jews' torturously protracted, morally ambiguous, confrontation with colonialism. Israel's connection to France's ill-fated, anti-FLN campaign in the 1950s is one striking instance of poignant ambiguities embedded in this confrontation. When viewed through one historical paradigm, the aforementioned Fifth Freedom model, Shimon Peres's dealings with officials in France's political-military establishment gain bluntly rough but genuine validation. Their ethical gist was "never again"—a cruelly isolated state in the hostile Middle East was doing whatever it had to do to procure unconventional weapons in order to preempt future Holocausts. Israel's subsequent, nontransparent policy of "nuclear ambiguity" should not (in my opinion) be shielded from criticism. Still, in view of Teheran's nuclear procurement policy in the twenty-first century, and the frightening demonstrations staged in mid-April 2024 and October 1, 2024, when this extremist Islamic state, whose policy avowedly calls for the destruction of the Jewish state, lobbed 300 missiles (the first time) and then 181 missiles (the second time) toward Israel, it is hard to dispute the "never again" rationale of Israel's passing alliance with France in the 1950s. However, when Peres's activity in France is viewed through the alternative prism, in keeping with the ethos and precepts of postcolonial theory, a radically different picture emerges. He hobnobbed with the selfsame sort of French officials, the suave executioners, who fill the screen in the *Battle of Algiers*. Peres and his Israeli cohorts therefore endowed the Jewish state with some level of complicity in a despicable and murderous clampdown of the FLN's anti-colonial campaign.

The FLN anti-France campaign became a mythologized prototype in postcolonial studies because its famed champions were morally selective in their partisanship. Figures like Fanon and Sartre are precursors whose courageous but debatable glorification of the FLN set the stage for the laudable, but nonetheless problematic, protest performances of college students on campuses in North America and Europe in spring 2024. In both cases, the champions of anti-colonial struggle supported organizations, the FLN and Hamas, which used terror indiscriminately against civilians. In both cases, these advocates endorsed the anti-colonial groups while knowing that their success would possibly (in the FLN case) or certainly (with Hamas) bring to power a radical Islamic regime inimical to democratic values which, among

---

54. Antonius, *Arab Awakening*, 412.

many other things, endowed French citizens in the 1950s, and American college students in our period, free speech rights to protest against their countries' presumptive role in colonialist oppression of Algerians, or Palestinians. In both cases, the protestors kept a Cheshire cat grin whenever anyone pointed out the implications of "from the river to the sea" sorts of rhetoric—that is, they seemed inscrutably detached from objections about how the unqualified success of the groups they were supporting would mean the extermination or full migratory dispersal of the pieds-noirs, or of Jewish Israelis.

Sartre's preface to Fanon's classic anti-colonial polemic, *The Wretched of the Earth*, is often considered an overly zealous rationalization of terror, but it seems to me that his writing offers the most cogent defense of the moral selectivity inherent in postcolonial theory.[55] Since all moral claims are selective in many ways, undoubtedly the best apology for the subjective partisanship of protests conducted in the spirit of postcolonial theory relies on the utilitarian measure of the greater good. Sartre makes this argument most clearly in his essay "A Plea for Intellectuals," which was originally promulgated in Japan in 1965.[56]

In "A Plea," Sartre justified partisan support for the colonized on the grounds that, relative to the colonizers, there are many more of them, and they are ordinarily miserable. His words—"a concrete and unconditional alignment with the actions of the underprivileged class"—delivered a "get out of jail free" pass of immunity to anti-colonial terror waged by an oppressed mass of people.[57] "A Plea" featured psychologically penetrating analysis of the self-doubting hesitation of intellectuals who come from privileged upper and middle classes, as they ally themselves in support of the protests and political struggles of masses in decolonizing parts of the world. Counterarguments, either about the rights of groups not aligned with militant anti-colonialists, or about possible nondemocratic outcomes of the anti-colonial struggle, were dismissed by Sartre as expressions of class interest. Intellectuals must "unconditionally" align with the anti-colonialists owing to the overwhelming scope of damage caused by Western power, he argued.

At the start of the anti-colonial struggle, Sartre declared in his preface to Fanon's book, the earth was divided between five hundred million men and 1.5 billion "natives."[58] Colonialism, Sartre proclaimed, professing to

---

55. Sartre, preface to *Wretched of the Earth*.
56. Sartre, "Plea for Intellectuals."
57. Sartre, "Plea for Intellectuals," 261.
58. Fanon, *Wretched*, vii.

speak in the voice of an African rebel, has for centuries "stifled virtually the whole of humanity." Championing Fanon's analysis, Sartre imagined that his existentialist radicalism was now hitched to the liberation of the oppressed masses, "virtually the whole of humanity." Lighting one match after another in an inflammatory essay, Sartre sounded gleeful: "Europe is done for."[59] His words rattled the consciousness of bourgeois Westerners who had been enjoying themselves for fifteen years after World War II: "You who are so liberal, so humane, who take the love of culture to the point of affectation, you pretend to forget that you have colonies where massacres are committed in your name."[60]

Relying on his dialectical phraseology, Sartre suggested that Western prosperity and cultural achievement depended on the barbarous deprivation of outsiders. In a twist he could not have anticipated, this anti-colonialist argument stifled the development of postcolonial studies on college campuses for about two decades. In "A Plea," the target audience for recruitment in anti-colonial campaigns was privileged Westerners, precisely the core enrollment group for university programs. But in the 1960s era, Sartre's framing of his anti-colonial polemic in a dialectic about how Western prosperity is an outgrowth of barbarism attracted attention among radical groups, like the Black Panthers in America or the PLO in the Middle East, who were positioned outside of the West's power establishment. In the Western mainstream, Sartre's patronage of Fanon's critique of colonialism went into deep freeze. It was thawed by the keffiyeh-wearing radical chic protestors at elite private universities (and elsewhere) during Israel's Gaza War, basically a lifetime after Sartre theatrically announced that decolonization's triumph would spell doom for the West.

This was because "dialectic of enlightenment" analyses positing that vicious exploitation was embedded within the West's cultural triumphs became a staple left critique whose validation was tracked to Auschwitz and other Holocaust symbols, not to the 1945 Setif and Guelma massacre in French Algeria, and other colonialist atrocities. Up to the culture wars and the rise of multiculturalism on college campuses at the end of the twentieth century, liberal-minded professors nursed the white middle-class guilt of impressionable students by teaching them to recite dialectical delicacies from Walter Benjamin's theses on the philosophy of history, most famously, "there has never been a document of history which is not simultaneously one of barbarism."[61] Benjamin, born into an assimilated German Jewish

---

59. Fanon, *Wretched*, ix.
60. Fanon, *Wretched*, xiv.
61. Benjamin, *Illuminations*, 256.

family, drafted such lines in Paris 1940, just before he tried to flee from Nazism.

In the year of Fanon's death, 1961, when his *Wretched of the Earth* was published, Israel staged the Eichmann trial in Jerusalem. Before this trial, opinion makers in the West had some incentive to circumscribe discussion of the Nazi crime (e.g., the desire to rehabilitate West Germany as a buffer against Soviet expansionism during the Cold War, or a desire to prolong a celebratory view of World War II as a democratic triumph unsullied by the abandonment of millions to genocidal violence). Commentators like Deborah Lipstadt and Peter Novick have demonstrated how the Eichmann trial overwhelmed fifteen years of discursive reticence, and for decades thereafter turned commemorative practices and consciousness about the Holocaust into an element of "civil religion" in the United States and elsewhere.[62]

Nobody noticed it at the time, but Holocaust awareness and colonialism awareness wrestled with one another through Fanon's career, each vying for the privilege of becoming the looking glass through which the privileged West would understand where its triumphs had come from, and what its triumphs had portended. Fanon, born in a Caribbean French colony, Martinique, became a psychiatrist thanks to his entitlements as a French citizen (he studied in Lyon), after becoming a decorated soldier fighting for France during World War II.[63] Rather than drawing inspiration from the victory against Nazism, Fanon's World War II–era experiences finalized his estrangement from the liberal democratic heritage of the French Revolution. Among many other things, Fanon's belief that French colonialism hypocritically subverted and nullified this heritage drew from his encounters with racism while he wore his French army uniform.

Fanon's clinical work as a psychiatrist intersected with Holocaust trauma on many levels. In the early 1950s, for instance, he worked in a clinic, Saint Alban in southern France, whose heroic reputation rested largely on its functioning years earlier as a refuge for Jews and others persecuted by Nazism.[64] Psychiatrists at this asylum, such as François Tosquelles, had trained under the influence of exiled European Jews, like Sandor Eiminder, who had been part of Freud's circle in Vienna. Adam Shatz's recent biography of Fanon is studded with examples of Fanon's professional interaction with Jewish Holocaust refugees. These Jewish colleagues were understandably intrigued by Fanon's principal theoretical innovation, "sociogeny," the

---

62. Lipstadt, *Eichmann Trial*; Novick, *Holocaust*.
63. Biographical information here relies on Shatz, *Rebel's Clinic*.
64. Shatz, *Rebel's Clinic*, 124–38.

idea that some forms of psychological suffering can be traced to exploitative social relations, rather than a particular individual's psychological makeup.

Fanon propounded this hypothesis in his 1952 volume *Black Skin White Masks*.[65] Developed by a philosopher-psychiatrist whose outlooks were forged out of personal experience with colonial racism, sociogeny was one of many proposals regarding how Freudianism might, or might not, be incorporated in a radical social theory like Marxism. Five years earlier, the Frankfurt school, comprised largely of German Jews whose lives were transformed by the Holocaust, issued a different view of the same problem, combining Marxism and Freudianism, in books like Theodor Adorno and Max Horkheimer's *Dialectic of the Enlightenment*.

Not just on this theoretical level but also in quite practical terms, Fanon's anti-colonialism overlapped with Jewish figures who became identified with the process by which Holocaust awareness penetrated the West's civil religion later in the twentieth century. One example is Claude Lanzmann, who gained fame in the mid-1980s for his lengthy documentary on the Holocaust.[66] As a left-wing journalist in the late 1950s, Lanzmann contributed to the dissemination of Fanon's anti-colonialism broadside, *The Wretched of the Earth*, under Sartre's patronage. In his work as a roaming FLN operative in Africa, Fanon joined forces here and there with Jewish idealists with Holocaust backgrounds who were involved in anti-colonial struggles, as exemplified by Herbert Weiss in Leopoldville.[67] Fanon's blistering *Wretched of the Earth* would subsequently inspire many radicals who viewed Jewish experiences and ideologies, especially Zionism, as part of the colonialist complex critiqued by the book; but examples such as Lanzmann and Weiss suggest that in formative experiences which led to the text's publication, anti-Semitic victimization and colonialist victimization were intertwined mostly in a creatively symbiotic way.

One factoid symbolizes how anti-colonialism and Jewish struggles against anti-Semitism blended constructively in the process which led to the composition of Fanon's landmark text. The title of Fanon's study, *Les Damnés de la Terre*, comes from a line in a poem written by Jacques Roumain, a Haitian Marxist who died during World War II. The climactic part of the poem, beckoning a redemptive uprising of the wretched of the earth, envisions a revolutionary alliance between decolonized Blacks and other victims, including Jews.

65. Fanon, *Black Skin*.
66. Shatz, *Rebel's Clinic*, 349–68.
67. Shatz, *Rebel's Clinic*, 325–28.

Critiques of Colonialism: The Wretched of the Earth

To position Fanon's outlook in our Talmudic terms, *The Wretched of the Earth* evokes Rashbi's categorical rejection of colonialism as unmitigated exploitation, but it reads as though Rashbi lived in an earlier period of the Bar Kokhba revolt when Tannaim like Rabbi Akiva believed in the practical efficacy of militant opposition to the Romans.

Sometimes using technical-sounding psychological terms ("disalienation"), Fanon attributed ethical-existential, and political, import to anti-colonial efforts. He suggested that such struggles transformed the downtrodden, whose identities had been downsized to an animal level by colonialism. Anti-colonialist struggle turned them into men.

The book's first part, "On Violence," whose bellicose tone still rattles readers some sixty-five years after its publication, explicitly identifies anti-colonial violence as catharsis integral to this process by which colonized victims disalienate themselves. Fanon defines decolonization as an "agenda for total disorder." At least for illustrative purposes, the chapter contrasts the colonizer and the colonized as Manichean prototypes, as "two congenitally antagonistic forces."[68]

Part parable, part political analysis, the writing in this chapter draws from Fanon's own philosophical reflection, and also from his practical work as an FLN activist spokesman. In the tradition of leftist Hegelianism, he viewed "congenital antagonism" between the two forces as a process by which slaves liberate themselves and become human by vanquishing their masters. In pragmatic political terms, his doings with the FLN taught him to view anti-colonial struggle as a violent zero-sum contest. The outcome of decolonization, he wrote, could be "summed up in the well-known words: 'The last shall be first.'" He explained that the "last can be the first only after a murderous and decisive confrontation between the two protagonists." And the decolonization agenda would never be realized by persons who "are not determined from the very start to smash every obstacle encountered."[69]

Fanon's opening chapter in *The Wretched of the Earth* has a generic, paradigmatic character. Readers nonetheless identify its descriptions as accurate snapshots of notorious contemporary or future colonialist ecosystems, of shanty towns in Apartheid South Africa, or of the socioeconomically egregious landscape on the West Bank created after Israel's 1967 and 1973 wars by messianic right-wing Jewish settlers, with massive state support.

---

68. Fanon, *Wretched*, 2.
69. Fanon, *Wretched*, 2–3.

Elaborating on an insight developed earlier by Albert Memmi, Fanon viewed colonialism as a system of vicious sociopsychological circularity wherein the colonized sublimate and envy the ethos and lifestyle of the colonizers. The colonists' sector, Fanon recorded, is comprised of "lights and paved roads, where the trash cans constantly overflow with strange and wonderful garbage, undreamed-of leftovers.... The colonists' sector is a sated, sluggish sector, its belly is permanently full of good things." It would be impossible to find in the "famished" sector of the colonized a single resident "who does not dream of taking the place of the colonist," Fanon wrote.[70]

Colonialism's chokehold on its victims could not be explained in basic Marxist terms of class struggle and economic exploitation. Instead, colonialism is a complicated swirl of racism, class, capital, and politics, Fanon argued. Whereas the Marxists viewed economic dynamics as the foundation upon which oppressive social practices and ideas are built, Fanon believed that a factor like racism also generated its own causal dynamics. Aphoristically, he explained, "In the colonies the economic infrastructure is also a superstructure. The cause is effect: You are rich because you are white, you are white because you are rich." Owing to such dynamic, multilevel causality, "Marxist analysis should always be slightly stretched when it comes to addressing the colonial issue."[71]

The key word in that sentence is "slightly." In the triangle between, first, colonialism's apologists, such as Rabbi Judah in the Talmud; second, Rashbi anti-colonial militants like Fanon; and last, "third way" realists in the tradition of Rabbi Jose, what separates these last two legs can be associated with Fanon's qualifier in this sentence, "slightly." Though he delivers on his promise to "stretch" Marxism in his book, Fanon only does so "slightly," and he remains ideologically orthodox about the moral and political necessity of anti-colonialism's violent triumph. In retrospect, the book's Achilles's heel is its dogmatic refusal to discuss how religious nationalism might engulf anti-colonial movements, such as the one led by the FLN in Algeria, in ways subversive to outcomes of social justice sought by progressives of many names, including Marxists. Fanon suggests many times that decolonization ultimately will lead to a future devoid of primordial, essentialist constructs like race, but he never explains how, in anti-colonial campaigns, the involvement of fundamentalist religious movements poses a threat to these outcomes. Fanon's reticence in this retrospect can be seen either as a consequence or betrayal of events in his own political career—he had firsthand experience relating to the problematic relationship between

---

70. Fanon, *Wretched*, 4–5.
71. Fanon, *Wretched*, 5

religious nationalism and progressive, secular-left, anti-colonial struggle. For instance, in a tragically complicated sequence, Abane Ramdane, an FLN leader closely allied to Fanon, was murdered in 1957 by an organizational faction led by Abdelhafid Boussouf; in lieu of the social revolutionary goals evoked in Fanon's famous book, this faction was associated with the agenda of restoring Muslim Algeria.[72]

In *The Wretched of the Earth*, Fanon sometimes camouflages his ideological rigidity in propagandistically lyrical writing. The focus of the book's second chapter is the countryside. The author confronts a classic problem that had riddled mid-nineteenth-century socialists of many persuasions, starting with Marx who sneered patronizingly in the *Communist Manifesto* about how bourgeois urbanization had "rescued a considerable part of the population" from the "idiocy of rural life," to Russian leftists like Alexander Herzen who, in an antithetical tone, developed the Narodnik theory of natural rural harmony that promoted the village commune (*mir*) as the foundation of future socialist development.[73] How, all such socialists and other leftists wondered, did the uneducated rural masses fit into a revolutionary situation, such as the decolonization struggle precipitated by the FLN's heroic campaign in Algeria?

Fanon offered a detailed analysis of how bourgeois colonizers cultivated political passivity among the masses, exploiting rural traditions and superstitions to set the stage for their colonialist plunder. These bourgeois predators encouraged "marabouts and witch doctors [to] prevent the sick from consulting a physician"; they manipulated local rural elder councils, *djemaās*, so that aggrieved commoners would not turn to lawyers to prosecute justifiable grievances; they gloated greedily as their monopolistic activity was strengthened when "local chiefs oppose the introduction of trade and new products in the name of religion and tradition."[74] In an analysis that combines conventional Marxist analysis of stage-by-stage revolutionary progression and outright romantic utopianism, Fanon explained that rural populations liberate themselves from such colonialist manipulation thanks to the intervention of déclassé activists from the cities. These déclassé rebels, he explains, "discover a coherent people who survive in a kind of petrified state, but keep intact their moral values and their attachment to the nation."[75]

---

72. Shatz, *Rebel's Clinic*, 197–233.
73. Marx and Engels, *Manifesto*, ch. 1. See also Herzen, *From the Other Shore*.
74. Fanon, *Wretched*, 65.
75. Fanon, *Wretched*, 79.

In his 1850 treatise, *From the Other Shore*, Herzen had romanticized the Russian people (or *narod*, meaning "people" or "nation"), identifying the "intact moral values" on the Russian communal *mir* as the engine of revolutionary socialist change.[76] In the same vein, Fanon hinged anti-colonialism's historic triumph upon a myth of rural altruism and ardor. Colonialism would be brought to its knees by the rural masses, "a generous people, prepared to make sacrifices, willing to give all they have, impatient, with an indestructible pride."[77]

Fanon's writing is almost willfully inconsistent. In his professional life as a psychiatrist, he switched roles constantly as a pitiless diagnostician and as a remedial therapist. This duality colored his political writing, adding to its creative complexity while also compromising its programmatic consistency.

Two extended parts of the book compromise its overall revolutionary optimism about anti-colonialism's inevitable moral and political triumph. One, based on the author's sobering observations as an itinerant FLN mobilizer in sub-Saharan Africa, features withering descriptions of how opportunistic leaders of decolonization struggles manipulate revolutionary rhetoric while local elite confederates line their pockets, creating zones for leisure playgrounds and extraterritorial plunder for overseas businessmen. The other, the concluding section called "Colonial War and Mental Disorders," chillingly evokes the impression that psychological scars left on traumatized victims of colonialism might never be effaced. Ending his book, Fanon implies that a postcolonial society is liable to be psychologically unhealthy.

Insights in this late chapter of Fanon's masterwork derive from the author's years of clinical experience, part of which featured collaboration with Jewish survivors. In the corpus of post–World War II writings lionized in academia as "critical studies," this concluding section in *The Wretched of the Earth* is the last place where postcolonial studies and Holocaust studies compatibly converge. These two fields thereafter took separate paths following the Eichmann trial and the controversies over Israel's conquests in the 1967 war. Many of the findings and conclusions of this late chapter in the *Wretched of the Earth* would sound the same, were one to replace each reference to "colonialism" with "Holocaust."

There is no small measure of identity posturing in *The Wretched of the Earth*. The author sometimes prefaces his pronouncements by writing "We Algerians" ("We Algerians during the course of this war have had the

---

76. Herzen, *From the Other Shore*, 183–86.
77. Fanon, *Wretched*, 79.

opportunity . . ."⁷⁸)—this phrasing can be excused as a professional habit, since Fanon used it in his work as an FLN spokesman when he mobilized the public and anonymously published editorials in the organization's journal, *El Moudjahid*. But as shorthand abbreviation of the author's own identity, the phrase is ridiculous because formative experiences in Fanon's life transpired in Martinique and France, as well as African locales other than Algeria.

Despite such distortions of self-presentation, and the mix of orthodox dogma and unfounded romanticism in its treatment of subjects like the political culture of the countryside, *The Wretched of the Earth* projects an overall sense of uncompromising realism. This dimension is underscored by the way the book departs from the detached philosophical radicalism of its patron, Sartre. Fascinated by the psychology and morality of political rebellion, Sartre euphemistically glossed internecine violence in revolutionary movements, starting with the Jacobin reign of terror after 1789—branding such violence "fraternity-terror," he never sullied his hands by detailing what such a phrase really means.[79] In contrast, Fanon wrote in a noticeably realistic, unapologetic key about the vortex of circumstances wherein revolutionaries, facing murderous reprisals from class or colonial enemies, become violently suspicious of one another. In unnervingly remorseless prose, he explained why nobody in the colonial power complex—e.g., self-proclaimed reformers who infiltrated trade unions and national parties from above, and promoted byzantine schemes for Algerian semi-autonomy—could be trusted by the FLN. Privately, Fanon confided to Sartre and Simone de Beauvoir feelings of complicity for the murders of two figures with whom he had politically allied, Abane Ramdane, and the alluring, ill-fated Congolese politician, Patrice Lumumba.[80] However, no such political remorse infiltrates the gritty prose of *The Wretched of the Earth*, and its shock-appeal street credibility derives from its uncompromising defense of anti-colonial revolutionary morality.

As an inaugural text in postcolonial studies, *The Wretched of the Earth* keeps a tenor of totalized objectivity that is lacking in counterpart volumes in Holocaust studies. When was the last time you read a book about the Holocaust which had anything interesting to say about the psychology and private inner worlds of Nazi oppressors? In contrast, in addition to detailing the traumas suffered by colonialism's victims, the disarming closing part of Fanon's book, "Colonial War and Mental Disorders," refers also to the

78. Fanon, *Wretched*, 131.
79. Shatz, *Rebel's Clinic*, 354.
80. Shatz, *Rebel's Clinic*, 331.

mental health states of the FLN's oppressors, utilizers of the *gégène* torture contraption, by which electrodes were applied to an interrogatee's genitals, among other outrages. In his working life, Fanon conscientiously treated such brutal colonial enforcers in his psychiatric clinics, dividing his time between care for them and treatment of victimized rebels from his own FLN movement (his biographer, Shatz, claims that Fanon refused treatment to only one such violent colonial oppressor). Owing to such professional scrupulousness, he garnered insight about colonists' mentalities and wrote about them with authority.

Fanon's life and work has inspired an impressive phalanx of admirers and followers. Astonished by the *Wretched of the Earth's* acrobatic feat of articulating uncompromising resistance to colonialism while evincing understanding of the psychology of the men who applied its brute policies, they regard Fanon as a revolutionary humanist. The term, in almost all contexts, is oxymoronic. But what else can you call a man who provided mental health therapy to men whose actions, he believed, had virtually destroyed the world?

What can be said about the loose ends left untied by *The Wretched of the Earth*? Fanon himself confessed that persons from irresponsible local elites in decolonized states in Africa and elsewhere were driving around in sports cars and investing resources plundered from home in foreign corporations. In their debauchery, such elites were destroying dreams of national liberation that had been fostered by anti-colonial struggles. In general, it is hard to read *The Wretched of the Earth* without wondering why the author is not worried about the prospect of fundamentalist Islam seizing power in postcolonial Algeria, undermining visions of socialist democracy that had attracted many to the FLN struggle. In view of his talent for diagnostic realism, why did Fanon believe that the democratizing capacity of anti-colonial liberation struggle would be sustainable over time, after colonial superpowers left the scene?

The obvious, postmodern, response to this query is emphatically *not* part of Fanon's ideological repertoire. His book does not articulate a relativistic attitude by which concerns about postcolonial democracy are dismissed as items in a bourgeois-built superstructure, or as irrelevant mind-messing wrought by pro-colonialism confusion-mongers (a phrase Fanon actually uses once). Though he was crushingly disappointed by France's inability to effectuate the citizenship ideals of 1789 in the new world that was being created after World War II, Fanon would never have said that concepts like "rights" or "democracy" are, in principle, unimportant constructs wrought entirely by the self-interested rhetoric of colonialist-capitalist elites. Instead, Fanon believed that the revolutionary idealism of postcolonial campaigns would be sustainable because he believed in the reality of existential leaps, and because he believed that revolutionary violence is inestimably cathartic.

In his professional work, the parallel to Fanon's political attitude might have been his enthusiasm for electroshock therapy. To be sure, innumerable psychiatrists through the 1950s utilized electroconvulsive treatment, but (if his biographers are to be believed) Fanon's faith in this method seems to have been excessive, as though he believed that madness could be blown out of physical systems by radical action. This point, admittedly, is a bit metaphorical and strained, but I am trying to call attention to the corporal radicalism of Fanon's attack on colonialism.

The agenda of *The Wretched of the Earth*, announced in its opening chapter, is to violently extirpate colonialism from the globe, and Fanon is evidently thinking in biological terms about an invasive operation—"decolonization is quite simply the substitution of one 'species' of mankind by another."[81] These words are worth repeating: "The substitution of one 'species' of mankind by another." Anti-colonialism will yield a new, utopian stage of history because it will destroy one (colonizer) type of man and create another (postcolonial) type of man, Fanon suggests. He is caught in a trap of pseudo-biological radicalism because he has no practical answer as to why it is reasonable to suppose that revolutionary anti-colonialism will produce ameliorative, sustainable outcomes. In this respect, he belies the humanist ethos of his revolutionary professional and political career, and opportunistically usurps modes of biological determinism which left a genocidal imprint on various nineteenth-century and twentieth-century ideologies.

Fanon fell into this trap because he was unwilling to ground a theory of revolutionary anti-colonialism on an interpretation of history. More plausible than biological determinism, a response to the question about the democratic sustainability of anti-colonial rebellion proposes that activist masses will take risks and endure sacrifices in anti-colonial rebellion, and then positively engage with the imperfect compromises and mundane realities of postcolonial state-building, because they believe that the revolutionary process coheres with the best ideals of their people's past, and might possibly revive them in a modern mode.

Of course, an ample scholarly corpus demonstrates how nationalist movements are not particularly scrupulous or admirable in their use of history. They typically "invent" national traditions as excuses to rationalize their pursuit of identifiable present-day (and future) policy goals.[82] Revolutionary

---

81. Fanon, *Wretched*, 1.
82. Hobsbawm and Ranger, *Invention of Tradition*.

movements, as exemplified by Islamists in Iran in the late 1970s, sometimes use and abuse historical precedents to warrant religiously fundamentalist, illiberal policies in the present. In other words, by injecting "history" into the discussion of the sustainability of anti-colonial idealism, we are hardly providing a money-back guarantee that a particular revolutionary struggle will yield a progressively liberal outcome. What we *are* saying is that it was reckless for Fanon not to rely, in some measure, on argumentation about history in an attempt to resolve problems that were palpably left hanging by the anti-colonial discussion in *The Wretched of the Earth*. However much it sounds like pretzel logic, one abiding truth of revolutionary circumstances is this: history itself teaches that rebellions invariably rely on examples from the past to warrant their campaigns for a particular vision of the future. It would be very hard to think of a significant revolutionary movement that did not gain mileage from a selectively interpreted "usable past."

This dimension, history, is underdeveloped in Fanon's argument for a specific reason, stemming from his critique of a particular aesthetic and political mode, negritude, in the broad anti-colonial movement. His ambivalent, mostly negative, assessment of negritude began close to home, since the movement was partly fashioned by a poet/politician from Martinique, Aimé Césaire. The story of Fanon's relationship with Césaire and negritude's evocation of Black history has been told elsewhere,[83] and it suffices here to recap what an attentive reader of *The Wretched of the Earth* will notice: Fanon believed that idealized references to historic pasts in negritude thought and art encouraged backward-looking passivity detrimental in recruitment campaigns launched by activist anti-colonial movements like the FLN. He believed that negritude was politically co-opted by opportunistic elites whose reformist agendas disguised an intent to prolong colonialism. In an ironic zigzag, negritude's appeals to hoary communal truths and triumphs of precolonial Africa encouraged ridiculous situations in the metropole wherein white elites preached patronizingly to colonial natives about the authenticity of their primitive art, Fanon observed.

Negritude, so to speak, got under the skin of Fanon's thinking about race and history. His political views faltered, in consequence. In early writings, he was so dismissive about the turn to history in negritude theorizing that he rejected appeals for reparations based on past injustices caused by colonialism to Africans. Yet in a few passages in *The Wretched of the Earth*, Fanon cites the precedent of Konrad Adenauer's affirmation in the Eichmann trial setting of West Germany's continuing willingness to pay Holocaust reparations. Adenauer's statement, Fanon declares, is a warrant for a

---

83. Shatz, *Rebel's Clinic*, 36–53.

future where world powers will necessarily make massive capital transfers to Third World countries as redress for how they profited historically from the plunder of their colonial networks.

In *The Wretched of the Earth*, such declarations about how the West profited from colonialism, and about the consequent imperative of reparations, are like a quick clap of thunder on a summer day that disappears without any rain. "The ports of Holland, the docks in Bordeaux and Liverpool owe their importance to the trade and deportation of millions of slaves," Fanon proclaims; thus, the capitalist powers "must pay up."[84] These passages are strikingly overreaching not because there was (or is) anything intrinsically implausible in reparations discussions regarding decolonized Africa (or regarding the enslavement of African Americans), but rather because the historical analysis in Fanon's book is so perfunctorily underdeveloped. By definition, reparations are compensations for abuses of the past, and they are thus awkwardly and falteringly supported in a book that minimizes the impact of history. For better or worse, Fanon's negative appraisal of leaders in the negritude movement shaped the way he critiqued colonialism. Mostly, he kept history out of the equation and presented contemporary violent struggles against colonial power as having cathartic power of their own making.

Critiques of Colonialism: The Two Alberts and the Third Way

Rabbi Jose's third way orientation in debates about colonialism was developed, with mixed success, in this late 1950s Algeria crisis by two Alberts: one, Albert Memmi, a Jew from Tunis, and the second, Albert Camus, an Algerian-born existentialist who regarded himself as being mostly French.

The first, Memmi, published his groundbreaking study, *The Colonizer and the Colonized*, in 1957, a few years before Fanon released his *Wretched of the Earth* (the two men never met), and so Memmi's work is sometimes regarded as being a point of origin in postcolonial theory.[85] As Fanon was to do, Memmi devoted considerable discussion to the mindset of the colonizers (as advertised by its title, *The Colonizer and the Colonized* has two halves, and Memmi's prose actually seems a little sharper when it refers to the oppressors, rather than the victims, in a colonial system). Though Memmi lacks Fanon's buoyant faith in anti-colonial rebellion as a soul-saving endeavor by which history leapfrogs to a liberated new stage, *The Colonizer and the Colonized* analyzes colonialism's self-defeating contradictions,

84. Fanon, *Wretched*, 57–58.
85. Memmi, *Colonizer*.

and categorically predicts its utter disappearance from historical reality. In this respect, Memmi's book, like Fanon's, is ideological and perhaps can be thought of as a precursor of "cultural Marxist" approaches that thinkers and researchers like E. P. Thompson developed in the last decades of the twentieth century.

More to the point, Memmi's uncompromising belief that colonialism is a doomed project unable to reform itself separates his writing from that of the second Albert, Albert Camus. In addition to his Nobel Prize–winning literary work (much of it based on allegorical or semirealistic Algerian landscapes), Camus published journalistic writings pleading for compromise formulas to the Algerian crisis that would protect the pied-noir population and also offer Algeria effective sovereignty within some sort of overall French political frame, while mitigating the political impact of FLN terror.[86] This particular difference between the two Alberts can be explained in a fashion that is sociologically reductive but nonetheless valid. Having grown up in Tunis's Jewish community, a stratum straddled on the border between, on the one hand, colonialist victimization and, on the other hand, significant though limited civil and socioeconomic opportunity offered by colonialism to privileged local groups, Memmi became irretrievably frustrated with French rule. His excellent autobiographical novel, *The Pillar of Salt*, published two years before *The Colonizer and the Colonized*, ends in rupture, its young protagonist severed from the traditional ways of his childhood Jewish milieu but unable existentially to pursue an undergraduate program of study in Paris for which he had been prepared on an assimilationist course as a scholarship pupil in Tunis.[87] Camus, in contrast, did not have this luxury of projecting an unrelenting sense of existential exhaustion bred by life in a colonial framework. The problem was not that he came from a privileged colonialist background—Camus's parents had murky European backgrounds sufficient for the possession of French civil entitlements in Algeria, but they were poor and unlucky (Camus's father died during World War I, and his mother was illiterate). Still, his mother remaining in a working-class district in Algiers, Belcourt, Camus kept tangible, avowed commitments to the pied-noir group's demand for a future in the country, until the circumstances and aftermath of Algerian independence quashed it. Camus appreciated Memmi's depiction of minority hardship under colonialism and wrote a preface to *Pillar of Salt*, but the two Alberts had different ideas about the necessity and viability of colonialism's reform. Memmi's theory of colonialism's inescapable self-contradictions joined him to the

---

86. Discussion on Camus draws from Carroll, *Albert Camus*.
87. Memmi, *Pillar of Salt*.

ideological diehards in the Sartre-Fanon camp, who mercilessly applauded FLN terror as the midwife of history's predetermined next, postcolonial, stage. Noticing Memmi's uncompromising attitude, Sartre gave a stamp of approval in his published preface to *The Colonizer and the Colonized* but also patronizingly criticized Memmi for the book's lack of Marxian analysis about colonialist oppression as a systematic phenomenon operating within an "apparatus" of class struggle.

Memmi argued that colonialism could never be reformed due to its perpetrators' unyielding social and psychological investment in it. Colonizers, he believed, were people of mediocre quality who were drawn out of the metropole by incitements of status and wealth offered by life in the colonies. Many arrived without long-term plans and lived rather lonely, unhappy lives in North Africa; nonetheless, owing to the relatively high style of life afforded to them by colonialism's plunder of local resources and its exploitation of local laborers, they remained. These colonizers were snubbed on return visits to the metropole but nonetheless articulated ultranationalist, patriotically French attitudes in the colonies. Memmi, in fact, depicts them as semifascists—by awarding privileges and riches to a small colonizer minority, while oppressing the colonized masses, colonialism is a fascistic system, he explicitly declares.[88]

Lacking any objective warrant for their privileged status, the colonizers rely on essentialist generalizations about the colonized. Memmi's elaboration of this point links him both to the argument about racism and colonialism developed several years earlier by Hannah Arendt, in her *Origins of Totalitarianism*, and also to the critique published some years later in Fanon's impactful book. Memmi was fascinated by the way colonizers who had professional credentials—as, for instance, physicians—ignorantly generalized about the supposed indolent lifestyle of the "natives" and furnished absurdly bogus biological explanations of this alleged trait. For Memmi, the similitude between such observations and passages in Fanon's later book, *The Wretched of the Earth*, irked suspicion. (Memmi's concerns were apparently allayed when he learned that Fanon had published a study of racism, *Black Skin, White Masks*, years earlier in 1951, incidentally the publication date of Arendt's book, *Origins of Totalitarianism*; it bears mention that Fanon's experience with the way colonizer racism rebooted in response to FLN insurgency, suddenly complaining that the natives are too restlessly activist rather than being passively indolent, contributed to a more supple and nuanced view of colonialist racism, compared to Memmi's *The Colonizer and the Colonized*.)

88. Memmi, *Colonizer*, 99.

In some of his writings, Memmi suggested that colonial society allowed, to some extent, crossings of ethnoreligious and class barriers. Pivoting on the Jewish situation in Tunis, his novel, *The Pillar of Salt*, documents a mother's involvement in premodern fertility and healing rituals with Berbers and Arabs; and it alludes to the success enjoyed by the protagonist's father, a tanner, in complicated ethnonational and economic class networks, before he succumbed to poverty and tuberculosis. However, in *The Colonizer and the Colonized*, Memmi's analysis of the political psychology of colonizers overlooks how it might have been tempered by such ethnonational or class border-bending in daily markets and social settings. As happened in the first chapter of Fanon's book, Memmi tended toward prototypical abstraction when he wrote about colonizers. For them, he insisted, no compromise was possible. Their operating assumption was this: should colonial rule introduce any measure of socioeconomic reform friendly to the colonized, the whole system of privileges enjoyed by the colonizers would collapse like a house of cards. Furthermore, Memmi argued, the *mission civilisatrice* ethos of French colonialism was a sham. However much they invested in educational programs or prattled about bringing civilization to the colonies, the colonizers would never allow locals to truly assimilate French norms and culture. This was because the basis of the colonizers' privilege was the imagined reality of their sociobiological separation from the colonized. Colonialism, Memmi, declared, lacked any capacity for revitalization: "Colonized society is a diseased society in which internal dynamics no long succeed in creating new structures."[89] This being the case, Memmi diagnosed, violent revolution is, and will remain, a permanent feature on the global decolonization landscape. "Far from being surprised at the revolts of the colonized peoples, we should be, on the contrary, surprised that they are not more frequent and more violent."[90]

Memmi's diagnosis, then, was quite similar to Fanon's. The essential difference between the two is that only the latter believed that this diagnosis was inherently remedial. Owing to his belief in the possibility of radical change in individual psychology and social reality, Fanon viewed anti-colonial revolution as a cleansing game changer. Memmi, in contrast, whose confusing life experiences as an ambitious Jew in Tunis who interrupted his pro-assimilatory investments by suspending his scholarship-funded studies (the fictionalized autobiography *Pillar of Salt* ends on this disillusioned note, whereas Memmi himself migrated to the metropole and eventually earned a doctorate at the Sorbonne), and who wrote a novel

89. Memmi, *Colonizer*, 98.
90. Memmi, *Colonizer*, 127.

about the complicated dynamics of his own mixed marriage,[91] never really believed that anti-colonial revolution and political independence in Algeria or anywhere else would truly decolonize the two players in the drama he depicted in his pathbreaking 1957 study. The colonizers were a lost cause, and the colonized would never become truly assimilated Frenchmen and Frenchwomen—depressingly, each group left a part of itself in the other, and political liberation would not remove the mutually enervating effects of colonialism. Using an analogy that would never have appeared in writings published by Fanon (who seems, incidentally, to have had a more relaxed mixed marriage than Memmi), *The Colonizer and the Colonized* envisions a decolonized future wherein these two groups will look like members of a divorced couple who look and act like one another after their formal estrangement. "At the height of his revolt, the colonized still bears the traces and lessons of prolonged cohabitation (just as the smile or movements of a wife, even during divorce proceedings, remind one strangely of those of her husband)," concluded Memmi, in an image that flatly contradicts the main equation in *The Wretched of the Earth*, holding that anti-colonial revolt equals human liberation.[92]

Memmi prescribed no magical remedies for the postcolonial era. "There is no question here of a wish but of an affidavit," he wrote in the short, concluding chapter of *The Colonizer and the Colonized*. He ended the book with some facile proclamations deriding "the famous and absurd incompatibility between East and West" and suggesting, in a wan modernization key, that engineering projects will help decolonized lands ("Science is neither Western nor Eastern. . . . There are only two ways of pouring concrete, the right way and the wrong way").[93]

Memmi wrote rather prolifically up to the end of his life (2020), and some of these later writings can be praised for their unpredictable realism. Cognizant of Memmi's background in an ethnoreligiously diverse North African milieu, and swayed by some nostalgic depictions at the start of *Pillar of Salt*, leftist Israeli post-Zionists sometimes try to co-opt Memmi as though his example reinforces their thesis that Arabs and Jews got along fine in the Middle East before Jewish nationalists, Zionists, came and ruined this Semitic lovefest. This interpretation is not tenable. Memmi's descriptions of Jewish life in closed-off venues like the urban *mellah* in Morocco are harshly unsparing. Never romanticizing Jewish settings in the Middle East,

---

91. Memmi, *Strangers*.
92. Memmi, *Colonizer*, 129.
93. Memmi, *Colonizer*, 132.

Memmi sometimes hinted about their resemblance to European ghettoes. He believed that challenges of Arab-Jewish interaction preceded Zionism.[94]

These later writings have flaws similar to pitfalls in Fanon's *Wretched of the Earth*. Memmi could be ideologically dogmatic. Because Jewish life in Europe and elsewhere in pre-Holocaust times shared attributes with the experiences of North African groups under French colonial rule, Memmi tended to think inflexibly of the Jews as an everlastingly colonized community. He never really processed evidence showing how, as a sovereign power in Israel, they have been slouching toward the other side of the equation as a result of conquests in the 1967 Six-Day War.

As a sensitive, intellectually precocious youth, Memmi was badly traumatized by his assimilatory efforts in Tunis, and he drew upon several unhappy personal memories when he rejected Fanon's soon-to-be propounded thesis about how revolutionary work would heal scars left by colonialism. A growing number of students and scholars, largely in the Jewish Studies field, who are rediscovering Memmi's work today, tend to think about his complicated background within contemporary multicultural rubrics wherein ideas like "diversity" and "hybridity" are associated with identity sophistication and human fulfillment. But Memmi was not merry when he wrote sentences like, "In the colonial context, bilingualism is necessary." In the nonfictional *Colonizer and the Colonized*, he inserted some clarifications, saying (with regard to bilingualism) that "the two worlds symbolized and conveyed by the two tongues are in conflict," and describing bilingual fluency as a "cultural catastrophe which is never completely overcome."[95] Such passing exclamations should be read in conjunction with Memmi's fictional work, particularly *The Pillar of Salt*. This first novel is filled with vivid, sometimes heart-wrenching, sequences of how the author turned into a rude, secularizing teenager who taunted his parents' Jewish traditionalism and fumbled in French as an assimilating scholarship pupil, rattling off misnomers as his mind raced frantically to translate thoughts that reached his mind in the nonliterary vulgate of the colonized.

Memmi's judgments can be assessed in a solely Jewish context. In Europe, modernizing Jewish intellectuals, called *Maskilim*, who frequently came out of the Russian empire to study philosophy or literature in German-speaking lands, published autobiographical writings which strongly echo many of Memmi's descriptions (one such late eighteenth-century Maskil, Salomon Maimon, described precisely the same linguistic

---

94. Silver, *Bi-shelihut ha-Ma'arav*, 221–36.
95. Memmi, *Colonizer*, 106–7.

experience[96]). But decades before the Holocaust, such European Maskilim attributed happy endings to their Europeanized modernization. They often adopted a carefree (in Maimon's case, a mocking) attitude toward Jewish religious study and observances. Memmi, who opens *Pillar of Salt* with a sentimental, loving description of Shabbat in his childhood home, never found cause for such enthusiasm about assimilatory modernization in his North African, colonized, setting.

This reading of Memmi is too narrow, however. Quickly catching the attention of figures like Sartre and Camus, Memmi's *Colonizer and the Colonized* was not written in a Jewishly parochial vein. Using his own Jewish background for demonstrative purposes, Memmi argued that the experience of Westernized modernization was necessarily traumatic for any colonized minority.

Doubting that Islamic nationalism would preserve safe spaces for non-Muslim minorities in a postcolonial future, Memmi was never gleeful about decolonization. Whether or not Fanon really believed the FLN's propaganda about its inclusiveness, the author of *The Wretched of the Earth* studiously avoided discussion about the implications of organized Islamic militancy within anti-colonial struggle. For Memmi, concerns about these implications were center stage. He made a point of framing them as anxieties shared by all secular progressive leftists, not just Jewish revolutionaries, in decolonizing North Africa. "Proclamations in the name of God, the Holy war concept," Memmi recorded, "throw the leftist off balance and frighten him." As though he were asking Fanon a question left unanswered in *The Wretched of the Earth*, Memmi, speaking as a "leftist," queried, "How can he fail to notice that when freed, the most newly liberated nations hasten to include religion in their constitutions?"[97]

We will leave Memmi standing exactly at this place, one where he has acutely identified social, moral, and political reasons that justify colonialism's elimination, and where he has also acknowledged that the campaign to eliminate it might be dangerous and even, in terms of his own identity, self-annihilating. Standing in this place, Memmi, a Franco-Tunisian writer, becomes the Jewish intellectual of modern times whose situation foreshadows the situation of liberal Jews in 2024. These Jews identify with the idealism of campus protests against Israel's Gaza War and share many of these demonstrators' criticisms of Israel's colonialist occupation of the West Bank; but they also dread a future that would arise should power brokers in

---

96. Maimon, *Autobiography*, 109.
97. Memmi, *Colonizer*, 33.

Washington (and other places) ever decide to fashion serious policy in tune with Hamas-inspired "from the river to the sea" campus radicalism.

In *The Colonizer and the Colonized*, Memmi insightfully diagnosed the necessity of decolonization. But from his own individual and Jewish communal standpoint, he knew that this diagnosis was self-defeating. For Memmi in 1957, and for liberal American Jews and center-leftist Israelis today, the most important sentence in this book is this acknowledgment: "There are, I believe, impossible historical situations, and this is one of them."[98] Memmi believed in the historic necessity of decolonization in North Africa but also forthrightly acknowledged how it might usher in Jihad radicalism ("holy war," as he phrased it), leaving no room for Jews, among others. Memmi was speaking about himself when he wondered aloud, "Why should he struggle for a social order in which he understands that there would be no place for him?"[99] But he is also speaking to all of us. He is speaking to liberal humanists, Jews and gentiles, who acknowledge the fundamental legitimacy of Israel's existence, as they watch the campus protests and try to recalibrate their identities and efforts.

Memmi offered no remedies, no policy path forward. In this sense of positive prescription, his work remains inscrutable, and reminiscent of the way Rabbi Jose listened silently while Rashbi and Rabbi Judah wrestled back and forth about whether Roman colonialism was good for the Jews. There is a message laden in such silences about colonialism, however. On the same path as Rabbi Jose, Memmi is saying to Jews in 2024, "Find a third way, or die." "Die," at least in the sense of remaining a vibrant group presence that has something better to do in history than wait for billionaires from the tribe to come and use their dollar donations as a truncheon that bludgeons away the free speech rights of college students and the administrative freedom of university presidents.

Our agenda here is to turn to contemporary issues of Israel and colonialism, but we should quickly complete the circle in this discussion of decolonization and North Africa. If you are looking for an affirmative third way platform in that context, try the other Albert—Camus. There, as in most other settings, the answer is called "humanism."

Because he opposed FLN terror activities and advocated compromise formulas, hoping to leave elements of French colonialism intact (including the pied-noir settlement in Algeria), Camus's work has been met with opprobrium among postcolonial critics. Adamant commentators like Conor Cruise O'Brien and Edward Said dismissed Camus's writing as an

---

98. Memmi, *Colonizer*, 39.
99. Memmi, *Colonizer*, 39.

apologetic for French colonialism in Algeria.[100] They disputed the writer's own hyphenated self-identification as a French-Algerian by arguing that the pieds-noirs constituted an extraterritorial colonialist excrescence, devoid of true Algerian roots.

The fulcrum of such criticism is the disarming inattention to Algeria's Muslim majority in Camus's best-known books. Very few Arabs or Berbers in Oran are pictured as recipients of treatment meted by the pragmatic pied-noir altruists who mobilize to fight the contagion in *The Plague*.[101] Similarly, the Arab murder victim appears in *The Stranger* as an instrumental device in a novel that is most intelligibly read not as an indictment of colonizer violence but rather as an existentialist satire about the absurdity of human institutions vested with the power to cast judgment and sanctimoniously enforce draconian procedures such as capital punishment.[102] Camus's literary parochialism *is* a problem, one reminiscent of how Israeli fiction often focuses exclusively on Jewish protagonists and issues, even when it addresses areas like Galilee, where I live, which retained large Arab populations even after the 1948 mass "Nakba" exodus. Literary flaws, however, do not always imply endorsement of persecution. That Camus's writing had blind spots and biases does not mean that it ought to be regarded as a malevolent apologetic for colonialist oppression. Camus can be faulted for his retention of wishful-thinking denial about the inevitability of FLN triumph right up to his 1960 death in an automobile accident; but a new generation of what might be called post-postcolonial critics, exemplified by the writing of David Carroll, has persuasively brushed away vituperative condemnations of Camus's literary and political writings on Algeria and decolonization.[103]

Fanon conceded that Marxist theory needed to be stretched "slightly" in view of colonialism's complicated realities. Camus, in contrast, recoiled from the FLN and revolutionary terror in Algeria because, as Cold War culture intensified, he believed that "slightly" was not enough—ideological dogmatism, on his view, posed a mortal threat to world culture. Camus had an obsessive objection to capital punishment, apparently based on a story about his father's experiences.[104] This bugbear, reflected in plot sequences, and the outlooks of a few characters, in his fiction, also fulcrumed Camus's distaste for revolutionary terror executions perpetrated by groups like the FLN. His extended 1951 essay *The Rebel* is essentially an anti-ideology

100. O'Brien, *Albert Camus*; Carroll, *Albert Camus*, 49–55.
101. Camus, *Plague*.
102. Camus, *Stranger*.
103. Carroll, *Albert Camus*.
104. Carroll, *Albert Camus*, 86–87.

polemic filled with historical-philosophical argumentation about the political crimes committed by intellectuals and radicals, such as Russian revolutionaries from the nineteenth century, in the name of various social theories.[105]

As an existentialist humanist, Camus believed that the burden of philosophical discussion and political action is to intelligibly offset the sheer absurdity of human mortality (this is the point of his 1942 booklet, *The Myth of Sisyphus*).[106] Unlike writers such as Fanon who implied that revolution would change everything, Camus championed social idealism even though its practitioners can never know whether their good deeds will ever achieve anything (if anything, Camus's heroes have a Sisyphean inkling about how the outcome of their altruism will not be sustainable). As Sartre implied in his less dogmatically Marxian moments, the gist of such existentialist humanism is a protagonist's empathetic intuition about which action, out of an array of alternatives, would likely bring the most benefit to the most people. In Camus's fiction, the personification of such humanism is Dr. Bernard Rieux, the Oran physician in *The Plague* who correctly diagnoses the dangers posed by the contagion before anyone else, and then spends the rest of the novel saving lives for no reason other than that there could be no better alternative, under the circumstances, than trying to prevent as many deaths as possible. Precisely because it is undogmatic, Rieux's pragmatic humanism operates as a kind of counter-contagion, mobilizing residents from Oran (described by Camus, in times before the plague, as a dreadful locale populated by awful money-grubbers) to overcome their own mediocrity and work together despite differences in their social station, and life experiences.

All of this has tremendous appeal to anyone who has a relatively optimistic view of human nature and believes, as Camus tried emphatically to illustrate in *The Plague*, that under the right circumstances, many people can rise above their own narrow egoism. But we cannot elaborate on Camus's brand of existential humanism here. The problem is not, as some postcolonial critics dubiously contended, that it apologetically warrants colonialist oppression. Neither Camus's fictional writings nor his well-known philosophical treatises do anything like that. When it comes to a discussion of colonialism and contemporary politics, my complaint with existential humanism is its tendency to float beyond the pedestrian facts of everyday history.

---

105. Camus, *Rebel*.
106. Camus, *Myth*.

Camus's fiction deserves praise for its absurdism and its allegory, not its realism. Most people read *The Plague* as an allegory about the French resistance to Nazi occupation; its readers are likely to come away with an inspiringly enlightened view of human potentiality, but that does not mean they will learn anything new about the Holocaust. And what does *The Stranger* really say about the inherent injustice of colonialism's judicial systems? Even in kangaroo courts of infamous colonial settings, say South Africa before 1991, Boers brought to trial on serious murder allegations were never going to be executed because they were boors who did not properly mourn their mothers deaths. Probing Camus's writing for suggestions about how to think about contemporary colonialism controversies like Israel's Gaza War is like reading Kafka's *Metamorphosis* as a guide for the reduction of greenhouse gas emissions.

THE 2023–2024 GAZA WAR AND THE DEBATE ABOUT ISRAELI COLONIALISM

Hamas's malevolent attack on October 7, 2023, transformed realities in Israel's decades-long conflict. For hours that day the IDF and other Israeli security forces displayed indescribable incompetence and cowardice, allowing Hamas fighters to rampage in small towns, communal villages, and an outdoor rave party on Israel's side of the southern border. Nukhba commandos, assisted by militarily untrained Gazans, captured hundreds of unassuming civilians, ranging in age from infants to octogenarians, as hostages, and killed twelve hundred persons (some of them foreign nationals).[107] Historians will compile troves of evidence showing how the attack should have been identified in advance, and preempted. For one thing, scenarios of surprise enemy attacks on Israel-controlled territory were on everyone's mind, since Hamas attacked at the time of the fiftieth anniversary of Egypt's stunning 1973 crossing of the Suez Canal and the subsequent Yom Kippur War—like many others, I had been to the cinema a few days before October 7 (this was an autumn holiday season) and watched one of several films released at the time that documented the grisly events that unfolded in October 1973 when Israel dropped its guard and allowed thousands of enemy Egyptians to pour into the Sinai Peninsula.

On a geopolitical level, historians will scratch their heads incredulously, wondering what politicians in Jerusalem and Washington, DC, were thinking weeks ahead of Hamas's offensive, when they gleefully announced an impending peace initiative. Supposedly, this initiative would stabilize

---

107. *Times of Israel*, "Israel Revises Death Toll."

Israel's situation in the Middle East by mitigating Iran's bellicosity via the forging of an alliance of Sunni states, led by Saudi Arabia, which have been worried about the Islamic radicalism of the Shiite regime in Teheran. This Saudi initiative expressly left the Palestinians in the cold. It would have continued and amplified a unilateral trend initiated by Donald Trump's first administration, which moved the US embassy to Jerusalem and made other pro-Israel moves in places like the Golan Heights, and also negotiated the Abraham Accords, normalizing relations between Israel and Bahrain, and Israel and the United Arab Emirates, without offering the Palestinians anything at all in recompense.

Israel's prime minister, Benjamin Netanyahu, who in the 1980s first gained international prominence by proclaiming expertise in the realm of terror prevention, giddily touted the newly proposed Saudi initiative as a major step in the process by which Israel would attain peace and stability in the Middle East in the absence of a two-state solution, or any other negotiated accommodation with the Palestinians. In an autobiographical memoir, published originally in English several months before the October 7 calamity, Netanyahu lavishly defended this doctrine envisioning a future of peace and stability for Israel while some three million Palestinians would continue to live under colonial occupation on the West Bank. Gloatingly saying that they anticipated the Trump-brokered Abraham Accords, Netanyahu quoted his own words at the UN General Assembly in 2014: "Many have long assumed that an Israeli-Palestinian peace can help facilitate a broader rapprochement between Israel and the Arab world. I think it may work the other way around."[108] Weeks before the October 7 Hamas attack, Netanyahu reiterated this theory during another UN address, intoning about how Israel can have peace while maintaining its occupation of the West Bank, and after the two-state formula becomes a forgotten relic of bygone diplomacy.[109]

Netanyahu's hubris in this second, pre–October 7, UN address had been inflated by the Biden administration. Biden's White House inexplicably rewarded a Netanyahu government that had bestowed senior ministerial positions to racist Kahanist politicians, and that had spent months drafting and legislating a scheme to overhaul the country's judicial branch and thereby undermine the checks and balances mechanisms of Israeli democracy. Deservedly, President Biden won widespread, renewed appreciation among Israelis and diaspora Jews for his administration's swift, generous, and strategically crucial responses to Hamas's October 7 attacks;

---

108. Netanyahu, *Bibi*, 525.
109. PBS NewsHour, "Israeli Prime Minister."

but the Biden administration's lobbying for the Saudi peace deal in weeks ahead of this Hamas offensive was one of its worst foreign policy blunders.

Since 1937, in the middle of Britain's Mandatory period in Palestine, diplomacy regarding what became the world's most intractable dispute has fulcrumed on the two-state, Jewish and Palestinian, formula. That Donald Trump would ignore this compromise formula's irreproachable logic, and the hefty historical precedents layered within it, may not have been a surprise, but Joe Biden, an experienced politician who is both a philosemite and a pragmatic realist, should never have slipped in the Saudi oil slick. The strengthening of Saudi-US networks would bring benefits to American citizens, but what good did it do to the world when the Biden administration added Israel to the Saudi deal framework, leaving the neglected Palestinians at the curb? After they were demonstrably removed from Middle East peace and development diplomacy, what alternative was left to the Palestinians other than to resume an armed struggle against the Jewish state? In months after October 7, this question could not be comfortably addressed by many commentators, particularly "pro-Israel" ones, because posing it seemed to rationalize rape, murder, and hostage-taking perpetrated by Nukhba fighters from Hamas's military wing; it also seemed to express ingratitude toward the United States at a troubled time when the Biden administration stood firmly by Israel's side. But as wartime passions subside, the question will be asked with mounting severity by historians, not to mention new political administrations in the White House.

Political-military investigations in years to come will focus on the excruciating issue of how exactly it came about that the IDF was nowhere to be found, for hours, at places like Kibbutz Be'eri and Kibbutz Nir Oz, when Nukhba men raped and murdered and scootered back to Gaza with young mothers and their babies in their paws. Yet it is worth mentioning what life was like in Israel in days *before* the Hamas attack. This aspect of the gruesome fiasco is likely to be overlooked by future commentators, but the nobility of spontaneous, grass roots, Israeli responses in days after October 7 cannot really be understood if it is not kept in mind.

The Hamas attack occurred on Simchat Torah, a holiday celebrating the conclusion of the annual cycle of synagogue Torah readings. Simchat Torah concludes a seven-day holiday, Sukkot ("The Festival of Booths"), an autumnal celebration commemorating pilgrimages in ancient days to the temple in Jerusalem, during which Jews happily take meals in a symbolically verdurous *sukkah*. In Israel, Sukkot is appreciated by youngsters as a reprieve that comes just a few weeks after the end of summer and their return to classrooms. Families appreciate the holiday as a period when beaches and nature trails and outdoor tables at restaurants can be utilized in much greater comfort than the situation five or six weeks earlier, during the last, swelteringly hot, days of August.

Sukkot in 2024 was different. Several weeks earlier, just before the spring legislative session of the country's parliament, the Knesset, shut down for the summer, the Netanyahu government had legislated a major, controversial plank of its judicial overhaul plan (disallowing the judiciary's use of a "reasonableness" standard to overturn dubious laws or public sector appointments). Believing that the Netanyahu government's self-proclaimed judicial system "reform" was effectively an antidemocratic coup perpetrated by the self-interested prime minister (who was himself dealing with criminal indictments on bribery and related charges and therefore had direct incentive to cauterize the judicial branch) and his cabinet ministers, tens of thousands of protestors had been in the streets for many months. The demonstrations centered on a weekly, Saturday night, mass show of peaceful dissent in central Tel Aviv, involving about one hundred thousand persons, sometimes more.

Demonstrations against the Netanyahu government reached their zenith in late July, just before the Knesset's summer recess, when the parliament rescinded this "reasonableness" standard. This Knesset spectacle was widely followed on live television broadcasts and social media platforms in the country. Thanks to his background, as a schoolboy in Philadelphia and a degree earner at MIT, Netanyahu has genuine familiarity with constitutional principles; in public statements made in Israel in earlier phases of his career, he overtly applauded the independence of Israel's judicial system. Nonetheless, during this fateful, late July 2023, parliamentary session, Netanyahu flitted in and out of the parliament to cast his vote in favor of this phase of the program to decimate Israel's judiciary. He looked a little pale, like an estranged husband who is relieved to sign a divorce agreement but worried about the alimony payments it enjoins. Giggling cabinet ministers huddled together to take selfies and celebrate having taken a giant step toward awarding themselves full immunity in a future de-democratized Israel where they would be able to do what they want, including the suspension of norms mandating the holding of national elections (pointedly, Netanyahu did not join this huddle).

Meantime, unforgettably, one liberal politician from a centrist party, representing many thousands of Israelis who never in their lives had imagined that the Jewish state would cease to operate as a democracy, wept openly when it was her turn to speak at the Knesset podium. Thereafter, the Knesset shut down in August and September; and so too were the mass protests against the Netanyahu government put on hold, pending the reignition of the power-grabbing Netanyahu government's legislative efforts. Everyone knew that in days after Simchat Torah, those efforts would resume. The Knesset would return to work and the government would proceed with the next planks in its program to neutralize judicial oversight of the cabinet and the parliament—schemes to allow a Knesset majority to overturn judicial decisions, to wrest control over judicial appointments, and so on. October 7 was a Shabbat, the last one in the foreseeable future when one hundred thousand or one hundred and fifty thousand concerned citizens would not have strong cause to demonstrate in the name of Israeli democracy in Tel Aviv.

When Hamas attacked Israel's southern communities on October 7, the soldiers, unassuming families, and young partygoers in this area represented a seriously demoralized body politic which, at that precise moment, was in a state of nauseous dread. Even many right-wingers who had supported the Netanyahu government's doings, by and large, were privy to this bedraggled state of consciousness (just as many patriotic, good-hearted Americans who support Trump do not experience schadenfreude when they see how his actions and policies are tearing the country apart, as in episodes such as the January 6, 2021, assault on Capitol Hill).

The way the Netanyahu government tore the fabric of Israeli democracy before the Gaza War is not exclusively a Jewish story. It is part of a global trend. As I write these lines, there is some glimmer of hope coming from Europe's oldest democracies, England and France, where centrist-left constellations have recently staved off challenges posed by the illiberal right. If the tides are now turning in favor of democracy, the story of the assault on liberalism will have an identifiable timetable—for instance, in Britain the timeline could be eight years, dating from the June 2016 Brexit vote to the recent parliamentary election in which the conservative Tories, who glorify the ghoulish fetishes of the global radical right (anti-immigrant xenophobia, predatory free market policy favorable to the wealthiest 1 percent, and so on), were finally voted out of power. But there are many strong reasons to doubt whether any turning points in our era of tweeted illiberalism are really on the horizon.

We live in a darkening world, the twilight of a centuries-long era when liberal optimism exercised authority, albeit of varying intensities in different places and times. Democracies will continue to erode so long as their uncalibrated economies block the revival and expansion of the middle classes. So long as these national economies remain divided between the 1 percent big elite, the 10 percent little elite, and an immiserated everyone else, global politics will be dominated by a populist left and a populist right. Global politics in our time is an ongoing mind-bend by which established elites fortify their control over capital and status by cultivating a theatrical anti-establishment style perfectly suited for social media. The shenanigans indulged by Netanyahu's government before the Gaza War are exactly like power-grabbing party games played in innumerable democracies (in fact, planks in the Netanyahu government's judicial overhaul scheme were relatively tame compared to the summer 2024 US Supreme Court decision in favor of presidential executive immunity).

Israel's situation is distinctive in just one way. The erosion of social morale caused by mind-bending, demagogic politics can be lethal in a democracy that faces an ongoing security crisis. Thus far, Israel is the world's first and only democracy to experiment with internally divisive illiberalism while inveterate enemies look on, sharpening their knives.

When considering Israel's contemporary predicaments, the surge in patriotic idealism we witnessed in days after October 7 ought to be an integral part of the equation, counterbalancing many other considerations which darkly shade Israel's Gaza War, and frame it as a lugubrious reflection of acute or irreparable flaws in the Jewish state. Like anyone else who lives in this country, I have many memories, mostly bleak, of how life felt around October 7, but only one of them sticks to my bones. I left my house the morning after the Hamas attacks and drove off past the Amiad junction, which separates Lower Galilee and Upper Galilee. This two- or three-kilometer stretch led to a pick-up point where busses had waited to gather civilians who were instantly re-outfitting themselves as IDF reservists. The busses had waited to take these reservists to their IDF units, many of which were organizing for fighting on the Gaza Strip. Cars were parked bumper-to-bumper on a side of this longish stretch of road. They belonged to men who had raced off from their homes to get to the army busses without taking the time to take out what was left on the car seats from holiday vacation trips—children's safety seats, candy wrappers, summer toys.

I have here a few suggestions for readers who belong to the non-Jewish sensible mainstream in America or elsewhere, who have for nine or ten months seen news reports of grisly IDF operations on the Gaza Strip that brought about the deaths of forty thousand Palestinians, most of them not Hamas militants. I want to talk to readers who—after decades of thinking about Israel as a pretty decent historical outcome whose existence redresses, to some extent, centuries of anti-Semitism—have wondered recently about whether the time has come to revise this sympathetic attitude. If you are in this group, perhaps you have been wondering about those thousands of college protestors who keep calling Israel a failed colonial project, and who chant about how Palestine ought to be purged of Zionists and liberated from the river to the sea. Perhaps, you are wondering, those kids have a point.

I am not here with an agenda of stifling such reflection. Instead, my aim is to point it in critical but constructive directions, ones which, writing as a historian, I think would be acceptable to a majority of my colleagues in Western countries, excluding ones who exhibit, in their research and writing, extremely partisan, pro-Israel or pro-Palestinian, views.

Americans are heavily invested in Israel. No other country gets such a proportion of their tax dollars. People who don't evaluate their investments from time to time are very foolish.

While much in the radical chic sloganeering, and guerilla warfare fashion choices, in these college protests makes me blanch, I welcome the invitation to a discussion of where Israel should go after the Hamas War and how its special relationship with America should proceed. Why not?

With predictable, regular inanity, Israeli news programs during this months-long Gaza War crisis keep pinpointing the failure of our global public relations effort (called *hasbara* in Hebrew) as one of the country's major failures in this period. If only we explained ourselves better, if only we had better hasbara, all those kids in keffiyehs on the Columbia University campus would change their minds and go home with a copy of the *Diary of Anne Frank* in one hand and a knish from the food truck in the other. That sums up the infantile and idiotic line of thinking here. Once in a while a maverick voice will point out that a major factor contributing to this perception of a hasbara gap is that international media provide ample visual and verbal coverage of Palestinian death and hardship in the Gaza War, whereas Israel's national media outlets studiously refrain from presenting images of Palestinian casualties. On one television evening news program, a panelist, a reporter who is identified with the secular left, stated baldly that she is not prepared to see a picture of a Palestinian casualty in an Israeli news report so long as Hamas keeps Israeli hostages captive on the Gaza Strip; the comment warrants mention both for its emotional candor and also as an example of addled professional thinking. This sort of media partisanship has wobbly warrant, but it is not really anomalous. If you are an American over the age of thirty, how many images of Iraqi suffering during the Second Persian Gulf War do you remember seeing in the mainstream media?

Neither Israel's internal media nor its international public relations spokespeople can be blamed for the swirl of chaos in global discourse about the 2023–2024 Gaza War. The problem has not been the *content* of the hasbara that floated off into social media or mainstream journalism outlets. Instead, the problem is that Israel in 2024 has no hasbara to sell at all. The country is unflinchingly united around the general Zionist principle concerning the rectitude of a Jewish state located in the Jews' ancestral homeland; most Israelis have well more than the minimal measure of contentment with their daily lives that is required for people to take arms and defend their established way of life. But we are a deeply divided people when it comes to thinking about how we have gotten to where we are, particularly over the last quarter century, and also about where we want to go over the next twenty-five or a hundred years.

In this fractious context, most Israelis (including myself) would reject a lot of what the college protestors were saying on American and European campuses in spring 2024. But that does not mean that a lot of us do not agree with many of the steps in the critique of colonialism voiced by these students (and their teachers). In fact, many of us would agree with conclusions reached by the protestors, though obviously not ones which creepily invert the unfounded accusation of IDF genocide in Gaza by calling for the transfer or effective genocide of Zionists in Palestine, "from the river to the sea." In other words, what liberal Israelis, whose nationalist outlook is not shared or well-understood by many liberal gentiles in America or elsewhere, need to have more of nowadays is *not* hasbara public relations. What they need to have is a real discussion.

I return to the long line of cars parked by the side of the road on October 8, 2023. Speaking to the reader as though he or she is an investor looking belatedly at the item in the portfolio after roughly seventy-five years, since Israel's establishment, the first, and perhaps only, thing that really needs to be understood about all of us in Israel, left-wing secularists and religious right-wingers, is that we are all stakeholders. No matter how badly we misbehave by anyone else's, or by our own Jewish, standards, we aren't going anywhere because this country is in our identities no less indelibly than any other component. The postcolonial theorists, and anti-Zionists from other intellectual denominations, can talk all they want about how Jewish rootedness in Eretz Israel is a Zionist invention. They can wheel out the occasional Israeli maverick, here a tenured historian from Tel Aviv University, there an internet blogger, who circulate evidence about how the Jews descend from the medieval Khazar Khaganate, or from anywhere else on earth apart from Jerusalem and other areas in Eretz Israel.[110] Such argumentation exudes a whiff of hypocrisy because it typically comes from the postmodern left, where identity is viewed as a volitional construct rather than a biological determinant; so by this logic, whether or not Zionists doctored evidence of Jewish settlement in Palestine over the ages is irrelevant. But the theoretical consistency and motivational inspirations of such anti-Zionists are not germane. You can measure the demography as though its truth is that Muslim Palestinians have dwelled in the land, on average, for

---

110. Sand, *Invention*.

six or ten generations, whereas the average for Jewish Israelis is two or four. For Israelis, such demography is incalculable because we are talking about a fraction whose numerator is the ideal of being Jewish, and the denominator is the entire history of that ideal. For us, no equation outside of the land of Israel can be ratiocinated. We are not going anywhere else.

Still talking about the half-full glass part of the investment, let me add a few words about people who live in the non-disputed, or lesser-disputed, parts of the country—that is, within Israel's pre-1967 Green Line borders—but who are not stakeholders in the Zionist conception of the Jewish state. About ten miles west of this junction which had turned into an elongated parking lot on October 8 is an area of Western Galilee which has a heavy concentration of Palestinian Arab towns and villages (on any day of the week, if you visit the shopping mall just outside of Karmiel, the largest Jewish town in this area, about two-thirds of the shop patrons and working staff will be Arab, not Jewish). The country was in chaos, but this northern region was relatively quiet because it took a few days before Lebanon's militant Shiite group, Hezbollah, started shelling Galilee as a show of support for Hamas in Gaza. Hundreds of hastily parked cars would have been easy picking for anyone whose political economy sanctions the looting of Zionists whenever a window of opportunity cracks open. These parked cars, however, remained untouched for days, until family members of the reservists came to bring them home.

Generally, during the long months of the Gaza War, Palestinian citizens who live within pre-1967 Israel refrained from activities that might reasonably have been construed as evidence of fifth column solidarity with the enemy (I am not giving much credence to various social media posts by a few such Palestinian citizens which disputed Israeli war narratives and stirred comment in Israel's media for a news cycle or two; such social media posting constituted a tempest in a teacup, compared to a scenario wherein a national minority is resolved to actively disrupt the majority's war effort). For the purpose of the current discussion, there is no incentive to overinterpret the meaning of this nondisruptive attitude among the country's Palestinian citizens. Maybe many of them, in their hearts and minds, proactively opposed Hamas's war action on October 7, meaning that they are to the political "right" of North American and European college protestors, who supported this action as legitimate anti-colonial "resistance." Maybe they refrained from disruptive acts out of pragmatic calculations unconnected to this issue of ideological and political viewpoints. Whatever their motivational reasoning, these Israeli Palestinians do not enact "resistance" in ways that would be consistent with the postcolonial analysis upheld by the college protestors on campuses in spring 2024.

Were we to hash out these points, I am sure that I would shamelessly pull rank at some point, imagining that I have some experience in support of my outlook (almost half of my classrooms for the past quarter century have been filled with Israeli Palestinian students, and I was involved in the founding of a Jewish-Arab school in Galilee, where three of my children studied). I concede that coming on too heavily in this way would be gaslighting. And the truth is that I am very critical of the way my own public college relates to its non-Jewish students—just to give one of many personal examples as to why I would not be inclined to romanticize about Arab-Jewish rapprochement in Galilee. So let's just stick to two big overlapping points.

First, were you to read materials written by teachers of these college protesters, or listen to their lectures, you would sometimes find that they dilute and obfuscate important differences between the civil status of Palestinians who live within Israel's Green Line, and Palestinians who live next to Jewish settlements, under colonial occupation, on the West Bank. For clarity's sake, I will call the groups involved in the distinction drawn here "Israeli Palestinians" and "West Bank Palestinians." Israeli Palestinians face all sorts of subtle and not-so-subtle forms of discrimination or disrespect in workplaces and in housing spheres (I know of one major realtor company in Galilee which does not work with Arab clients), and in encounters with bureaucrats and law enforcement officers (police work vis-à-vis the Arab minority was a huge issue in Israel's pre–October 7 political arena, and it is likely to revive after the Gaza War—the crux is the large number of unregistered firearms). Israeli Palestinians also have a few important advantages unavailable to the Jewish majority, mostly stemming from the fact that their teenagers are not compelled to serve in the IDF. In formal legal-civil terms, Israeli Palestinians have equal status—this is exactly the status that Israeli settler colonialism has denied to millions of West Bank Palestinians. Israeli Palestinians vote in elections and have political parties whose Knesset members are far from shrinking violets, and who have rights of parliamentary immunity, exactly like their Jewish counterparts.

Second, were you to visit regions like Galilee or the Negev and engage truthful discussions with Israeli Palestinians, the moment of truth would come were you to ask, "If a Palestinian state were to arise on the West Bank and Gaza Strip, would you move to it?" Not very many would answer in the affirmative. Postcolonial theorists and other radical anti-Zionists might rationalize this finding in a number of ways ("Palestinians would hold the fort in Galilee for some future day when their state encompasses it," etc.), but these would be disingenuous. Israeli Palestinians have political rights and enjoy socioeconomic opportunities in ways which are not easy to come by in the Middle East, and which may never arise in a Palestinian state if an organization like Hamas gains control over it. They are not stakeholders in the Zionist vision of the Jewish state, but they are also not colonized in ways evoked in Frantz Fanon and Albert Memmi's descriptions of French rule in North Africa.

To tell the truth, this line of pro-Israel apologetic only goes so far. Perhaps you will agree that Jews in Israel are stakeholders who love their country, and are not going anywhere else, and that their state provides full democratic rights to Israeli Palestinians, roughly 20 percent of the total population, even though it also condones a troubling measure of socio-economic discrimination towards members of this group. Maybe that is enough to warrant your investment over the past seventy-five years, but I myself am not really buying it.

There is a "benefit of the doubt" way of looking at the Jewish state whose analytic starting point is always relentless violent Arab intransigence toward it. On this perspective the fact that, faced with such pressure and provocation, the Jews have been able to sustain democratic realities for most (or a lot) of people who have come under the purview of its state is fundamentally laudable; and any IDF misstep begetting "collateral damage" is excusable because the Jews are doing the best they can under intolerable circumstances. In the case of the Gaza War, such circumstances include Hamas's cynical use of civilian populations as "human shields" in ways that invite and amplify such collateral damage. The Jews deserve merit badges because other peoples, under such circumstances, would have protected themselves by establishing minatory, fascistic regimes just months after their state's establishment in a sea of terroristic hostility.

Israel's hasbara advocates often settle in this paradigmatic groove. You could hear it after October 7 when they began their YouTube perorations with rhetorical questions like, "What would the Americans have done had some Canadians crossed into Maine, murdered a few thousand folks at Fort Ken, and brought a few hundred kidnapped hostages across the Saint John River into New Brunswick?" (You can multiply these numbers to account for differences in scale between Israel and the United States.)

The upside of this "benefit of the doubt" argumentation is that its starting point is as reasonable as any other possibility. There isn't a clear-thinking Jew in the world who wasn't viscerally offended in spring 2024 by the way admirably idealistic college students lionized Hamas terrorists, who kidnapped elderly Jews and Jewish infants and who raped Jews and murdered Jews, as freedom fighters in the Middle East akin to Che Guevara in the Cold War/Third World setting, or Patrick Henry and the Minutemen, in the anti-colonial American frame. When Palestinian terror is the point of departure in your discussion of the Arab-Israeli conflict, such college campus grandstanding looks repugnant; but this realistic, benefit of the doubt, perspective provides much more mileage than that. It throws light upon the way terror strikes perpetrated by Iranian-backed groups like Hamas and Hezbollah are not "only" cruelly reprehensible but also the products of an opportunistic *strategy*.

Under the leadership of Arafat and the PLO, Palestinian nationalism wrested significant territorial concessions from Israel during the 1990s Oslo peace process and thereafter (Israel's pullout from Gaza under Ariel Sharon's leadership in 2005 can be seen as a by-product of the Oslo process, which was predicated upon the "land for peace" mechanism, and adopted as its inaugural slogan, "Gaza First"). Arafat, however, demurred when a comprehensive "two-state" deal, featuring Israeli withdrawal from over 90 percent of the two most controversial post-1967 areas, Gaza and the West Bank, was offered to him at the 2000 Camp David Summit by Israel Prime Minister Ehud Barak, with heavy backing from the Clinton administration. The Palestinians then launched the violent Second Intifada (2000–2005) whose terroristic activists were spurred by Tanzim guerillas, who operated under the aegis of Fatah, the military arm of the Arafat-led PLO. Previously, at junctures of the Oslo peace process, as in a documented example of an address at a Johannesburg mosque in 1994, Arafat suggested that peace negotiations were merely a tactic. Inspired by the precedent of an agreement signed by Muhammad with the Quraysh at Mecca, Palestinians were grabbing some land from Israel before proceeding to other tactics, like terror, in order to attain the ultimate goal of destroying Israel once and for all, Arafat suggested.[111] Just as the Second Intifada was winding down, pro-Palestinian groups launched the BDS (Boycott, Divestment and Sanctions) campaign, whose goal is to punish Israel economically and isolate it diplomatically.

For most Israelis, it was beginning to look as though the Palestinians were using one technique after another—"land for peace" diplomacy, Second Intifada terror, BDS boycotts—in a maximalist strategy of uncompromising opposition to the Jewish state, however its borders come to be defined. This interpretation became consensual in Israel, even among Jews who had just several years earlier ardently supported the Yitzhak Rabin government's engagement in the Oslo process. Following the Sharon government's dismantling of settlements in the Gaza Strip in 2005, Hamas, a militant Islamic group, quickly rose to power in this densely populated, indigent coastal region. Rather than seizing an opportunity to build a social welfare infrastructure that could be the foundation of future Palestinian

---

111. Palestinian Media Watch, "Arafat."

sovereignty in a two-state solution with Israel, Hamas lobbed thousands of rockets at Israel's southern locales for eighteen years. And it built a bizarrely expansive labyrinth of subterranean tunnels as a below-earth military base for its fighters, as a storage locker for Jewish hostages, and as an underground bridge for crossing into Israel in jack-in-a-box attacks. Then Hamas launched the October 7 attacks.

This analysis glosses some secondary considerations. For instance, during this post-Oslo period, the Palestinian Authority (PA) leadership on the West Bank, which has enjoyed semi-autonomous authority over zones in this region not pockmarked by Jewish settlements, cooperated with Israeli security forces, by and large (Oslo produced a Byzantine charting of A, B, and C zones on the West Bank in which the Palestinians have security and political control, or political control, or nothing). The PA demonstrated its potential as the foundation of the Palestinian part of a future two-state solution (over the years, PA leader Mahmoud Abbas delivered mixed messages about this scenario). Precisely for this reason, Netanyahu, who expediently paid lip service to a two-state solution in a speech delivered at Bar Ilan University in 2009 but is nonetheless an inveterate opponent of the two-state formula, avoided becoming publicly affiliated with the PA (Israel's security cooperation with the Palestinians on the West Bank mostly engages its Shin Bet security service, whose work cannot be transparently visible). For Netanyahu, any photo opportunity with Abbas would have been seen as a token of support for a two-state solution (Israel's hard right-wing constituency has never forgiven Netanyahu for being photographed with, and for negotiating with, Arafat during his first, 1996–1999, term as prime minister, but this happened because Netanyahu was mercilessly arm-twisted by the Clinton administration until Israel agreed to a few concessions over Hebron, and compliance with what was called the Oslo 2 agreement, in excruciating negotiations that were finished at the Wye River in fall 1998). So, in a divide-and-rule tactic, Netanyahu authorized, via Qatar, the delivery of suitcases of money for Hamas, despite this Islamic group's track record of continuing missile attacks on Israel and the mounting evidence of its investment in tunnels—that is, in the creation of an underground military state for war against the Zionists.

Think about that. To stand one hasbara tactic on its head, what would Americans have done after September 11, 2001, had it turned out that the Bush administration, via Qatar, had delivered suitcases of cash to Al-Qaeda before the Twin Towers attack? In normal, liberal political environments that lasted in the West after 1776 and 1789, until everyone went crazy on Facebook, Instagram, and the site formerly known as Twitter, and until the British voted for Brexit and the Americans voted for Trump, Netanyahu's pro-Hamas strategy would have become a devastating political liability after October 7, 2023. Historians will not overlook how this right-wing politician launched his career in the 1980s and 1990s by branding himself as an expert on international terror and then, through bribes, nourished an enemy that on October 7 perpetrated the gravest terror attack on the Jews in the post-Holocaust era. Israel's public, to date, has been more indulgent and forgiving toward Netanyahu than historians are likely to be. At any event, Netanyahu's policies were often misbegotten, but they were not crafted with genocidal intent.

Much wrangling and mutual recrimination goes on whenever commentators discuss what happened between Palestinians and Israelis in the 1948 war, but since the 1990s—that is, in the lifetimes of college protestors of spring 2024—a rejectionist or annihilationist strategy can be ascribed to the Palestinians, but not to the Israelis. Israel zigzagged in this period. It elected two pro-peace governments in the 1990s (in 1992, under Rabin, and 1999, under Barak) which negotiated within the frame of the land for peace principle and the two-state solution. And consider the case of Ariel Sharon. In the IDF, Sharon gained recognition in the 1950s when he led a special "101" unit that carried out brutal reprisal raids against Arabs. In politics, Sharon became the on-the-ground architect and engineer of the settlement movement in the post-1967 territories. Most notoriously, a national inquiry panel, the Kahan Commission, imputed to Sharon, then Israel's defense minister, "indirect responsibility" for the massacre of Palestinian refugees in the Sabra and Shatila camps at the end of the First Lebanon War. This selfsame Sharon, a controversial right-wing icon, supervised Israel's most significant territorial withdrawal since the 1967 war, dismantling the Gaza Strip settlements in 2005. Sharon, in short, quintessentially personifies Israel's zigzag approach to its conflict with Palestinians.

The land for peace formula lost credibility among Israelis, meaning that no left-wing politician could ever have been elected prime minister for a generation or two after the Oslo process collapsed. Nonetheless, anytime a right-wing leader other than Netanyahu grabbed the leadership reins in Israel, the country engaged American-brokered talks for a revival of the two-state formula. This is exemplified by the meeting between Prime Minister Ehud Olmert with PA leader Mahmoud Abbas at the Annapolis Conference in 2007.

None of this means that Israel has been a staunchly peace-oriented country in the twenty-first century, firmly committed to a two-state compromise solution with the Palestinians. It has not been that. Far from it. Very strong cases could be made mitigating the thrust of examples I have just cited. Sharon's pullout from Gaza, for instance, was motivated largely by personal expediency—he had incentive to win supporters among center-left Israelis and thereby intimidate state prosecutors, who were busily investigating corruption charges against Sharon and his family. The truth is that Yitzhak's Rabin second term as prime minister constituted the last time Israel had a leader whose policies for Israeli settlement withdrawal were not adulterated by such considerations, and whose pro-peace policies seemed credible to a majority of Israelis thanks to his reputation as an army hero—and this was thirty years ago (Rabin was assassinated, while serving as prime minister, in 1995). Nonetheless, the sequence we have traced here—Arafat's "Quraysh" instrumental approach to Oslo, the turn to violent terror in the Second Intifada following Arafat's decision not to sign on the dotted line and finalize Oslo, the rise of BDS as the extension of Palestinian nationalist warfare against the Jewish state by economic means, and Hamas's conversion of Gaza into a subterranean anti-Zionist military camp the moment Israel dismantled its aboveground settlements and left the strip—is thought-provoking. It offers strong justification for using Palestinian extremism and Palestinian terror as the starting point in discussions of how the two sides got to the Gaza War crisis of 2023–2024.

And this starting point strongly encourages discussants to give Israel the benefit of the doubt. When you look at what Hamas has *really* said and done since its formation during the First Intifada, when you look at the quality of Arafat's leadership up to the Second Intifada (if you're not sure what to make of Arafat, have a look at what his contemporaries, other leaders in the Middle East, thought of him), and when you consider that even blue-ribbon anti-Zionists from passing generations, such as Noam Chomsky, have criticized the BDS movement's right of return advocacy,[112] it is hard to avoid the aforementioned conclusion: "Give the Jews a break. Other peoples might have done much worse, under the circumstances."

This "benefit of the doubt" approach is an apologetic that has reasonable footing in empirical reality. However, being an apologetic, it does not break new ground. With a quarter of the twenty-first century soon to be in the books, the Jews cannot afford to stay where they are, in an increasingly hostile world.

The Gaza War controversies on college campuses and elsewhere ominously ushered in a new era whose clearest precedent is the 1870s in Europe, just after Jews won formal "emancipation" civic rights in the new state of Germany, and elsewhere, but worried as the modern anti-Semitic movement concurrently sprang to life. In those days, Jews sought security

---

112. Chomsky's criticism of BDS tactics is carefully and wordily articulated in Chomsky, "BDS Movement."

via the strategy of integration in European nation-states, believing that the attainment of formal citizenship rights would suffice as collateral. Since the Holocaust, the Jews have sought security by investing in Israel, believing that a special relationship with the United States will suffice as collateral. In the first case, European Jewry after the 1870s, the rise of organized anti-Semitism was the game changer. Today, anti-Zionism's depiction of Israel as a colonialist state is a game changer, owing to the view's mounting acceptability in powerful settings like the left wing of the Democratic Party and college campuses.

No precedent for this development is to be found in American Jewish history. Prior to this newly fashionable view of Israel as a genocidal colonial power, no malignant view of a Jewish cause, interest, or collective ever gained firm status in reputable and influential settings in the United States. A century ago, elite universities like Harvard maintained a semi-declared quota policy limiting Jewish enrollment, and Henry Ford marshaled the resources of his motor company for the dissemination of the forged anti-Semitic tract, the *Protocols of the Elders of Zion*. Such actions constituted a nuisance for Jews, but they were not fraught with menacing potential comparable to contemporary developments on college campuses, on social media, and in some circles of the Democratic Party. This is not a time for Jews to stand still by updating and polishing old apologetics. We tried that before, in Europe before the world wars, and look where that got us.

When it comes to how gentiles hear Jews, the "benefit of the doubt" approach is tone-deaf.

Essentially, the Christian world is divided into two when it comes to core Jewish concepts and symbols. In recent years, in responses to anti-Zionist initiatives like BDS and the 2024 campus protests, this division is reflected in differing, pro and con, attitudes evinced by American Protestants in the liberal mainline churches, as opposed to American Protestants in the conservative Evangelical movement. Some gentiles plainly resent "chosen people" rhetoric in the Old Testament. They take that doctrine seriously, but they view the entirety of Old Testament prophecy as metaphor that was superseded and universalized in Jesus' mission, as documented in the New Testament Gospels. Fast-forwarding from medieval church disquisition about this supersession doctrine to contemporary disputes about Israel, Christians in this camp resent how pro-Israel spokesmen argue that the Jewish state deserves the benefit of the doubt because its majority has not yet turned it into North Korea. "*That* is what happened to the chosen people doctrine in modern times?" such Christians privately wonder, churlishly or not. Essentially this is a complaint about how the Jews seem to keep asserting that they deserve more out of history than anyone else gets.

If you want an example of how this complaint is sublimated within polemic ostensibly directed at twenty-first-century issues regarding US foreign policy and Israel, have a look at the book *The Israel Lobby and U.S. Foreign Policy*, published in 2007 by two distinguished US academics, John Mearsheimer and Stephen Walt. The book, which boosted the anti-Zionist movement, develops a critique of how lavish American diplomatic, security, and economic assistance for the Jewish state is (allegedly) the product of pressure tactics deployed by the "Israel lobby," not the result of Judeo-Christian values and democratic ideals shared by Israel and the United States. To burnish this analysis, the authors litter the text with a series of assertions and analogies, such as this: "With the partial exception of Soviet support for Cuba, it is hard to think of another instance where one country has provided another with a similar level of material aid over such an extended period."[113]

One group of gentile readers will peruse such a statement and think, "Wow," viewing it as confirmation of a nagging private feeling that the Jews have been pushy about their place in the world ever since their Bible proclaimed them to be the chosen people. Such readers are the target audience for authors of books like *The Jewish Lobby*. But another group will get to the end of the statement thinking, "So what?"

Members of this second group applaud the conveyance of disproportionately high levels of "material aid" for Israel because the Jews have been disproportionately abused in history by Christians, among others. Disproportionate aid for Israel is meritorious compensation, these gentiles believe—after all, had America altered its nativist immigration policies in the 1920s and 1930s, Hitler's genocide would have reached far fewer than six million Jews. Sure, democracy in the Jewish state is imperfect, but the same can be said about America; and look at what the Jews are up against in the Middle East! Americans have two oceans, and Mexicans and Canadians, at their borders. Israelis have Hamas in the south, Hezbollah in the north, and other variants of Shiite and Sunni hatred everywhere else (this long reach of malice was recently exemplified by Houthi missile attacks on the Jewish state launched from Yemen).

Having taken the leadership reins in this second group, the Evangelicals clutch a rigidly literal approach toward the chosen people conundrum. Its fundamentalism has worked to the advantage of the Jewish state, or at least to the right-wing leaderships that have held power in it over the past quarter century, the period when the illiberal Evangelicals became a gushing fountain of philanthropic and political support for the Jewish state. These

---

113. Mearsheimer and Walt, *Israel Lobby*, 36.

Evangelicals cite biblical passages such as Gen 12:3 which promise punishment to nations of the world hostile to the chosen people. Here is how John Hagee, a prominent pro-Israel Evangelical, interprets such passages: "Every nation that presumes to interfere with God's plan for Israel, including the United States, stands not only against Israel but also ultimately against God."[114]

These generalizations about Christian attitudes toward the Jewish state can, of course, be parsed rather differently, but that does not alter the main point. Familiar pro-Israel apologetics are not breaking new ground at a moment when the surge of anti-Zionism is a call to action to all self-respecting Jews in Israel, the United States, and anywhere else. These are apologetics whose contents tell Christians who have preexisting positive dispositions toward the Jewish state what they want to hear, just as they mean nothing to Christians who have preexisting negative dispositions toward the Jewish state.

When the "benefit of the doubt" apologetic is thought of philosophically, my own thoughts turn to objections expressed by terms like "slippery slope," or "situational ethics." When I immigrated to Israel in my early twenties, in the mid-1980s, I brushed up my acquaintance with luminaries of Zionist thought and politics—Theodor Herzl, Ahad Ha'am, Chaim Weizmann, David Ben-Gurion. Various differences of temperament and Jewish self-identification separate such figures, but all of them shared the same thought regarding the overall moral implications of sovereign Jewish statehood. However clichéd it was, all of them talked about a Jewish state serving as a "light unto the nations." I did my regular IDF service not too long after the First Lebanon War and after the Kahan Commission of Inquiry concluded that then Defense Minister Ariel Sharon and others had "indirect responsibility" for the cold-blooded massacre of Palestinians at Sabra and Shatila. I resumed IDF service in the reserves exactly in the weeks when the First Intifada erupted, and Israel was met with global opprobrium owing to its crackdown on Palestinian teenagers on the Gaza Strip and the West Bank who were throwing rocks in what was widely regarded as a legitimate form of civil disobedience (Yitzhak Rabin, who later became my own Zionist hero, was then the defense minister and won notoriety for telling IDF soldiers to "break the bones" of such teenagers; I didn't listen, but formally, the message was directed at me and all other IDF soldiers). As will be recalled, it was at this time, throughout the 1980s, when pro-Israel supporters of Yitzhak Shamir's Likud-led government changed the terms of hasbara apologetics. Disastrously, these terms remained in effect

---

114. Hagee, *Jerusalem Countdown*, 201.

for the next thirty-five years, culminating in the pathetic social media howling at the moon executed by self-designated, and officially anointed, Israeli spokespeople during the 2023–2024 Gaza War.

During the First and Second Intifadas, Israeli hasbara spokespeople praised our country and its army for not behaving like Jordan during Black September 1970—the reference is to a brutal pacification campaign in which King Hussein's forces killed several thousand fighters from Arafat's PLO. It seemed as though we had tumbled on the slippery slope from being a light unto the nations, to being a worthy ally of America's liberal democracy because we did not (at least, for the time being) behave like France's anti-anti-colonial oppressors, with their *gégène* torture methods.

How low can the bar go before we start to look for new modes of thinking about the practices and purposes of the Jewish state? During the periods of the Netanyahu government's attempted judicial overhaul, and the Gaza War, Israel's police minister has been Itamar Ben-Gvir. This politician, who has authority over protest demonstrations and the prison conditions of security prisoners, is a racist who earned his stripes in Meir Kahane's Kach movement, which advocated the transfer of Arabs from Israel (as an indication of descending morality in Israeli politics, when I arrived in Israel, the Kach party was considered so obscenely extremist that Kahane was barred from the Knesset; today his protégé is Israel's "National Security" minister). When he entered politics, Ben-Gvir had hanging in his living room a picture of Baruch Goldstein, the American Jewish settler who massacred twenty-nine Palestinians at Hebron's Cave of the Patriarchs in 1994.[115] Under the apologetic logic of Israel's hasbara campaigns, here is how the country's spokesmen would rationalize such phenomena: "Let's give Israel the benefit of the doubt about Ben-Gvir. At least he's not Hitler." Is that the way we want our grandchildren to hear us talking about the Jews' most important achievement in modern times, Israel?

The Recreant Generation

Two atrocities can be associated with October 7, 2023. One was committed that day by Hamas against Jews. The other was committed for almost a quarter century by Jews against themselves, and its results became manifest in weeks and months after October 7.

In one generation, between the collapse of the Oslo peace process in September 2000 and Hamas's attack against the Supernova Sukkot festival, Kibbutz Be'eri, Kibbutz Nir Oz, and other southern locales in October 2023,

---

115. *Times of Israel*, "Ben-Gvir Responds."

Jews lost their liberalism. They moved from being at the forefront of liberal social change in modernity to being the rear guard of neoconservative retrenchment in postmodernity. Their thinking and activity about Israel, and in Israel, became neocolonialist. Their philanthropy was weaponized by nouveau riche, Jewishly ignorant, billionaires and put to uses abusive to liberal democracy in America and in Israel. Their educators were co-opted by these philanthropists; in turn, these billionaires were co-opted by Israel's self-interested, illiberal political leaders. The Jewish settlers on the colonialist West Bank settlements commanded everyone. Israel's electoral system failed its democracy. American Jewish organizations which lobbied for Israel by arguing that it is the only democracy in the Middle East failed common sense.

Behold the legacy of the Jews' recreant generation.

Pre-1967 Israel, whose borders were wrought by the efforts of secular Labor Zionists whose idealism has appeal to liberal-minded diaspora Jews today, has contracted on its southern and northern ends. Because Israel is one of the world's few democracies that does not have regional representation in its elected national assembly, nobody who was on the scene after October 7 to plead the causes of one hundred thousand northerners who had to evacuate their homes, and of thousands of southerners who were murdered, maimed, raped, and kidnapped, did so on the basis of an electoral mandate to represent these constituencies.

In contrast, settlers in the illegally occupied West Bank maintained ample representation in Netanyahu's governmental cabinets. Some portion of relief funds allotted for the border Gaza communities were gerrymandered and redirected to the West Bank settlements, under the patronage of Netanyahu's finance minister, Bezalel Smotrich, an outspoken racist who has groused about Jews having to share space in hospitals with Arabs, and who views settlers as his prime constituency. Hours before Hamas's October 7 attack, some portion of the IDF's deployment in the south, two battalions according to reports, were redirected to the West Bank to protect settlers. This redeployment became a priority due to the antics of politicians and activists connected to Netanyahu's coalition. They featured a rabble-rouser from Smotrich's party (Zvi Sukkot) who, with his boss, gallivanted around the West Bank town of Huwara, which had been ravaged by settlers over the preceding months in episodes described in Israel's liberal media as settler pogroms. In days before October 7, such right-wing extremists displayed intentions of setting up a Jewish holiday tabernacle in Huwara (half a year earlier, Smotrich publicly advocated "wiping out" this town).[116]

---

116. To witness what caught the attention of world media *one day* before Hamas's

To reiterate, peripheral ends of the pre-1967, internationally recognized, borders of Israel, which had been created largely by the labor of secular pioneers whose outlooks are compatible with most members of the global, "pro-Israel" network, who are secular liberals, contracted. In tandem, in the key post-1967 part of Israel, the occupied West Bank, the focus of acute international controversy, growth continued on the settlements, which are the product of an illiberal, messianically irredentist, ideology. Crafted by two rabbis, father and son, Abraham Isaac Kook and Zvi Yehuda Kook, that ideology is profoundly repugnant to most people in this pro-Israel network.

By July 2024, nine months after the October catastrophe, the IDF reported a manpower loss of ten thousand soldiers, due to death or disability.[117] The army desperately sought reinforcements, there being a strong possibility of war erupting on the northern border against Hezbollah, an Iranian proxy which reportedly has a cache of one hundred and fifty thousand missiles and rockets of various range lengths.[118] The army manpower shortage was so dire that IDF spokesmen spoke about it openly in the media, despite the morale boost delivered by such discussion to the country's enemies, including Hamas, which was still at war with Israel and in possession of the bodies of one hundred and twenty hostages, perhaps a third of them still alive.

These being the circumstances, of course the time was ripe for Orthodox parties in Netanyahu's coalition to press for legislation that would formalize the military service exemptions given to Haredi (ultra-Orthodox) men who study in yeshivot and profess that Torah study is their vocation. Reports disclosed that some sixty-six thousand Haredim had such exemptions in the year of the judicial overhaul crisis and the Gaza War.[119]

These army exceptions for the religious have been considered part of a semi-official secular-Orthodox "status quo" arrangement in Israel whose roots extend back to policies sanctioned by David Ben-Gurion in the early years of the state.[120] But they were not numerically significant until the period after 1977, when right-wing Likud governments, first led by Menachem Begin and then, from 2009 (with brief interruption) by Netanyahu, forged coalition alliances with these Orthodox parties, which vigilantly guard

---

Simchat Torah attack, see Knell, "Huwara." For Smotrich's minatory rhetoric about Huwara, see Bachner, "Israel."

117. I24News, "Defense Minister."
118. Yaron, "150,000 Missiles."
119. Liveblog, "Record High."
120. For origins of the status quo arrangement, see Friedman, "This Is the History."

these IDF exemptions for their constituencies. Following deliberations that stretched into the period of the Gaza War, Israel's High Court has ruled that these IDF exemptions had no solid legal footing in the so-called status quo. The court ordered the government to regularize them in legislation.

The timing of this court directive was not fortuitous for the ultra-Orthodox. For Israel's secular population, along with rapidly growing numbers of people in the national religious camp (an Orthodox sector which, unlike that of the ultra-Orthodox Haredim, is uniformly patriotic and whose members serve in the IDF, with rising numbers in recent decades advancing to high officer ranks), the military manpower depletion resulting from the Haredi service exemptions is seen both as a moral outrage and as a strategic liability. In summer 2024, Israel's direction on this topic was hard to discern. Quite possibly a sea change was in motion whereby an acute anomaly in Israel's social system would be removed thanks to the conscription of thousands of Haredi men. On the other hand, since it was Israel's High Court that scuttled the army exemption arrangement, it seemed likely that the ultra-Orthodox parties would regroup as soon as the Gaza War ended and compel Netanyahu's coalition to codify and sanction the IDF Haredi exemptions via proper legislation. The coalition might do that by ramping up its assault on the legal system in its judicial overhaul program. This means that the chances of Israel becoming a less democratic, and more socially inegalitarian, country after many exhausting and excruciating months of warfare on the Gaza Strip are quite viable. It bears mention that an Orthodox politician who has spearheaded the campaign to legalize IDF exemptions is Aryeh Deri, from Shas (a religious party comprised mostly of Mizrahi Jews—that is, Jews of North African–Middle Eastern descent). In court rulings and plea bargain deals, Deri has twice been convicted on financial impropriety charges and disqualified from holding office as a senior cabinet minister (in principle, Deri disputes this disqualification, but he has refrained from formally holding a ministerial portfolio in Netanyahu's government). Operating behind the scenes, Deri's input on this IDF exemption issue has added a touch of ex parte, recidivist criminality to the innately iniquitous Haredi position.

Worse than anything else, after the October 7 attack, the recreant generation demonstrated how Israeli colonialism on the West Bank has corrupted Jewish culture. When you read the writings of Memmi and Fanon about colonizer mentality, about how the pieds-noirs and the French army officers and politicians responded to the challenge of FLN guerilla warfare, you are reading about how all of Israel—its mainstream media outlets, its social media tweeters and bloggers, its government coalition politicians, and its opposition politicians—responded to the Hamas attacks.

To its credit, the IDF warned civilian populations in Gaza, routinely delaying important anti-Hamas operations until residents moved southward from their homes. Clichés that circulate widely in Israel's mainstream about how the IDF is the "most moral army in the world," mostly constitute self-serving propaganda; nonetheless, the IDF's conscientiousness about providing warnings to civilian populations in Gaza is significant and noteworthy. But its actions can never elevate morally above the way the country's mainstream culture thinks about the enemy.

For months, Gaza was regarded generically in Israeli public discussion as a nest of Hamas terror. No serious distinctions were drawn between three groups: first, Nukhba guerillas who actually crossed the border and carried out attacks, much of them heinously vicious and directed against civilians; second, Gaza residents who aided and abetted Hamas; third, the majority of Gazans whose overall sympathy for the Islamic movement in no palpable, actionable way renders them complicit for the attack ordered by Yahya Sinwar and his confederates in the Hamas leadership. All Gazans are Hamas, and Hamas is ISIS, and so all Gazans are ISIS: such Monty Python–esque logic tolled devastatingly cruel consequences. You kill forty thousand Gazans in redress for fifteen hundred Israeli casualties when you think this way. When you think like a colonizer, you don't need to see facts that might bother you. Thanks to such thinking, Israelis never saw on their own media outlets images of Palestinian suffering in Gaza.

A day or two after October 7, Naftali Bennett, who had a brief one-year term as prime minister (2021–2022), introduced an additional way of thinking colonialistically of Gaza as a generic for terror. Bennett is a capable, decent-sounding character with a distinguished IDF track record, and also a financial fortune under his belt due to his stint working in the high-tech start-up field. Exploiting how years of Netanyahu governance had utterly exhausted Israel's friends in North America and Europe, Bennett used smoke and mirrors in the West to project his term at Israel's helm as an extension of his own reasonable pragmatism.[121] In fact he is a militant extremist who is more deeply implicated in Israeli colonialism than any leader in the country's history—before he became prime minister, Bennett served a term as the head of the Jewish settlers' main lobbying and policy forum, the Yesha Council. Bennett toured Israel's battered Gaza border locales shortly after the October 7 massacres and collated evidence of rapes and butchery, which at that time circulated graphically, but nonetheless uncertainly, in the

---

121. To see one columnist's extraordinary feat of spoon-feeding insouciance, see Stephens, "Naftali Bennett's Exit Interview."

social media. Interviewed on one of the nightly news programs, he set a new standard in public rhetoric about Gaza, branding Hamas men "Nazis."[122]

This became a favorite epithet despite, or because of, its illogical relationship to the way Israelis and other Jews think about their own history. Much as African Americans have zero tolerance for anyone who uses the N-word, Jews become extremely agitated when anyone tries to mitigate the unique horror of the Nazi crime by making hazy analogies to other reprobate, though not racially genocidal, situations. Halfway into the Gaza War, an intelligent, although understandably overwrought, Israeli Palestinian woman was blindfolded and handcuffed and hauled into a police station for using a Holocaust analogy in reference to IDF operations on the Gaza Strip.[123] Meantime not an hour went by in Israel's mainstream media without someone calling Gazans "Nazis."

Zvi Yehezkeli, then the Arab affairs commentator on the most liberal of Israel's four television networks, Channel 13, went on record declaring that Israel should have killed one hundred thousand Palestinians at the start of the Gaza War. Ram ben Barak, a Knesset politician from the largest opposition party, which is considered centrist, and a former deputy head of the Mossad, Israel's overseas intelligence agency, stated in a television interview that the transfer of Gazan civilians to other Middle East locales ought to be seriously considered, presumably since that would obviate the nuisance of killing them as collateral damage in bombings and raids targeted against properly identified Hamas fighters (writing with a hard-line Likud member of Knesset, he shared his insight with the outside world in a *Wall Street Journal* op-ed).[124] Then came a comically revealing twist. Ben Barak belongs to a party that had been run essentially as a one-man show by a charismatic and popular former media personality, Yair Lapid (who also served a months-long term as prime minister, following Bennett's tenure). Months into the Gaza War, as a window-dressing display of democratization, Lapid decided to hold party primaries for the first time. Members of Israel's leading moderate party rewarded Ben Barak for talking about the transfer of Palestinians by putting him within just a few votes of ousting Lapid.

Meantime, cabinet members in Netanyahu's coalition posted and vocalized abusive comments about Gazans, whose incendiary character was cited in the South Africa–inspired prosecution of Israel for genocide at the International Court of Justice, in the Hague. You can Google those. The ICJ

---

122. Bennett, "Bennett on Channel 12."
123. Hashmonai, "Israeli Woman Detained."
124. Danon and Ben-Barak, "West Should Welcome."

trial was a politically motivated sham, and when countries go to war they should be judged in terms of the war's political and moral merits, not for the intemperate remarks made by their politicians about the enemy. However, whether or not you Google these comments consider how pervasively the anti-colonial critique articulated by thinkers and activists like Fanon and Memmi now applies to Israel. Hateful statements made by Netanyahu's confederates are an outgrowth of a colonialist culture in which it becomes customary, even at times of peace, to talk about people on the other side in thoughtlessly derogatory terms, as an undifferentiated, inferior collective. To be sure, Hamas's outrageous provocations on October 7 changed the temper of public discussion in Israel. However, Israel's media pundits and political figures, from all sides of the spectrum, regularly talked about the killing of thousands of Gazans, most of them unidentified with Hamas terror actions, in pitilessly fatuous euphemisms because decades of colonial occupation, before 2005 on the Gaza Strip and consecutively since 1967 on the West Bank, had fashioned such thought and discussion. The killing of forty thousand Palestinians in Gaza was "mowing the lawn," or "giving Gaza a haircut." These words were sounded, over and over and over. By Jews. They are the mantra of the recreant generation.

The Third Way, Jewish History, and Israel's Strategic Crisis

When Rashbi and Rabbi Judah were arguing, Rabbi Jose was thinking about how they were both right, and how they were both wrong. He knew that in his own everyday reality, there were plenty of Jews who thought like Rashbi, just as there were plenty of Jews who thought like Rabbi Judah. The Jews had lost sovereignty in their own land after trying to bolster it during two revolts against Rome. Now there were Romans everywhere. Through the Bar Kokhba revolt, the Romans kept one army legion, Legio X Fretensis, in Palestine, but now they had added a second one, around Megiddo (a northern locale in the Jezreel Valley known for biblical end of days prophecy, as heard in its cognate, Armageddon), Legio VI Ferrata.[125]

Jews were docile in dealings with these Roman warriors. Whenever they upheld their religious scruples in encounters with these soldiers, they were careful not to seem insubordinate. The Talmud records incidents in which the soldiers succored Jews—this happens in an incident in Sepphoris when a soldier intervenes and helps a flustered Jewish customer buy a piece of meat from a recalcitrant butcher. In another incident, in Sikhnin (today a large Arab town in Western Galilee, Sakhnin), soldiers arrive to douse

125. Safrai, "Relations"; Avi-Yonah, *Jews*, 36.

a blaze at the home of a Jewish notable, Joseph ben Simai—because it is a Shabbat, the observant Jew declines such assistance but later pays a token of gratitude to the Romans.[126]

Meantime Emperor Hadrian, who ruled through the end of the Bar Kokhba revolt, ordered the construction of a road leading from the new legion base at Megiddo to Sepphoris. So Rabbi Judah was right about how such projects made life easier for the Tannaim and for the oft-maligned Jewish laymen (*amei ha'aretz*) in Galilee.

But Rashbi was right when he suspected that projects like the Megiddo-Sepphoris road had an agenda of tightening the Romans' grip on Palestine and thereby thwarting dreams that lingered in some Jewish hearts for Third Temple restoration and resumed Jewish semisovereignty in the land. Besides, Rashbi could have said, supplementing his argument, such Roman "improvements" came with a price tag.[127] The Talmud refers to taxes and other burdens imposed on Jews, in support of the Roman soldiers. These include the *angaria*, or compulsory labor stints, and the *arnona* (a malapropism for *annona*), which required Jews to supply provisions to Romans as they patrolled around Palestine.

Rabbi Jose was thinking about how conflicts within colonial contexts are a zero-sum game. Unlike Fanon, he could not have glorified anti-colonial terror because its application in the 66–70 revolt foretold national disaster, not national liberation. Nobody, not even Cecil B. DeMille, has been able to produce a successful Battle of Algiers–type movie mythologizing the Sicarii, one of the spin-offs from the militant anti-Roman Jewish group called "zealots" by the historian Flavius Josephus. Sicarii militants hid daggers under their cloaks before stabbing the Romans, and their collaborators. Such anti-colonial terror was brushed aside as pinpricks by the Romans, who replenished their siege on Jerusalem and ended up chasing the few remaining Jewish rebels, zealots, to Herod's old winter palace, Masada, around the Dead Sea. Writing retrospectively under Roman patronage, Josephus had personal and professional reasons not to mythologize Sicarii anti-colonial terror, which had backfired and contributed to the calamitous loss of Jewish sovereignty in the land. The glossiest spin he could give to the zealot saga was to concoct a tale of zealot collective suicide at Masada. However, the heroic tone in Josephus's account seems inconsistent (as will be recalled, in an earlier section of his epic history, recording his doings as a commander of the Jewish revolt in Galilee, he praises himself for escaping

---

126. For the Sepphoris and Sikhnin incidents, see Silver, *Galilee, 47 BCE to 1260 CE*, 165.

127. Silver, *Galilee, 47 BCE to 1260 CE*, 165–67.

from a collective Jewish suicide pact identical to the one he describes at Masada). The Masada narrative's details strain credulity, and some of them appear to be boilerplate items that can be found in several other historical writings in antiquity. Unimpressed, Jews ignored Josephus's Masada story for some eighteen hundred years until the Zionists revived it.[128]

Sicarii behavior mimicked how Romans brutalized Jews. With such observations in mind, while Rashbi and Rabbi Judah debated, Rabbi Jose, like Memmi, was thinking about the cunning logic of colonialism whereby the colonized end up acting like the colonizers whom they despise. Josephus's famous *Jewish War* underscores this point in consciously deliberate, and also inadvertent, ways (recall that both the overall perspective, and innumerable polemical details, of *The Jewish War* were shaped by Josephus's belonging to an elite Jerusalem priestly caste that was never fully resolved about the wisdom of the anti-Roman revolt). The author of *The Jewish War* inserted scenes in which his own power rivals, like John of Gischala, indulge scandalous debaucheries within the Second Temple's grounds, acting as licentious Romans.[129] Caught up in his own egoism, Josephus injected far-fetched descriptions about how he organized a huge Jewish rebel army in Galilee—more than he realized, Josephus is saying that the Jewish rebellion he himself helped command had characteristics of the enemy it opposed.

Rabbi Jose was thinking about how the irrational passions stirred by the Jews' confrontation with Roman colonialism led some of their more obtuse elites toward flamboyant, utterly self-destructive demonstrations of national honor. According to Oxford University scholar Martin Goodman, the entire calamity of the Jews' revolt against Rome can be traced to a bad joke perpetrated in 64 CE, two years before the actual fighting started, by some youngsters from the Jewish Jerusalem elite. These young hotheads were upset when the Roman governor, Gessius Florus, raided the temple treasury for funds—in an ill-advised prank, the Jewish youths carried about a beggar's basket, asking for funds for Florus, as though he were a mendicant. The parents of these youths disobeyed the Romans' demand that the insolent pranksters be handed over.[130] Thereafter, Jewish elites were locked in an insubordinate but conflicted mode, as persons who had much to lose, socioeconomically, in the rebellion but who continually jockeyed, one against the other, reaching for leadership glory in an anti-colonial revolt that was an irrational and improbable exercise from the start (Goodman's analysis identifies the in-fighting and failed leadership of the Jews' Judean

---

128. Ben-Yehuda, *Masada Myth*; Cohen, "Masada."
129. Josephus, *J.W.* 4.556–66.
130. Goodman, "Bad Joke."

elite as the primary cause of the revolt's eruption, and of its disastrous outcome).[131]

Is it fair and judicious to impose such vast political import to acts of anti-colonial insolence, such as the Florus prank recorded by Josephus? What about the antics of confederates in Netanyahu's coalition during the 2023–2024 judicial overhaul crisis and the Gaza War? What about the foreign minister, Eli Cohen, who baited US Vice President Kamala Harris for criticizing the overhaul plan, even though its antidemocratic gist would be patent to anyone who has an elementary school education in civics. Harris hasn't read a single clause in the overhaul program, sneered Cohen.[132] Mocking the US president who, after the start of the Gaza War, rallied in support of the Jewish state by sending two aircraft carriers to the region, and who enacted a series of other vastly impactful pro-Israel measures, Itamar Ben-Gvir, the Kahanist police minister, exercised his emoji skills and tweeted about how Biden loves Hamas.[133]

Are the Jews innately accommodating toward colonialism, as Rabbi Judah suggested? Are they innately antagonistic to it, as Rashbi declared? How did Rabbi Jose think about these questions? With hindsight not available to Rabbi Jose, we can say, for Rashbi, that the Jews' unruly anti-colonialism lasted in Eretz Israel with even greater durability and pungency than what is implied in the highly nationalistic narratives of Zionism, which are premised upon the concept of a "two thousand year" exile, following the two failed anti-Roman rebellions. In fact, just as Constantine was Christianizing the Roman Empire, Jews in Galilee in 351 CE staged a third rebellion, starting in Sepphoris (then known as Diocaesarea), and led by a little-known rebel named Patricius. Though it was a lost cause from the start, this third revolt can be seen as evidence of how Jewish striving for national independence in their own land continued to inspire group action, decades after Rashbi stridently advocated such anti-colonialism. Patricius and his band managed to drift south from Galilee and reach Lydda. This fleeting demonstration of Jewish rebel power must have disturbed the Romans to some degree since they recapitulated pacification measures they had used during the 66–70 revolt. The Romans sent forces from coastal Acre (Ptolemais) into Galilee in 351, just as Vespasian had used Acre as a launching pad for his assault on the Josephus-led forces in Galilee in the year 67.[134]

131. Goodman, *Ruling Class of Judea.*
132. Magid, "FM on Kamala Harris."
133. *Times of Israel*, "Ben-Gvir Hammered."
134. Silver, *Galilee, 47 BCE to 1260 CE*, 186–87.

Overlooking such episodes, supporters of Rabbi Judah's pragmatism can expose bluffs and hypocrisy in Rashbi's anti-colonial militancy. The story of his thirteen-year hideaway in the cave, needless to say, is Aggadah—Jewish superhero myth. Supposedly Rashbi hid from Roman oppressors in the cave with his son, Eleazar ben Simon. However, insofar as we know, Eleazar ended up plying vocationally as a public order commissar for the Romans.[135]

With all such information in his view, or anachronistically imputed to him for the pedagogic purpose of highlighting the acuity of the dilemma, we can hypothesize that Rabbi Jose was thinking about a third way. His thought was that colonialism does not lend much honor to anyone, Jews included. It is a zero-sum game for the colonizer and the colonized.

Here is what Rabbi Jose would tell us today: if the first way is college students, Jews and gentiles, protesting about Israeli colonialism, and the second way is the manipulation of the pro-Israel crowd by which American Jewish billionaires are brought in to arm-twist university presidents and compel them to shut down the protests, no matter that a significant portion of the students' complaint is plainly true, we better find a third way.

Pro-Israel Jewish Liberals: Disunite and Survive!

One of the most extraordinary and revealing aspects of the Jewish cultural response to the Hamas October 7 attack was its ongoing attestation of surprise. Setting aside the issue of the detestable acts Hamas perpetrated after its Nukhba men crossed into Israel, which must be subjected to condemnation whatever moral standards you choose, what was noteworthy in responses of Israelis and overseas Jews was the utter inability to imagine why Palestinian nationalism could conceivably choose a path of forcible resistance against Israel.

Here we arrive at what is probably the most explosively fraught point in contention, one that creates seemingly unbridgeable gaps between the anti-Zionist college protests and the pro-Israel outlook. When the college students talked about Hamas "resistance," Israel and its supporters retorted that these protestors were rank anti-Semites. The college students can be faulted for not fashioning an easily accessible disclaimer that would have distanced them from condonation of the vicious brutality utilized by Nukhba men in their attack (however much such disclaimers were, in fact, vocalized on campus compounds, or posted in social media, wearing keffiyehs and chanting "from the river to the sea" might not have been the best way

---

135. Silver, *Galilee, 47 BCE to 1260 CE*, 168.

to reinforce them). Nonetheless, the overall orientation of the college protests is easy to elucidate sympathetically, their moral sincerity being quite evident. In contrast, the feigned outrage of Israeli spokespeople and of pro-Israel groups reflects the recreant character of contemporary Jewish culture.

I am happy to be living in a world where the killing of forty thousand persons by a country whose self-description as a liberal democracy serves as a warrant for its receipt of disproportionate assistance from the United States does not escape the notice of thoughtful young Americans who are trying to figure out what they want out of their country in the present and future. I am a Jew and a patriotic Israeli; but I am not happy right now to be living in a world where citizens in my country, and our supporters in America and Europe, profess surprise and consternation about how Palestinians decided to revive the path of resistance, viewing it as a logical option in circumstances where their decades-long conflict with the Jewish state remains unresolved, partly because of Israel's continuing illegal settler occupation on the West Bank.

As Israel sees it, following its 2005 pullout from the Gaza Strip, subsequent circumstances in this region are entirely of the Palestinians' own making. When the anti-Zionists refer to pre–October 7 suffering on the Gaza Strip as a consequence of Israel's continuing "occupation" of it, they are exploiting technicalities about who retains formal authority for Gaza after the 1967 Six-Day War; but, in a substantive sense, the anti-Zionists are simply lying when they refer to Israel's "occupation" of Gaza. That occupation ended in September 2005 when Ariel Sharon supervised Israel's pullout, a move applauded in liberal public opinion around the globe. Subsequent hardships suffered by Gaza residents resulting from Israeli military blockades at various Gaza entry points are not Israel's fault. The blockades were (and are and will be) imposed and enforced by Israel as reasonable security measures that would be taken by any country were an enemy to constantly lob missiles into its territory, and invest prodigal resources in the construction of underground tunnels through which its fighters aim to burrow through for future terror attacks. Stating the matter another way, Israel closed Gaza's borders because Hamas receives massive weapons allotments from, among other sources, Iran, a country expressly committed to the destruction of the Jewish state, which also arms Israel's other major enemy, the Shiite Hezbollah organization in Lebanon, across Israel's northern border.

From Israel's standpoint, choked-off, blockaded realities of life in Gaza for hundreds of thousands of people who may not proactively support Hamas are obviously lamentable, but they are just as obviously the consequence of Hamas's own policy choice to continue violently terroristic acts of national resistance against the Zionists. Had representative Palestinian groups not selected this option, there is nothing in Israel's Zionist ideology that would have preempted a very different socioeconomic reality in Gaza, a region where Palestinians have full internal autonomy. On the contrary, back in the Oslo days, Israeli peacemakers like Shimon Peres envisioned a future of Palestinian prosperity on the West Bank and Gaza Strip. Peres articulated this outlook in a volume called *The New Middle East*, whose overall utopianism and faith in the power of free-market globalization seems daft in retrospect.[136] Nonetheless, in real life Israel, with Turkey, became engaged during Oslo in the construction of an industrial zone at the Erez Crossing for the promotion of economic growth in Gaza. Years later, even after pro-peace enthusiasms in Israel were dampened by the violent terror attacks during the Second Intifada, some leftist diehards thought of Israel's 2005 withdrawal as an invitation for international capital to turn the Gaza Strip into the Monte Carlo of the Middle East.

No doubt, such Israeli idealists were deluded for thinking that the legacy of their country's almost forty-year occupation on the Gaza Strip would be economic prosperity. Their distance from the political mainstream was comparable to that of extremists on the Israeli right, including settlers who, under compulsion, grudgingly evacuated their settlement homes in Gaza, and who howled about how this 2005 withdrawal was outright political and theological apostasy.

In the ensuing period, almost twenty years, the viewpoint of the pro-settler far right picked up steam in Israel. In fact, during the 2023 judicial overhaul crisis, a number of familiar media personalities could be seen nightly on television news programs articulating this extreme right-wing, pro-settler viewpoint and doctoring facts of the 2005 Gaza withdrawal in Aesopian arguments which supposedly justified the Netanyahu government's illiberal policies on legal reform and other issues. Simply put, well before October 7, 2023, most Israelis regarded Sharon's unilateral pullout from Gaza as a bad move because it gave uninhibited latitude to Hamas to launch terror attacks against the Jewish state. Also, granting Palestinians unlimited internal autonomy over an entire region hampers the ability of Israel's security service, the Shin Bet, to collect intelligence needed to stave off terror—this point was gruesomely proven by the events of October 7.

However, none of these attitudes and developments undermine the validity of Israel's overall position regarding the Gaza Strip prior to October 7. During this near-twenty-year period, before the 2023–2024 Gaza War, Israel did not occupy the region. Gaza's atrocious socioeconomic circumstances were, in the main, a by-product of ideological and policy choices

---

136. Peres, *New Middle East*.

reached by the Palestinians themselves. And while a fringe minority of Israelis openly advocates renewed Jewish settlement construction on the Gaza Strip (months into the Gaza War, some figures on the Israeli right staged public demonstrations in this key), Israel is unlikely to recolonize the Gaza Strip after the painful, protracted 2023–2024 war. The "colonialism" concept is not an appropriate standard of criticism for Israel's policies toward the Gaza Strip after 2005; therefore its use by college protestors as a rationalization to warrant Hamas's violence on October 7 was out of bounds.

All of this is true, although many micro-level objections could be made in an exposure of how this conventional Israeli, and "pro-Israel," perception about the Gaza Strip glosses many inconvenient facts and realities. The real problem is that this conventional Israeli argument happens to be utter rubbish because Palestinians (and other peoples) do not operate in reality as though their lives are unfolding in a political legal brief. That is another way of saying that the real failure of pro-Israel public relations hasbara during the Gaza War crisis is that most Jews in the world actually believed it.

In one century after another, life as a minority required Jews to promulgate formal apologetic accounts of their circumstances. They seamlessly transferred this format to the Israeli-Arab conflict. Through the 1970s and 1980s, this format was applied mostly by the pro-Israel lobby in the United States, basically because the Israelis were too self-involved to bother much about hasbara. The format can be found in this period in primers put out by AIPAC-affiliated writers under titles like "Myths and Facts About the Israeli-Arab Conflict."[137] Writing as a Jew, I have to say that these are wonderful handbooks because we always win in them. Their contents boil down to legalistic claims, which sound like this: Palestinians ought to be reconciled with their circumstances on the Gaza Strip because their leaders rejected Britain's 1937 partition plan, which would have given them a lot more than Gaza and the West Bank, as would have the UN's 1947 partition plan, which the Palestinians also rejected, never missing an opportunity to miss an opportunity for success.

After I became a historian, I gained some knowledge about the veracity of contents in these pro-Israel primers, or lack thereof. But one does not have to go to graduate school to discern how these pro-Israel pamphlets are a rococo mix of courtroom advocacy, Capitol Hill lobbying, and merciless frontiersman ethics. Saying that one group deserves to be miserable because it descends from persons who rejected proposals that were thrust upon them, and fashioned by another group's foreign way of thinking, is

---

137. The format is exemplified by Bard, *Myths and Facts*. By far the most influential iteration of this approach during the 2023–2024 Gaza crisis was Tishby, *Israel*.

an outrage. It is akin to the scandal of early twentieth-century American history textbooks which implied that Native Americans deserved what they got because their ancestors sold Manhattan for a few beads.

That this sort of AIPAC apologetic is anachronistic and patronizing made it a perfect fit for the recreant generation. After Oslo's collapse, Israeli spokesmen co-opted the AIPAC rhetoric. By the time of the October 7 "surprise," Israelis were living in a Middle East of their own imagination, one where the Palestinians were consigned indefinitely to purgatory thanks to a political-legal brief that was comprehensible only to their enemies. Gazans deserved to live in squalor because they descended from intransigent leaders like Arafat who rejected reasonable compromise formulas in episodes like the 2000 Camp David Summit.

No doubt, perceptions and claims raised in the writings of anti-colonial figures like Fanon and Memmi help account for Israel's military failure on October 7. Israeli contractors gouged the public treasury for tens of millions of shekels, building (among other things) a bogus security fence on the Gaza border, and Israeli army officers and politicians signed off on failed security measures and projects because of dynamics of greed and administrative mediocrity that are memorably detailed in Memmi's account of colonizers in his famous 1957 volume. And, again, lazy racist generalizations about the character of colonized masses undergird episodes like October 7. As happened in the case of Egypt's Suez crossing in the October 1973 Yom Kippur War, Nukhba fighters crossed over from Gaza fifty years later, in October 2023, because Israeli intelligence, on many different levels, operated on the basis of cultural presumptions that can be related to colonialism. But I am proposing that the best explanation of why Israel was so surprised on October 7 is to be found on a somewhat different cultural level. Israel was persuaded by its own hasbara propaganda. For Jews, public apologetics are invariably a honey trap. Israel nestled in the logical lap of a political-legal brief whose methodologies and claims were never shared by Palestinians.

The third way path out of the crisis stirred by the 2023–2024 war is to stare realistically at the salient cultural and political traits of the recreant generation, and to forge reasonable correctives to them.

The kids are all right. That is, the spring 2024 college campuses ought to be seen as a constructive challenge to America's pro-Israel community. That should be the point of departure on the third way. It is a very different place to start, compared to the *bubbe-meises* which Israel and its lobby will try to sell as soon as the wars against Hamas in the south, and Hezbollah in the north, are ended, or suspended, and Jewish hostages are returned, dead or alive.

Israel's propaganda campaign started moments after the Hamas attacks, with the promulgation of slogans about Jewish unity ("Together, we will beat Hamas"). Such slogans retained validity as a mobilizing device when tens of thousands of soldiers, many of them civilians transforming as reservists, needed to fight in response to what Hamas had done, and to what Hezbollah had yet to do. But the unity slogan is vapid in a time of relative quiet. As months went by in the Hamas war, the slogan became unbearably hypocritical since it was propagated by a Netanyahu government that had willfully ripped the delicate fabric of Israeli democratic constitutionalism (which has no standing in a particular document) and shaped policies in line with the interests and orientations of its own "base" electorate, roughly 50 percent of the country.

Israel's Gaza War was extraordinary in the history of modern democracy in that one of its two major objectives was the ransoming of dozens of hostages (liquidating Hamas was the other), but everyone in the country tacitly understood that the anomaly did not end there. The unspeakable truth of the Gaza War is that it would have been fought differently, quite possibly with a much better outcome for the hostages and their families, had the brunt of Hamas's captives been right-wingers and religious Zionists of the varieties which comprise the electoral base of the parties in Netanyahu's coalition, rather than left-center secularists, largely associated with the kibbutz movements, a constituency that has not strongly and consistently been represented in government cabinets since Likud's rise to power in 1977.

This is a fearful, uncomfortable scenario for anyone in Israel to think about, so it was vocalized in an implicit, shorthand way. Apart from loyal Likud members, everyone in the country verbally abused Netanyahu, who became an effigy scapegoated to expiate the death of nonpartisan patriotism, called *mamlakhtiyut*, in Israel. Netanyahu has done much over the years to attenuate mamlakhtiyut, but the incessant chirping during the Gaza War about how a hostage release deal was stalled repeatedly, due to the self-interested concerns of a prime minister who is under criminal indictment, attested to much more than an issue-specific critique of Netanyahu's spectacularly disappointing performance as Israel's prime minister in this late phase of his political career. His public pillorying reflected broad anxiety about how barely a full lifetime, eighty years, went by after the Holocaust before the Jews found a way to make a mockery of the idea of national unity.

The traditional explanation for the hurban catastrophe two thousand years ago by which the Jews lost their Second Temple, and political sovereignty, hinges on this concept of national unity. It is called *sinat hinam*, baseless hatred. Invented by Talmudic rabbis who were musing about something they knew nothing about, political sovereignty, sinat hinam has always been an antiseptic, mostly useless way of thinking about the political world. It has the diagnostic acuity of a parent saying that a child is having a vomiting fit because of an upset stomach.

In a world of grotesque income inequality, where slogans about communal unity regularly serve the interests of small cadres of economic and political elites who enjoy comfortable and protected lives, the credibility of the national unity standard is tarnished in many places, and is not really a distinctive problem of Jewish politics. Ultimately, however, the moral and political failures of Jews in this recreant generation can be traced to a mischievous interpretation of Jewish history that was cultivated after the Holocaust by co-opted classes of Jewish intellectuals, academic scholars, and media-enabled commentators. These recreant thinkers and academics became increasingly indebted to sources of private capital in the Jewish world as five decades went by between Israel's colossal intelligence failures in the October 1973 Yom Kippur War and the October 2023 Simchat Torah war.

This interpretation of Jewish history teaches that before the Holocaust, it was a very bad idea for Jewish groups in diaspora lands to try to organize in opposition to one another. The unity myth governed politicized historiography in every subfield of Jewish history. Its imposing presence in American Jewish history research and writing is familiar. On this interpretation, American Jews, who have had a relatively placid history, now and then experimented with organizational principles other than the axiom of Jewish unity. The experiments failed. One example is American Jewish affairs at the end of the nineteenth century, when spokesmen from the settled Jewish population, comprised mostly of Jews with Sephardic or Central European roots, publicly presented themselves as a type of Jew that ought to be distinguished from the *Ostjuden*, masses of Jewish newcomers from Eastern Europe. Soon enough, American Jews found strong reasons not to express and organize themselves as though there really are two, or more, unlike groups of Jews in the world.

The Jews' entry into modernity, in early nineteenth-century Europe, was characterized by complex networks of rivalry between subgroups, two of them eventually identified as "Orthodox" (*Mitnagdim* and *Hasidim*), and one (*Maskilim*) comprised of semisecularized modernizers. In reality, the prevailing Jewish circumstance in this setting was disunity, and a salient phenomenon in Jewish politics was alliances forged by leaders of one of these three subgroups to advance its values and interests in contest against the other two groups. This situation can be gleaned in Jewish history research produced since the Holocaust, but its complexities and legacies have been interpreted selectively. In Israel, for instance, where religious Zionism and its offshoot in the colonialist settlements are heavily endowed by state funding, including state-supported academic institutions within the Green Line (Bar-Ilan University) and in the occupied territories (Ariel University), scholars have systematically downplayed the moral, political, and social challenges posed by secularization, within the Haskalah (Jewish Enlightenment) movement and beyond it. In such scholarship, the Haskalah's proponents, the Maskilim, typically appear as slightly modified Orthodox Jews. Their relationship to identity clusters, such as Reform Judaism (whose legitimacy is routinely snubbed in Israeli academia, just as it has been in Israeli politics), is left shrouded in mystery, whereas developments among what became ultra-Orthodox groups, like the Hasidim, are researched in an intense but romantically selective fashion.

Developing an analysis of how such scholarship serves political interests in Israel, particularly among the religious Zionists who want to show how their pet projects in the settlements, along with how the explosive growth of ultra-Orthodox communities (whose members usually do not serve in the IDF), ought not to be worrisome in a state that projects itself to the world as a liberal democracy, would take us too far afield. Here it suffices merely to point out that the unmitigated allegiance to myths of Jewish unity, not just among Jewish Studies scholars, has developed in recent decades in diametrical opposition to past and contemporary sociopolitical realities in the Jewish world. Perhaps you have, as I do, a number of liberal-minded Jewish family members and friends in North America and Europe. How many of them are comfortable with what they hear about the behavior of Orthodox Jewish groups in their home countries and Israel? How do they feel about the stories regarding how public money from the New York State treasury, and from Israel's state budget, has been manipulatively handled in these Orthodox communities so that, in the end, the funds support fundamentalist school curricula and anti-modern, unsafe, or illiberal public behavior in fields of public health, on West Bank settlements, and elsewhere? Does the concept of Jewish unity, as it has been developed in state-supported scholarship in Israel and by philanthropically endowed Jewish studies departments in North America, apply to the way these secular Jewish liberals, still a majority in the United States, really feel and respond to such developments?

The idea of Jewish unity was developed after the Holocaust by honorably-intentioned scholars, activists, rabbis, and others who believed it would become a communally empowering concept. Undeniably, eighty years later, its dogmatic institutionalization has weakened the Jews. Israel's 2023–2024 Gaza War, and global responses to it, have exposed how vulnerable the Jews have become due to gaps yawning between the way they privately feel and the way they publicly present themselves.

Israel's conduct in the war was hardly beyond reproach; but its own self-generated evaluations, challenging the Palestinian casualty toll (forty thousand) cited internationally and insisting that a large portion of the casualties had identifiable connections with Hamas terror, have validity, albeit not as absolute truth. From our own, Israeli, standpoint, the vastly circulated allegation condemning the war as genocide is tantamount to a blood libel.

Trying to climb somewhat beyond this parochial perspective, I am suggesting here that the genocide accusation is best understood not really as a blood libel but rather as an *absurdist* statement whose referents transcend well beyond humanitarian concern for the welfare of Palestinians on the Gaza Strip.

The genocide accusation reflects the resentful anxiety of anti-Semites about the chosen people concept ("look at what those superior-minded Jews are up to in Israel"). More important than that, the accusation became possible in a world where ideologically-driven groups could exploit obvious gaps between the ways secular-liberal Jews really think and the public presentation of collective Jewish interests, particularly Israel.

One such group is the postcolonial theorists, whose livelihood and professional field developed, often unwittingly, in rivalry with Holocaust studies, as we have seen. Nothing could better validate the ascendance of postcolonial theory, compared to Holocaust studies among other things, and nothing could better proclaim this theory's status as the politically correct way of thinking about the world, than to assert that Israel is guilty of genocide. In lieu of the conventionally accepted rationale of Israel's establishment, as a worthy political and moral response to the Holocaust, Israel is now seen as a colonialist entity that seeks and effects the genocidal Holocaust of Palestinians. The genocide accusation's wide-scale acceptance, on college campuses and many other places, attests to the triumph of a *theory*—not anti-Semitism but rather postcolonial theory whose complex determinants and traits are far more readily associated with liberal humanism than with illiberal malevolence.

Some of these determinants and traits have been discussed here, but we should add some final words about why the genocide accusation became inspirational to Jewish subgroups, including young American Jewish college students, whose presence in the campus protests was conspicuous. Absurdist statements become attractive as alternatives to conventionally produced dogmas, such as the idea of Jewish unity, whose untruth can no longer be concealed. To say that Israel's killing of forty thousand

Palestinians on the Gaza Strip was genocide makes some sense, whereas to say that following more than half a century of colonial occupation on the West Bank, Israel is "the only democracy in the Middle East" makes no sense at all. For idealistic young Jews in the diaspora, who are publicly identified with Israel whether they like it or not, the only escape hatch from such mendacious propaganda is the absurd. Linked by the dogma of Jewish unity to colonialist Israeli behavior that their teachers have, understandably, taught them to abhor, what recourse would have been more logical for such young Jews other than protest? In the skewed circumstances of Jewish life in 2023–2024, the participation of such Jews in absurdist demonstrations about Israeli genocide was probably the most logical occurrence. *The kids are all right* because their college protests have forced recreant Jewish adults to stop playing make-believe games about Jewish unity.

So what are the best takeaways from the college protests against Israel's Gaza War?

We can start with one of the most egregious developments in the recreant generation: from the liberal viewpoint, still upheld by a majority of American Jews, *it is not okay, it is not cute, it is not a necessary evil* that Evangelicals who support Donald Trump, and who oppose LGBTQ rights, have become a powerful philanthropic and political lobbying presence supportive of Israel's right-wing governments. That the Evangelicals are waiting for the rapture and the subsequent conversion of 144,000 of us, perhaps in a scenario facilitated by apocalyptic nuclear war between Israel and Iran, does not add elegance to the Evangelicals' arrangement with the Jewish state. But theology, as the kids have taught us, is not the problem. Colonialism is.

The Evangelicals have become a major source of support for Israel's illegal and illiberal occupation of the West Bank via the maintenance and expansion of Jewish settlements in this region. The Evangelicals are friends of your enemy if you belong to the liberal majority of American Jews, or are part of the 40 percent or so of Israel's Jewish population which has been firmly opposed to the settlement movement since its formation by the Gush Emunim group after the 1973 Yom Kippur War. The Evangelicals have no place in a new American Jewish organizational world that must reformat (and, in all likelihood, fragment) under the realization that the myth of Jewish unity is not a solution, but part of the problem.

From the liberal viewpoint, still upheld by a majority of American Jews, *it is not okay, it is not cute, it is not a necessary evil* that billionaires have taken possession of the mainstay of the Jewish lobby, AIPAC, along with a wide swath of other institutional networks important in American Jewish-Israel interaction, and have promoted agendas supportive of Israeli colonialism on the West Bank. The most indelible image of the recreant generation is this: your average Israeli *shlimazel* left his apartment in the morning with a free newspaper, *Yisrael Hayom*, in his hand, while your average American Jewish teenager enjoyed a free junket tour of Israel on the Birthright program, both freebies being subsidized by Sheldon Adelson, a parvenu with billions to burn from his casino businesses. Adelson was the largest donor to Donald Trump's 2016 campaign and also a lavish patron of Israeli right-wing politics which, via Netanyahu, finds colonialist expression in the maintenance and expansion of the West Bank settlements.

Adelson's most ostentatious maneuver in the Jewish world happened when he used his philanthropic muscle to coax the Trump administration to move the US embassy to Jerusalem in May 2018. At the embassy cornerstone ceremony, Evangelical leader John Hagee blessed the world. What "Good News" for the Jews! Adelson's embassy move taught the world that Jews can be rewarded for their philanthropy in unilateral diplomacy. Thanks to the almighty power of the Jewish billionaires, America can be persuaded into taking unilateral moves on symbolic or substantive issues in the Arab-Israeli dispute, without any semblance of consultation with, or consent from, the Palestinians.

Netanyahu, deliriously happy, turned this into a doctrine—his theory that Israel would have peace and prosperity in the Middle East without worrying about Palestinian demands. For all his distaste for Donald Trump, President Biden drew inspiration from this embassy move, foolishly promoting the Saudi initiative in a fashion that drove the isolated Palestinians into a corner.

In history's causal nexus, the distance between Adelson's embassy move and the Hamas October 7 attack isn't even a long walk. It's a short skip. And it's the price Jews paid for depositing their politics with their billionaires, with an illiberal pro-Israel oligarchy.

In the 1980s, signs of Israeli political malfeasance in its settlement occupation of the West Bank and Gaza Strip were mounting, and they were about to compromise dogmatic precepts of pro-Israel lobbying, such as the canard about Israel being "the only democracy in the Middle East." A series of fiascoes and scandals—the Pollard espionage affair, wrangling about "who is a Jew," etc.—reached a crescendo when the First Intifada erupted in 1987. Backlash about Israel's colonialist crackdown on Palestinian teenagers who threw rocks at IDF tanks was voluminous and devastating (in essence, the smokescreen thrown by the pro-Israel lobby over settlement colonialism in the post-1967 territories was lifted by two groups of teenagers, Palestinians during the First Intifada, and American and European undergraduates on campuses in spring 2024). There appeared to be no way for pro-Israel lobbying to persist in its format submissive to Likud's pro-settlement policies, especially after the brief interregnum of international popularity enjoyed by Israel under the pro-peace Rabin and Barak Labor governments in the 1990s ended abruptly with Oslo's collapse and the eruption of the Second Intifada.

The answer to the riddle of how pro-Israel lobbying lasted through the Gaza War on the basis of threadbare slogans and the indulgence of settlement colonialism on the West Bank is this: AIPAC billionaires brought the lobby out of the quagmire, allowing it to dust off the old saw about Israel as the Middle East's sole democracy. The slogan had no truth the moment you strayed beyond Israel's 1967 Green Line, but this was counterbalanced by the fact that the billionaires kept the Netanyahu governments happy and well-nourished, and provided donations to US politicians who had no problem rubbing AIPAC snake-oil over their campaigns, so long as their treasure chests filled with dollars.

In turn, this trend of pro-Israel billionaire philanthropy is an outgrowth of socioeconomic trends in 1980s Reaganite America, whose legacy poses a grave danger to the future of American democracy as a whole. The gist of these trends is the concentration of capital thanks to deregulatory and privatization policies. These policies opened up playing fields for entrepreneurs and financiers from groups who were not quite in the Wall Street establishment, including Jews, some of whom were willing to experiment with innovative financial items, such as junk bonds and leveraged buyouts (LBOs); in cases such as those of Michael Milken and Ivan Boesky, such financial experimentation and innovation straddled between breathtaking, American dream success and outright white-collar crime.

The dots between these phenomena—AIPAC billionaire philanthropy conducive to West Bank settlement colonialism, predatory capitalism, and threats to American democracy posed by the inordinate socioeconomic and political power wielded by the wealthy 1 percent—are simple to connect. And they are the link between this volume's first essay and the current one. With some important exceptions (Bernie Sanders pops right to mind), few people in the recreant generation would connect them before the college protestors came around.

In the mid-2020s, liberal Jewish politics in America is mirroring larger trends of politics in the country as a whole. Problems that arose in the Gilded Age and which found solutions, of sorts, in the Progressive 1930s are recycling a century later. So, too, in Jewish politics. The first important American Zionist leader was Louis Brandeis, who also became the first American Jew to attain a seat on the bench of the Supreme Court in the same World War I era when he became a Jewish nationalist. Brandeis won renown in American politics for his dire warnings about the antidemocratic implications of the concentration of capital in banks and corporations—what he called "the curse of bigness." He infused this same perspective in Zionist politics, demanding decentralization and power sharing in Jewish nationalist affairs, much to the chagrin of European Zionists.

It would be well for liberal American Jews to keep this Brandeis example in mind as they search for a third way. They are likely to be deterred and intimidated, at first, by the way a newly organized challenge against illiberal American Jewish groups and organizations, and against West Bank settlements, is castigated as an affront to Jewish unity, as baseless hatred, as *sinat hinam*. But sinat hinam has always been a myth; deference to it in a political world where liberalism as a whole has many dangerously empowered enemies would spell the death of the sort of liberal Jewish identity we ourselves, along with our parents and our grandparents, have cherished.

In the broadest senses of American democratic ideals and of Jewish vitality, doing what has to be done after the Gaza War crisis is a tribute to unity, not to fractiousness, not to sinat hinam. Reforms that need to be done in Jewish life and reforms that need to be done in American democracy are synergetic. This is because the socioeconomic source of all our ills, of Jewish settlement colonialism, of anti-constitutionalism in Trump's MAGA movement, can be traced to back to one place, to the curse of bigness, exactly as Brandeis taught.

From the liberal viewpoint, still upheld by a majority of American Jews, *it is not okay, it is not cute, it is not a necessary evil* that Israeli settlers and their signature institutions gained acceptance in the American Jewish organizational mainstream. From their inception under Gush Emunim in the mid-1970s, the settlements have been a profoundly anti-American phenomenon. In the political sphere, their gist is an aggressive campaign to undermine pro-peace American diplomacy predicated on the "land for peace" formula. Jewish settlers have willfully acted to sabotage American foreign policy since the days of Secretary of State Henry Kissinger's shuttle diplomacy effort on behalf of limited Israeli withdrawal on the Sinai Peninsula after the Yom Kippur War (an effort that incidentally cemented the special relationship between Israel and the United States), and through the Oslo peace process years. The settlement movement's campaign against American foreign policy was noxiously aggressive in the period of Obama's two terms—in one well-known episode, then Vice President Biden was greeted on a visit to Israel with an announced infringement of a settlement freeze supposedly agreed to by the Netanyahu government. During the current Gaza War, this settler subversion of liberal American foreign policy initiatives has continued in a gruesomely officious fashion. Settlers and their confederates have dumped over truckloads of humanitarian aid arranged by the Biden administration for starving civilians on the Gaza Strip.

The colonialist settlement movement is not only anti-American in this political sense of planting "facts on the ground" (i.e., Jewish enclaves) in disputed, post-1967 territories for the purpose of forestalling land for peace initiatives promoted in American foreign policy. The settlement movement has always been anti-American in ethos. From its start in the 1970s, its prominent rabbinical figures have spoken about America's socioeconomic system in a vein of grossly stereotypical exaggeration, drawing specious contrasts between the supposed spiritual purity of Greater Israel settlement and degraded American materialism. Their rhetoric is reminiscent of juvenile remonstration about the West and America apprehensible in the tantrums of radical fundamentalist leaders from the Islamic Brotherhood in Egypt, or the Islamic revolution in Iran. This anti-American ethos applies also to many of the confused souls, American Jewish immigrants on the West Bank (and formerly on the Gaza Strip) who constitute 10 percent of the total settlement population. Before they stroll over to the swimming pool on suburbanized West Bank enclaves like Efrat, such immigrants can be heard ranting about the ills of American materialism or American foreign policy with stridency they would never have dared vocalize in front of their Christian neighbors in their pre-Israel lives. Whether or not such persons are very bad Jews has been in dispute in Israel for fifty years, but there has never been cause to doubt that they are self-hating Americans.

The kids are all right because they have forced the hand of the American Jewish organizational establishment, whose members remain, for the time being, mostly Democratic Party liberals. Those organizations, reformatted or not, cannot afford to be a tail that is wagged by officials from the State Department and the White House at times when these officials initiate and enforce much tougher policies toward especially illiberal renegade settler groups. Should it persist in Washington after the 2024 elections, liberal American Jews must race ahead and be at the *front* of this much-belated policy trend. Tax exemption privileges should be annulled in the cases of American Jewish foundations or individuals who contribute money to settlement colonialism on the West Bank. Selective boycotts in the supply and demand of products to and from the settlements ought to be initiated, as a few courageous voices of dissent in the recreant generation (i.e., Peter Beinart, or the founders of Ben & Jerry's) have proposed in past years. There should be a shutdown of interchange between US academic bodies and Israeli academia so long as a rogue settler educational entity at Ariel on the West Bank remains accredited with university status in Israel's higher education system. The trade association of global Jewish studies, called the Association of Jewish Studies, should be boycotted or suspended so long as it extends membership and speaking privileges to academics from this settler institution at Ariel. Philanthropically endowed Jewish studies centers at American universities that have had substantive affiliation with Ariel University should be put on probation until those ties are irrevocably severed.

This last suggestion warrants brief amplification. The spring 2024 crackdowns on campus protestors who chanted "from the river to the sea" may or may not have been justifiable, but they inarguably applied to ephemeral, symbolic irritants. In contrast, the maintenance of Jewish studies institutes that are supportive of Zionist colonialism on the West Bank is a systematic problem. It ought to be actionable under campus policy stricter than the crackdown on the spring 2024 protests.

Pro-Israel right-wingers who have lobbied in recent years for anti-democratic measures clamping down on BDS activists might argue that self-described Jewish leftists are being hypocritical when they advocate boycotts against West Bank academic or commercial enterprises since such boycotts infringe free trade rights, academic freedom, and the like. The argument is disingenuous. BDS activism might be objectionable and worth opposing on many grounds, but it is not, in principle, illiberal to boycott colonialism. On the contrary, the use of boycotts in anti-colonialist politics is essentially a *liberal* maneuver aimed at protecting the rights of an outsider group (in this case, Palestinians) that is abused by state power.

The legislative and advocacy climate in Washington is likely to alter significantly in the event of a Trump victory in the upcoming elections. Powerful organizational and philanthropic interests will launder soiled realities of the Gaza War. They will obscure how, as Israeli hostages languished or perished, the war was prolonged for months because the Netanyahu government was worried about how a post-war resolution might strengthen the hand of relatively moderate groups in the Palestinian Authority—should such groups prove to be governmentally responsible, the Netanyahu government's case for prolonged Jewish settler control on the West Bank, and against a two-state solution, would attenuate. Endlessly protracting the Gaza War, even when retired, high-ranking IDF officers appear on television night after night and insist that there is no military rationale for the fighting's continuance, the Netanyahu government is playing for time, hoping that a new Trump administration in Washington will sanction Israel's annexation of the West Bank, if not Jewish resettlement on the Gaza Strip.

What does the future hold in store? Feeling threatened in an increasingly uncivil and anti-Semitic world, many Jews will circle the wagons defensively and resist changes in long-standing organizational and lifestyle patterns. Such instinctual, self-defensive conservatism might not set the tone, however. In terms of reformatting institutions and patterns of Jewish life, the events of 2023–2024 could prove to be no less transformative than those of the 1967–1973 (Six-Day War and Yom Kippur War) period. In months and years ahead, there will be no shortage of Jewish religious and organizational leaders who will take cues from right-wing Israeli governments that are invested in settlement colonialism on the West Bank. They will declaim sententiously about the perils of sinat hinam. Such profoundly illiberal messaging could (and should) be met by pushback of newfound strength, however.

The likelihood of four more years of Trump governance will present a vexing array of challenges to American Jews who remain liberals. Despite innumerable counterpressures, these Jewish liberals will have powerful practical incentive to resist "life goes on" acquiescence toward continued Israeli settlement colonialism on the West Bank, or toward its possible renewal on the Gaza Strip. The events of 2023–2024 taught these liberals an indelible lesson. They showed them how they get hit where it hurts the most by exhibiting "life goes on" passivity toward the Jewish organizations which supposedly represent them. American Jews can no longer send their children to the country's most prestigious universities and colleges in the warmly encouraging, confidently safe atmosphere that preceding generations of American Jews assumed had become part of their social contract with the country's constitutional democracy.

Moving beyond that weighty consideration, we arrive at the inchoate realm of politics, where practical self-interest and genuine values converge. It is in this Jewish political realm where liberal American Jews, many of them descendants of scrupulously hard-working immigrants, or of second generation types who found it convenient to pretend that there is no such things as Jewish politics, will have to take their stand. Dealing courageously with complexities of a possible new Trump era, they will have to withstand the sinat hinam blandishments of apologists for Israel's pro-settlement governments. For both moral and practical reasons, it will be the post-recreant imperative of the coming generation of generation of Jews, in America and in Israel, to abandon resorts to illiberal methods of protecting presumed Jewish goals and interests. No more state legislature initiatives to overturn rights of BDS activists (even though many of them are anti-Semites), no more billionaires flexing their muscles to dump university presidents (even if some of them acted like nincompoops when the Gaza War campus protests erupted); the foundation of a new Jewish politic must be that such illiberalism is wrong, even when it seems to work for a spell.

On a practical level, such recreant recourse to illiberalism was a colossal strategic blunder. It will ineluctably spawn anti-Semitism backlashes in the long term, perhaps of power more menacing than any presumed danger to Israel, or to any other Jewish interest, that it forestalled in the short term. No less gravely, for American Jews, such illiberalism is ideational and existential self-slander. Apart from the community's quasi-fundamentalist fringes, contemporary American Jews are heirs to persons who believed that by judiciously and selectively upholding the parts of their religious and cultural traditions they cherished, they would ultimately promote universal purposes, as well as parochial Jewish ones. For these early, optimistic entrants in modernity, the notion that Jewish survival must be leveraged upon the dismissal of core universal values of American democracy, such as the right to free speech or the right to protest, would have been perceived leerily as strange metaphysical incongruity. That the passing generation of American Jewish and Israeli activists and leaders saw things otherwise was its recreant essence.

Bibliography

Adorno, Theodor, and Max Horkheimer. *Dialectic of Enlightenment*. London: Verso, 1997.
Alterman, Eric. *We Are Not One: A History of America's Fight over Israel*. New York: Basic, 2023.
American Jewish Committee. "5 Reasons Why the Events in Gaza Are Not 'Genocide.'" Updated Dec. 5, 2024. https://www.ajc.org/news/5-reasons-why-the-events-in-gaza-are-not-genocide.
Anderson, Betty. *The American University of Beirut: American Nationalism and Liberal Education*. Austin, TX: University of Texas Press, 2011.
Antonius, George. *The Arab Awakening: The Story of the Arab National Movement*. London: Hamish Hamilton, 1938.
Applegate, Debby. *The Most Famous Man in America: The Biography of Henry Ward Beecher*. New York: Doubleday, 2006.
Arendt, Hannah. *The Origins of Totalitarianism*. New York: Meridian, 1962.
Aridan, Natan. *Advocating for Israel*. Lanham, MD: Lexington, 2017.
Ariel, Yaakov. *An Unusual Relationship: Evangelical Christians and Jews*. New York: New York University Press, 2013.
Aschheim, Steven. *Brothers and Strangers: The East European Jew in German and German-Jewish Consciousness*. Madison, WI: University of Wisconsin Press, 1982.
Aslan, Reza. *Zealot: The Life and Times of Jesus of Nazareth*. New York: Random House, 2013.
Auletta, Ken. *World War 3.0: Microsoft and Its Enemies*. New York: Random House, 2001.
Aviad, Janet. *Return to Judaism: Religious Renewal in Israel*. Chicago: University of Chicago Press, 1983.
Aviam, Mordechai. "Christian Galilee in the Byzantine Period." In *Galilee Through the Centuries: Confluence of Cultures*, edited by Eric Myers, 285–94. Winona Lake, IN: Eisenbrauns, 1999.
Aviam, Mordechai, and Peter Richardson. "Josephus' Galilee in Archaeological Perspective." In *Flavius Josephus*, edited by Steve Mason, 177–200. Leiden: Brill, 2003.
Avi-Yonah, Michael. *The Jews of Palestine: A Political History from the Bar Kokhba War to the Arab Conquest*. Oxford: Basil Blackwell, 1976.
———. "The Missing Fortress of Flavius Josephus." *Israel Exploration Journal* 3.2 (1953) 94–98.

BIBLIOGRAPHY

Bachner, Michael. "Israel Should 'Wipe Out' Palestinian Town of Huwara, Says Senior Minister Smotrich." *Times of Israel*, Mar. 1, 2023. https://www.timesofisrael.com/israel-should-wipe-out-palestinian-town-of-huwara-says-senior-minister-smotrich/.
Bain, Robert E., et al. *Earthly Footsteps of the Man of Galilee*. New York: N. D. Thompson, 1894.
Baldwin, Neil. *Henry Ford and the Jews*. New York: PublicAffairs, 2001.
Bard, Mitchell. *Myths and Facts: A Guide to the Arab-Israeli Conflict*. Chevy Chase, MD: American-Israeli Cooperative Enterprise, 2002.
Bar-On, Mordechai. *The Gates of Gaza*. New York: St. Martin's, 1994.
Bartels, Larry. *Unequal Democracy: The Political Economy of the New Gilded Age*. Princeton: Princeton University Press, 2008.
Barton, Bruce. *The Man Nobody Knows: A Discovery of the Real Jesus*. Indianapolis: Bobbs-Merrill, 1925.
Baruch, Bernard. *Baruch: My Own Story*. New York: Holt, 1957.
Becker, Carl. *The Declaration of Independence: A Study in the History of Political Ideas*. New York: Harcourt, Brace, 1922.
Beecher, Henry Ward. *The Life of Jesus, the Christ*. New York: J. B. Ford, 1871.
Beit-Hallahmi, Benjamin. *Despair and Deliverance: Private Salvation in Contemporary Israel*. Albany, NY: State University of New York Press, 1992.
Benjamin, Walter. *Illuminations*. New York: Schocken, 1969.
Bennett, Naftali. "Bennett on Channel 12: Don't Do the Expected." [In Hebrew.] Uploaded Oct. 9, 2023. Video, 10:15. https://www.youtube.com/watch?v=Yw7YCoIwBDk.
Ben-Yehuda, Nachman. *The Masada Myth: Collective Memory and Mythmaking in Israel*. Madison, WI: University of Wisconsin Press, 1995.
Berkowitz, Michael. "The Madoff Paradox: American Jewish Sage, Savior and Thief." *Journal of American Studies* 46 (Feb. 2012) 189–202.
Biale, David, et al. *Hasidism: A New History*. Princeton: Princeton University Press, 2018.
Boas, Adrian, ed. *Montfort: History, Early Research and Recent Studies*. Leidin: Brill, 2017.
Boesky, Ivan. *Merger Mania: Arbitrage; Wall Street's Best Kept Money-Making Secret*. New York: Holt, Rinehart & Winston, 1985.
Brandeis, Louis. *The Curse of Bigness*. New York: Viking, 1934.
———. *Other People's Money and How the Bankers Use It*. New York: Frederick Stokes, 1932.
Brenner, Michael. *Prophets of the Past: Interpreters of Jewish History*. Princeton: Princeton University Press, 2010.
Brewerton, David. "Bruce Wasserstein Obituary." *Guardian*, Oct. 22, 2009. https://www.theguardian.com/business/2009/oct/22/bruce-wasserstein-obituary.
Burrough, Bryan, and John Helyar. *Barbarians at the Gate: The Fall of RJR Nabisco*. New York: Harper Collins, 2008.
Cambell, Jim. *Madoff Talks*. New York: McGraw Hill, 2021.
Camus, Albert. *The Myth of Sisyphus*. New York: Knopf Doubleday, 2012.
———. *The Plague*. London: Penguin, 2002.
———. *The Rebel: An Essay on Man in Revolt*. New York: Knopf Doubleday, 2012.
———. *The Stranger*. New York: Knopf Doubleday, 2012.
Cardin, Shoshana. *Shoshana*. Baltimore: Jewish Museum of Maryland, 2008.

Carenen, Caitlin. *The Fervent Embrace: Liberal Protestants, Evangelicals, and Israel.* New York: New York University Press, 2012.
Carnegie, Andrew. *His Autobiography and His Essay "The Gospel of Wealth."* Boston: Houghton Mifflin, 1920.
Carroll, David. *Albert Camus, the Algerian: Colonialism, Terror, Justice.* New York: Columbia University Press, 2007.
Case, Shirley Jackson. *Jesus: A New Biography.* Chicago: University of Chicago Press, 1927.
Chafets, Zev. *A Match Made in Heaven: American Jews, Christian Zionists, and One Man's Exploration of the Weird and Wonderful Judeo-Evangelical Alliance.* New York: Harper Collins, 2007.
Chancey, Mark. *The Myth of a Gentile Galilee.* New York: Cambridge University Press, 2002.
Chernow, Ron. *The House of Morgan: An American Banking Dynasty and the Rise of Modern Finance.* New York: Macmillan, 1990.
———. *Titan: The Life of John D. Rockefeller.* New York: Vintage, 1998.
Chomsky, Noam. "Noam Chomsky on the BDS Movement." Address to the United Nations, Oct. 14, 2014. Video, 4:48. https://www.youtube.com/watch?v=O4YwG6Z9NpU.
Clarke, Howard. *The Gospel of Matthew and Its Readers: A Historical Introduction to the First Gospel.* Bloomington, IN: Indiana University Press, 2003.
CNN. "Watch Obama Roast Trump." White House Correspondents' Dinner. Uploaded Apr. 28, 2016. Video, 5:09. https://www.youtube.com/watch?v=HHckZCxdRkA.
CNN Politics. "Fact-Checking the ABC News Presidential Debate." Sept. 11, 2024. https://edition.cnn.com/2024/09/10/politics/fact-check-debate-trump-harris/index.html.
Cohan, William D. *Money and Power: How Goldman Sachs Came to Rule the World.* London: Penguin Books, 2011.
Cohen, Avner. *Israel and the Bomb.* New York: Columbia University Press, 1998.
Cohen, Hermann. *Religion of Reason: Out of the Sources of Judaism.* New York: F. Ungar, 1972.
Cohen, Naomi. *Jacob H. Schiff: A Study in American Jewish Leadership.* Hanover, NH: Brandeis University Press, 1999.
Cohen, Shaye. *Josephus in Galilee and Rome.* Leiden: Brill, 2002.
———. "Masada: Literary Tradition, Archaeological Remains, and the Credibility of Josephus." *Journal of Jewish Studies* 33.1–2 (Spring–Autumn 1982), 385–405.
Cohn, Haim. *Mavo ishi: Autobiografiya* [Personal introduction: an autobiography]. Or Yehuda: Kinneret, Zmora-Bitan, 2005.
———. *The Trial and Death of Jesus.* New York: Harper & Row, 1971.
Cole, Bret. *M&A Titans: The Pioneers Who Shaped Wall Street's Mergers and Acquisitions Industry.* Hoboken, NJ: Wiley, 2008.
Cooper, John Milton. *The Warrior and the Priest: Woodrow Wilson and Theodore Roosevelt.* London: Belknap, 1983.
Danon, Danny, and Ram Ben-Barak. "The West Should Welcome Gaza Refugees." *Wall Street Journal*, Nov. 13, 2023. https://www.wsj.com/articles/the-west-should-welcome-gaza-refugees-asylum-seekers-hamas-terrorism-displacement-5d2b5890.

BIBLIOGRAPHY

Davis, John. *The Landscape of Belief: Encountering the Holy Land in Nineteenth Century Art and Culture*. Princeton: Princeton University Press, 1996.
Davis, Moshe, ed. *America and the Holy Land*. Vol. 4 of *With Eyes Toward Zion*. New York: Praeger, 1995.
———. *The Emergence of Conservative Judaism*. Philadelphia: Jewish Publication Society of America, 1963.
———, ed. *Scholars Colloquium on America-Holy Land Studies*. Vol. 1 of *With Eyes Toward Zion*. New York: Arno Press, 1977.
———, ed. *Themes and Sources in the Archives of the United States, Great Britain, Turkey and Israel*. Vol. 2 of *With Eyes Toward Zion*. New York: Praeger, 1986.
Davis, Lottie, and Moshe Davis. *Land of Our Fathers: Biblical Names in America from the Old Testament*. Illustrated by Charles Harper. 1954. George Glazer Gallery. https://www.georgeglazer.com/wpmain/product/map-united-states-pictorial-land-of-our-fathers-biblical-names-judaica-vintage-print-1954/.
Deutscher, Isaac. *The Non-Jewish Jew and Other Essays*. London: Oxford University Press, 1968.
De Vise, Daniel. "The Top 1 Percent of American Earners Now Own More Wealth than the Entire Middle Class." *USA Today*, Dec. 6, 2023. https://www.usatoday.com/story/money/2023/12/06/top-1-american-earners-more-wealth-middle-class/71769832007/.
Dodge, Bayard. *The American University of Beirut*. Beirut: Khayat, 1958.
Eddy, Paul Rhodes, and James K. Beilby, eds. *The Historical Jesus*. Downers Grove, IL: InterVarsity Academic, 2009.
Ehrlich, Judith Ramsey, and Barry J. Rehfeld. *New Crowd: The Changing of Jewish Guard on Wall Street*. Boston: Little, Brown, 1989.
Ehrman, Bart. *Lost Scriptures: Books That Did Not Make It into the New Testament*. New York: Oxford University Press, 2003.
Eliav, Aryeh. *Eretz hatzvi* [Land of the hart]. Tel Aviv: Am Oved, 1972.
Eren, Colleen. *Bernie Madoff and the Crisis*. Stanford, CA: Stanford University Press, 2017.
Fanon, Frantz. *Black Skin, White Masks*. New York: Grove, 1967.
———. *The Wretched of the Earth*. New York: Grove, 2004.
Fenichell, Stephen. *Other People's Money: The Rise and Fall of OPM Leasing Services*. Garden City, NY: Anchor, 1985.
Ferguson, Fergus. *Sacred Scenes: Notes of Travel in Egypt and the Holy Land*. Glasgow: Thomas Adamson, 1864.
Ferguson, Niall. *Empire: How Britain Made the Modern World*. London: Allen Lane, 2003.
Festinger, Leon. *When Prophecy Fails*. Minneapolis: University of Minnesota Press, 1956.
Fitzgerald, F. Scott. *The Great Gatsby*. New York: Scribner's Sons, 1953.
Flusser, David, and Steven R. Notley. *The Sage from Galilee: Rediscovering Jesus' Genius*. Grand Rapids: Eerdmans, 1997.
Flynn, John. "Standard Oil and Microsoft—Intriguing Parallels or Limping Analogies?" *Antitrust Bulletin* 46.4 (Winter 2001) 645–743.
Fosdick, Harry Emerson. *The Living of These Days*. London: SCM, 1957.
———. *A Pilgrimage to Palestine*. New York: Macmillan, 1927.

Foster, Paul. *The Apocryphal Gospels: A Very Short Introduction*. New York: Oxford University Press, 2009.
Foxman, Abraham. *Jews and Money*. New York: St. Martin's, 2010.
France, John. *Hattin*. New York: Oxford University Press, 2015.
Fredriksen, Paula. *When Christians Were Jews: The First Generation*. New Haven: Yale University Press, 2018.
Friedman, Menachem. "And This Is the History of the Status Quo." In *Hama'avar miyishuv l'medina, 1947–1949* [Transition from yishuv to state, 1947–1949], edited by Varda Filofski, 47–64. Haifa: Haifa University Press, 1990.
Friedman, Murray. *The Neoconservative Revolution: Jewish Intellectuals and the Shaping of Public Policy*. New York: Cambridge University Press, 2005.
Friedman, Thomas. *The Lexus and the Olive Tree*. New York: Anchor, 2000.
Freyne, Sean. *Galilee, Jesus and the Gospels: Literary Approaches and Historical Investigations*. Philadelphia: Fortress, 1988.
Fukuyama, Francis. *The End of History and the Last Man*. New York: Avon, 1993.
Fuller, Adam. *Israel and the Neoconservatives: Zionism and American Interests*. Lanham, MD: Lexington, 2019.
———. *Taking the Fight to the Enemy: Neoconservatism and the Age of Ideology*. Lanham, MD: Lexington, 2012.
Gandossy, Robert. *Bad Business: The OPM Scandal and the Seduction of the Establishment*. New York: Basic, 1985.
Gates, Bill. "Bill Gates: Microsoft Antitrust Deposition Highlights." United States Court of Appeals for the District of Columbia Circuit. Recorded Aug. 27, 1998. Video, 39:27. https://www.youtube.com/watch?v=gRelVFm7iJE&t.
Geiger, Abraham. *Judaism and Its History in Two Parts*. New York: Block, 1911.
Gilad, Moshe. "Ben-Gurion Saw This Kibbutz as a Symbol of Israeli Steadfastness: It's Abandoned Now." *Ha'aretz*, Jan. 18, 2024. https://www.haaretz.com/israel-news/2024-01-18/ty-article-magazine/.premium/ben-gurion-saw-this-kibbutz-as-a-symbol-of-israeli-steadfastness-its-abandoned-now/0000018d-1280-dac4-a9cf-52fb789a0000.
Gladwell, Malcolm. "The Uses of Adversity." *New Yorker*, Nov. 2, 2008. https://www.newyorker.com/magazine/2008/11/10/the-uses-of-adversity.
Golani, Motti. *Israel in Search of a War*. Brighton: Sussex Academic Press, 1998.
Goldberg, Michelle. "A Grotesque Spectacle in Jerusalem." *New York Times*, May 14, 2018. https://www.nytimes.com/2018/05/14/opinion/jerusalem-embassy-gaza-protests.html.
Goldhagen, Daniel. *Hitler's Willing Executioners: Ordinary Germans and the Holocaust*. New York: Vintage, 1997.
Goldman, Shalom. *God's Sacred Tongue: Hebrew and the American Imagination*. Chapel Hill, NC: University of North Carolina Press, 2004.
———. "The Holy Land Appropriated: The Careers of Selah Merrill, Nineteenth Century Christian Hebraist, Palestine Explorer and US Consul in Jerusalem." *American Jewish History* 85.2 (June 1997) 151–72.
Goldman Sachs. "Sidney Weinberg Leads the Firm for More than Three Decades." https://www.goldmansachs.com/our-firm/history/moments/1930-sidney-weinberg-leads.html.
Goodman, Martin. "A Bad Joke in Josephus." *Journal of Jewish Studies* 36.2 (1985) 195–99.

———. *Josephus's The Jewish War: A Biography*. Princeton: Princeton University Press, 2019.
———. *The Ruling Class of Judea: The Origins of the Jewish Revolt Against Rome, A.D. 66–70*. Cambridge, UK: Cambridge University Press, 1987.
———. *State and Society in Roman Galilee, A.D. 132–212*. London: Vallentine Mitchell, 2000.
Goodwin, Doris Kearns. *The Bully Pulpit: Theodore Roosevelt, William Howard Taft and the Golden Age of Journalism*. New York: Simon & Schuster, 2013.
Gordis, Daniel. *We Stand Divided: The Rift Between American Jews and Israel*. New York: Harper Collins, 2019.
Goren, Haim. *The Loss of a Minute Is Just So Much Loss of Life: Edward Robinson and Eli Smith in the Holy Land*. Turnhout: Brepols, 2020.
Gorenberg, Gershom. *The Accidental Empire*. New York: Times, 2006.
———. *The End of Days: Fundamentalism and the Struggle for the Temple Mount*. Oxford: Oxford University Press, 2000.
Gorton, T. J. *Renaissance Emir: A Druze Warlord at the Court of the Medici*. Northampton, MA: Olive Branch, 2014.
Graetz, Heinrich. *History of the Jews: From the Reign of Hyrcanus (135 B.C.E.) to the Completion of the Babylonian Talmud (500 C.E.)*. Vol. 2 of *History of the Jews*. Philadelphia: Jewish Publication Society of America, 1893.
Green, Arthur. *A Guide to the Zohar*. Stanford, CA: Stanford University Press, 2003.
Greene, Graham. *The Quiet American*. London: Penguin, 1971.
Grose, Peter. *Israel in the Mind of America*. New York: Knopf, 1983.
Grove, Andrew. *Only the Paranoid Survive: How to Exploit the Crisis Points That Challenge Every Country and Career*. New York: Doubleday, 1996.
Habib, Bilal, et al. "The Distribution of Household Income in 2020." Congressional Budget Office, Nov. 2023.
Hacker, Jacob S., and Paul Pierson. *Winner-Take-All Politics*. New York: Simon & Schuster, 2010.
Hagee, John. *Jerusalem Countdown: A Warning to the World*. Lake Mary, FL: FrontLine, 2006.
Halamish, Aviva. *The Exodus Affair: Holocaust Survivors and the Struggle for Palestine*. London: Vallentine Mitchell, 1998.
Halbfinger, David, and Michael Wines. "Is B.D.S. Anti-Semitic?" *New York Times*, July 27, 2019. https://www.nytimes.com/2019/07/27/world/middleeast/bds-israel-boycott-antisemitic.html.
Hansen, Marcus L. "The Problem of the Third Generation Immigrant." *Commentary* 14.5 (1952) 492–500.
Hashmonai, Adi. "Israeli Woman Detained, Blindfolded Over Social Media Posts Criticizing War." *Ha'aretz*, May 31, 2024. https://www.haaretz.com/israel-news/2024-05-31/ty-article/.premium/israeli-woman-detained-blindfolded-over-social-media-posts-criticizing-war/0000018f-cee4-da41-a9cf-dffe8ad90000.
Haung, Laura. *Edge: Turning Adversity into Advantage*. New York: Penguin Random House, 2020.
Hawkins, Richard. *Progressive Politics in the Democratic Party: Samuel Untermyer and the Jewish Anti-Nazi Boycott Campaign*. London: I. B. Tauris, 2022.
Heilemann, John. *Pride Before the Fall: The Trials of Bill Gates and the End of the Microsoft Era*. New York: Harper Collins, 2002.

Henriques, Diana B. *The Wizard of Lies: Bernie Madoff and the Death of Trust*. New York: St. Martin's Griffin, 2012.
Henry, Patrick. "'And I Don't Care What It Is': The Tradition-History of a Civil Religion Proof-Text." *Journal of the American Academy of Religion* 49.1 (Mar. 1981) 35–49. https://doi.org/10.1093/jaarel/XLIX.1.35.
Herberg, Will. *Protestant-Catholic-Jew: An Essay in American Religious Sociology*. Garden City, NY: Doubleday, 1955.
Herzen, Aleksandr. *From the Other Shore*. London: Weidenfeld & Nicolson, 1956.
Herzl, Theodor. *Old-New Land*. Princeton: M. Wiener, 1997.
Heschel, Susannah. *The Aryan Jesus: Christian Theologians and the Bible in Nazi Germany*. Princeton: Princeton University Press, 2008.
Hickman, W. Braddock. *Corporate Bond Quality and Investor Experience*. Princeton: Princeton University Press, 1958.
Higham, John. *Strangers in the Land: Patterns of American Nativism, 1860–1925*. New Brunswick, NJ: Rutgers University Press, 2002.
Hirst, K. Kris. "Did Henry Ford Really Say History Is Bunk?" ThoughtCo, updated Sept. 4, 2019. https://www.thoughtco.com/henry-ford-why-history-is-bunk-172412.
Hixson, Walter. *Israel's Armor: The Israel Lobby and the First Generation of the Palestine Conflict*. Cambridge, UK: Cambridge University Press, 2019.
Hobsbawm, Eric. *Primitive Rebels: Studies in Archaic Forms of Social Movement in the 19th and 20th Centuries*. New York: Norton, 1965.
Hobsbawm, Eric, and Terrence Ranger, eds. *The Invention of Tradition*. Cambridge, UK: Cambridge University Press, 1992.
Hofstadter, Richard. *The Paranoid Style in American Politics and Other Essays*. New York: Knopf Doubleday, 2008.
Hollinger, David. "Communalist and Dispersionist Approaches to American Jewish History in an Increasingly Post-Jewish Era." *American Jewish History* 95.1 (Mar. 2009) 1–32.
Horsley, Richard, and John Hanson. *Bandits, Prophets, and Messiahs*. Harrisburg, PA: Trinity, 1999.
Hubbard, Elbert. *A Message to Garcia and Thirteen Other Things*. East Aurora, NY: Roycrofters, 1901.
———. *Selected Writings of Elbert Hubbard*. East Aurora, NY: Wise & Co., 1922.
Huberman, Hagai. *Hanan Porat: Biographiya* [Hanan Porat: a biography]. Tel Aviv: Yediot Aharanoth, 2013.
Hurlblut, Jesse, and Charles Foster Kent. *Palestine Through the Stereoscope*. New York: Underwood & Underwood, 1914.
Huss, Boaz. *She'alt kiyuma shel ha-mistika ha-yehudit* [The riddle of the existence of Jewish mysticism]. Jerusalem: Hakibbutz Hameuhad, 2016.
Ilan, Shahar. *Haredim be'am* [Haredim LTD]. Jerusalem: Keter, 2000.
I24News. "Defense Minister Gallant: IDF Needs 10,000 More Soldiers." July 1, 2024. https://www.i24news.tv/en/news/israel/society/artc-defense-minister-gallant-idf-needs-10-000-more-recruits.
Jansen, Jan, and Jurgen Osterhammel. *Decolonization: A Short History*. Princeton: Princeton University Press, 2017.
Joinville, Jean. *The Memoirs of the Lord of Joinville*. London: Murray, 1906.
Josephson, Matthew. *The Robber Barons: The Great American Capitalists, 1861–1901*. New York: Harcourt, Brace, 1934.

Josephus. *The Jewish War*. Translated by Martin Hammond. Oxford: Oxford University Press, 2017.

Kaell, Hillary. *Walking Where Jesus Walked: American Christians and the Holy Land Pilgrimage*. New York: New York University Press, 2014.

Kahn, E. J. "Director's Director." *New Yorker*, Sept. 7, 1956. https://www.newyorker.com/magazine/1956/09/08/directors-director.

Kahn, Roger. *The Passionate People: What It Means to Be a Jew in America*. New York: Morrow, 1968.

Kampen, John. *Matthew Within Sectarian Judaism*. New Haven: Yale University Press, 2019.

Keefe, Patrick Radden. *Empire of Pain: The Secret History of the Sackler Family*. New York: Knopf Doubleday, 2021.

Kessler, Oren. *Palestine 1936: The Great Revolt and the Roots of the Middle East Conflict*. Lanham: Rowman & Littlefield, 2023.

Kimmelman, Reuven. "Identifying Jews and Christians in Roman Syria-Palestine." In *Galilee Through the Centuries: Confluence of Cultures*, edited by Eric Meyers, 301–34. Winona Lake, IN: Eisenbrauns, 1999.

Klausner, Israel. *Opozitsyah le-Hertsl* [Opposition to Herzl]. Jerusalem: Ahiever, 1944.

Klausner, Joseph. *Jesus of Nazareth: His Life, Times and Teaching*. London: Allen & Unwin, 1925.

Klein, Naomi. *No Logo*. New York: Picador, 2009.

———. *The Shock Doctrine: The Rise of Disaster Capitalism*. New York: Henry Holt, 2007.

Knell, Yolande. "Huwara: Violence Flares in Flashpoint West Bank Town." BBC, Oct. 6, 2023. https://www.bbc.com/news/world-middle-east-67032419.

Kolsky, Thomas. *Jews Against Zionism: The American Council for Judaism, 1942–1948*. Philadelphia: Temple University Press, 1990.

Konvitz, Milton. *Judaism and the American Idea*. Ithaca, NY: Cornell University Press, 1978.

Kotz, H. David. "Investigation of Failure of the SEC to Uncover Bernard Madoff's Ponzi Scheme." US Securities and Exchange Commission, Case No. OIG-509, Aug. 31, 2009. https://www.sec.gov/files/oig-509-exec-summary.pdf.

Kraft, Barbara. *The Peace Ship: Henry Ford's Pacifist Adventure in the First World War*. New York: Macmillan, 1978.

Kraines, Oscar. *The Impossible Dilemma: Who Is a Jew in the State of Israel?* New York: Bloch, 1976.

Krugman, Paul. *The Return of Depression Economics and the Crisis of 2008*. New York: Norton, 2009.

Kuznets, Simon. "Economic Growth and Income Inequality." *American Economic Review* 45.1 (Mar. 1955) 1–28.

Landau, Noa. "Bibi Netanyahu Is Failing Ever Upward." *New York Times*, Dec. 19, 2024. https://www.nytimes.com/2024/12/19/opinion/netanyahu-israel-power.html.

Lau, Binyamin. *Hakhamim: Tekufat ha-galil* [The wise scholars: the Galilee era]. Tel Aviv: Yedioth Aharonoth, 2008.

Lazarowitz, Arlene. "Different Approaches to a Regional Search for Balance: The Johnson Administration, the State Department and the Middle East, 1964–1967." *Diplomatic History* 32.1 (Jan. 2008) 25–54.

Lederhendler, Eli. *American Jewry: A New History*. Cambridge, UK: Cambridge University Press, 2017.

Le Goff, Jacques. *Saint Louis*. Notre Dame, IN: Notre Dame University Press, 2009.

Levin, Geoffrey. *Our Palestine Question: Israel and American Jewish Dissent, 1948–1978*. New Haven: Yale University Press, 2023.

Levine, Lee. "R. Simeon b. Yohai and the Purification of Tiberias: History and Tradition." *Hebrew Union College Annual* 49 (1978) 143–85.

Lewin, Kurt. *Resolving Social Conflicts: Selected Papers on Group Dynamics*. Washington, DC: American Psychological Association, 1997.

Linfield, Susie. *The Lions' Den: Zionism and the Left from Hannah Arendt to Noam Chomsky*. New Haven: Yale University Press, 2019.

Lipstadt, Deborah. *The Eichmann Trial*. New York: Schocken, 2011.

Lipton, Martin. "Pills, Polls, and Professors Redux." *University of Chicago Law Review* 69 (Summer 2002) 1038–65.

Little, Douglas. "The Making of a Special Relationship: The United States and Israel, 1957–1968." *Journal of Middle East Studies* 25 (1993) 563–85.

Liveblog. "In Record High, 66,000 Haredim Received Exemption from Military Service in the Past Year." *Times of Israel*, Feb. 21, 2024. https://www.timesofisrael.com/liveblog_entry/in-record-high-66000-haredim-received-exemption-from-military-service-in-past-year/.

Lucas, Robert. "Why Doesn't Capital Flow from Rich to Poor Countries?" *American Economic Review* 8.2 (May 1990) 92–96.

Lupfer, Jacob. "100 Years Later, Fosdick's Question, 'Shall the Fundamentalists Win?' Still Echoes." *RNS*, May 20, 2022. https://religionnews.com/2022/05/20/100-years-later-fosdicks-question-shall-the-fundamentalists-win-still-echoes/.

Luz, Ulrich. *The Theology of the Gospel of Matthew*. Cambridge, UK: Cambridge University Press, 2012.

Magid, Jacob. "FM on Kamala Harris: 'Wouldn't Be Able to Name One Overhaul Clause That Bothers Her.'" *Times of Israel*, June 7, 2023. https://www.timesofisrael.com/fm-on-kamala-harris-wouldnt-be-able-to-name-one-overhaul-clause-that-bothers-her/.

Maimon, Solomon. *The Autobiography of Solomon Maimon*. Princeton: Princeton University Press, 2019.

Mann, Brian. "Supreme Court Tosses Out Bankruptcy Plan for Purdue Pharma and Sackler Family." NPR, June 29, 2024. https://www.npr.org/2024/06/27/nx-s1-5021713/supreme-court-tosses-out-bankruptcy-plan-for-purdue-pharma-and-sackler-family.

Markopolos, Harry. *No One Would Listen: A True Financial Thriller*. New York: Wiley, 2011.

Marty, Martin. *Righteous Empire: The Protestant Experience in America*. New York: Dial, 1970.

Marx, Karl. *Capital: A Critique of Political Economy*. London: Penguin, 1981.

Marx, Karl, and Frederick Engels. *Manifesto of the Communist Party*. 1848. Marxists Internet Archive. https://www.marxists.org/archive/marx/works/1848/communist-manifesto/.

Mason, Steve, ed. *Flavius Josephus: Life of Josephus*. Leiden: Brill, 2003.

Mathews, Shailer. *The Social Teachings of Jesus: An Essay in Christian Sociology*. New York: Macmillan, 1897.

BIBLIOGRAPHY

McAlister, Melani. *Epic Encounters: Culture, Media, and U.S. Interests in the Middle East, 1945–2000*. Berkeley, CA: University of California Press, 2001.
McCraw, Thomas. *Prophets of Regulation*. London: Belknap, 1984.
McDougall, James. *A History of Algeria*. Cambridge: Cambridge University Press, 2017.
Mearsheimer, John, and Stephen Walt. *The Israel Lobby and U.S. Foreign Policy*. New York: Farrar, Straus & Giroux, 2007.
Meislish, Shaul. *Hazara b'teshuva* [Returning to religion]. Givatayim: Masada, 1984.
Melamed, Leo. *Escape to the Futures*. New York: Wiley, 1996.
Memmi, Albert. *The Colonizer and the Colonized*. Boston: Beacon, 1991.
———. *The Pillar of Salt*. Boston: Beacon, 1992.
———. *Strangers*. New York: Orion, 1960.
Merrill, Sellah. *Galilee in the Time of Christ*. London: Religious Tract Society, 1885.
Merrill Lynch. "Chief Investment Office: Capital Market Outlook." Sept. 3, 2024. https://mlaem.fs.ml.com/content/dam/ML/ecomm/pdf/CMO_Merrill_09-03-2024_ada.pdf.
Meyers, Eric, ed. *Galilee Through the Centuries: Confluence of Cultures*. Winona Lake, IN: Eisenbrauns, 1999.
Milanovic, Branko. *The Haves and the Have-Nots: A Brief and Idiosyncratic History of Global Inequality*. New York: Basic, 2010.
Miller, Stuart. "The Minnim of Sepphoris Reconsidered." *Harvard Theological Review* 86.4 (Oct. 1993) 377–402.
Mitzman, Arthur. *Sociology and Estrangement*. New Brunswick, NJ: Knopf, 1973.
Monbiot, George, and Peter Hutchison. *Invisible Doctrine: The Secret History of Neoliberalism*. New York: Crown, 2024.
Morgan, David. *The Forge of Vision: A Visual History of Modern Christianity*. Oakland, CA: University of California Press, 2015.
———. *Protestants and Pictures: Religion, Visual Culture, and the Age of American Mass Production*. New York: Oxford University Press, 1999.
Morris, Benny. *Tikun ta'ut: Yehudim ve-aravim be-Erets Yisrael 1936–1956* [Correcting a mistake: Jews and Arabs in Eretz Israel, 1936–1956]. Tel Aviv: Am Oved, 2000.
Mowry, George. *The Era of Theodore Roosevelt and the Birth of America, 1900–1912*. New York: Harper & Row, 1958.
Moynihan, Colin. "Guggenheim Targeted by Protestors for Accepting Money from Family with OxyContin Ties." *New York Times*, Feb. 9, 2019.
Muller, Jerry Z. *Capitalism and the Jews*. Princeton: Princeton University Press, 2010.
Muravchik, John. *Making David into Goliath: How the World Turned Against Israel*. New York: Encounter, 2015.
Myers, Jody. *Kabbalah and the Spiritual Quest: The Kabbalah Centre in America*. Westport, CT: Praeger, 2007.
Netanyahu, Benjamin. *Bibi: My Story*. New York: Threshold, 2022.
Noah, Timothy. *The Great Divergence: America's Growing Inequality Crisis and What We Can Do About It*. New York: Bloomsbury, 2012.
Novick, Peter. *The Holocaust in American Life*. New York: Houghton Mifflin, 1999.
O'Brien, Conor Cruise. *Albert Camus: Of Europe and Africa*. New York: Viking, 1970.
Oppenheimer, Aharon. *Ha-galil be'tekufat ha-Mishnah* [Galilee during the Mishnah period]. Jerusalem: Shazar Center, 1991.
———. *Yehuda Ha-nasi* [Judah Hanasi]. Jerusalem: Shazar Center, 2007.

Oren, Michael. *Power, Faith, and Fantasy: America in the Middle East, 1776 to the Present.* New York: Norton, 2007.

Overman, J. Andrew. *Matthew's Gospel and Formative Judaism: The Social World of the Matthean Community.* Minneapolis: Fortress, 1990.

Paget, James Carleton. "Albert Schweitzer and the Jews." *Harvard Theological Review* 107.3 (2014) 363–98.

Palestinian Media Watch. "Arafat Compares Oslo Accords to Muhammad's Hudaybiyyah Peace Treaty." May 10, 1994. https://palwatch.org/page/8.

Paul VI. *Nostra Aetate.* Delivered on Oct. 28, 1965. Vatican.va. https://www.vatican.va/archive/hist_councils/ii_vatican_council/documents/vat-ii_decl_19651028_nostra-aetate_en.html.

PBS NewsHour. "Israeli Prime Minister Benjamin Netanyahu Addresses the 2023 United Nations General Assembly." Sept. 22, 2023. Video, 25:55. https://www.youtube.com/watch?v=kNH85jgzJoY.

Penslar, Derek. *Shylock's Children: Economics and Jewish Identity in Modern Europe.* Berkeley, CA: University of California Press, 2001.

Peres, Shimon. *The New Middle East.* New York: Holt, 1993.

Pew Research Center. "A Portrait of Jewish Americans." Oct. 1, 2013. https://www.pewresearch.org/religion/2013/10/01/jewish-american-beliefs-attitudes-culture-survey/.

Pietrusza, David. "Ku Klux Klan in the 1920s." Bill of Rights Institute. https://billofrightsinstitute.org/essays/the-ku-klux-klan-in-the-1920s.

Pontecorvo, Gillo. *The Battle of Algiers.* Los Angeles: Allied Artists, 1966.

Prime, William C. *Tent Life in the Holy Land.* New York: Harper & Brothers, 1857.

Prothero, Stephen. *American Jesus: How the Son of God Became a National Icon.* New York: Farrar, Straus & Giroux, 2003.

Radosh, Rob. "A Tale of Two Mezvinskys." Campus Watch, Aug. 10, 2010. https://www.meforum.org/campus-watch/a-tale-of-the-two-mezvinskys.

Rajak, Tessa. *Josephus.* London: Duckworth, 2004.

Rappoport, Jason, et al., eds. *The Sefaria Midrash Rabbah.* Translated by Joshua Schreier. 2022. https://www.sefaria.org/texts/Midrash/Aggadah/Midrash%20Rabbah.

Raz, Avi. *The Bride and the Dowry: Israel, Jordan, and the Palestinians in the Aftermath of the June 1967 War.* New Haven: Yale University Press, 2012.

Reich, Robert. "Academic Freedom Is the Loser When Big Donors Hound University Presidents." *Guardian,* Dec. 12, 2023. https://www.theguardian.com/commentisfree/2023/dec/12/us-college-donors-influence-gaza-israel.

Reinhart, Carmen, and Kenneth Rogoff. *This Time Is Different: Eight Centuries of Financial Folly.* Princeton: Princeton University Press, 2009.

Renan, Ernest. *The Life of Jesus.* London: Watts, 1935.

Risen, Clay. "Peter Grose, Veteran Correspondent, Dies at 88." *New York Times,* Jan. 13, 2023. https://www.nytimes.com/2023/01/13/us/peter-grose-dead.html.

Robins, Walker. "Cultural Zionism and Binationalism Among Liberal American Protestants." *Israel Studies* 23.2 (2018) 142–67.

Robinson, Edward, and Eli Smith. *Biblical Researches in Palestine, Mount Sinai and Arab Petrea in 1838,* vol. 3. London: John Murray, 1841.

Rosenthal, Steven. *Irreconcilable Differences? The Waning of the American Jewish Love Affair with Israel.* Hanover, NH: University Press of New England, 2001.

Routely, Nick. "Ranked: The World's Top 25 Websites in 2023." Visual Capitalist, May 25, 2023. https://www.visualcapitalist.com/ranked-the-worlds-top-25-websites-in-2023/.
Rubin, Robert. *In an Uncertain World: Tough Choices from Wall Street to Washington.* New York: Random House, 2003.
Rubinstein, Danny. *Mi la-H. elai: Gush emunim* [On the Lord's side: Gush Emunim]. Tel Aviv: Hakibbutz Hameuchad, 1982.
Safrai, Shmuel. "The Relations Between the Roman Army and the Jews of Eretz Yisrael After the Destruction of the Second Temple." In *Roman Frontier Studies*, edited by Shimon Applebaum, 224–30. Tel Aviv: Student's Organization of Tel Aviv University, 1971.
Said, Edward. *Orientalism*. London: Penguin, 1995.
Saldarini, Anthony. *Matthew's Christian-Jewish Community.* Chicago: University of Chicago Press, 1994.
Sales, Ben. "Bernie Madoff, Whose Ponzi Scheme Devastated the Jewish World, Dies in Prison at 82." *Jewish Telegraphic Agency*, Apr. 14, 2021.
Sand, Shlomo. *The Invention of the Jewish People.* New York: Verso, 2020.
Sanders, Bernie. "Episode 8: Naomi Klein." In *Bernie: The Podcast*. Uploaded May 29, 2024. Video, 47:47. https://www.youtube.com/watch?v=_3-CSRTVwys&t.
Sarna, Jonathan. *Jacksonian Jew: The Two Worlds of Mordecai Noah.* New York: Holmes & Meier, 1980.
Sartre, Jean-Paul. "A Plea for Intellectuals." In Sartre, *Between Existentialism and Marxism*, 228–85. New York: Pantheon, 1974.
———. Preface to *The Wretched of the Earth*, by Frantz Fanon, iii–lxiii. New York: Grove, 2004.
Schafer, Peter, et al. *Toledot Yeshu ("The Life Story of Jesus") Revisited.* Tubingen: Mohr Siebeck, 2011.
Schaff, Philip. *Through Bible Lands*. London: Henderson, Bait & Fenton, 1878.
Schiffman, Lawrene. "Was There a Galilean Halakah?" In *The Galilee in Late Antiquity*, edited by Lee Levine, 143–55. Cambridge, MA: Harvard University Press, 1992.
Schwain, Kristin. *Signs of Grace: Religion and American Art in the Gilded Age.* Ithaca, NY: Cornell University Press, 2008.
Schwartz, Seth. *Imperialism and Jewish Society: 200 B.C.E. to 640 C.E.* Princeton: Princeton University Press, 2001.
Schweitzer, Albert. *The Quest of the Historical Jesus: A Critical Study of Its Progress from Reimarus to Wrede.* London: A & C Black, 1910.
Senor, Dan, and Saul Singer. *Start-Up Nation: The Story of Israel's Economic Miracle.* New York: Grand Central, 2011.
Shafat, Gershon. *Gush Emunim*. Bet-El: Sifriyat Bet-El, 1994.
Shamir, Milette. "Encounters of a Third Kind: Mark Twain, William C. Prime and American Holy Land Narratives." *Issues in Contemporary Jewish History* 6 (2016) 33–51.
Shatz, Adam. *The Rebel's Clinic: The Revolutionary Lives of Frantz Fanon.* New York: Farrar, Straus & Giroux, 2024.
Shay, Felix. *Elbert Hubbard of East Aurora.* New York: Wise & Co., 1926.
Sheleg, Yair. *Hahut ha-meshulash: Kitzur toldot hatziyonut hadatit* [Triple thread: a brief history of religious Zionism]. Hevel Modi'in: Kinneretz, Dvir, 2024.

Silk, Mark. "Notes on the Judeo-Christian Tradition in America." *American Quarterly* 36.1 (Spring 1984) 65–85.

Silver, M. M. *Bi-shelihut ha-Ma'arav* [In the service of the West]. Tel Aviv: Hakibbutz Hameuchad, 2014.

———. *The History of Galilee, 1538–1949*. Lanham, MD: Lexington, 2022.

———. *The History of Galilee, 47 BCE to 1260 CE*. Lanham, MD: Lexington, 2021.

———. *Louis Marshall and the Rise of Jewish Ethnicity in America*. Syracuse, NY: Syracuse University Press, 2013.

———. *Our Exodus: Leon Uris and the Americanization of Israel's Founding Story*. Detroit, MI: Wayne State University Press, 2010.

———. *Zionism and the Melting Pot*. Tuscaloosa, AL: University of Alabama Press, 2020.

Smith, Roy C. *The Money Wars: The Rise and Fall of the Great Buyout Boom of the 1980s*. New York: Truman Talley, 1990.

Sombart, Werner. *The Jews and Modern Capitalism*. New Brunswick, NJ: Transaction, 1982.

Sorkin, Andrew Ross. *Too Big to Fail*. London: Penguin, 2011.

Stephens, Brett. "Naftali Bennett's Exit Interview." *New York Times*, June 21, 2022. https://www.nytimes.com/2022/06/21/opinion/naftali-bennetts-exit-interview.html.

Stewart, James B. *Den of Thieves*. New York: Simon & Schuster, 2010.

Stidham Rogers, Stephanie. *Inventing the Holy Land: American Protestant Pilgrimage to Palestine, 1865–1941*. Lanham, MD: Lexington, 2011.

Strange, James. "First Century Galilee from Archaeology and from the Texts." In *Archaeology and the Galilee: Texts and Contexts in the Graeco-Roman and Byzantine Periods*, edited by Douglas Edwards and C. Thomas McCollough, 39–49. Atlanta, GA: Scholars, 1997.

Straus, Oscar. *The Origin of the Republican Form of Government in the United States of America*. New York: Putnam, 1885.

Suskind, Ron. *Confidence Men: Wall Street, Washington, and the Education of a President*. New York: Harper Collins, 2012.

Sutton, Matthew Avery. *American Apocalypse: A History of Modern Evangelicalism*. Cambridge, MA: Harvard University Press, 2014.

Tarbell, Ida. *The History of the Standard Oil Company*. New York: Norton, 1966.

Taylor, Joan. *Christians and the Holy Places: The Myth of Jewish-Christian Origins*. Oxford: Clarendon, 1993.

Teveth, Shabtai. *The Cursed Blessing: The Story of Israel's Occupation of the West Bank*. New York: Random House, 1970.

Thomson, William M. *The Land and the Book*. London: T. Nelson & Sons, 1865.

Times of Israel. "Ben-Gvir Hammered by President, Opposition Over Tweet." May 9, 2024. https://www.timesofisrael.com/ben-gvir-hammered-by-president-opposition-over-hamas/.

———. "Ben Gvir Responds to Bennett: Fine, I'll Take Down Baruch Goldstein's Picture." Jan. 15, 2020. https://www.timesofisrael.com/liveblog_entry/ben-gvir-responds-to-bennett-fine-ill-take-down-baruch-goldsteins-picture/.

———. "Israel Revises Death Toll from Oct. 7 Hamas Assault, Dropping It from 1,400 to 1,200." Nov. 11, 2023. https://www.timesofisrael.com/israel-revises-death-toll-from-oct-7-hamas-assault-dropping-it-from-1400-to-1200/.

Tishby, Noa. *Israel: A Simple Guide to the Most Misunderstood Country on Earth.* New York: Simon & Schuster, 2021.
Troy, Gil. *Moynihan's Moment: America's Fight Against Zionism as Racism.* New York: Oxford University Press, 2013.
Turchin, Peter. *Elites, Counter-Elites, and the Path of Political Disintegration.* New York: Penguin, 2023.
Twain, Mark. *The Innocents Abroad or the New Pilgrims' Progress.* Hartford, CT: American Publishing Co., 1869.
Uberti, David. "Americans Have More Investment Income Than Ever Before." *Wall Street Journal,* June 5, 2024. https://www.wsj.com/economy/americans-have-more-investment-income-than-ever-before-84b7a6c6.
Urofsky, Melvin. *Louis D. Brandeis: A Life.* New York: Pantheon, 2009.
Van Dyke, Henry. *Out-of-Doors in the Holy Land.* New York: Scribner's Sons, 1908.
Veblen, Thorstein. *The Theory of the Leisure Class.* New Brunswick, NJ: Transaction, 1992.
Vise, David, and Steve Coll. *Eagle on the Street.* New York: Scribner's Sons, 1991.
Vogel, Lester. *To See a Promised Land: Americans in the Holy Land in the Nineteenth Century.* University Park, PA: Pennsylvania State University Press, 1993.
Watts, Steven. *The People's Tycoon: Henry Ford and the American Century.* New York: Vintage, 2005.
Weber, Max. *The Protestant Ethic and the Spirit of Capitalism.* London: Routledge Classics, 2001.
Weinberg, Steve. *Taking On the Trust: The Epic Battle of Ida Tarbell and John D. Rockefeller.* New York: Norton, 2008.
Weiss, Anthony. "AJ Congress Crippled by Madoff Scandal." *Forward,* Jan. 8, 2009. https://forward.com/news/14905/ajcongress-crippled-by-madoff-scandal-03132/.
Weiss, Johannes. *Jesus' Proclamation of the Kingdom of God.* Philadelphia: Fortress, 1971.
Wertheimer, Jack. "Breaking the Taboo: Critics of Israel and the American Jewish Establishment." In *Envisioning Israel: The Changing Ideals and Images of North American Jews,* edited by Allon Gal, 397–419. Detroit: Wayne State University Press, 1996.
Wilkinson, Alissa. "The *Left Behind* Series Was Just the Latest Way America Prepared for the Rapture." *Washington Post,* July 13, 2016. https://www.washingtonpost.com/news/act-four/wp/2016/07/13/the-left-behind-series-was-just-the-latest-way-america-prepared-for-the-rapture/.
Wilsey, John. *God's Cold Warrior: The Life and Faith of John Foster Dulles.* Grand Rapids: Eerdmans, 2021.
Wilson, John Francis. *Caesarea Philippi: Banias, the Lost City of Pan.* London: I. B. Tauris, 2004.
Woodward, Alex. "Fake News: A Guide to Trump's Favorite Phrase." *Independent,* Oct. 2, 2020. https://www.independent.co.uk/news/world/americas/us-election/trump-fake-news-counter-history-b732873.html.
Wrede, William. *The Messianic Secret.* Cambridge, UK: James Clarke, 1971.
Wu, Tim. *The Curse of Bigness: Antitrust in the New Gilded Age.* New York: Columbia Global Reports, 2018.
Yaron, Oded. "150,000 Missiles Aimed at Israel: How Far Does Hezbollah's Deadly Arsenal Reach?" *Ha'aretz,* Oct. 23, 2023. https://www.haaretz.com/

israel-news/security-aviation/2023-10-23/ty-article-magazine/150-000-rockets-and-missiles-the-weapons-israel-would-encounter-in-a-war-with-hezbollah/0000018b-573d-d2b2-addf-777df6210000.

Zeitlin, Solomon. "Who Were the Galileans? New Light on Josephus' Activities in Galilee." *Jewish Quarterly Review* 64.3 (Jan. 1974) 189–203.

Zertal, Ideth, and Akiva Eldar. *Lords of the Land: The War over Israel's Settlements in the Occupied Territories, 1967–2007.* New York: Nation, 2007.

Index

Abbas, Mahmoud, 271–272
Abraham Accords, 100, 260
Acre (Akko), 139–140, 143–144, 165, 286
Adenauer, Konrad, 248
Adorno, Theodor, 240
Adelson, Sheldon, 100, 297
Afghanistan, 181, 219
Agudath Yisrael Party, 202
AIPAC (American Israel Public Affairs Committee), 20, 98, 100, 156, 206, 290–291, 296, 298
Aish Hatorah (Yeshiva), 199
Akiva (Rabbi), 241
Algeria, 232–234, 238, 242–246, 249–250, 253, 256–257
Al-Husseini, Haj Amin (Mufti of Jerusalem), 224
Allen, Woody, 67, 229
Allende, Salvador, 63
Al-Qaeda, 181, 271
Amal, 147
American Dream, 22, 46, 66, 86, 95, 97, 108, 113, 154, 193, 298
American Jewish Congress, 91–92
American Jewish Historical Society, 157
American University of Beirut, 146, 165
   Syrian Protestant College, 165
Amsterdam, 29
Ansari, Aziz, 194
Anti-Defamation League, 90
Anti-Semitism, 7, 18, 21, 27–28, 30–31, 34, 36, 55, 64–68, 72–73, 90–91, 93–96, 101, 111–112, 115, 129, 134, 158, 177, 180, 196, 219, 225, 232, 240, 264, 274, 301

modern variant, 64, 128, 273–274
money-related, 22, 67, 69, 74, 90, 99
regarding Israel, 65, 102, 151, 218, 220, 222, 224, 231, 274, 287, 295, 302–303
Antonius, George, 235–236
Arafat, Yasser, 149–150, 229, 270–271, 273, 277, 291
   See Also PLO
Arbitrage, 21, 80–81, 85, 87
Arendt, Hannah, 225, 251
Ariel University, 294, 300–301
   See Also West Bank
Ariel, Yaakov, 160, 198
Armstrong, Lance, 114, 182
Arnold, Benedict, 179
Aslan, Reza, 9, 11, 133
Association of Jewish Studies, 301
Athens, 106–107, 202
Augustus, 119, 123
Auschwitz, 238
Aviad, Janet, 199
Aviam, Mordechai, 138
Ayn Jalut, 144
   See Also Mongols

Backward glance, 25, 101
Bagatti, Bellarmino, 10
Balfour Declaration, 169
Barak, Ehud, 270, 272, 298
Bar-Ilan University, 271, 294
Bar Kokhba Revolt, 138, 141, 2-7-208, 210–211, 216, 241, 283–284
Barton, Bruce Fairchild, 11–13
   The Man Nobody Knows, 11
Baruch, Bernard, 71
Battle of Algiers (Movie), 232–233

321

INDEX

Bear Stearns, 43, 81
Beatles, 4, 26
  See also Harrison, George
Becker, Carl, 157
Beecher, Henry Ward, xv, 170–171, 174, 176
Be'eri (Kibbutz), 261, 277
Begin, Menachem, 149–151, 205, 226, 229, 279
Beinart, Peter, 300
Beirut, 38, 150–152, 164–165, 228
Bekka Valley, 173
Ben Barak, Rami, 282
Ben-Gurion, David, 151, 155, 208, 227, 234–235, 276, 279
Ben-Gvir, Itamar, 148, 277, 286
Ben Hur See Wallace, Lew
Benjamin, Walter, 238
Bennett, Naftali, 281–282
Ben Simon, Eleazar, 215, 287
  See Also Rashbi
Berkowitz, Michael, 83, 87, 90–91
Bernard of Clairvaux, 140
Bernstein, Carl, 114
Bethlehem, 119–120
Bethsaida, 120, 123
Biden, Joe, 112, 117, 155, 260–261, 286, 297, 299–300
Black, Jack, 91
Blackstone, William, 155, 177
Bnei Brak, 200
Boesky, Ivan, 20–22, 74, 78, 80–82, 87, 89, 94, 97, 298,
  and Wall Street film, 20–21, 82
Bonds, Barry, 114
Bordeaux Pilgrim, 138
Boussouf, Abdelhafid, 243
Bouteflika, Abdelaziz, 232
BDS (Boycott, Divestment, Sanctions), 117, 270, 273–274, 301
Brandeis, Louis, 23–24, 26–28, 67–68, 74, 85, 186–188, 298–299
  Other People's Money (book), 24, 28, 68, 187–188
Brandeis University, 67
Breaking the Silence (Organization)
Breira (Organization), 231
Brexit, 263, 271

Brooklyn, 66, 69, 79, 201
Brown, John, xv
Bultmann, Rudolph, 130
Burckhardt, Ludwig, 166
Burke, Edmund, 155
Burnett, Carol, 235
Bush, George W., 187, 271
Bushnell, Horace, xv

Caesarea Philippi (Banias), 119, 123–124, 138, 167, 171
Calling of Saint Matthew (painting), 3, 99
Calvinism, 31–33, 35, 171, 174, 176
  See also Caravaggio
Camp David Summit (2000), 270, 291
Camus, Albert, 249–250, 255–259
  See Also: Fanon, Frantz, Memmi, Albert
Canaanite Woman, 121
Capernaum, 2–6, 9–12, 22, 26, 99, 119–120, 122–123, 138, 171
Caravaggio, 3–5, 99
Carenen, Caitlin, 177
Carmel, Moshe, 145
Carnegie, Andrew, 170, 185
Carroll, David, 257
Carter, Jimmy, 117, 149, 153, 226
Case, Shirley Jackson, 7–8
Césaire, Aimé, 248
Chabad, 199, 201
Chafets, Zev, 203
Chamberlain, Houston Stewart, 6
Chancey, Mark, 6–7
Chicago Tribune, 178–180
Chin, Denny, 92
Chomsky, Noam, 273
Churchill, Winston, 116, 225
CIA (Central Intelligence Agency), 52, 63
Clarke, Howard, 15
Clayton Antitrust Act, 186
Clinton, Bill, 44, 48, 85, 117, 155, 182, 270–271
Clinton, Chelsea, 112
Clinton, Hillary, 112
CNN, 55, 109
Cohen, Eli, 286

322

INDEX

Cohn, Roy, 94
Congress (US), 91, 112, 116, 155, 193
Congressional Budget Office, 190
Conservative Judaism, 28, 153, 158, 229
Costner, Kevin, 192
Council on Foreign Relations, 153
Crimean War, 162
Crossan, John Dominic, 4
Cohen, Hermann, 36
Cohn, Haim, 126
Cold War, 37, 42, 50, 52–54, 66, 94, 110–111, 148, 150, 152, 181, 192, 225, 239, 257, 269
Columbia University, 212, 265
Constantine, 125–126, 138, 213, 286
Council of Nicaea, 125
Cronkite, Walter, 114
Crucifixion, xiii, 2, 10, 25, 64–65, 95, 125–126, 131–132, 138
Crusades, 5, 111, 139–140, 142–144, 208

Daniels, George H., 57
Darwinism, 41, 64, 175
Davis, Moshe, 153, 155–161, 163
Dayan, Moshe, 226–227
Dead Sea, 134, 184
De Beauvoir, Simone, 245
Decapolis, 121–122
Deconstructionism, 18
De Gaulle, Charles, 233–234
De Leon, Moses, 215
DeMille, Cecil B., 284
Depression (1930s), 14, 47–48, 65, 68, 108, 178, 184
Democratic Party, x, 27, 66, 96, 186, 274, 300
Deri, Aryeh, 280
Deutscher, Isaac, 36–37
Dickens, Charles, 59, 93
Dimona, 234
Dodge, Horace, 72
Dodge, John, 72
Donovan, William, 72
Dreyfus Affair, 93
Druze, 144
Dubnow, Simon, 36

Dulles, John Foster, 235
Dyke, Henry van, 168–169

Earthly Footsteps of the Man of Galilee, 174–175
Eden, Anthony, 234
Efrat, 300
 See Also West Bank
Egypt, 139, 149, 226, 228, 234, 259, 291, 300
Eichmann Trial, 63, 223, 225, 239, 244, 248
Eiminder, Sandor, 239
Eisenhower, Dwight, 111, 117, 234–235
Elon Moreh, 228
 See Also West Bank
Emhoff, Doug, 112
 See Also Harris, Kamala
Epstein, Jeffrey, 94
EPZ (Export Processing Zone), 58–60
 See also: Naomi Klein
Eren, Colleen, 83–84
Erez Crossing, 289
Eshkol, Levi, 151
Essenes, 135, 143
Evangelicalism, xi, 65, 96, 106–107, 116, 158, 160, 175–178, 197–198, 200, 202–206, 274–276, 296–297

Facebook, 114, 271
Fakhr al-Din, 144
Fanon, Frantz, 233, 236, 249–250, 269, 284
 and Camus, 257–258
 and Memmi, 251–255, 280, 283, 291
 Biography of, 239–240
 Wretched of the Earth, 237, 241–249, 255
Fatah, 149
 See Also PLO
Federal Trade Commission, 186
Ferguson, Fergus, 140
Ferguson, Niall, 223
Festinger, Leon, 17

INDEX

Fifth Gospel, 107, 162–175, 177–178, 192, 204
Fitzgerald, F. Scott, 113
FLN (National Liberation Front), 232–236, 240–246, 248, 250–251, 255–257, 280
Flusser, David, 131
Ford, Henry, 67–68, 72–73, 178–179, 182
  anti-Semitism and, 28, 66–67, 72–73, 180, 274
  history is bunk, 178–180
Ford, Henry II, 73
Ford Motor, 21, 67–69, 72–73, 77
  See also Sidney Weinberg
Foreign Affairs, 153
Fosdick, Harry Emerson, 169, 170, 175
Foxman, Abe, 90–91
France, 42, 93, 139, 209
  and Algeria, 232–234, 236, 239, 245–246, 263, 277
Franciscans, 10, 138, 140
Franklin, Benjamin, 32, 154, 184
  See also Weber, Max
Friedman, Milton, 46–47, 52, 63,
Friedman, Thomas, 37–56, 59, 62–63
  and economic inequality, 45–48
  and Golden Straightjacket, 39, 42, 46, 49–51, 55–56, 59, 63
  Jewish aspects, 53, 55–56
  and *Lexus and Olive Tree*, 39, 41, 49–52, 54
Freyne, Sean, 4
Fredriksen, Paula, 132
Fukuyama, Francis, 47, 53
Fuller, Charles, 178

Gadot, Gal, 156
Galilee, xv, 10, 105–107, 127–128, 131–133, 149, 183, 203, 257
  Fifth Gospel, 162–175
  Gaza War Period, 146–148, 264, 267–268
  History of, 133–145
  Jesus and Early Christianity, 2–9, 12, 16, 25, 65, 118–125

Jews and Second Temple Period, 125, 129–130, 209–217, 283–284
Galilee of the Gentiles, 6–8
Gates, Bill, 188–189
Gaza Strip, x, xiii, 99, 118, 145–147, 149, 156, 208, 218–219, 221, 222, 226, 228, 230, 235, 259, 261, 264–268, 270, 272–273, 276, 278–283, 288–291, 295–297, 300–302
Gaza War, x, xi–xii, 10, 21, 65, 96, 98, 101, 117, 145–146, 152, 162, 202, 218–220, 235, 238, 255, 259, 263–265, 267–269, 273, 277, 279–283, 286, 289–290, 292–294, 296, 298–299, 301–302
Geiger, Abraham, 128–130
Gemayel, Bashir, 149
Gilded Age, 23, 85, 162–163, 168–171, 173–175, 185, 298
Gladwell, Malcolm, 70
Golan Heights, 123, 138, 199, 260
Goldhagen, Daniel, 65
Goldman Sachs, 5, 21, 24, 43, 68–71, 73, 75, 79, 85
Goldman, Shalom, 154
Goldstein, Baruch, 277
Goldstein, Mordecai, 199
Goodman, Martin, 135, 212–213, 285
Goodman, Myron, 86
  See Also OPM
Gordis, Daniel, 161
Gorenberg, Gershon, 198
Graetz, Heinrich, 36, 129–130
Grant, Ulysses S., 162
Green, Arthur, 215
Greene, Graham, 113
Grose, Peter, 153–161, 163
Gush Emunim, 151, 226–227, 296, 299
Gush Etzion, 227
Guy of Lusignan, 139

Ha'am Ahad, 276
Hadid, Gigi, 156
Hadrian (Emperor), 217, 284
Hagee, John, 203–204, 276, 297
Haley, Alex, 196

INDEX

Hamas, x, xii, 10, 99, 117, 145–147, 204, 218–219, 221–222, 230–231, 236, 256, 259–265, 267, 269–273, 275, 277–283, 286–292, 295, 297
Hansen, Marcus Lee, 195
  Hansen's Law, 196, 199, 201
Hardalim (Orthodox Jewish group), 202
Harrison, Benjamin, 177
Harper's Illuminated Bible, 172
Haung, Laura, 70
Harper's Weekly, 24
Harris, Kamala, 109, 112, 286
Harrison, George, 4, 26
See also Beatles
Harvard University, 41, 44, 57, 70, 75, 79, 274
Hasbara, 150, 158–160, 205, 271, 276–277
  First Lebanon War, 151–152
  Gaza War, 265–266, 269, 290–291
Hasidism, 2, 36, 293–294
Haskalah (Jewish Enlightenment Movement), 93, 209, 294
Hattin, 140
  Battle, 139, 144
Hayek, F.A., 46–47, 52,
Hebrew University of Jerusalem, 131–133, 142, 153, 158
Hebron, 204, 271, 277
Hedge funds, 40, 44–45, 50, 55, 63, 88
Hendrix, Jimi, 200
Henriques, Diana, 87–88, 92
Heraclius, 138–139
Herberg, Will, 115, 153
  Protestant-Catholic-Jew, 115
Herod, 8, 9, 123, 215, 284
Herod Antipas, 9, 215
Herzen, Alexander, 243–244
Herzl, Theodor, 202, 210, 227, 276
Hezbollah, x, xiv, 10, 124, 146–149, 222, 267, 270, 275, 279, 288, 291–292
Hickman, W. Braddock, 75
Higham, John, 176
Hillula, 141–142, 215
  See Also: Rashbi, Meron

Hitler, Adolf, 65, 178, 275, 277
Hobsbawm, Eric, 8, 131
Hofstadter, Richard, 187
Hollinger, David, 161
Holocaust, xiii, 5, 18, 20–21, 28, 64–65, 92–93, 98, 100–102, 105, 107, 111, 126, 130–132, 134, 142–143, 148, 156, 178, 184, 196, 200, 202, 208, 232, 238–240-248, 254–255, 259, 272
  and Economics, 21, 66, 68, 78, 95
  and Israel, xii, 117, 220, 222–224, 230, 236, 274, 282, 292
  and scholars, 7, 244–245, 293–295
Hofstra University, 83
Horkheimer, Max, 240
Horsley, Richard, 8–9
House of Shammai, 216
Houthis, 275
Hubbard, Elbert, 56–58, 60–62
  and a "Message to Garcia," 56–58
Huleh Valley, 166
Huwara, 278
  See Also West Bank
Hussein (King of Jordan), 277
Hutchison, Peter, 47

IDF (Israel Defense Forces), 86, 147–148, 151–152, 199, 205, 229, 235, 297, 301
  and Gaza War, 208, 218, 259, 261, 264, 266, 268–269, 272, 276, 278–282, 294
IMF (International Monetary Fund), 41, 44, 63
Immigration and Nationality Act (1965), 114
Inquisition, 5, 29, 111, 141, 208, 221
International Court of Justice (ICJ), 219, 282–283
International Criminal Court (ICC), 116
Intifada (First, from 1987), 151–152, 159, 183, 224, 228–231, 173, 276, 297
  Second (from 2000), 65, 273, 289, 298

INDEX

Iran, x, 52, 203, 222, 248, 260, 288, 296, 300
Islamic Brotherhood, 300

Jackson, Thomas Penfield, 189
Jazz Singer, 194
Jefferson, Thomas, 184
Jerusalem, 38, 64, 100, 105–106, 126, 131–132, 134, 138–141, 143–145, 149, 155, 159–160, 162, 168, 171–172, 175, 177, 183, 198–199, 20, 203–204, 209, 223–224, 230, 235, 239, 259–260, 266, 297
  in Second Temple period, 6, 8, 22, 105, 119–120, 124, 129–130, 132–133, 168, 207, 211–212, 214–215, 261, 284–285
Jesus, 5–8, 18, 98, 101, 105–107, 116, 133
  Backward Glance, 25–26
  Capernaum and, 2–3, 9–11
  Corporate Style, 11–14
  Eschatological Interpretation, 14–17
  Fifth Gospel and, 162–175
  Galilee Events and, 119–125
  Historical Jesus, 26
  Jews Relate to, 125–132, 162, 213
  Matthew and, 2,3
  Money and, 4, 22–23, 29, 35, 55
  Sermon on the Mount, 137, 140
Jewish Theological Seminary, 28
John (Gospel of), 132, 175
John of Gischala, 285
Joinville, Jean, 139
Jordan (country), 227, 277
Jordan River, 3, 121, 123, 173
Jose ben Halafta, 216–217, 222, 242, 249, 256, 283–284, 286–287
Joseph (Saint), 119
Joseph, Frederick, 75
Josephus, 8, 124, 133–137, 141, 147, 284–286
  Jewish War, 134–136, 285
  Life, 136
  in Galilee, 8, 134, 286
Jotapata (Yodfat), 134, 136
J Street (Organization), 218, 231

Judah bar Ilai, 210, 214–217, 236, 242, 256, 283–287
Judah ben Bava, 217
Judah Hanasi, 141, 210–211, 217
Judeo-Christian Civilization, xiv, 18, 105–107, 110–113, 115, 118–119, 121, 124–125, 128, 130, 133, 137–138, 140, 142–143, 145, 148, 152–156, 159, 161–162, 183–184, 197, 198, 200, 202, 204–206, 275
Judas Iscariot, 97, 120

Kabbalah, 36, 142–143, 215–216
  Lurianic, 41
  in Safed, 141–144
Kafka, Franz, 259
Kahane, Meir, 277
Kahn, E.J., 71
Kahn, Roger, 66–68
Karmiel, 267
Keynes, John Maynard, 51
  Keynesian economics, 45
King David Hotel, 223
King, Martin Luther, 169, 204
Kiryat Shmona, 149
Kissinger, Henry, 299
Klausner, Joseph, 131–133
Klein, Naomi, x, 37–38, 44, 47, 50–51, 58–63, 221
  No Logo, 58–62
  Shock Doctrine, 44, 47, 62–63
Knesset, 229, 262–263, 268, 277, 282
Know Nothing Party, 171
Konvitz, Milton, 157
Kook, Abraham Isaac, 279
Kook, Zvi Yehuda, 279
Krugman, Paul, 44–45
Ku Klux Klan (KKK), x, 176
Kuznets, Simon, 47

Labor Party (Israel) 151, 230, 298
Lake Tahoe, 173
Lanzmann, Claude, 240
Lapid, Yair, 282
Last Supper, 120, 123
LBOs (Leveraged Buyouts), 21, 74, 77–80, 89, 298

INDEX

Lebanon, x, xiv, 10, 121–124, 146–147, 149–150, 164, 166, 173, 222, 267, 288
   Lebanon War (1982), 146–150, 152–153, 159, 205, 228–229, 272, 276
Left Behind (novels), 203
Le Goff, Jacques, 139–140
Lehman Brothers, 21, 27, 43
   Kuhn, Loeb, 27
Letelier, Orlando, 63
Levine, Dennis, 22
Lewin, Kurt, 220
Lewinsky, Monica, 114
Levy, Gus, 85
Likud Party, xi, 20, 54, 149–151, 177, 198, 205, 221, 226–227, 230, 276, 279, 282, 292, 297
Lincoln, Abraham, 162
Lindsey, Hal, 203
Lipstadt, Deborah, 239
Lipton, Martin, 78
London, 29, 231–232
London School of Economics, 44
London Times, 92
Lord's Prayer, 15, 120
Los Angeles, 54, 105, 178
Louis IX (King, Saint), 139
Lucas, Robert, 45
Luke (Gospel of), 2, 101, 119, 122
Lumumba, Patrice, 245
Luria, Isaac, *see Kabbalah*
Luz Ulrich, 25

Madoff, Bernard, 21, 74, 76, 80, 82–84, 86–95, 97
   and anti-Semitism, 74, 85, 90–94
   BLMIS (Bernard L. Madoff Investment Securities), 83, 87–89
   Ponzi fraud, 21, 76, 87, 89, 96
Madoff, Peter, 83
Madoff, Ruth Alpern, 83
Maher, Jim, 79
Maimon, Salomon, 254–255
Make America Great Again (MAGA), x–xi, xiv, 27, 97, 109, 112, 176, 190, 299
Malhotra, Neil, 93
Manara (Kibbutz), 146–147

Manhattan Project, 111
   See Also Oppenheimer, Robert
Margalit, Yoltam, 93
Margolin, Deb, 92
Mark (Apostle), 1
Mark (Gospel of), 2, 4, 6, 101
Markopolos, Harry, 88
Maronites, 149–150
Martinique, 239, 245, 248
Marxism, 5, 31,115, 240, 242–243, 250–251, 257–258
Marx, Karl, 41, 51, 53, 63, 243
Mary (Mother of Jesus), 119
Masada, 124, 134, 284–285
Matthew (Apostle), xiii, 1–5, 12, 22, 26, 51, 55
Matthew (Gospel of), 2–5, 7, 15–16, 18, 20, 22, 24–25, 37, 55, 98, 101, 119, 122–123, 125, 140, 211
Mathews, Shailer, 9, 177
McCarthy, Joseph, 94
McClure's, 185
McDonald's, 42, 54
McGwire, Mark, 182
McKinley, William, 56
Mearsheimer, John, 155–156, 275
Megiddo, 283–284
Meir (rabbi, Tanna), 210, 216–217
Meir, Golda, 151
Meir, John, 130, 213
Melamed, Leo, 78
Memmi, Albert, 242, 249, 251, 269, 280, 283, 291
   and Camus, 250, 256
   Biography, 250
   Colonizer and Colonized, 251–256
Merrill Lynch, 190
Merrill, Selah, 134
Merkaz Harav (Yeshiva), 126
Merkin, Ezra, 92
Meron, 141–142, 215–216
Mezvinsky, Marc, 112
Milanovic, Branco, 45, 50
Milken, Lowell, 77
Milken, Michael, 21–22, 75–82, 87, 89, 94, 97, 298
   and Drexel Burnham Lambert, 21, 75–76, 82
   junk bonds, 75–76

INDEX

Miller, William, 17
  Millerism, 17
Mills, C. Wright, 61
Mishnah, 141, 210, 212, 216
  See Also Talmud
Mohammad, Mahathir, 43
Monbiot, George, 46, 52
Mongols, 144
Monroe Doctrine, 179
Montfort (Castle), 140
Moody Monthly, 176
Morgan, David, 172
Morgan, J.P., 24, 26, 28, 68, 70–71
Morris, Benny, 145
Morocco, 228, 253
Morris, William, 57
Moses, 123, 128, 154, 184
Mossad, 156, 282
Mount of Beatitudes, 140
Moynihan, Daniel Patrick, 225
Muckrakers, 23–24, 185, 188,
Muller, Jerry, 33
Myerson, Bess, 111–112

NAACP, 201
Nakba (Palestinian 1948 Catastrophe), 144–145, 257
Napoleon, 144, 167, 178
NASDAQ (National Association of Securities Dealers Automated Quotations), 87
Nasser, Gamal Abdel, 225, 234
Nathanson, Roby, 205
Nazareth, 3, 6–7, 9, 103, 106–107, 119–120, 130–131, 138, 213,
  and Fifth Gospel, 168–170
Nazism, x, 5–6, 30, 64, 223–225, 231–232, 235, 239, 245, 259, 282
Netanyahu, Benjamin (Bibi), 49, 116, 146, 205, 220, 230, 260, 271–272, 280–281, 286, 292
  and Big Donors, 100, 298
  and Evangelicals, 203–204
  and Gaza War, 99, 204, 218, 262, 282, 301
  and Israeli politics, xi, 145, 150, 260, 263–264, 277, 279, 289

and West Bank settlements, 117, 278, 283, 297, 299
Netanyahu, Sara, 148
Netflix, 91, 156
Neusner, Jacob, 135
New Deal, 52, 66, 97
  See also Roosevelt, Franklin
New Testament, 2–4, 8, 13, 15–16, 37, 95, 101, 106, 112, 119, 122–125, 128, 130–132, 136–137, 155, 162–165, 168–170, 172, 175, 211, 213, 274,
New York City, xii, 1, 27, 86, 92, 189, 199
New Yorker, 69–71, 85
New York State, 17, 24, 57, 294
New York Times, 38–39, 44, 49, 86–87, 153, 203, 229
Nir Oz (Kibbutz), 261, 277
Nixon, Richard, 83, 150, 182
Noah, Mordecai, 155, 158
Noah, Timothy, 46–48, 50
North Korea, 52, 274
Novick, Peter, 239
Nukhba, 259, 261, 281, 287, 291
  See Also: Hamas
NYSE (New York Stock Exchange), 83, 87

Obama, Barack, 117, 179–180, 187, 299
O'Brien, Conor Cruise, 256
Occupy Wall Street, 26
Ohio, 164–165
Ohr Sameah (Yeshiva), 199
Old Testament, 2–3, 6, 13, 29, 35, 37, 105–106, 112, 123, 128, 154–155, 157–160, 162, 168–170, 172, 175, 184, 201, 204, 207–208
Olmert, Ehud, 272
OPEC (Organization of the Petroleum Exporting Countries), 78, 90, 150
Operation Hiram, 144–145
OPM (Leasing Company Affair), 85–87
Oppenheimer, Aharon, 211
Oppenheimer, Robert, 111–112

INDEX

Oran, 257–258
Oren, Michael, 154, 163
Oslo Peace Process, 65, 99, 101, 156, 205, 220, 227, 229–230, 270–273, 277, 289, 291, 298–299
Ostjuden, 129–130, 293
Outlook (journal), 13, 173
Overman, J. Andrew, 25

Palestinian Authority, 146, 271, 301
Palmach, 208
Pan (Greek God), 123
Patricius, 286
Paul (Apostle), 131, 133
Penn Central Transportation Company, 84–85
Penslar, Derek, 29
Perella, Joseph, 79
Peres, Shimon, 151, 230, 234, 236, 289
Peter (Saint), 119–120, 122–123, 167
Phalangists, 149
Pharisees, 4–5, 7, 22–23, 25, 95–96, 101, 121, 125, 129, 135, 143
PLO (Palestinian Liberation Organization), 149–150, 225, 228–231, 238, 270, 277
Pnyx, 103, 106–107
Podhoretz, Norman, 225
Pollard, Jonathan, 94, 228, 297
Pontecorvo, Gillo, 233
Porat, Hanan, 227
Pornhub, 114
Powell, Colin, 182
Preminger, Otto, 224
Prime, W.C., 172
Prohibition, 104, 174–175
Prothero, Stephen, 11
Protocols of the Elders of Zion, 28, 180, 274
Pryor, Roger, 189
Pseudepigrapha, 119
Pujo Committee, 26–28
Purdue Pharma, 96–98
 See Also Sackler Family
Puritans, ix, 31–32, 35, 154, 159, 169

Qatar, 271

Rabin, Yitzhak, 117, 150–151, 270, 273–273, 276, 298
 See Also Oslo Peace Process
Ramdane, Abane, 243
Rashbi (Shimon bar Yochai), 141, 210, 217
 Debate about Colonialism, 216, 236, 241–242, 256, 283–287
 In Cave, 215, 287
 Tomb, 141–142, 215
 Author of Zohar, 215
Raymond III (of Tripoli), 139
Reagan, Ronald, 20, 22, 52, 74, 78, 85, 89, 94, 97, 152, 159–160
Recreant Generation, 146–147, 220, 277–278, 280, 283, 291, 293, 296, 298, 300, 303
Red Sea, 128, 154, 184
Reform Judaism, 1, 128–129, 209, 229, 294
Reich, Robert, 99
Reinhart, Carmen, 48
Reles, Abe, 93, 93
Renan, Ernest, 26, 128, 171
Republican Party, xi, 11, 51, 79, 96, 109, 117, 176, 186–187, 198
Riesman, David, 61
Riklis, Meshulam, 77
Riley, William Bell, 176–177
Robinson, Edward, xv, 10, 17
Rockefeller, John D., 170, 176–177, 185–186, 188–189
 and Standard Oil, 176. 185–188, 189
Rogoff, Kenneth, 48
Roman Empire, 4, 6–9, 17, 95, 101, 119, 121, 123–124, 126, 131–136, 141, 169, 207–217, 236, 241, 256, 283–287
Rome, 3, 138, 183
Roosevelt, Franklin D., 11, 72, 225
Roosevelt, Theodore, 13, 157, 185, 187–188
Rosenberg, Ethel, 93–93
Rosenberg, Julius, 93–94
Rosenthal, A.M., 229
Roth, Philip, 67, 195
Rothschild, Amschel, 35

INDEX

Roumain, Jacques, 240
Roycroft, 57–58, 60–61
  See also: Elbert Hubbard
Rubin, Robert, 43–44, 85
Ruth, Babe, 182

Sabra and Shatila (massacre), 38, 149,
  150, 272, 276
Sackler Family, 96–98
Sadat, Anwar, 149, 151, 226
Sadducees, 135, 143
Safed, 147, 157, 215
  See also: Kabbalah
Said, Edward, 226, 256
Sakhnin, 213, 286
Saladin, 139
Saldarini, Anthony, 25
Sarna, Jonathan, 158
Sanders, Bernie, 27, 46, 221, 298
Sanhedrin, 126, 211–212
Sapiro, Aaron, 180
Sartre, Jean-Paul, 233, 236, 258
  and Fanon, 237–238, 240, 245
  and Memmi, 251, 255
Saudi Arabia, 260–261
Schaff, Philip, 168–169
Schiff, Jacob, 27–28
Schmegegge, 161
  Economics and, 184–186
  Evangelicalism and, 175, 178,
    200–206
  Definition of, 181–183
Scholem, Gershom, 142
Schwartz, Seth, 212–213
Schweitzer, Albert, 14, 15, 17, 19, 25,
  127, 129
  The Quest of the Historical Jesus,
    14, 127
Schwimmer, Rosika, 179
Scopes Trial, 175
Sderot, 218
Sea of Galilee, 3, 10, 16, 119, 122, 128,
  136, 167, 173, 215
Second Great Awakening, 17, 158,
  163, 175
Second Persian Gulf War (Iraq War),
  63, 181, 265

Second Temple, xiii, 6, 8, 22, 25, 38,
  101, 105, 119, 122, 131, 133, 135,
  138, 143, 166, 174–175, 183, 207,
  212, 214–215, 261, 285, 292
  Hurban, 25, 101, 138, 143, 183,
    212, 214, 292
  See also Jerusalem
Second Vatican Council, 65, 126
Securities and Exchange Commission
  (SEC), 76, 80, 82–84, 91, 97
Sefer Toledot Yeshu (Book of the Life
  of Jesus), 127
Sepphoris (Tzippori), 6–7, 9, 137, 139,
  210–211, 213, 216, 283–284, 286
Sermon on the Mount, 2, 7–8, 15–16,
  24, 120, 137, 140, 168–170
Settlements, *See* West Bank
Seventh-Day Adventist *See* Millerism
Seward, William, 162
Shad, John, 88
Shamir, Yitzhak, 230, 276
Sharett, Moshe, 151
Sharon, Ariel, 149–150, 270, 272–273,
  276, 289
Shatz, Adam, 239, 246
Sherman Antitrust Act, 188
Sh'faram, 210
Shiite Islam, 146, 149, 166, 260, 267,
  275, 288
  See Also Hezbollah
Shin Bet (Security Service), 271, 289
Sicarii, 284–285
Sidon, 122
Siegel, Martin, 22, 81
Silverman, Sarah, 91
Sinai Peninsula, 151, 199, 226
  Revelation, 104, 207
  Yom Kippur War, 259, 299
Sinai War (1956), 151, 234–235
Sinat Hinam, 292, 299, 302
Sinwar, Yahya, 281
Six-Day War (1967), 20, 65–67, 115–
  116, 150, 160, 175, 177, 183–184,
  199, 204, 220, 223–224, 226, 228,
  235, 256, 288, 302
Smith, Adam, 51, 59
Smith, Eli, xv
Smotrich, Bezalel, 148, 278

INDEX

Sombart, Werner, 28–38, 61, 159
  and Nazism, 30–31
  and Weber, 31–33, 38, 64, 95, 159
  Jews and Modern Capitalism, 28, 31–32, 36
South Improvement Company, 189
  See Also: Rockefeller, John D.
South Lebanon Army (SLA), 147
Soviet Union, 37, 47, 52, 72, 111, 150, 181, 239, 275
Squadron, Howard, 92
Stanford, Robert Allen, 92
Statue of Liberty, 193
Steinberg, Saul, 77
Stewart, James B., 22, 77, 82,
  Den of Thieves, 22
Stewart, Lyman, 176–177
Stiles, Ezra, 154, 158
Stone, I.F. 224
Stowe, Harriet Beecher, xv
Straus, Oscar, 157–158, 179
Strauss, David Friedrich, 171
Suez Canal, 234, 259, 291
Sukkot, Zvi, 278
Supernova (Festival), 277
Supreme Court (US), 23, 98, 112, 264, 298
Sutton, Matthew Avery, 176, 178
Synoptic Gospels, 55, 101, 122, 125, 132, 136–137
  See Also Mark, Matthew, Luke
Syria, 138, 149, 219

Taft, William Howard, 186
Talmud, 36, 141–142, 215, 221, 292
  and colonialism, 207–210, 213–214, 216–217, 236, 242
  and Galilee, 131, 138, 141, 210–212, 283–284
  and money, 33–35, 37
Tanakh, *see* Old Testament
Tannaim, 138, 141, 209–212, 214–215, 241, 284
Tarantino, Quentin, 109
Tarbell, Ida, 185–186
Taylor, Joan, 10
Teheran, 148, 204, 236, 260
Tel Aviv, 262–263, 266

Temple Mount, 198
  See also Jerusalem
Teshuvah (Newly Orthodox Jewish), 197, 199–205
Testa, Emmanuele, 10
Teutonic Order, 140
Teveth, Shabtai, 227
Thatcher, Margaret, 20
Thompson, Dorothy, 224
Thompson, E.P., 250
Thomson, W.M., 163–168, 170
Tiberias, 6, 9, 137–138, 141, 209, 211, 215
Tissot, J. James, 174
Titus, 124, 135
Tolstoy, Lev, 194
Tosquelles, Francois, 239
Truman, Harry, 72
Trump, Donald, ix–xiii, 27, 95, 97, 112, 117, 146, 176, 190, 193, 198, 271, 296, 299, 302
  and Middle East, 260–261, 297
  and Truth, 107, 109–110, 114, 178–180, 182, 185, 188
  2024 Elections, x, xiv, 147, 187, 301
Trump, Ivanka, 112
Tunis, 150, 229, 249–250, 252, 254
Turchin, Peter, 48
Turner, Frederick Jackson, 13, 191
Tuscany, 144
Twain, Mark, 113, 167, 172–173
  Innocents Abroad, 113, 167, 172–173
Twenties (1920s), 13–14, 27–28, 47, 58, 66–67, 104, 158, 163–164, 168, 171, 175–177, 193, 195, 235, 275
Tyre, 122

Uncle Tom's Cabin, 164
  See Also Stowe, Harriet Beecher
United Nations, 71, 138, 182, 219
University of Chicago, 7, 9, 45
Untermyer, Samuel, 27–28
Uris, Leon, 223–224
Usha, 141, 210–211, 214, 217

INDEX

Vance, Cyrus, 153
Veblen, Thorstein, 185
Vespasian, 124, 135, 286
Vietnam War, 74, 78, 108, 113, 233

Wallace, Lew, 13, 173
Wall Street, 24, 28, 68–82, 85–86, 89, 93, 282, 298
Wall Street Journal, 86, 282
Walt, Stephen, 155–156, 275
Wanamaker, John, 174
Washington, DC, 1, 66, 100, 150, 159, 256, 259, 300–301
Washington Naval Conference, 181
Washington Post, 114, 180
Wasserstein, Bruce, 79–80
Watergate Affair, 84, 108, 113–114, 182
   See Also Nixon, Richard
Weber, Max, 31–38, 61, 64, 95, 159, 185
   The Protestant Ethic and the Spirit of Capitalism, 31–32, 185
   See Also Sombart, Werner
Weinberg, Helen Livingston, 70
Weinberg, Noah, 199
Weinberg, Sidney, 67–73, 77, 85
   and Ford Motor, 72, 73
   biography of, 69–70
Weiss, Herbert, 240
Weiss, Johannes, 15, 19
Weissmann, Mordecai, 86
Weizmann, Chaim, 276
   See Also OPM
West Bank, xi, xiii, 20, 38, 96, 98–99, 117, 145–146, 160–161, 198, 226–228, 241, 255, 260, 268, 270–271, 276, 278–280, 283, 289–290, 296, 300
   Jewish settlements on, x–xi, 20, 38, 98–100, 117, 148–149, 197–198, 220–221, 228, 230, 278, 288, 294, 296–302
Who is a Jew (controversy), 229–230, 297
Wiesel, Eli, 91–92

Wilkie, Wendell, 72
Wilson, Charles, 72–73
Wilson, Woodrow, 168, 179, 181, 186–187
Winfrey, Oprah, 182
Winthrop, John, 169
Woods, Rose Mary, 182
Woodward, Bob, 114
World War I, 36, 38, 107, 178, 250
   and America, 23–24, 26–28, 66, 68, 72, 92, 113, 170, 178, 187–188, 298
   and Mandatory Palestine, 10, 208
World War II, 222–223, 238–240, 244–246
   and America, 47, 72, 93, 110–112, 118, 178, 192, 194, 220
   and Holocaust, xiii, 107
   and Israel, 222–223, 238–240, 244, 246
Wrede, William, 137

Yad Vashem, 224
Yale University, 154, 184
Yaqut al-Hawami, 138
Yarmuk (Battle), 138–139, 144
Yavne, 208
Yehezkeli, Zvi, 282
Yesha Council, 281
Yeshiva University, 67, 86, 91–92
Yohanan Ben-Zakkai, 208
Yom Kippur War (1973), 86, 116, 148, 150, 199, 259, 291, 293, 296, 299, 302

Zionism, 149, 158, 160, 201, 208, 235, 254, 286
   American Jews and, 27–28, 230
   Anti-Zionism, 220, 240, 274, 276
   Christian Zionism, 116, 160, 177, 203–204
   Fifth Freedom and, 225, 228
   Labor Zionism, 151
   Religious Zionism, 177, 202, 293
Zohar (Book of Splendor), 215
   See Also Rashbi

www.ingramcontent.com/pod-product-compliance
Lightning Source LLC
Chambersburg PA
CBHW071228230426
43668CB00011B/1354